The Norton Guide to Equity-Minded Teaching

The Norton Guide to Equity-Minded Teaching

Isis Artze-Vega
Valencia College

Flower Darby
University of Missouri

Bryan Dewsbury
Florida International University

Mays Imad
Connecticut College

W. W. NORTON & COMPANY
Celebrating a Century of Independent Publishing

W. W. Norton & Company has been independent since its founding in 1923, when William Warder Norton and Mary D. Herter Norton first published lectures delivered at the People's Institute, the adult education division of New York City's Cooper Union. The firm soon expanded its program beyond the Institute, publishing books by celebrated academics from America and abroad. By midcentury, the two major pillars of Norton's publishing program—trade books and college texts—were firmly established. In the 1950s, the Norton family transferred control of the company to its employees, and today—with a staff of five hundred and hundreds of trade, college, and professional titles published each year—W. W. Norton & Company stands as the largest and oldest publishing house owned wholly by its employees.

Editor: Justin Cahill
Senior Associate Editor: Anna Olcott
Project Editor: Thea Goodrich
Developmental Editor: Beth Ammerman
Managing Editor, College: Marian Johnson
Production Manager: Jane Searle
Media Editor: Ariel Eaton
Managing Editor, College Digital Media: Kim Yi
Ebook Producer: Emily Schwoyer
Marketing Managers: Julia Hall, Michele Dobbins
Design Director: Rubina Yeh
Book Designer: Justin Rose
Director of College Permissions: Megan Schindel
Permissions Specialist: Josh Garvin
Composition: MPS North America, LLC
Illustrations: MPS North America, LLC
Manufacturing: Sheridan Books

Permission to use copyrighted material is included in the credits section of the book, which appears on p. 285.

ISBN: **978-0-393-89371-7** (pbk)

W. W. Norton & Company, Inc., 500 Fifth Avenue, New York, NY 10110
    www.wwnorton.com
W. W. Norton & Company Ltd., 15 Carlisle Street, London W1D 3BS

3 4 5 6 7 8 9 0

To our students and mentors
who have guided us in this important work,
and to you, our faculty partners, with love

BRIEF CONTENTS

INTRODUCTION   **An Invitation to Equity-Minded Teaching**   xvii

Section One: Design for Equity   1

UNIT 1   **Relevance and Rigor** *Connect Courses to Students' Lives and Challenge Them*   3

UNIT 2   **Transparency** *Create an Equity-Minded Assessment and Grading Strategy*   31

UNIT 3   **Welcome and Support Students** *Design an Inclusive Syllabus and Online Course*   55

Section Two: Inclusive Day-to-Day Teaching   91

UNIT 4   **Relationships** *Earn and Maintain Students' Trust*   93

UNIT 5   **Belonging** *Validate Students' Presence and Abilities*   117

UNIT 6   **Structure** *Plan Ahead to Support Student Learning and Success*   139

UNIT 7   **An Inside Look** *Examples of an Equity-Minded Online Class and In-Person Classroom*   169

Section Three: Learning through Critical Reflection   203

UNIT 8   **Reflection** *Take the Time to Look Inward and Engage with Student Ratings Data*   205

UNIT 9   **Inquiry** *Gather and Learn from Additional Student Feedback*   225

CONCLUSION   **A Learning Sanctuary**   245

CONTENTS

ABOUT THE AUTHORS   xv

INTRODUCTION **An Invitation to Equity-Minded Teaching**   xvii

SECTION ONE: Design for Equity   1

UNIT 1   **RELEVANCE AND RIGOR** *Connect Courses to Students' Lives and Challenge Them*   3

What Does the Research Say about Relevance?   4

How Motivation Drives Learning   4

On Culturally Relevant Teaching and Its Predecessors   8

What Does the Research Say about Rigor?   11

How Rigor Facilitates Learning   12

On Rigor and Equity   13

Putting the Research to Work | Equity-Minded Course Design   17

Step 1: Analyze the Course Context   18

Step 2: Develop Learning Objectives   20

How Can I Get Started?   28

UNIT 2   **TRANSPARENCY** *Create an Equity-Minded Assessment and Grading Strategy*   31

What Does the Research Say about Assessment and Grading?   32

Purpose   32

Authenticity   34

Transparency   35

On Equitable Grading   37

Putting the Research to Work | Identifying Primary Assessments and a Grading Structure   41

Step 3: Determine What Evidence of Learning You Will Collect   41

Additional Assessment Design Considerations for Online Classes   45

Updating Your Grading System   47

How Can I Get Started?   52

UNIT 3   **WELCOME AND SUPPORT STUDENTS** *Design an Inclusive Syllabus and Online Course*   55

What Does the Research Say about the Syllabus?   57

The Inclusive Syllabus: Essential in All Modes   60

Putting the Research to Work | Final Stages of Course Design and Syllabus Upgrades   62

Step 4: Identify Your Main Learning Activities and Tie It All Together   63

Equity-Minded Design Considerations for Online (and Online-Enhanced) Courses   81

How Can I Get Started?   88

SECTION TWO: Inclusive Day-to-Day Teaching   91

UNIT 4   **RELATIONSHIPS** *Earn and Maintain Students' Trust*   93

What Does the Research Say about Relationships and Trust?   94

Who Trusts Whom?   98

Earning and Restoring Trust   99

The Power of Wise Feedback   101

On Cultivating Trust Online   103

Putting the Research to Work | Building and Maintaining Trust   107

1. Get to Know Your Students (Even before Day 1)   108

2. Help Students Get to Know *You*   112

3. Wisen-Up Your Feedback   113

How Can I Get Started?   115

UNIT 5   **BELONGING** *Validate Students' Presence and Abilities*   117

What Does the Research Say about Belonging?   119

The Historical and Social Context for Belonging in Higher Education   119

The College Context for Belonging   122

How Does Belonging Impact Students?   124

Faculty-Facing Factors That Impact Belonging   125

What Do We Know about Belonging in Fully Online Courses?   127

Putting the Research to Work | Creating Contexts of Belonging   129

1. Tell Students Your Belonging Story   129

2. Ask Students to Work in Diverse, Interdependent Groups   130

3. Ask Students to Wrap an Assessment   133

4. Explicitly Assess Belonging   134

How Can I Get Started?   136

UNIT 6   **STRUCTURE** *Plan Ahead to Support Student Learning and Success*   139

What Does the Research Say about Structure?   141

Putting the Research to Work | Foundational Structures and Key Strategies   144

Alignment   144

Active Learning Strategies and Practice   145

On Active Learning Online   147

Putting the Research to Work | Specific Structural Strategies for Advancing Equitable Outcomes   158

1. Try Using a Lesson or Module Template   158

2. Add Structure to Existing Activities   162

3. Scaffold Something Sticky   165

4. Schedule an Intervention (and/or a Shout-Out)   167

How Can I Get Started?   168

UNIT 7   **AN INSIDE LOOK** *Examples of an Equity-Minded Online Class and In-Person Classroom*   169

How Do I, Flower Darby, Teach My Asynchronous Online Class?   170

A Few Considerations before I Start   170

Right before the Semester Begins   171

On Day 1   176

On Day 3   177

During a Regular Week (after Week 1)   177

Before the First Project   181

After the First Project   182

Approaching the Finish Line and Requests for Deadline Extensions   183

After the Semester Ends   184

Flower's Concluding Thoughts   185

How Do I, Bryan Dewsbury, Teach My Large, In-Person Class?   186

A Few Considerations before I Start   186

Right before the Semester Begins   187

On Day 1   193

A Typical Class Session   196

Assessments and Grading   199

Intervention Week   200

Beyond Biology   200

At the End of the Course   200

Bryan's Concluding Thoughts   202

SECTION THREE: Learning through Critical Reflection   203

UNIT 8   **REFLECTION** *Take the Time to Look Inward and Engage with Student Ratings Data*   205

What Does the Research Say about Student Course Evaluations?   207

Do SETs Give Us Insight into "Teaching Effectiveness" and Student Learning?   209

Bias Affects SET Results   210

Putting the Research to Work | Starting with Reflection and Engaging with Student Perspectives in SET Data   214

1. Examine SET Results Systematically and Holistically   214

2. Lean In to Negative Feedback   216

3. Mitigate Bias from the Start   218

4. Empower Students to Complete SETs—and More Effectively   219

5. Advocate for Change   219

How Can I Get Started?   223

UNIT 9   **INQUIRY** *Gather and Learn from Additional Student Feedback*   225

What Does the Research Say about Gathering Student Data and Feedback outside of SETs?   226

Readily Available Data beyond SETs   227

Putting the Research to Work | Filling in Your Data Gaps   228

Four Equity-Minded Ways to Gather, Engage with, and Respond to Data   228

Taking the Time to Act   242

How Can I Get Started?   243

CONCLUSION **A Learning Sanctuary**   245

ACKNOWLEDGMENTS   253

APPENDIX   257

Formulating Significant Learning Objectives   258

Course Planning Map   260

The Grounded Model: Building Student-Teacher Trust in a "Beating the Odds" U.S. Urban High School   262

The "Who's in Class?" Form   263

NOTES   265

CREDITS   285

ABOUT THE AUTHORS

Isis Artze-Vega (lead author and editor) serves as College Provost and Vice President for Academic Affairs at Valencia College in central Florida, a Hispanic-Serving Institution long regarded as one of the nation's best community colleges. She provides strategic leadership in the areas of curriculum, assessment, faculty development, online learning, career and workforce education, and partnerships for educational equity. Prior to joining Valencia, Isis served as Assistant Vice President for Teaching and Learning at Florida International University and taught writing at the University of Miami. She is coauthor of *Connections Are Everything: A College Student's Guide to Relationship-Rich Education* (2023).

Flower Darby is an Associate Director of the Teaching for Learning Center at the University of Missouri. In this role she builds on her experience teaching in person and online for over twenty-six years, as well as experience gained in her previous roles as Director of Teaching for Student Success and Assistant Dean of Online and Innovative Pedagogies, to empower faculty to teach effective and inclusive classes in all modalities. Flower is the author, with James M. Lang, of *Small Teaching Online: Applying Learning Science in Online Classes* (2019), and she is an internationally sought-after keynote speaker.

Bryan Dewsbury is Associate Professor of Biology and Associate Director of the STEM Transformation Institute at Florida International University. He is the Principal Investigator of the Science Education and Society (SEAS) research program, a team blending research on the social context of teaching and learning, faculty development of inclusive practices, and programming to cultivate equity in education. Previously, he was at the University of Rhode Island. Bryan is a Fellow with the John N. Gardner Institute, where he assists institutions of higher education cultivate best practices in inclusive education.

Mays Imad is an Assistant Professor of Biology and Equity Pedagogy at Connecticut College. Prior to that, she founded the Teaching & Learning Center at Pima Community College in Tucson, Arizona, where she also taught for over ten years in the department of life and physical sciences. A Gardner Institute Fellow and an American Association of Colleges and Universities Senior Fellow, Mays's research focuses on stress, biofeedback and self-regulation, critical feeling, and cultivating resilience, and how these impact student learning and success. A nationally recognized expert on trauma-informed teaching and learning, Mays works to promote inclusive, equitable, and contextual education—all rooted in the latest research on the neurobiology of learning.

INTRODUCTION

AN INVITATION TO EQUITY-MINDED TEACHING

Welcome to the *Norton Guide to Equity-Minded Teaching*, an invitation to join faculty and higher education professionals from across the country and globe who strive to realize more equitable outcomes for students. That includes us, the author team. We have worked as full-time faculty in several disciplines, taught in varied modalities and classes of different sizes, and importantly, spent a great deal of time partnering and learning with faculty from across the United States and beyond. (To learn more about our individual areas of expertise and experiences, see About the Authors.) Knowing firsthand that faculty life is busy and complex—and that those who share this mission are often hard-pressed for resources and time—we've curated the findings of scholars and practitioners from varied fields on equity-minded education and student success. We have also prioritized practical application. After all, even when we know something isn't quite right in our class and want to make it better—when we want to be intentional about advancing equity—it's not always clear *what* we can or should do. And because online learning and teaching with technology are now ubiquitous, we have also infused modality and technology considerations and guidance throughout the guide.

Overall, in this guide we propose that **equity-minded** faculty (1) design their online and in-person courses with attention to relevance, rigor, and transparency; (2) teach by fostering student belonging and trust and by facilitating learning in well-structured and highly relational physical and virtual environments; and, particularly at the end of each term, (3) reflect on students' and their own experiences and outcomes, using reflection and data to identify areas for further enhancement.

equity-minded:
Describes teaching practices that strive to realize equal outcomes among all students.

How do these practices relate to equity? As we'll explain, the emphasis on *relevance*, *rigor*, and *transparency* reflects the fact that many minoritized students* enter learning spaces where it is unclear how content and assessments are relevant to their lives or aspirations, where the implicit assumption is that they are not intellectually capable of rigor, and where expectations for success are largely opaque or invisible. Similarly, attention to *belonging* and *trust* reflects the fact that both are necessary for student success, yet students from marginalized backgrounds often do not feel a sense of belonging in our courses or institutions and can be distrustful of colleges and of their professors. *Structure*, in turn, refers to the design of course elements such as online modules, daily learning plans, and group exercises. Increased structure is both a strategy for inclusion and an opportunity to ensure and monitor the use of equity-minded practices. Finally, *reflecting* on students' and our own learning is how we determine the impact of our teaching—including how experiences and outcomes vary among our students. It's also how we identify what to do differently when we teach again.

As distilled in the following infographic "*The Norton Guide to Equity-Minded Teaching* at a Glance," the guide's structure mirrors these key ideas, which also align with primary phases of the faculty teaching cycle: designing or refining a course before the term begins (Section One), implementing and refining your strategies in real time once the semester is underway (Section Two), and reflecting post-term on the teaching/learning experience and outcomes (Section Three). As the guide progresses, we'll discuss the relationship among these topics and approaches. Recognizing that each of our students, and each of us, navigates higher education in the context of an unjust social order, in the Conclusion we depict a more beautiful future, one in which we as educators intentionally empower students to co-create meaning, purpose, and knowledge—what we call a *learning sanctuary*.[1]

You may be wondering why we leave this vision of the future to the Conclusion, that is, why we focus our efforts and guidance in the body of the guide on working *within* existing systems and structures. We admit to having struggled with this very question. Ultimately, we determined that we have a responsibility today and every day to serve the students who are in our courses and counting on us. And we know that teaching, here and now, can make an enormous difference. So the Conclusion is where we imagine an aspirational

---

*We use the term *minoritized* here and throughout the guide to refer to students historically excluded from higher education. As equity scholar Shaun Harper writes, the term minoritized signifies "the social construction of underrepresentation and subordination in U.S. social institutions, including colleges and universities." He clarifies that "persons are not born into a minority status nor are they minoritized in every social milieu (e.g., their families, racially homogeneous friendship groups, or places of religious worship). Instead, they are rendered minorities in particular situations and institutional environments that sustain an overrepresentation of whiteness." At the same time, we recognize the limits of this and other terms. Shaun R. Harper, "Race without Racism: How Higher Education Researchers Minimize Racist Institutional Norms," in "Critical Perspectives on Race and Equity," ed. Estela Mara Bensimon and Robin Bishop, Supplement, *The Review of Higher Education* 36, no. 1 (Fall 2012): 9–29.

The Norton Guide to Equity-Minded Teaching at a Glance

Equity-focused educators teach classes in which a student's personal history and identities do not predict success. We design with intention, teach with care, and learn and grow from critical reflection to improve future teaching.

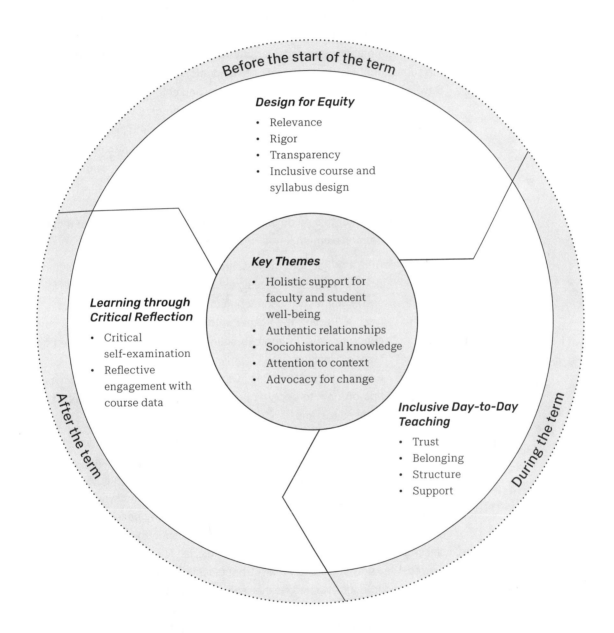

future, and where we issue both an invitation and a call to action to join us in making that vision a reality.

How do we know these principles and practices *work*? Throughout the guide, we synthesize and point you to research on each component of equity-minded teaching we've just outlined. For now, we'll highlight a study conducted by coauthor Bryan Dewsbury and a group of his colleagues at the University of Rhode Island.[2] Their study results showed that the introduction of inclusive and active pedagogies, such as those described in this guide, resulted in not only more equitable student learning and success gains in the short term—that is, gaps in attainment were considerably reduced—but also improved success in the subsequent biology course. For two additional examples, see studies by Sat Gavassa and colleagues and by Sarah Eddy and colleagues.[3] At the same time, we feel strongly that empirical studies are not the only valid source of knowledge. There's a great deal we can learn from theorists and practitioners, including one another. Therefore, to support and inform the suggestions we present we draw extensively on theoretical frameworks, on historical evidence of inequity, and on our own, other educators', and our students' lived experiences (both in and out of class).

Each section of this guide includes two to four units, and within most units, you'll find common elements:

- first, a "What Does the Research Say?" section in which we summarize findings from several categories of research on teaching and learning and examine their connection to equitable student outcomes;
- next, a "Putting the Research to Work" section in which we suggest concrete ways to improve online and onsite teaching based on the research insights; and
- finally, a short "How Can I Get Started?" section in which we provide tips on how to apply key recommendations from the unit if you're pressed for time.

The "How Can I Get Started?" section is further divided into four common modalities and contexts because they sometimes require adaptations or different approaches. And indeed, throughout the guide, you'll find suggestions for in-person classes of all sizes, as well as for asynchronous and synchronous online modalities.[4] These common scenarios don't cover every possible option, but we hope you find ideas that you can tweak, remix, and apply in your physical or virtual classroom, especially as the lines between modalities have become increasingly blurred. We know you'll likely learn from teaching in one modality—for example, online synchronous—how to further enhance your teaching in another context, such as when you have some students in the classroom and some participating in class via Zoom.[5] In each unit, we also weave in brief examples from our own teaching. To augment these examples, Unit 7 features a distinct structure: two extended case studies that illustrate what it looks like when the practices shared in the previous units come together in the day-to-day work of teaching.

How you engage with and use the research and practices we share in this guide is up to you, of course, but here are three general suggestions:

1. *Prioritize yourself.* Although we hope you'll be motivated to implement many of these ideas, please keep in mind your capacity to make changes and your current context (e.g., how many courses you're teaching and your faculty position type, personal life, etc.) to ensure that your journey toward more inclusive teaching doesn't compromise your wellness or negatively impact your career.

2. *Start small.* Popularized by James Lang's book *Small Teaching*, the "small teaching" approach entails making modest but powerful evidence-based teaching adjustments.[6] This strategy can help with the previous suggestion, as one of the ways we contribute to our own exhaustion is by trying to do too much and all at once.

3. *Don't do it alone.* Whether redesigning a course, trying out a new assessment or activity, identifying or creating new instructional materials, or examining the impact of a practice, potential partners abound. In addition to your faculty peers, consider collaborating with departmental leaders, faculty developers, instructional designers, librarians, counselors, student affairs colleagues, and institutional researchers. In the context of equity, partnering with students and sharing responsibilities with them can not only alleviate some of the pressure we feel to do it all ourselves but also be an important step toward disrupting power dynamics that tend to reflect the broader social order.[7]

The What and Why of Equity *and Other Terms*

Educational equity is both an aspiration and a commitment to action. It means recognizing that each student is starting from a different place and that many of the teaching practices that may have worked for us when we were students are not serving our current students equally well. Equity-minded educators work to ensure that every student has the opportunity to learn, succeed, and thrive. This work involves making adjustments to account for the imbalances in students' experiences and access to resources. Equity-minded educators strive to prepare students for active engagement, success, wellness, and joy in a world still characterized by injustice. When will we have achieved educational equity? When students' identities and social histories do not predict their academic outcomes.

In this guide, we define *equity-minded teaching* as teaching that is informed by principles, practices, and historical understandings that aim to realize equal outcomes among all students, with particular attention to students of minoritized races and ethnicities. To unpack this definition a bit, the focus on *outcomes* reminds us that good intentions are not enough; we have a responsibility as faculty to recognize that our teaching has enormous impact on students and thus to monitor the outcomes of our practice. Key outcomes include *student success* (measured using common criteria like grades, reenrollment, credit accumulation, and graduation) and *learning* (as measured by our assessments). As coauthors we chose to stress the focus on learning because students will reap the benefits of our improved teaching practices only if our efforts result in more and deeper learning. Without enhanced learning, there is no equity, and any claim of *student success* improvements rings hollow.

The second part of our definition of *equity-minded teaching* signals that students of all identities and lived experiences were in our minds and hearts as we wrote this guide. Many, if not most, of the practices we describe are known to support learning and success for all students. Yet our definition also acknowledges that as an author team, we decided to focus disproportionately on the outcomes of students from marginalized racial and ethnic backgrounds. Of course, we recognize the limitations of this emphasis. For example, race and ethnicity are only two identity categories, and each of our students, like each of us, represents the intersection of several identities. The inadequate categories of race and ethnicity also fail to account for the nuances within each. And in some cases, students' socioeconomic realities, gender, and familial experience with college (among other factors) have a greater impact on students' success than does their race or ethnicity. This is one of the reasons why throughout this guide we emphasize the importance of taking time to learn about the lived experiences and outcomes of the actual students we teach versus relying on our assumptions or generalizations.

Our focus on students of historically marginalized races and ethnicities is meant neither to minimize the importance of other identity variables nor to suggest that these aspects of students' identities exist in a vacuum. Instead, it reflects the fact that, over time, data from across higher education institutions, disciplines, and modalities show the most pronounced inequities in the outcomes of Black and Latinx students. As Tia Brown McNair, Estela Mara Bensimon, and Lindsay Malcolm-Piqueux affirm, "Despite our best intentions to be equitable toward all students, our ways of 'doing' higher education continue to produce racial inequity in educational outcomes."[8] In other words, many of our colleges and universities are sites of inequitable racial and ethnic outcomes that have persisted for far too long.

You'll also find that we sometimes use the term and share research on *inclusive teaching*. Inclusive teaching experts Viji Sathy, professor of psychology and neuroscience, and Kelly Hogan, professor of biology, define *inclusive teaching* as "embracing student diversity in all forms—race, ethnicity, gender, disability, socioeconomic background, ideology, even personality traits like introversion— as an asset. It means designing and teaching courses in ways that foster talent in all students, but especially those who come from groups traditionally excluded in higher education."[9] Inclusion is therefore a core component of equity.

One way to differentiate inclusive from equity-minded teaching is to think of inclusion as what we can do now; it is focused on the present. Equity, on the other hand, looks at both the past and the future, and it works to agitate or transform the system. Many efforts to encourage inclusive teaching have focused on science, technology, engineering, and mathematics (STEM) fields and faculty. As STEM scholars write, this focus is largely a result of the considerable "exodus of students from STEM fields, especially the leave-taking of women and students of color" and the recognition that the causes of STEM attrition are complex, including the "complicity of poor teaching by faculty."[10] Despite this disciplinary focus, the findings and practical suggestions we've gathered from research on *inclusive teaching* can be helpful to faculty across disciplines.

We provide additional guidance on equity-minded and inclusive teaching drawn from various frameworks, using terminology such as *multicultural*, *justice-oriented*, *culturally competent*, *culturally responsive*, and *culturally sustaining* teaching practices. Your discipline may have its own terms too—and it can get overwhelming (and/or irritating) to keep track of them all. We have found that it's best to avoid getting too caught up in the distinctions among the terminology. Instead, we often think of these frameworks as varied means to the same end—equal outcomes among all student groups—and we draw on and honor the insights provided by each body of research.

Suggestions, but No "Solutions" or Quick Fixes

Finally, we are humbled and energized by the efforts and insights of those who have devoted their professional careers to these topics, as well as by the urgency with which many faculty have recently embraced equity-minded teaching. And we are confident that, as was never clearer than in our collective response to the pandemic, college faculty care deeply about students and their learning, and can make miracles happen. We faculty will need to sustain this urgency and momentum to accomplish our lofty goals. The fact that you're engaging with this guide at all indicates your willingness to put in the work—thank you! At the same time, we owe you honesty: Yes, there's a great deal you can do to cultivate equal outcomes among your students, and this guide offers many research- and practice-informed suggestions, but there are no quick fixes.

Realizing changes in your students' outcomes will require an investment of time, a high level of intentionality, and a great deal of courage. It will also necessitate reflection, not just on your teaching practices, but on *yourself*, the very core of your being. *You* are a crucial factor in your equity-minded practice, so if you seek to become an equity-minded educator, we strongly encourage you to begin or continue looking inward. Skipping this step of personal reflection comes with considerable risk. In their study on college and university efforts toward inclusion, Jan Arminio, Vasti Torres, and Raechele L. Pope found that educators' lack of reflective practice was a key reason why the institutions made only moderate progress on their goals. As they explain in their 2012 book *Why Aren't We*

There Yet?: Taking Personal Responsibility for Creating an Inclusive Campus, "Self-knowledge is the first necessary element.... Only after educators are honest and knowledgeable about their own cultures, beliefs, values, privileges, and biases can they begin to interact with others authentically in their daily contexts."[11] In short, the authors suggest that using new practices without also reflecting on ourselves can result in a lack of authenticity that can undermine our teaching aspirations and enhancements.

There's no shortcut for investing time and energy in yourself. Whether you look inward by taking implicit associations tests[12] and reflecting on your results, reading and reflecting on the ideas in books that describe personal experiences exploring identity such as Ibram X. Kendi's *How to Be an Antiracist* or Debby Irving's *Waking Up White*, partnering with a trusted colleague or relative to discuss your experiences and beliefs, or participating in another form of reflective practice, self-knowledge is key. And it's rarely easy. As activist and community organizer Leslie Mac acknowledges, "It takes intention, deliberate action, accountability and humility to do this internal work."[13] Looking inward can also elicit discomfort, as it tends to uncover beliefs and actions inconsistent with our values. If you find yourself feeling shame or guilt, remember that neither is productive and channel your feelings into action, perhaps by trying out one of the suggestions in this guide.

Modality and Technology Matter

Course modality may not seem like a key consideration for equity-minded teaching, so we want to explain why we've made modality, and the intentional use of widely available technology, such as Zoom, Canvas, D2L, and other learning management systems (LMSs), core elements of this guide. For one, it seems that the abrupt, wholesale shift to online instruction as a result of the pandemic has forever changed how we teach. Many of us are using our campus LMS and tools like Zoom more than ever to enhance teaching and learning in in-person courses as well as in **hybrid** and online modes.[14] Jenae Cohn, a teaching with technology scholar, argues that, post-pandemic, *all* classes are online classes.[15] Because an LMS and a platform such as Zoom are generally available for every class, and considering the growth of online textbook materials and activities, every course can benefit when instructors intentionally include tech-mediated structures and tasks that advance equitable outcomes.

Further, the proportion of online courses offered at many of our institutions has also changed. Most of us have not returned to our pre-COVID reliance on in-person courses. It's fair to say that, as a result of the pandemic shift to online instruction, many of us are including in our classes, regardless of modality, more online elements such as recorded mini-lecture and explainer videos, audio or video feedback on student work, and automated quizzes.[16] It is also likely that asynchronous classes will continue to be the most commonly offered online modality because they offer the most flexibility and access to students

hybrid: A course format that combines in-person and online instruction.

who would not otherwise be able to pursue a college degree. Yet this modality can also be a site of inequity. Although we can work to plan and teach learner-centered, engaging, and inclusive asynchronous classes, the lack of real-time interactions means that students must exert more independence and autonomy to be successful.[17] This absence of in-person support is one reason why students who may be less prepared for college due to opportunity gaps are likely to fare worse in online classes. For instance, research has found that students have higher withdrawal rates in fully online courses, compared with in-person or hybrid courses—and that these disparities are often greatest among students of color.[18] Plus, technology requirements and tools can be difficult for some students to access or use effectively without our guidance. Our online students deserve just as much support as those who learn in person.

With students' need for support in mind, we combine careful attention to online course design with the use of technology in teaching. Two frameworks are particularly beneficial to this effort, as they enhance equitable online design and inform the suggestions in this guide: **Universal Design for Learning (UDL)** and the **Community of Inquiry (CoI)** framework. You may be familiar with UDL in the context of online course technology and design that supports students with varying levels of abilities, but UDL also provides critical guidance for equity-minded instructors of in-person courses. Books like Andratesha Fritzgerald's *Antiracism and Universal Design for Learning* (2020) and Mirko Chardin and Katie Novak's *Equity by Design* (2020) argue that UDL can advance equity for all students, as each student brings to the class unique attributes, including individual histories, aspects of neurodivergence, and mental health trauma, that may raise barriers to learning. As authors Thomas J. Tobin and Kirsten T. Behling explain in their 2018 book *Reach Everyone, Teach Everyone*, when we bake options and supports that acknowledge learner variability into the design of our class (in any mode), we're working to lower barriers for all.[19]

The CoI framework, in turn, was proposed in 2000 based on the research of Randy Garrison and his colleagues, who wanted to understand what goes into effective and engaging asynchronous online classes, and what prevents them from feeling like electronic correspondence courses.[20] Although this framework originated from the study of asynchronous classes, the approach applies in synchronous online, hybrid, and in-person classes too. The implication for equity-minded teaching, as we explain later in this guide, is that online environments can sometimes feel cold and unwelcoming, so it takes additional intentionality to center presence and connection when teaching online.

Universal Design for Learning (UDL): An evidence-based framework to account for individual learner variability and lower barriers to learning for all students.

Community of Inquiry (CoI): A research-informed theoretical framework to guide the development and teaching of vibrant online courses that prioritize interactions with other people in the class.

Join Us!

We wrote this guide fueled by a heartfelt conviction that through their teaching, faculty members can make the greatest difference for students and their attainment of equitable outcomes. Yes, teaching is only part of the equation. Students' college experiences and outcomes are influenced by many factors, including the students' prior schooling experience, family situation, and knowledge level, as well as by our college environments and students' busy, complex lives. However, as Sylvia Hurtado and colleagues write, "For students who do not have time for traditional college involvement or do not have as much peer contact, . . . they get their cues from faculty and staff about whether the educational environment is inclusive and welcoming."[21] College students can circumvent many of our services, initiatives, and even our colleagues, but their experiences will always center on *you* and your teaching.

We are grateful to Norton for seeking us out to share what we've learned about equity-minded teaching and encouraging us to further develop and articulate our suggestions and practices in the form of a guide for faculty. Norton's Inclusion and Equity-Minded Teaching website (http://seagull.wwnorton .com/equity) describes the publisher's commitment to ensuring that its books and resources are inclusive and promote equity-minded teaching. However you choose to engage with the research, suggestions, strategies, and tools in this guide, please don't forget to pause and celebrate your successes along the way—and to share your successes with your students and colleagues, to foster collaborative learning with and from each other. And with that, students are waiting; let's get going!

Isis Artze-Vega
Flower Darby
Bryan Dewsbury
Mays Imad

SECTION ONE

DESIGN FOR EQUITY

"I never teach my pupils; I only attempt to provide the conditions in which they can learn."

—Albert Einstein

This part of the guide is meant to support you in designing or updating a course before the term begins. Whether you have a couple of summer months, several weeks, or only a few days between terms to work on your course, you'll find varied ways to infuse inclusive elements into it. Course design may not seem like an obvious site for enhancing equity, yet it represents a powerful set of tools for increasing students' level of engagement, their learning, and their overall success. It's likely that some of your current courses are hand-me-downs of sorts, inherited from your department or a colleague, so you may not have yet had the chance to craft a course that is aligned with your values and expertise. Course design also provides an essential foundation for equity-focused day-to-day teaching, and intentional design is inextricable from inclusive online teaching.

At the same time, we know wholesale course design or redesign is not always possible or permitted—for example, in colleges or departments that rely on course templates. Faculty have told us that they nonetheless find the principles of design described in this section helpful because they are applicable in other parts of their teaching, whether when shaping class discussions or motivating students to complete an assignment. Plus, the research summaries in each unit have implications for teaching far beyond course design, and the "How Can I Get Started?" suggestions at the end of each unit do not require course design changes.

Given that students who choose online courses and programs often have particularly complex lives—for example, juggling part- or full-time work, childcare, and/or other responsibilities with their coursework—it is particularly important that your asynchronous course is fully developed before Day 1. That's why this section also introduces evidence-based online course design frameworks, such as Universal Design for Learning, as well as online design rubrics and their supporting organizations, including the Quality Matters Rubric, the Online Learning Consortium Quality Scorecard, and the Peralta Equity Rubric.[1] These have been specifically designed to support holistic student success in asynchronous classes, and we hope that in these systematic tools you'll also find inspiration to guide alignment and equity-focused strategies for in-person, synchronous, and hybrid course modes.

This section comprises units that each address one or more core elements of course design: learning goals, assessments, grading schemes, and course materials. Unit 1 spotlights *relevance* and *rigor,* demonstrating how to enhance your learning objectives accordingly. Unit 2 focuses on creating relevant, rigorous, and *transparent assessments* as well as an *equitable grading scheme.* Since many of the decisions we make about course design materialize in our course syllabi, Unit 3 describes how to create an *inclusive syllabus* that welcomes and engages students via an emphasis on their success, the illustration of the course's relevance, and a careful selection of course materials. Unit 3 also provides extended guidance for online course design, since we generally plan and create the entire course before the start of the term.

1

RELEVANCE AND RIGOR
Connect Courses to Students' Lives and Challenge Them

Students are motivated and empowered to learn when we help them see value and purpose in what they're learning and have high expectations for them.

Whether you're seeking to refine an existing course or embarking on the design of an entirely new one, attending to relevance is one of the most important steps you can take to advance student learning and cultivate more equitable student outcomes. By **relevance**, we mean the degree to which learners can identify themselves in a course. Relevance advances equitable outcomes primarily because it is key to motivating students and to ensuring that they feel seen and that they matter. We have also seen that a lack of perceived relevance can influence students' decision-making about their educational journeys. As coauthor Mays Imad describes, "I have watched talented, creative, high-potential students walk away from the sciences because STEM curriculum [often] lacks ethical, political, and creative significance."[2]

We hope that after reading this unit you'll see that increasing the personal relevance of your course to students doesn't mean you try to make everything interesting to them or limit your teaching to what's practical in the "real world." It also does not require that you become deeply familiar with the experiences and backgrounds of each of your students every semester. Rather, enhancing relevance is a mindset, a set of practices, and an opportunity to get to know your students.

Equity-minded course design also requires a commitment to **rigor**, by which we mean academic challenge that supports student learning and growth.[3] We recognize that the term *rigor* is sometimes coded language signaling that "some students deserve to be here, and some don't," as University of North Carolina, Chapel Hill, professors Jordynn Jack and Viji Sathy have noted.[4] So why have we chosen to center this concept? First, because rigor is

relevance: The extent to which a student can see their goals, interests, or experiences reflected in their learning.

rigor: Academic challenge that supports student learning and growth.

a pervasive academic construct that is essential to learning. Second, because we want to challenge the common presumption that equity-mindedness requires a reduction of rigor or standards. This notion is not only inaccurate; it is also deficit minded, reflecting the belief that some students are intellectually deficient or limited, and that the only way to improve their success and remedy performance gaps is to lower our standards or expectations. Third and relatedly, because maintaining rigor empowers students to live up to their potential, defy stereotypes about their abilities, and thrive in their future lives and careers.

This unit begins with a synthesis of research on both educational relevance and rigor. It then introduces two models of course design that will be referenced throughout this section, pointing out opportunities to enhance both relevance and rigor in your course learning goals, which are the anchors of course design. (Ideas on how to enhance relevance and rigor in other parts of your course are provided in later sections.)

What Does the Research Say about Relevance?

Research on educational relevance is extensive, so we've broken down our summary into two components: theories of motivation and what is known as culturally relevant pedagogy.

How Motivation Drives Learning

When students submit lackluster work, keep their cameras off, don't reach out to you for help, and so forth, you may think to yourself, "If only they were motivated!" And on the one hand, you're right: your sense that motivation is key to learning and success is supported by ample research. On the other hand, these student behaviors can be misleading and are often more indicative of the complexity of students' lives than anything related to the course. What can appear to be a fixed state of disengagement or lack of motivation can likewise be misleading, as levels of motivation are not static. When it comes to student engagement, there's a great deal we as faculty can influence through our teaching—so much so that Susan Ambrose and colleagues isolate motivation as one of their seven research-based principles most applicable to college teaching. "Students' motivation determines, directs, and sustains what they do to learn," they summarize.[5] Other scholars have echoed this conviction, calling motivation the very "engine" of learning.[6]

So how does this engine work? In the most general terms, the National Academies of Sciences, Engineering, and Medicine explains in *How People Learn II* that students come to our courses with a wealth of knowledge and experiences, and they are often seeking an entry point into the new material that will connect it to what they already know.[7] From a neuroscientific perspective, on a day-to-day basis, our brains have limited energy to process and store information. Our ability to simplify, distill, and make sense of information is thus not only an innate energy-conserving (or efficiency) skill but also a survival skill. When we are emotionally engaged, the same brain system that helps keep us alive (our brain stem) is activated.[8] In other words, the more we feel connected to a story or topic, the more we are engaged. As faculty, our responsibility in teaching is to optimize motivation and emotional engagement by creating "room for learners to interpret tasks and assessments in ways that broadly leverage their individual strengths, experiences, and goals"—in short, by creating learning experiences students relate to and value.[9]

Motivation researchers isolate two specific variables that influence behavior: *expectancy of success* and *perceived task value*. Expectancy of success refers to the confidence that one can accomplish a task, and perceived task value refers to the degree to which one finds importance or value in a task. It follows that students will perceive importance or value in tasks that reflect their perspectives and priorities—that is, those they consider relevant to their lives. Research suggests that students are more likely to choose to learn something if they perceive the assignment as valuable or relevant, while their levels of engagement will be highest when they feel they can accomplish it successfully. For example, an assignment that makes a connection to topics many students care about, like social media or environmental sustainability, could feel more relevant to your students and thus motivate them. And if you provide clear guidelines and/or an opportunity for them to improve their work based on your feedback (as we will discuss in Unit 2), your students will be more hopeful that they can accomplish the task successfully and thus be even more motivated to complete it.

Motivation and Modality

Although the general principles of motivation apply in all modalities, it can be helpful to strike a balance between intrinsic and extrinsic motivation in fully online courses.

The need for extrinsic motivation is often expressed by experienced online educators in the refrain "Online students don't do optional."

Why? A primary reason students take online courses and enroll in online programs is their inherent flexibility. Many students juggle work and family obligations; indeed, attending classes online is often their only avenue for pursuing a college credential. Given the reality of limited time, they may be more motivated to devote time to other tasks and responsibilities. It's also the case that when we provide guidance, tips, and reminders for success when teaching in person, we feel somewhat confident that students in the room heard us. Yet online, when we send announcements, comment on assignments, or record and post videos, it can feel like sending out messages into the void. Building specific requirements into courses can thus encourage student progress. For example, after a reading or mini-lecture video, you could include a two-question reading-check quiz worth two points. Or you could use the conditional release function in your learning management system (LMS) so that students submit an ungraded self-check in order to open the next element in your online course. A measure of additional extrinsic motivation, or to put it another way, an extra layer of accountability, may be helpful in online courses to help students prioritize their online learning and benefit from your guidance.

Motivation scholars suggest focusing on issues that are personally meaningful to students, such as those that relate to their cultural experiences, goals, and interests. Yet, as we mentioned earlier, your goal is not to make everything in the class interesting. Instead, we can help students see the larger purpose of what they're learning. The title of an article by David Yeager and colleagues illustrates this point: In "Boring but Important," the scholars share the results of several studies that collectively demonstrate that students with a purpose for learning that extends beyond their own interests and goals (as in making a difference in their communities) stay more focused when they face challenges or frustration, even when completing tedious or uninteresting tasks. The authors' findings also caution us not to rely on assumptions about students' motivations. For instance, in their study, students from low-income backgrounds did not prioritize education as a means to earn more money; they wanted to contribute to the world around them.[10]

Pause to Consider

- What do you know about why *your* students are in college? In your class? How do you know this?

- What additional small steps could you take to learn more about their motivations and goals?

It may seem obvious, but it's important not only to add content, assignments, or activities you think students will find relevant but also to describe or explain this relevance to them. Students won't always know about the connections to future coursework, civic life, or a profession. Before you share your observations and insights on relevance and value, it's helpful to ask students what they notice or imagine. For example, when starting a new unit or topic Mays always asks her students, "Why should you care? Why should you invest brain energy in this? How's this going to help you toward your goals?" This has the added benefit of prompting students' reflection on their aspirations, helping to remind them of their educational goals and to reconnect with their purpose. We each have an innate desire to matter in life, so Mays suggests you think of each of these reminders as a micro-affirmation of the value of each student's existence.

One common (and controversial) idea is that education should be made relevant to learners' career aspirations.[11] We don't suggest that relevance be *limited* to students' career goals; however, it seems prudent to tap into this source of relevance in addition to others, given that the overwhelming majority of college students indicate that a primary reason for attending college is to secure a job after graduation.

Making connections between your course and your students' career goals is easier than you may think. Take, for instance, the National Association of Colleges and Employers' list of the attributes most important to employers: teamwork and problem-solving skills, analytical and both verbal and written communication skills, and initiative, leadership, and technical skills. These attributes are likely already features of your course, so just by pointing out to your students that employers also value these competencies, you could make the material more relevant. Given the increasing prevalence of remote and hybrid work, helping students develop skills in online communication, relationship building, and teamwork—and explicitly pointing out how these skills will benefit them in their future jobs—is another key way to increase students' sense of the relevance of class activities, especially in online environments.

A related and underutilized source of relevance is students' current employment, particularly now that so many students are working their way through college. If your class helps prepare students with communication skills, for instance, students might reflect on the role of oral and written communication in their workplace. As a specific example, in an online organizational psychology class, you could ask students to consider whether they've ever had a job where their boss evidenced toxic leadership and, if so, what that was like and how their experience helps them understand concepts such as the bystander effect in the assigned reading. As students engage with other students' workplace stories, their understanding of complex theories will become more real and relatable, enhancing their learning.

One last reminder from motivation scholars: learners are often presented with various tasks at once and have limited time to devote to them, such that perceived value is usually a relative matter. Imagine a college student who has a part- or full-time job and is enrolled in several courses; their competing goals might include studying for an upcoming biology exam, revising an essay draft, and working extra hours so they can help their family pay for groceries. According to motivation theory, this college student will be more motivated to devote time to the goal(s) they value most—and working on your class won't always come first.

On Culturally Relevant Teaching and Its Predecessors

Now we turn to a parallel body of research and practice that centers the importance of relevance in student learning and is foundational to equity-minded teaching. Although it's beyond the scope of this guide to describe all forms of culturally relevant teaching, our summary would be incomplete without first acknowledging and honoring the work of Black educators in the nineteenth century. As Jarvis Givens, author of *Fugitive Pedagogy: Carter G. Woodson and the Art of Black Teaching*, writes, these individuals often put their own safety at risk by teaching students about the most salient parts of their lives: oppression, the ongoing struggle against it, and "elements of human life that were essential for Black children to flourish in a hostile world."[12] Their teaching was relevant in the purest sense of the word: students could identify themselves and the darkest parts of their realities in these fugitive classrooms, but they also saw and felt hope for a radically different future and were reminded of their boundless potential for greatness.

Countless educators engaged in relevant and liberatory practices in the subsequent decades. It was not until the early 1990s, however, at a time when U.S. learners were swiftly becoming more diverse, that education scholars developed new approaches to teaching attuned to this growing diversity.[13] Gloria Ladson-Billings, for instance, noticed a troubling misalignment between predominant educational cultures and students' home cultures, and she studied effective teachers of African American students.[14] The teachers were identified based on both traditional achievement measures like grades and other factors such as parents' sense that they were respectful to students and able to prompt student enthusiasm about learning. The effective teachers varied in their racial and ethnic identities (and included White teachers), and Ladson-Billings's analysis of their practices resulted in her seminal approach to teaching known as *culturally relevant pedagogy*.

Ladson-Billings isolates three specific criteria for culturally relevant pedagogy: (1) Students should experience academic success. (2) Students should develop and/or maintain *cultural competence*, which involves appreciating their own cultures and gaining fluency in at least one other culture.

(3) Students should develop a *critical/sociopolitical consciousness*, which involves applying their learning to societal problems. Implicit in these criteria is Ladson-Billings's conviction that, for students from historically underserved racial or ethnic groups, relevant teaching results in intellectual growth and traditional academic achievement—but that this attainment alone is insufficient. Her third criterion echoes fugitive educators' insistence on helping students exist in an inequitable society and work toward a more just future.

Ladson-Billings's ideas have been reinforced by scholars and practitioners during the nearly three decades since she articulated them. For instance, Stephen John Quaye and Shaun Harper conducted their research in 2006, long after the publication of Ladson-Billings's foundational study, and with an entirely different student group.[15] They interviewed more than two hundred high-achieving Black male undergraduates at forty-two predominantly White colleges and universities across the United States. Their goal was to identify the institutional agents, policies, programs, and resources that helped Black students achieve their desired educational outcomes. Quaye and Harper's findings validate Ladson-Billings's criteria for culturally relevant pedagogy because the students they studied were academically successful and developed both cultural competence and a critical consciousness. How did these students do it? Interestingly, the study found that the high-achieving students themselves supplemented assigned course readings with essays written by Black authors and other scholars of color. Seeing the impact of these supplemental readings on student achievement, the authors encourage faculty to assume responsibility for culturally inclusive curricula and pedagogy, particularly when teaching students from minoritized groups.

More recently, culturally relevant teaching garnered attention as part of both our national reckoning with racial justice and faculty responses to the COVID-19 pandemic. In late March of 2020, Luke Wood and Frank Harris III, San Diego State education professors and codirectors of the Community College Equity Assessment Lab, conducted a webinar for faculty on equity-minded and culturally affirming teaching in online courses.[16] They urged faculty to be culturally relevant and affirming and to be race conscious. Referencing Gloria Ladson-Billings's work, they explained that students of color often find that their voices are absent from course readings, assignments, and assessments, and that even the images used in PowerPoint presentations tend to be of White individuals. Wood and Harris used the term *mirroring* to stress the importance of students seeing themselves in course content, perspectives, and materials.

One way to help students see themselves in our online courses comes from a 2019 study by René F. Kizilcec and Andrew J. Saltarelli that examines the effect of inclusive images in asynchronous courses.[17] They created two mock online advertisements for two courses: Probability and Statistics and Computer Science 101. In one case, images in the ads were technology related, showing a graph on a screen for the first and a photo of an open laptop on a desk for the second. The experimental ads featured an image of a woman at a computer and of a group of women of diverse racial and ethnic identities. The authors found an increase in click-through rates among women who viewed the experimental ads. From these findings we can extrapolate an important lesson: intentional placement of images that enable students to see themselves in the discipline (or profession) may go a long way to promote academic engagement.

With respect to race consciousness, Wood and Harris implore us to "be intentional about providing opportunities to engage racial and equity issues within the context of the course," reminding us that inequities are prevalent across disciplines. Wood and Harris also echo Ladson-Billings's and Quaye and Harper's implication that race, as a central feature of our identities, is a key source of relevance.[18] Carter G. Woodson and his fellow practitioners of fugitive pedagogy knew this all too well.

Among the many scholars who have built on Ladson-Billings's work are Margery Ginsberg and Raymond Wlodkowski, who developed a model of culturally responsive teaching specifically for college faculty.[19] The impetus for their work, like Ladson-Billings's, was the demographic changes they were observing in the student and faculty profiles of U.S. higher education: increased student diversity yet limited faculty diversity. As they write in their book *Diversity and Motivation*, these demographic shifts have resulted in colleges and universities in which students' identities differ markedly from those of their professors. Ginsberg and Wlodkowski also found a tension between their research on intrinsic motivation and what they saw as many faculty members' reliance on extrinsic models of reinforcement, such as emphasizing grades and conducting competitive assessments. Based on intrinsic motivation, their model affirms that we will be much more effective in motivating diverse students if we enhance our communication with and respect for them, seeking to understand and draw on their strengths.

culturally responsive teaching: Instructional mindsets and practices through which educators leverage their students' diverse cultural backgrounds, identities, and lived experiences as assets for learning.

The Ginsberg and Wlodkowski model of **culturally responsive teaching** consists of four conditions for optimizing student motivation:

1. *Developing attitude*: creating or affirming a favorable disposition toward learning through personal relevance and choice

2. *Establishing inclusion*: creating a learning atmosphere in which we feel respected by and connected to one another

3. *Enhancing meaning*: creating engaging and challenging learning experiences that include students' perspectives and values

4. *Engendering competence*: creating or affirming an understanding that students have effectively learned something they value and perceive as authentic to their real world

Although relevance cuts across the four conditions, it is especially important to conditions 1 and 3: helping students develop a positive attitude toward learning and find meaning in what they're learning. Ginsberg and Wlodkowski indicate that offering students choices based on their experiences, values, needs, and strengths is one of the primary ways faculty can help students develop this type of attitude. They counsel faculty to, instead of presuming to know what students will find personally relevant, offer enough flexibility and choice to allow students themselves to ensure the relevance of their learning tasks. Students might apply a course idea to a societal issue that's important to them or be invited to relate a course topic or competency with one of their career goals or interests. Both condition 3, enhancing meaning, and condition 4, engendering competence, explicitly reference students' perspectives and values, reinforcing the inextricability of motivation and relevance. (Some of Ginsberg and Wlodkowski's specific recommendations for how to increase course relevance will be provided later on.)

What Does the Research Say about Rigor?

Before delving into the research on rigor, it seems important to elaborate on what we mean by rigor, and to expand on some of the ways the term *rigor* is used and misused. Common descriptions of rigor associate it with volume (like the number of assignments or hours spent studying) or curricular level (as in, calculus is more rigorous than algebra). Some think of rigor as thoroughness or accuracy, while others imagine severity or strictness, as in demanding, difficult, or extreme conditions. As Jack and Sathy write, "Far too many faculty members still think a challenging course should be like an obstacle race"—one in which "you, as the instructor, set up the tasks and each student has to finish them (or not) to a certain standard and within a set time. If only a few students can do it, that means the course is rigorous."[20] Professor emeritus of biology Craig Nelson famously reflects on ideas he dubs "dysfunctional illusions of rigor" that had informed his teaching practices, describing his personal realization that many so-called rigorous practices disadvantage students.[21]

Pause to Consider

- How do you define or describe *rigor*?

- How does your version compare to the one provided in this unit, and what might account for the differences?

We define rigor as academic challenge that supports student learning and growth, and we contend that it is essential to equity-minded teaching for the three reasons noted previously: to highlight rigor's relationship to learning, to counter the deficit-based belief that inclusion means lowered standards, and to affirm that students have boundless potential best tapped by high standards and support. After isolating a few key insights from the research on how rigor facilitates learning, we will summarize perspectives on the relationship between rigor and equity.

How Rigor Facilitates Learning

How does being challenged support learning? One well-established connection was developed by Russian and Soviet psychologist Lev Vygotsky in the 1930s. Vygotsky described the optimal level of challenge—the "sweet spot" for learning—as a theoretical space existing between what an individual can learn independently and what they can learn with guidance or in partnership with others. This sweet spot is known as the *zone of proximal development*; see figure 1.1. For us as educators, one of the key takeaways from

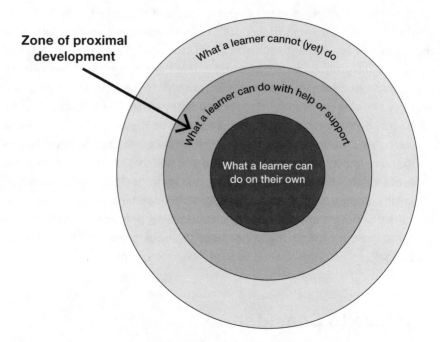

FIGURE 1.1 The Zone of Proximal Development

According to psychologist Lev Vygotsky, the "zone of proximal development" describes the space between what a learner can already do and what they can't yet do. Finding the "sweet spot" in the middle involves balancing rigor with support.

this connection is that to maximize learning, we must appropriately challenge students. If we aim too low, students won't devote sufficient effort or time to the learning task, and if we aim too high or offer insufficient support, students may think the task is impossible and disengage. Identifying the appropriate level of challenge can be difficult and usually takes time to calibrate (but don't despair: low- or no-stakes assessments can help, especially early in the semester). Vygotsky's theory also counters the perspective that providing students with support represents a reduction in rigor.[22] Even the toughest critics of active learning and group work might be excited to find out that they can pose more cognitively demanding challenges to students if they provide adequate support.

At the same time, equity-minded faculty pair rigor with support. We must not overlook the importance of enabling students to achieve success when facing academic challenges *with* the guidance of or in partnership with others. Students' ability to succeed with support is a primary reason why meaningful, well-structured collaborative learning experiences can be so effective. Intentionally designed and facilitated discussion forums can serve this purpose in both online and in-person courses, but they're especially helpful in fully online classes, where other forms of collaboration (like group projects) tend to pose challenges for students with shifting work schedules or busy home lives. We'll share specific examples and recommendations in Unit 2 on transparency and in Section Two when we consider what equity-focused online teaching looks like on a day-to-day basis.

Bloom's taxonomy (see figure 1.2) also helps make the connection between learning and rigor. It describes six levels of cognitive demand—from the recalling of facts to analysis, evaluation, and creation. When Benjamin Bloom and fellow educational psychologists studied the questions commonly posed to students in college settings, they found that more than 95 percent of test questions required students only to recall information. The resulting taxonomy (first published in 1956 and updated in 2001) has since been used by educators at all levels in the design of curriculum and assessments that include varied levels of cognitive challenge.

On Rigor and Equity

As we've alluded to previously, rigor is a complex and contentious topic. In relation to equity, the research suggests that rigor is both a critical problem and a key solution. Perhaps the most critical problem is that many teachers and faculty, often without being aware of it, continue to have lower academic expectations for their students of color. Implicit in this practice is the sense that some students are capable of rigorous work while others are not—and importantly, that an individual faculty member can immediately tell the difference.

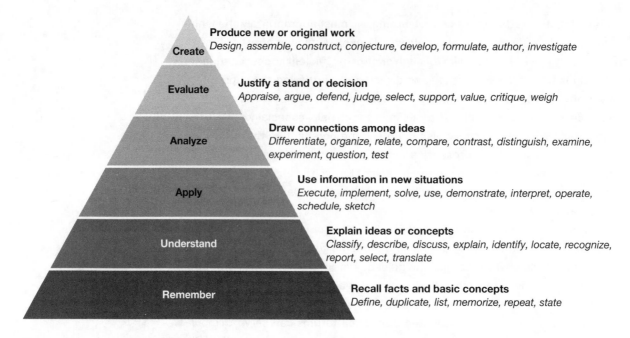

FIGURE 1.2 Bloom's Taxonomy

This widely used learning framework, developed in 1956 and later refined, envisions learning activities along a continuum from basic fact recall to complex thinking and ideation.

Source: Vanderbilt University Center for Teaching.

Given how little we know about our students and their actual abilities and lived experiences when they enroll in our courses, it seems we might be conflating students' capabilities with what we can observe, whether their background knowledge or our assumptions based on their identities.

In terms of race, psychologist and multiculturalism expert Derald Wing Sue and his colleagues refer to the latter as the "ascription of intelligence"—the act of "assigning intelligence to a person of color on the basis of their race," a common **racial microaggression**.[23] They explain that microaggressions are "brief, everyday exchanges that send denigrating messages to people of color because they belong to a racial minority group."[24] Racial microaggressions, specifically, are "brief and commonplace daily verbal, behavioral, or environmental indignities, whether intentional or unintentional, that communicate hostile, derogatory, or negative racial slights and insults toward people of color." As equity-minded faculty, we recognize that students will enter our classrooms with varied levels of academic preparation and knowledge of our specific disciplines. Yet we also engage in self-examination, get to know our students, and resist making assumptions about their capabilities. Instead, we believe in and demonstrate our belief in students' potential, set the bar high, and increase support structures.

racial microaggression: A brief incident, act, or remark that discriminates against or insults someone based on their race.

Although the impact of teacher expectations on student learning and performance has been famously difficult to study, many scholars have drawn a direct line between the two. As Kingsborough Community College professor of English Emily Schnee states plainly, "Low teacher expectations of Black students are well-documented and theorized to be a significant contributing factor in suppressing Black students' academic achievement."[25] Similarly, Zaretta Hammond, a leading scholar of culturally responsive teaching, correlates rigor and so-called "achievement gaps." She cites classroom studies that document the fact that underserved English learners, low-income students, and students of color routinely receive less instruction in higher-order skills development than other students do. As a result, Hammond argues, many of these students are dependent learners who are not yet ready for the academic challenges they encounter in college.[26] Most recently, a comprehensive study conducted by the National Bureau of Economic Research found a strong correlation between teacher expectations and college completion as well as evidence of racial bias in teachers' expectations, affirming that "white teachers, who comprise the vast majority of American educators, have far lower expectations for Black students than they do for similarly situated white students."[27]

Daniel Solorzano, Miguel Ceja, and Tara Yosso provided a vivid illustration of this damaging phenomenon via one student's retelling of an experience with a faculty member:

> I was doing really well in the class, like math is one of my strong suits. . . .
> We took a first quiz . . . and I got like a 95. . . . He [the professor] was like,
> "Come into my office. We need to talk," and I was like, "Okay." I just really
> knew I was gonna be [told] "great job," but he [said], "We think you've
> cheated. . . . We just don't know, so we think we're gonna make you
> [take the exam] again." . . . And [then] I took it with just the GSI
> [graduate student instructor] in the room, and just myself, and I got a
> 98 on the exam.[28]

Despite acknowledging the prevalence and impact of experiences like this one, leading scholars and practitioners of equity-minded teaching—past and present—insist that we cannot attain equitable outcomes without rigor. In the Jim Crow era, Black educators, as well as those who sought to stop them from teaching Black students and/or to limit these students to technical or applied content, understood the power of education and of critical thought.[29] Civil rights leader and educator Bob Moses uses the term "sharecropper education" to describe the limited, preassigned roles for which Black individuals were allowed to be prepared.[30]

A rigorous education counters the historical legacy of these societal forces and their contemporary manifestations. bell hooks recalls that she was taught that a "devotion to learning, to a life of the mind" was a form of resistance. Moses took a rigorous, discipline-based approach to empowering students to succeed in a postindustrial society. In 1982, he found out his eighth-grade daughter, Maisha, would not learn algebra because it was not offered at her school.[31] He knew that without this foundation she would be ineligible for honors math and science classes in high school—which would limit (or at least delay) her STEM literacy and career prospects. Believing firmly that math proficiency is a gateway to equality, Moses in 1982 founded the Algebra Project, a nonprofit dedicated to teaching algebra in culturally relevant ways to students who were often tracked into less rigorous classes. As of 2021, the Algebra Project had helped more than 40,000 students in hundreds of schools nationwide,[32] with results ranging from higher scores on district and state-level exams to confidence in math ability and placement into higher levels of math courses.[33]

The combination of rigor paired with support exemplified by the Algebra Project features prominently in Hammond's model of culturally responsive teaching. "While the achievement gap has created the epidemic of dependent learners," she writes, "culturally responsive teaching is one of our most powerful tools for helping students find *their* way out of the gap."[34] In fact, Hammond includes a "Ready for Rigor" framework within her book and her approach. Similarly, Luke Wood, in his text *Black Minds Matter*, focuses on the education of Black males and urges us to establish and convey high expectations "to counter pervasive messages that Black learners receive from educators, peers, family, and society at large that communicate their inability to succeed academically."[35] He also reminds us that students need to know we believe in them and that rigor needs to be balanced with support. Through an inclusive approach to rigor, we empower students and create the conditions in which *they* can strengthen their cognitive skills, surpass all expectations regarding their ability, and reap the liberatory benefits of learning.

These summaries of contemporary theories of motivation and culturally relevant (or responsive) teaching and of the literature on rigor only skim the surface of vast bodies of research. Yet they underscore the centrality of relevance and rigor to student learning and success, particularly for students with minoritized identities. An important caveat is that the implementation of these tools must be approached with authenticity and depth. When motivation is reduced to students' interests, versus their values or goals, or when culturally relevant teaching is reduced to superficial, symbolic tasks such as eating ethnic or cultural foods or listening to ethnic or cultural music, it will not reap its intended benefits. Rigor, in turn, must reflect actual cognitive challenge and be coupled with both our support and our belief in students' capacity for success. The section that follows homes in on a potent yet often untapped opportunity to increase learning equity via the power of relevance and rigor: course design, drawing on the key research principles on relevance we have just distilled.

Equity-Minded Course Design

For many of us faculty, the course-design process involves using or adapting a departmentally approved or another colleague's syllabus or online course and then making small tweaks each time we teach the course, often in the areas of course policies (which are addressed explicitly in Unit 3). Only rarely do we revisit our course learning goals or primary assessments and activities. And why would we, when we have so many other responsibilities to take care of both in and outside of teaching? However, careful course design provides an essential foundation for inclusive day-to-day teaching in all modalities.

This unit invites you to focus on course design or refinement using ideas found in L. Dee Fink's *Creating Significant Learning Experiences* and introduces key principles and practices from the Universal Design for Learning (UDL) course-planning approach.[36] Fink outlines a systematic process for designing courses that aims to ensure that learning lasts long after a semester has ended. The core components of the process may sound familiar: examining the context of the course, crafting learning goals, identifying assessment processes, and selecting the teaching/learning activities. What distinguishes Fink's model and makes it especially well-suited to inclusive teaching (and, in particular, to increasing a course's level of rigor and perceived relevance) is its comprehensive taxonomy of learning goals—that is, a broader, deeper conception of college-level learning.

Meanwhile, UDL, a neuroscience-based framework first developed in the 1980s, is predicated on the concept of universal design in the built environment. Picture a "curb cut"—the small ramp on sidewalks. It helps not only individuals who use wheelchairs but also those pushing strollers, using walkers, or rolling luggage. When we plan courses (in all modalities) with UDL in mind, we similarly build in supports and options that help all learners. UDL can be particularly important in online spaces, as these guidelines help us account for student diversity and intersectional identities that may not be visible to us. For example, videos without captions or transcripts prevent Deaf and hearing-impaired students from getting the material in the videos. PDF files that are not compliant with optical character recognition (OCR; such as a textbook chapter or article that was scanned on a department office copy machine) appear as meaningless images to screen-reader software, restricting access to our blind or vision-impaired students. In this unit we'll consider UDL principles as they relate to designing effective learning objectives, and we'll revisit both UDL and Fink's model throughout this section of the guide.

The remainder of this unit describes ways to enhance both rigor and perceived relevance, with an emphasis on your learning objectives.

Step 1: Analyze the Course Context

First, Fink encourages us to examine our course context. Although you can engage in this part of the process independently, it's also an excellent opportunity for collaboration with colleagues and departmental leaders. The latter can often access data more easily, for instance. Consider elements such as what role your course plays in students' sequence of courses or within their major, how it relates to other courses, and how many students are enrolled in each section. Also consider how long the class is scheduled to run. Is it a full semester or term? Or is it an accelerated duration?

Next, reflect on the characteristics of your learners. These are key to laying the groundwork for increased course relevance and enable us to build in supports to account for learner variability, in line with UDL. Here are a few questions to get you started:

- What do you know about the students who will take or have taken the course you're seeking to design or refine? For example, are they more likely to be traditional-age students (broadly defined as eighteen to twenty-four years old), or is it more commonly the case that your students are working professionals? Are they balancing schoolwork with jobs and family responsibilities?

- What sources of data are available to you? For instance, could your institutional research office provide you with a demographic profile of the students who have taken the class or are enrolled in your program of study? Have you or has your institution collected any qualitative data from your students, so that you can read about students' experiences in their own words?

- What is happening in the context of your students' communities/world as well as at your institution, including events related to the course context or content?

- If you have taught the class before, have you noted any patterns regarding the students' employment situations, their professional goals, and/or their assumptions or feelings about the subject matter?

The importance of pausing to reflect on what is happening in the world (or state, city, or college) was never more evident than during the pandemic. Recall that our brains are programmed to keep us alive—they're constantly scanning the environment, looking for and responding to threats and dangers. While it can be tempting to ignore any "elephants" in the room, don't underestimate their educational value or the impact of talking about them with students. For instance, the COVID-19 pandemic presented an opportunity to connect with our students based on our shared experiences of fear and uncertainty, as well as to remind students to consider the sources of their news and to beware of the large amount of misinformation. At the same time, less widespread occurrences, including campus-based incidents, can also have a pronounced impact on students.

The last question in our list, regarding students' feelings about the subject matter, may be especially important for faculty who teach introductory or general education courses. Unfortunately, many students question the relevance of introductory courses, as a team of MIT physics education researchers discovered in 2009.[37] These researchers were conducting a study on what students should learn in introductory physics, but their most significant finding turned out to be the stark contrast between student and faculty responses. In their words:

> We instructors seem to be saying, "We are going to make you into expert physicists," and the freshmen seem to be replying, "Before we commit to that much hard work, tell us how physics connects to the world around us and to society's problems, and teach us new things we haven't studied before."

The researchers concluded that, in order to secure and maintain students' attention, physics faculty should demonstrate the relevance and utility of physics to students' lives and careers. This strategy aligns with the UDL guideline related to affective learning. Helping students see that our material is interesting and relatable often results in more buy-in and engagement. Better learning is likely to be the result.

Another important data set for faculty teaching general education courses is the content of students' related high school courses. These data were key to the success of the Carnegie Math Pathways, a reform effort that resulted in student achievement consistently three to four times higher than in the traditional math sequence. The Carnegie curricular designers recognized that lower-level mathematics courses often focus on the same content students have previously struggled with in high school, so they created new curricula based on mathematics that students will use in their everyday lives—for instance, calculating car loan payments and understanding the Electoral College results. The emphasis is on having students apply statistics or quantitative reasoning skills to real-life situations, such that they engage in math that is meaningful and useful for them. For faculty teaching general education courses, we discern three key takeaways: (1) It's especially important to devote additional effort to helping students find value in the course content and outcomes. (2) When doing so, it's helpful to consider the courses and learning experiences students may have had before your course as well as those that will follow. (3) You don't have to go it alone: consider partnering with colleagues to revise a class.

Increasingly important contextual considerations include your teaching modality and your use of technology. Virtually all courses have access to Canvas or another LMS, and publisher materials and apps abound to enhance learner engagement and time on task. Yet technology use can itself be a site of inequity, raising barriers in potentially unforeseen ways. The following questions may prompt you to think more deeply about how your students are engaging with your course through technology:

- Are you teaching in person? If so, how often and for how long does the class meet?
- If you're teaching the class fully online, is the class asynchronous or synchronous?
- Is your class scheduled as a hybrid or other combination of modes (such as HyFlex or dual streaming)?
- Wherever you're teaching, how might you incorporate technology to enhance students' ability to achieve course learning objectives? How can your LMS or electronic publisher materials offer opportunities for practice, interaction, and application of new concepts and skills?
- As you consider synchronous or asynchronous technologies for your class in any mode, pause to reflect on UDL guidance related to individual learner variability and differing access. If you use a particular technology tool to increase engagement, for example, who are you excluding by making that decision? Who won't be able to use that tool due to internet availability, assistive technology limitations, or complex lives?

The growing variations of course modalities and available technologies call for more deliberate planning, and we also know that these flexible class offerings are essential as we strive to ensure greater access to a college education. Today's new majority students (those who were once considered the "minority" but who now represent the growing majority of college students) may be able to attain a college credential only by taking online or hybrid classes. To increase access, learning, and completion in an equitable way, we must plan for students who are juggling multiple obligations and competing demands on their time. Failing to do so implies that only students who don't have to work one or more jobs (as an example) are welcome in our classes—an implication that can get in the way of student belonging and trust (see Section Two).

Step 2: Develop Learning Objectives

Now that you've examined the context for your course, pause to consider the same questions Fink has posed to faculty across the country for decades: What is the lasting impact you would most like to have on your students? One or two years after the course, what would differentiate your students from those who did not benefit from your teaching?[38] As you ponder these questions, it's best to avoid looking at your current course learning objectives. After all, our years of dedication to our disciplines mean that, to us, our course content and goals are inherently and unambiguously relevant. It can be hard to imagine how anyone could question their importance or utility!

UDL guidelines likewise encourage us to reflect on long-lasting implications of student learning in our courses. A primary UDL- and neuroscience-based question to ask yourself is, "Why will my students care about what they're learning?" Careful consideration of this question may lead to creating supplemental objectives, or revising existing ones, in ways that significantly enhance the value and relevance of our course materials and activities.

When Phillip Carter, professor of linguistics at Florida International University, engaged in this reflective exercise, he thought about the lasting impact of the Modern English Grammar course he was assigned to teach.[39] Because many of his students would become teachers and work in ethnically and linguistically diverse schools, he felt they most needed to learn perspectives on grammar in writing, or information about the grammar of nonstandard varieties of English, including those spoken by their future students. He was also concerned about the ethics of a grammar course within a linguistically diverse, minority-serving institution, knowing that grammar had likely played a policing role throughout his students' education (picture lots of red ink correcting errors). Professor Carter also saw an opportunity. His Modern English Grammar course would be, for many students, their only encounter with the formal study of language and thus represented a chance for him, as a linguistics professor, to relate the course to the language found in students' homes and communities. His overall, long-term goal therefore became to empower his students by shifting their perspectives on what grammar is.

What If I'm Required to Use Standard Learning Objectives?

We know that updating learning objectives is not always feasible. Here are two ideas:

1. *Double up!* That is, when possible, include two sets of learning objectives. Directly after his student-friendly learning objectives, biomedical engineering professor Dr. Brian Helmke's syllabus reads, "Want to see these objectives in the geeky language of academics and ABET? Click here." This directs students to the end of the syllabus, where he complies with his institution's requirement to list the course's standard objectives.

2. *Translate them*. Learning objectives are often full of jargon and sound sterile, making it difficult for students to understand them. You can leave the official objectives as-is and translate (or partner with students to co-translate) them into learning goals that make sense to students, and get them excited about what they will know and be able to do as a result of your course.

The "How Can I Get Started?" ideas at the end of this unit provide additional ways to encourage student engagement with learning objectives.

How do you translate your teaching dreams into course learning objectives? In Professor Carter's case, he introduced what he calls the "critical goals of the course," which now appear front and center on his course syllabus. Whereas a traditional learning objective for a grammar course might sound something like, "Demonstrate an understanding of register, accent, and dialect in modern English," Carter instead asks his students, "What is grammar? What does it mean to talk about 'good' and 'bad' grammar? Who benefits from such distinctions? Who suffers? Where do notions of 'grammatical correctness' come from in the first place?" It's not hard to imagine that students would be more motivated to work toward Professor Carter's critical goals, as these relevant objectives exemplify Ladson-Billings's criterion of critical consciousness.

After reflecting deeply on your overarching goals for student learning, take a step back, especially if you've taught a particular course for years, and scrutinize the existing learning objectives as they appear on the syllabus. Sometimes, learning objectives become irrelevant over time; this irrelevance contradicts UDL-based guidelines and Fink's model and is a missed opportunity to advance equity. For example, coauthor Flower Darby rewrote her educational technology curriculum and objectives in a required online graduate course after realizing that approximately half of her students were not instructors and likely never would be. With curriculum committee approval, she redesigned the class to focus on effective use of technology—no matter where students would ultimately work. A periodic close review of learning objectives that you've lived with for years may reveal opportunities to make similar revisions to ensure that course experiences and outcomes are relevant for today's students, as Professor Carter and Flower did.

If you're wondering whether students will even notice your new course learning objectives, recall our pandemic-induced collective experiment in online learning. It's true that in fully in-person classes, many students engage with our course syllabi and thus our course learning goals only on the first day of class. However, a key feature of intentionally designed online courses, especially those built in line with rubrics such as Quality Matters or the Online Learning

Consortium (OLC) OSCQR Course Design Review Scorecard (more on these in Unit 2 and beyond), is the prominence of learning objectives at the module level, which serve as a visible course outline. This more detailed outline not only helps students organize their learning but also helps us as faculty monitor student progress on the objectives and ensure that our learning activities, assessments, feedback, and all other course features are aligned with the specific learning objectives at hand.

To develop your own course learning objectives, ones that may supplement officially approved language and that align with your long-term aspirations for your students, use the categories in Fink's taxonomy to guide your brainstorming.[40] The three categories on the right side of figure 1.3 may seem familiar, as they resemble Bloom's taxonomy of learning (see figure 1.2). Fink developed the categories on the left-hand side of the figure based on his analysis of faculty's long-term aspirations for their students. For instance, many

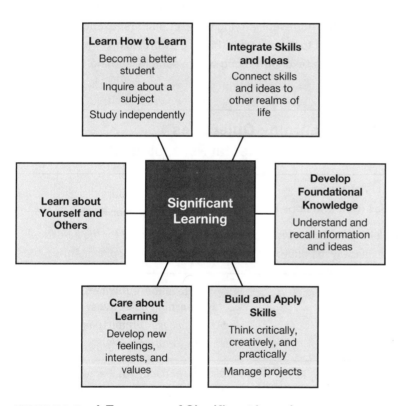

FIGURE 1.3   A Taxonomy of Significant Learning

L. Dee Fink's taxonomy has some similarities with Bloom's taxonomy, especially in the categories on the right, but Fink presents learning in a broader way. The categories on the left describe long-term aspirations for students.

Source: Adapted from L. Dee Fink, "A Self-Directed Guide to Designing Courses for Significant Learning," Dee Fink & Associates, accessed March 22, 2022, https://www.deefinkandassociates.com /GuidetoCourseDesignAug05.pdf.

faculty hoped students would apply what they had learned in class to their future studies and/or work, continue learning about the subject, and see themselves as change agents or problem solvers.

Across all of the categories, Fink insists on the importance of relevance: "Each category of significant learning contains several more specific kinds of learning that are related *and, in some way, have a distinct value for the learner.*"[41] In the same way, UDL guidelines remind us that "individuals are rarely interested in information and activities that have no relevance or value." To further enhance students' willing investment in course concepts and activities, consider including one or more learning objectives that promote individual reflection, prompting students to articulate how what they're learning aligns with and advances their personal values, goals, and interests. In line with UDL principles, invite students to contemplate these topics in their choice of formats: written reflections in paragraph form, bulleted lists, concept maps, videos, and more. Finally, to ensure high standards for your students, make sure you include learning objectives that represent varying levels of Bloom's taxonomy.

Table 1.1 is intended to prompt your thinking by providing Fink's questions for each category in his taxonomy along with a sample learning objective for

TABLE 1.1   Formulating Significant Learning Objectives
Guiding Questions and Samples from a Developmental Psychology Course

Your long-term aspirations for your students
A year or more after the course concludes, I want and hope that students will _____.

Sample response: "describe key factors, including parents, schools, and society, that account for the individual differences that develop between us; engage civically in policy matters associated with development."

Category of significant learning	Questions to consider	Relevance-enhanced learning objectives *After successfully completing this course, you will:*
Foundational knowledge	• What key information—including key ideas regarding minoritized identities—is important for students to understand and remember in the future? • What key perspectives—including diverse scholarly perspectives—are important for students to understand in this course?	• Describe some of what science can tell us about development, from conception to adolescence, and how those changes are shaped by culture and context. • Describe select theories and findings by diverse influential scientists, both past and present, that help us understand human development.

Application	• What kinds of thinking are important for students to learn?	• Question whether important development phenomena or research findings are relevant or even applicable across different groups of people.

Application

- What kinds of thinking are important for students to learn?
  - » critical thinking, in which students analyze and evaluate
  - » creative thinking, in which students imagine and create
  - » practical thinking, in which students solve problems and make decisions
- What important skills do students need to gain?

- Question whether important development phenomena or research findings are relevant or even applicable across different groups of people.
- Use key developmental ideas to craft questions and hypotheses associated with challenges you see the parents in your families or communities confront.

Integration

- What connections (similarities and interactions) should students recognize and make
  - » among ideas within this course?
  - » among the information, ideas, and perspectives in this course and those in other courses or areas?
  - » among material in this course and the students' own personal, social, and/or work life?

- Explain how environmental (e.g., income level) and genetic factors interact to shape individual development.
- Notice how key developmental ideas are reflected in current debates about early childhood education.

Human dimension

- What could or should students learn about themselves?
- What could or should students learn about understanding others and/or interacting with them?

- Identify some of the factors from your early environment and heredity that may have influenced and will continue to influence your development, particularly the ones that have contributed to your wellness and strengths.
- Identify some of the factors from the early environment and heredity of one of your peers from a different cultural background than yours that may have influenced their development (cultural competence).

Caring

- What changes/values do you hope students will adopt?
- What feelings do you want them to have about the subject matter?

- Commit to carefully examining policy matters that relate to development (like early childcare) and to becoming sufficiently informed when voting on related policies.

Learning how to learn	• What would you like students to learn about 　» how to be a successful student in a course like this? 　» how to learn about this particular subject? 　» how to become a self-directed learner of this subject (i.e., have a learning agenda of what they need/want to learn and a plan for learning it)?

• Find reliable sources when developmental questions arise in your life.
• Borrow/adapt some of the methods used by developmental scientists for your own study habits.

Source: Adapted from Robyn L. Kondrad, "Example of a Well-Designed Course in Developmental Psychology" (designed using Fink's model), Design Learning, *accessed March 22, 2022, http://www.designlearning.org/wp-content/uploads/2014/04/Kondrad-R.-Submission-Mar.-30.pdf.*

each that is informed by the relevance research we covered previously. For now, focus on the substance of your objectives instead of worrying about whether they conform to a set of standards, such as being concrete, action-oriented, and measurable. (There's plenty of time to wordsmith later!)

One specific way to update your objectives for equity is to consider, for each category of Fink's taxonomy, whether an explicitly equity-minded or justice-oriented learning objective aligns with your long-term goals for your students. In a literature class, for instance, one of your "integration" objectives might be for students to describe the role canonical literature in *x* time period plays in reinforcing or interrupting ideas about race and racial stereotypes. Adding racial literacy objectives like this one legitimizes critical thinking about race in historical context as content to be learned, not a set of opinions, explains English professor Allison Parker.[42] If you're still unsure how to connect your objectives to race, equity, or inclusion, an online search may likely reveal ideas and inspiration from your discipline. For example, in the "Lesson" section of "Classroom Resources," you can filter by your discipline at Learning for Justice, a project of the Southern Poverty Law Center: https://learningforjustice.org. Brief discipline-focused articles like Steven Meyers's "Putting Social Justice into Practice in Psychology Courses" (which helped inform table 1.1) are also plentiful. And Meyers offers one high-level question that may help all of us generate equity-minded, relevant ideas: "What are the implications of [your] traditional course information for society and the disenfranchised?"[43]

One last bit of advice for this phase of your course design/redesign journey. As coauthor Bryan Dewsbury puts it, "Be brave and reduce content."[44] As you look over and update your course learning objectives, consider what they include or suggest about the amount of content in the class, and whether you may need to cut down on coverage to allow for depth of learning and time for the equity-minded day-to-day teaching practices we will describe in Section Two. Building in time for deep engagement supports the UDL principle of designing for transferability, too. **Learning transfer** refers to students' ability to apply what they learned in our classes to new situations in the workplace, in the community, and at home. The ability to transfer learning to novel contexts and problems is the hallmark of deep and durable learning and is thus essential to equitable education.

We realize content "coverage" is the subject of a long-standing debate in many disciplines. Joel Sipress and David Voelker, for example, chronicle the genealogy of the coverage model in the teaching of history survey courses.[45] They conclude that coverage has never resulted in the intended historical learning gains, arguing instead for a new introductory history course focused on significant historical questions and historical argumentation. Similarly, Dewsbury and colleagues' study found that reducing content in an introductory biology course to allow for inclusive and active pedagogies not only resulted in student learning and success gains in the short term but also resulted in improved success in the subsequent biology course.[46] In short, cutting content does not necessarily compromise future learning. We encourage you to be mindful of the amount of content in your course as you proceed to the next steps in course design.

Examining your course content is also a great opportunity for collaboration with departmental colleagues. For example, when Mays began to look for ways to reduce the course content in her physiology courses, she reached out to colleagues in her department who teach microbiology, which many students take concurrently. Having that conversation and learning what they were covering in their respective courses helped her, in an evidence-informed way, cut down duplicated content in order to focus more on processes and mechanisms that are unique to physiology.

Your course context and student population, your learning objectives, and your course modality are all important aspects of course design that centers equity. And truly, there's no substitute for reconstituting or refining your course learning objectives as part of working toward more equitable teaching because they are the basis for all other course design decisions. However, if you're unable to devote a great deal of time to this work in the short term, the following ideas are meant to be implemented with little to no prep.

learning transfer:
A student's ability to apply what they learned in the classroom to new situations in the workplace, in the community, and at home.

HOW CAN I GET STARTED?

The following suggestions are intended to prompt implementation ideas for classes in all disciplines and enrollment sizes. Although we've categorized them into common modalities, we expect you'll find inspiration across modes; for example, an idea in one category may spark an idea in a different modality. We encourage you to tweak, remix, and apply in ways that make the most sense in your context.

For Any Class

- Review your course learning objectives and (1) make small tweaks to help students see the course's relevance to their lives, and/or (2) check for varying levels of Bloom's taxonomy to ensure students will be cognitively challenged.

- On the first day, or in an introductory video or post, let students know how the course learning goals will help them in their future courses and/or how they will be valued by employers. You might also point to one of the more rigorous goals, one that may intimidate students, and explain why you've included it as well as how you will support them in attaining it. Explain that you have the utmost confidence that every student in the class will be able to attain it if they devote sufficient time and effort.

- Revisit the previous practice periodically throughout the duration of the course. It's not enough to draw students' attention to the relevance of what they're learning in the first week, when students are likely overwhelmed by the daunting tasks in front of them. Similarly, discussing your confidence that students will be able to achieve the challenging goals in your class has limited impact in Week 1. Frequently communicate both of these crucial messages. For example, you can review them at the start of each new unit, topic, or module, or before beginning major assignments such as papers and projects. Record or write short announcements and send them to online or in-person students through the LMS (some LMSs allow you to preschedule these messages). If teaching in person, deliberately schedule class time to talk about these principles and how they benefit your students.

For In-Person Classes

- As the basis for an in-class discussion, adapt Steven Meyers's question: "What do you think the implications of this course content and goals are for society and the disenfranchised?"[47]

- In the first week or two of class (but not on Day 1, when students are likely overwhelmed by the flood of information), ask students to do a freewrite on notebook paper on a range of questions related to your learning objectives; ask several, and let them choose which to respond to. Example questions might be, "What learning objective are you most excited about (or anxious about) and why?" or "Based on the learning objectives for this course, how might you use what you learn here in your personal, academic, or professional life?" or "Where do you see yourself, your family, or your local community in these course learning objectives?" After students have had a few minutes to think and write, pair them to discuss their responses. Coach them to offer suggestions to each other if appropriate.

For Asynchronous Online Classes

- In an asynchronous discussion, ask students to consider how the textbook, literature, primary texts, or accepted canon disrupts or reinforces racial stereotypes. Encourage them to find and share additional resources that can be incorporated in class to represent a wider, more diverse range of perspectives. After all of your students have contributed, identify a few themes and examples to share back with the whole class.

- In a whole-class or small group discussion board, implement the reflection questions in the second bullet point of the previous list. Consider whether to select the "post-first" setting, which requires students to submit an original post before they can read others' contributions (this can encourage originality). Ask students to reply and offer encouragement and strategies to other students in the discussion.

For Synchronous Online Classes

- Think-Pair-Share: Ask students to review the course learning objectives and jot down a few notes about how the objectives might be helpful to them in their lives, future courses, or careers. See additional example questions in the "For In-Person Classes" list. Then send them to two- or three-person breakout rooms and ask them to discuss these notes with a peer. For added accountability, ask students to complete a prompt, such as sentence stems in a shared document or slide, to note takeaways from their conversation (e.g., "The learning objectives we discussed are . . . ."; "We talked about the following strategies to successfully accomplish these learning goals: . . . ."). When everyone is back in the main room, the small groups can take turns sharing some of their ideas with the whole class, whether aloud or in the chat.

- Ask students to consider how the views of members of majority-population groups have shaped your discipline, what voices have been left out, and how they might identify potential contributions from people who, historically, have been marginalized. Have the students form breakout groups, and then prompt them to discuss their thoughts and complete a synchronous online activity such as posting on a Padlet or a Google Jamboard, or populating a designated slide with their responses. Review the contributions once students are back in the main room, drawing out important points and highlighting meaningful ideas.

2

TRANSPARENCY
Create an Equity-Minded Assessment and Grading Strategy

Clear, authentic assessments enhance student learning and allow both faculty and students to better track learning, while equitable grading practices honor the significance of grades in students' educational experience.

Picking up where we left off in the course design/refinement process outlined in Unit 1, this unit focuses on the equity-minded principle of transparency. After you develop more relevant and rigorous course learning objectives, it's essential that you ensure that your main assessments—whether they're tests, essays, projects, portfolios, and so on—are also relevant, rigorous, and well aligned with your learning objectives. These assessments represent your and your students' main sources of data regarding their learning growth. (Equity-minded faculty also consistently use student assessment data to reflect on and refine their practice; see Section Three.) Because assessment research is vast and can be quite jargon-ridden, this unit focuses on three important characteristics of inclusive assessments: *purpose*, *authenticity*, and *transparency*.

Given the significant impact of grades on student learning and success, we also distill research on equitable grading. Grading can feel much more personal than other course design and instructional practices, so much so that grading practices are often left out of professional development opportunities for faculty. Yet, as the research summary in the following pages will demonstrate, grades bear significantly on student learning and success, particularly for students from minoritized groups. After we discuss the research on inclusive assessments, we'll turn to implementation, revisiting the course design process introduced in Unit 1 and suggesting how to identify your primary assessments and create an equitable grading scheme in any modality.

What Does the Research Say about Assessment and Grading?

Many faculty think of assessment as separate from instruction and learning. If you've ever thought to yourself, "I love teaching; I just hate grading," you might have a classic "testing" view of assessment. This common approach entails testing students after providing instruction to measure what and how much they know, usually using multiple-choice and fill-in-the-blank type quiz and test questions. Although quizzes and tests continue to be helpful assessment tools, advances in cognitive science have revealed that completing them is far from a passive activity for students. Indeed, assessments can be powerful opportunities to promote and deepen learning. This research summary begins with an overview of three key assessment features: purpose, authenticity, and transparency, noting opportunities to enhance equity in each. It then distills research on equitable grading.

Purpose

In the "testing" view of assessment mentioned previously, the purpose of assessments is to find out how much students know or can do, and this information is represented by a grade. You may have heard of the term **summative assessment** to describe this approach. Summative assessments focus on generating a measure or score, usually after a period of instruction. On the other hand, **formative assessments** usually entail evaluating learning over time and have a different core purpose: improvement. Contemporary research has established that assessments are most effective when they provide students (and faculty) with feedback on their learning in relation to the course learning objectives.[1] Formative assessments align with the fact that learning is an iterative process and a "work in progress." It's also true that the line between formative and summative assessments is often blurred: an activity, project, or quiz can both result in a grade and provide students with feedback on their progress.

Inclusive teaching experts Viji Sathy, professor of psychology and neuroscience, and Kelly Hogan, professor of biology, encourage faculty to use multiple formative assessments during a course. They explain that "students . . . might not realize that they are struggling to retain the material until they fail the first exam" and that multiple assessments give students practice evaluating their own progress. Sathy and Hogan add that, as faculty members, we too benefit from the immediate feedback. If a formative assessment shows us that only a fraction of our students have understood a key concept, for instance, we can develop additional exercises or practice opportunities to improve learner comprehension.[2]

Formative assessments also go hand in hand with **low-stakes assessments**, that is, assessments that carry relatively little weight in the course

---

summative assessment: A form of assessment that generates a score or measure after a period of instruction.

formative assessment: A form of assessment that evaluates learning over time and is focused on improvement.

low-stakes assessments: Assessments that carry relatively little weight in the course grading system and may occur frequently during a course.

grading system. These take the pressure off students so they do not become overwhelmed by the consequences of any one score. Lowering the stakes of any individual assessment is another important practice in inclusive teaching. Historically, faculty with a "testing" approach to assessment, particularly those with large class sizes, may have relied on **high-stakes assessments**. Under this approach, by using only a handful of assessments, each one ends up carrying a lot of weight in students' grades. In a class with highest-stakes assessments, a student's final grade might be calculated based mostly on midterm and final exam grades. Even if a course grade is determined by students' score on four exams, a student who fails just one exam cannot mathematically earn an A in the class—regardless of their grade on the other three.

This high-stakes assessment model excludes students rather than promoting equitable outcomes. Students have no way to recover from a poor midterm grade, which often causes them to disengage from or drop the class. In the case of students from minoritized identities, the psychological consequences of this situation can be equally profound as the educational results. Linda Nilson makes this point poignantly, writing that some students believe "they do not belong in this strange culture of higher education, and any poor or mediocre grades they get 'prove' it."[3] (**Sense of belonging**, the feeling of acceptance and support that comes with knowing that one is part of a group, is central to equity-minded teaching and is the subject of Unit 5.)

Formative assessments can promote both equity and academic integrity, because there tend to be more of them during a course. While completing lower-stakes assessments, students feel less anxiety (which is important because anxiety hinders their ability to show their learning, as often occurs in high-stakes assessments) as well as less temptation to cheat. Further, the use of multiple quizzing or testing moments in a course has been shown to support long-term learning by a series of studies on what has been dubbed the *testing effect*. In a nutshell, the testing effect indicates that students learn new material better and can remember it longer when they are tested on it (or test themselves), compared to when they reread the material.[4] Each time you quiz or test your students, or encourage them to quiz themselves as a way to study, you are asking them to retrieve the information or ability from their brain, strengthening the associated memories. Coauthor Isis Artze-Vega has taught her students about the testing effect, and she schedules weekly "retrieval time": when her students participate in ungraded, formative quizzes to help them retain course content. Not surprisingly, students seem to prefer retrieval time to a pop quiz. Course design decisions such as these that support deep and durable learning are equity-focused in that they equip every student for success—in your course and downstream classes, in life, and on the job.

high-stakes assessments: Assessments that carry substantial weight in the course grading system and may occur only a handful of times during a course.

sense of belonging: The feeling of acceptance and support that comes with knowing that one is part of a group. In an academic setting, it refers to a student's feeling of acceptance, inclusion, support, and respect in a learning environment.

Authenticity

authentic assessments: Assessments in which students demonstrate their learning in ways that are meaningful and purposeful.

Authenticity relates to the equity-minded concept of relevance described in Unit 1. **Authentic assessments** are those in which students demonstrate their learning in ways that are meaningful and purposeful. A traditional exam may rely on multiple-choice questions that ask students to recall information, such that students' performance does not accurately gauge or represent their knowledge and skills. The results are also limited in what we as faculty glean regarding student learning and may more accurately assess whether students are effective test-takers or whether they experience performance-reducing test anxiety.

Pause to Consider

- What are you hoping to accomplish when testing your students or assigning a major writing assignment or project?

- How well is your current approach to assessment aligned with those objectives?

Authentic assessments, in turn, are more realistic and give us rich data on student learning. Grant Wiggins, who coined the term, insists that authentic does not simply mean "real-world" or "hands-on."[5] He indicates that an assessment is authentic if it accomplishes the following:

- includes engaging, worthy, and complex problems or questions of importance

- asks students to use or apply their knowledge effectively and creatively

- replicates or resembles problems and situations seen in "real life"—whether by adults and consumers or working professionals

For example, students in a history class might be asked to examine a primary source (from a virtual or in-person archive) in order to craft an argument that informs a public hearing regarding a local landmark or issue of their choice. Students in a marketing class might be asked to analyze a case study in which a recent campaign was less successful than anticipated and then develop solutions for improvement.

Wiggins writes that when he introduced authentic assessments he heard critiques from those who teach "pure" versus "applied" sciences. Mathematicians, specifically, worried that authentic assessments rule out the use of "pure" math problems and the idea of assessing pure mathematical ability. In response, Wiggins shared his favorite math example, one that involves the Pythagorean theorem:

> We all know that $A^2 + B^2 = C^2$. But think about the literal meaning for a minute: The area of the square on side A + the area of the square on side B = the area of the square on side C. So here's the question: does the figure we draw on each side have to be a square? Might a more generalizable version of the theorem hold true? For example: Is it true or not that the area of the rhombus on side A + the area of the rhombus on side B = the area of the rhombus on side C? Experiment with this and other figures.
>
> From your experiments, what can you generalize about a more general version of the theorem?[6]

He explains that this assessment represents "doing" mathematics: "looking for more general/powerful/concise relationships and patterns—and using imagination and rigorous argument to do so, not just plug and chug." Wiggins's math example also illustrates that the principles of authenticity can be used in conjunction with a traditional test; they don't require a completely different assessment format. You can make an exam more authentic by increasing the authenticity of individual test questions.

In addition to promoting equitable outcomes via the centrality of relevance to motivation, authentic assessments can promote academic integrity and provide a means of data collection for inclusive teaching. Studies of academic dishonesty have found that people (not just students) are more likely to cheat when they lack a strong sense of the value or utility of the work they're doing.[7] Assessments that students find relevant therefore maximize motivation and learning while likely minimizing academic dishonesty. (Given faculty concerns over academic dishonesty in online classes, it may be especially prudent to use authentic assessments in fully online courses. We expand on ways to promote academic integrity later in the unit.) Additionally, since many authentic assessments give students the opportunity to choose how to demonstrate their learning, we can then take the time to notice what they choose. This insight helps us get to know our students more deeply, finding out what they find relevant and collecting rich data we can use to further refine our practices.

Transparency

Transparency refers to the extent to which information that is often implicit or unknown to students regarding an assessment is made explicit or transparent to them. Mary-Ann Winkelmes, founder and director of the Transparency in Learning and Teaching project (known as TILT Higher Ed), isolates three hallmarks of a transparent assessment: letting students know the purpose of an assessment (the "why"), breaking down how to effectively complete the assessment (the "how"), and providing students with criteria for success, as in a rubric that articulates what they should do to succeed (the "what").[8] Creating transparency can take the form of updating the written instructions for an assessment; the TILT website provides a detailed template and samples from across disciplines. Benefits of "TILT-ing" are most powerful when faculty provide students with clarity on the "why," "how," and "what" of each assessment, both in writing and via discussion.

Researchers from the TILT project found that in courses where students perceived assignments as more transparently designed, gains were realized in three areas that are important predictors of success: academic confidence, sense of belonging, and mastery of skills that employers value most when hiring. Those benefits were larger for first-generation and low-income students, as well as for students historically underrepresented in college. A little can go a long way: the study found meaningful results even when participating instructors "TILT-ed" (or added transparency) to only a handful of assignments. An added benefit of transparency is that it helps gain and maintain students' trust, the topic of Unit 4.

One reason for the benefits of transparency comes from the clarification regarding purpose. As we described in Unit 1, relevance is key to motivating students, so when we take the time to help them see why an assessment matters, we prompt their motivation to complete it. Also, as experts in our fields, certain tasks have become second nature to us, and we often fail to notice their complexity: for example, we might ask for an annotated bibliography or a lab report without detailing what we expect from our students. Deciphering what professors want and why they want it can be frustrating for students and can compromise their self-efficacy and motivation, leading to giving up or dropping the class in defeat. Thus, clearly communicating our expectations helps students succeed and creates a more equitable learning environment. As we saw with authenticity and fostering integrity, transparency can be especially helpful in fully online courses; in the following pages we will provide ideas for transparency when teaching online.

The principles of transparency apply to tests and exams too. Creating transparent assessments entails carefully constructing exams and individual questions, ensuring that they are purposeful and closely aligned with course learning objectives. It's also best to take time to describe the exam purpose, parameters, format, and scoring process to students. (If you worry that making your assessments more transparent could result in a reduction of rigor, revisit Unit 1 and recall that an assignment or test's level of rigor should represent the challenging cognitive tasks you are assessing, *not* whether students can infer the purpose of the assessment or interpret your instructions.)

On Equitable Grading

Mindful grading practices are essential to inclusive teaching. Just as most of us are never formally taught how to design effective courses, we are rarely taught how to develop grading schemes. Most faculty are also quite skeptical about the use of grades as indicators of learning. These challenges are compounded by the fact that grades have a profound impact on students—including their learning, academic progression, employment, and sense of self-worth. Students, particularly those from minoritized backgrounds, often view poor grades as proof that they are inadequate or do not belong in college.[9] Sathy and her colleague Jordynn Jack add that when many students earn an unsuccessful grade on an exam or class they think their only choice is to drop the class or change majors.[10] Further, the time it takes to receive grades in online classes may lag behind that in onsite classes, exacerbating grade-related inequities.[11] Faculty, in turn, can see patterns in student attainment as evidence that some students are more or less likely to achieve based on their identities, reinforcing **deficit thinking**.

Grading and assessment expert Joe Feldman is even more emphatic about the impact of grades on equitable outcomes. He writes:

> *We know that students' family income [and other variables] have a huge influence on achievement, but at the end of the day, it's their grades—our description of students' academic performance—that opens doors or closes them. We can learn a new curriculum or a new instructional strategy, but if our grading doesn't change, nothing for our students, particularly those most vulnerable, will really change, and the achievement and opportunity gaps will remain.*[12]

We agree not only based on our collective experiences but also in a mathematical/computational sense. Take, for instance, educational inequities in the form of college graduation rates. One of the strongest predictors of these graduation rates is students' grade point averages. These grade point averages, in turn, are the mathematical results of grades in individual classes. In this way, the connection Feldman makes between grading practices and achievement and opportunity gaps is spot-on. Certainly, our grading practices are not the *only* parts of our teaching that influence more equitable outcomes; however, they have a direct impact on many important educational outcomes and therefore warrant our thoughtful attention.

In his study of failing grades, Asao Inoue, professor of rhetoric and composition in the College of Integrative Sciences and Arts at Arizona State University, describes a different, parallel way in which grades impact students' lives. "Failure is constructed through the ways educational institutions, employers, and others outside of schools use the products of their assessments—the

deficit thinking:
The belief that some students are intellectually deficient or limited.

codes, numbers, grades, and other marks that signify student performance and ability," he writes.[13] In essence, much of the power of grades lies in their use and misuse outside of our classrooms. An employer might dismiss a student's résumé, for instance, equating their GPA with readiness for the job or overall capacity or intelligence.

One of the limitations of common grading practices is that they have remained largely unchanged for decades. In fact, most of our practices originated in the early twentieth century, when researchers noted a lack of consistency in teacher grading and tried to make grades more scientific.[14] One of teachers' primary goals in grading was therefore to realize the normal distribution, what we call "grading on a curve." Psychology and education professor Robert Glaser's work on grading in the 1960s lives on in classrooms across the globe. He explained there are two ways to interpret a test score: in relation to others' performance (as in grading on a curve) or to a standard level of expected performance (as in a driver's license exam).[15] This latter approach coincided with Bloom's conviction that educators should strive to have as many students as possible achieve at a high level. Many of us use a combination of these approaches when grading student work.

Pause to Consider

- How confident are you that the grades you give students in your class reflect their learning and their achievement of your course learning objectives?

- What do or would you say to a student who did not successfully complete your class, or who did so poorly, about their performance and its relationship to their abilities and potential?

Recently, grading has reemerged as a topic of interest. A handful of colleges have replaced numerical and categorical grading with student contracts that define success or a combination of self-reflection and faculty-written evaluations.[16] Alternative approaches to grading have also been proposed. Teaching scholar Linda Nilson has devised "specifications grading," which entails grading assignments and/or tests using the categories satisfactory/unsatisfactory or pass/fail: if their work meets carefully crafted specifications, students earn full credit.[17] If not, they earn no credit for that task. Importantly, Nilson strongly recommends allowing students to resubmit work for full credit. This kind of approach, whereby students can learn from mistakes on an assessment and subsequently demonstrate improved achievement, is a crucial characteristic of equity-focused grading.

Notre Dame anthropology professor Susan Blum has played a leading role in what's known as "ungrading," the latest innovation, of sorts, in postsecondary grading.[18] It may sound extreme, but in essence, ungrading means that we de-emphasize grades and refocus our own and students' energies on learning. When we ungrade, we redirect time and attention to learning via such tactics as self-assessment, self-grading, and formative feedback (more to come on the connection between ungrading and equity).

Some inclusive teaching experts warn that competitive grading, such as grading on a curve, limits motivation.[19] Jack and Sathy are more emphatic, referring to "curving" as an outright exclusionary practice. It signals to students that "most of them won't make the cut for an A," they write, and that the "instructor does not see all students as capable of success and is intent on sorting those who can succeed from those who cannot."[20] This approach also fosters competition among students and can limit collaboration since students' grades are based on their peers' level of success. Psychology professor Adam Grant has written, "At best, it creates a hypercompetitive culture, and at worst, it sends students the message that the world is a zero-sum game: Your success means my failure."[21]

Grading for Equity author Joe Feldman echoes many of these sentiments and argues that grading practices must "counteract institutional biases that have historically rewarded students with privilege and punished those without."[22] He proposes a model of equitable grading with three pillars: mathematical accuracy, bias-resistance, and motivation. By *accuracy*, Feldman means that grades truly reflect students' learning and performance. At the core of *bias-resistance* is the need to base grades on students' knowledge and abilities, and to minimize the impact of the instructor's interpretations of student behaviors and environmental factors on students' grades. *Motivation* hearkens back to the research we reviewed in Unit 1 regarding the centrality of motivation to learning. Feldman suggests that equitable grading practices should motivate students to achieve academic success, support a "growth" orientation to learning, and give students hope via redemptive practices. (His specific practices are embedded under the heading "Updating Your Grading System.")

Returning to our discussion on ungrading and its connection to equity, cognitive psychologist and teaching-with-technology scholar Michelle Miller cites helping marginalized students as one of the main benefits of ungrading.[23] Writing professor and digital pedagogy expert Jesse Stommel, a longtime ungrader, contends that ungrading is not inherently inclusive but that it can absolutely work to advance equity.[24] "Grades reinforce teacher/student hierarchies . . . while exacerbating other problematic power relationships," he explains. Stommel warns, however, that a risk in removing grades altogether is that course success could then rely on a "hidden curriculum"—the opposite of the transparent and explicit approach to grading and assessment we describe in this unit. To mitigate these challenges in his version of ungrading, Stommel does the following:

- shares and discusses data about bias in grading with his students
- actively challenges his biases and reflects on his own privilege/marginalization
- adapts his course learning outcomes, policies, and assessments based on his specific students, recognizing they are complex and not interchangeable

It's important to keep in mind that students have been conditioned to rely on grades, such that ungrading can elicit anxiety. In fact, when implementing *any* alternative grading approaches, we'll need to be patient and offer students a great deal of support and reassurance.

We concur with Miller's sense that faculty are increasingly in agreement on the principles of alternative grading approaches yet are still unclear on how to implement them or even get started. So in the following part of this unit, we'll share some of Miller's "ungrading-adjacent" suggestions for trying it out. For now, as a final note about ungrading and equity, we want to share a caution from Chavella Pittman and Thomas Tobin's account of how implementing inclusive practices affects instructors differently based on their identities.[25]

Pittman and Tobin use the implementation of ungrading as an example of an inclusive practice that was experienced in a markedly different way by Tom, who identifies as a White male professor, relative to a tenured professor of color who chose not to reveal her name. Whereas Tom's students were understandably anxious and requested clarification, students in the other professor's class responded with resistance that was "widespread and confrontational." Excerpts from an email exchange illustrate the latter:

> How do you not [have] grades? I'm sorry but this is getting a little ridiculous. . . . I understand your grading policy but as a student, I am reaching out to you to get my grade. . . . I'm sorry but I don't agree with how you do things. I think I'm going to reach out to the dean of students. I pay way too much money.

We know how much is at stake for each of you in your teaching—including your livelihood and your wellness—so we share this account not only because it happened in the context of ungrading but also because it is important to us that you make careful, informed decisions about all of the changes you may make in the name of equity. Our best counsel is to start really small and cautiously when considering ungrading (or alternative grading) approaches, for the sake of both your own and your students' well-being.

Identifying Primary Assessments and a Grading Structure

In Unit 1, we synthesized the first two steps of L. Dee Fink's course design process: analyzing the course context and developing learning objectives. Here, we describe his step three, drawing on the assessment and grading research to suggest ways to continue designing courses and assessments for equity.

Step 3: Determine What Evidence of Learning You Will Collect

With your new or updated course learning objectives in hand, shift your attention to determining how your students and you will gauge their progress toward these objectives. Fink often encourages faculty to use a simple three-column table as a tool for mapping their learning goals onto the associated evidence of learning (and learning activities; see step four of Fink's course design process in Unit 3). With the learning objectives as an anchor in the left-hand column, the middle column represents an opportunity to reflect on each objective and ask, How will my students and I know they are making progress toward or have attained the learning objective?

This mapping strategy also corresponds with the Online Learning Consortium (OLC) OSCQR Course Design Review Scorecard[26] and Quality Matters (QM) rubrics.[27] Both of these evidence-based tools focus on online courses. They can also be useful as a systematic way to take a step back from your class and get a fresh look at the alignment among elements of your course design. Returning to Fink's question in the previous paragraph, we know that relying on midterm and final exams to assign a course grade is limited in its impact on learning and represents a missed opportunity to advance equitable outcomes. Instead, consider the following four approaches to developing or updating your assessments.

Look Forward

One way to develop authentic assessments is to "look forward"—that is, to imagine a moment in your students' future lives (whether academic, personal, or professional) when you expect or hope they will use what they learned in your class.[28] You can then use this real-life, future context to construct a project or assignment, or in the case of tests or quizzes, to craft individual questions. For instance, physics education researchers have encouraged physics faculty to select illustrative examples involving "physics applied to everyday life/things" and "science in the news and society," using topics such as air resistance and aeronautics for moving mass problems, and relating mechanics to the energy crisis.[29] These relevant examples would work as well in individual test questions as they would in the design of a group project.

Consider also one of the learning objectives for the psychology class introduced earlier (see table 1.1): "Identify some of the factors from your early environment and heredity that may have influenced and will continue to influence your development, particularly the ones that have contributed to your wellness and strengths." In response, students could write or record a brief reflection, post what they learned about their wellness and strengths in a discussion board, read their peers' posts, and craft a brief synthesis of what they learned from reading or watching other students' submissions.

Connect to the Present

English teacher Brian Mooney taught his students how to analyze the rapper Kendrick Lamar's album *To Pimp a Butterfly* and assessed their learning by asking them to compare the lyrics to Toni Morrison's 1970 novel *The Bluest Eye*.[30] This assessment exemplifies both authenticity and several features of culturally relevant pedagogy: it builds on students' strengths, race consciousness, and critical consciousness. Mooney's rationale for the assignment also reminds us that equity-minded teaching brings opportunities to connect with and empower our students:

> *If I pedagogically ignored Kendrick's album release at a time when my students were reading Toni Morrison alongside articles about Mike Brown, Ferguson, #BlackLivesMatter—and considering the disposability of black bodies in an America that constructs a standard of beauty based solely on whiteness—I would have missed an opportunity to engage them in a pivotal conversation about race, hope, and justice. I would have missed an opportunity to speak to their hip-hop sensibilities—their hip-hop ways of being and knowing. I would have missed a chance to develop a set of profound connections to a popular culture text that is part of their lives.*

Offer Students Choices

Raymond Ginsberg and Margery Wlodkowski suggest another approach to developing authentic assessments: create assessments that offer students choices.[31] This recommendation is also directly in line with UDL guidelines, which remind us that it's unlikely that individual students will be interested in the exact same topic or issue, and that individuals have varying strengths and skills that enable them to best demonstrate their learning in differing ways. No two learners are exactly alike. Offering choice where possible acknowledges this fact and empowers unique individuals to succeed.

Recall the sample psychology objective in table 1.1: "Use key developmental ideas to craft questions and hypotheses associated with challenges you see the parents in your families or communities confront." To gauge their progress/mastery, students can be asked to choose a specific parenting challenge important to them and submit annotated questions and hypotheses, describing how they used developmental ideas to generate these questions and hypotheses. You could give students additional choice in the format of these submissions. For enhanced relevance, they might present these questions or hypotheses in infographic or concept map form, which would allow practice for students who want to learn basic visual design skills for future employment opportunities.

In one of her online graduate education classes, coauthor Flower Darby creates groups using the self-sign-up option in Canvas (other LMSs have a similar feature too). Then, to maximize student motivation and engagement, she identifies five timely and relevant topics for a deeper-dive project with both collaborative and individual components. Topics have varied from year to year based on what is emergent in the literature: virtual reality, use of mobile devices (such as iPads) in middle and high school classes, and so on. On a first-come-first-served basis, students sign up for the topic they're most interested in.

Lean into Technology

By 2018, smartphone ownership had become a nearly ubiquitous element of teen life; 95 percent of teens reported they had a smartphone or access to one, and nearly half of teens disclosed that they are online almost constantly.[32] Regular internet usage is up across all age groups.[33] Using technology in assessments to increase relevance could take a number of forms: technology can be part of the content, competencies, and/or the product. For instance, students could analyze a concept as depicted on a social media site. Or, given that video-conferencing skills will be increasingly important in the workplace (as in interviews, meetings, and presentations), we might ask students to record informal and more polished videos to demonstrate their learning.

Further, technology-enabled practice and assessment options are readily available in your LMS and publisher courseware. Equity-focused instructors deploy purposeful tech-mediated assessments, including auto-graded quizzes, publisher-provided homework sets, asynchronous discussions that allow you to "scan the room" and check for understanding, and synchronous tools such as clickers in a physical classroom or Zoom polls online. These options have the potential to enact powerful gains in student learning, so we'll further explore the use of tech in equity-minded teaching later in this unit and in Section Two as well.

Aim for Greater Transparency

The Transparency in Learning and Teaching (TILT) project offers many resources to help with transparent assessment design. Chief among them is a template for creating transparent assessments. As described in table 2.1, the template prompts us to craft assignments that specify to students the purpose of the assignment, what steps to take to successfully complete it, and our criteria for evaluating their success. The TILT project website also includes templates and sample assignments from varied disciplines.[34]

Transparency also applies to test design. This entails being more intentional when designing each exam, as well as clarifying to students your goals for each test, helping them effectively prepare for the test, and anticipating their questions about the test content, form, and scoring (award/deduct points, etc.). In terms of test construction, a helpful tool is the table of specifications (TOS), or test blueprint. You may have heard of the TOS with respect to a high-stakes, standardized assessment, yet it can also help with typical class-based tests. In essence, a TOS is a table that helps you align the learning objectives you're assessing with the individual questions or items in the test. Using a TOS

TABLE 2.1   The TILT Framework

Transparent assignment template

Purpose	• What is the instructional purpose of this assignment? What knowledge and skills will students gain from doing it?
	• Why complete it at this point in the course? How does it relate to other coursework and assessments?
	• How are the knowledge and skills gained from this assignment significant beyond the course: in later courses, in a career, or in life?
Task	• What exactly do you want students to do, perform, or create?
	• Will students understand your description of the task? What concepts or processes need to be defined?
	• What is the process for completing the task? When and how should students complete each step? What support or resources might they need to do so?
Criteria	• What does successful performance look like?
	• What are the characteristics of an excellent final product?
	• Where can students find annotated examples? How can they analyze and evaluate examples themselves?

Source: Adapted from Mary-Ann Winkelmes, "Transparent Assignment Template," TILT Higher Ed, 2013, https://tilthighered.com/assets/pdffiles/Transparent%20Assignment%20Template.pdf.

can help you ensure that (1) the number of questions per topic reflects that topic's level of importance and (ideally) how much time students have spent learning it, (2) the cognitive level of the questions aligns with the level at which you taught the concepts, and (3) you can trust that your students' grades will reflect their level of understanding of the corresponding learning objectives.[35]

The Clemson University Office of Teaching Effectiveness and Innovation's Test Blueprint Guide includes sample TOSs and step-by-step guidance.[36] In addition, the University of Waterloo Centre for Teaching Excellence's website includes an article titled "Preparing Tests and Exams," which also provides helpful suggestions on the qualities of a good exam, tips on talking to students about the test purpose and parameters, and ideas for gathering information after students complete a test.[37]

Additional Assessment Design Considerations for Online Classes

Online environments present unique assessment challenges. First, academic integrity is a valid and ongoing concern. Research suggests that cheating may be more prevalent in online exams than in-person ones, and a 2021 study of STEM courses found that contract cheating in online assessments increased by 196 percent from 2019 to 2020.[38] Second, from a student perspective, it's all too often unclear what we're asking students to do on an assignment or an exam, mostly because they can't ask questions about and get clarification on instructions in the moment they're working on the task in front of them (or even the next day, as in an in-person class). This lack of clarity may contribute to students feeling more anxiety and increased temptation to cheat.

We'll explore these challenges in more depth with three additional suggestions specific to online assessment.

Design for Integrity

During her presentations at all kinds and types of colleges, Flower is frequently asked how to prevent cheating in online quizzes and exams. She often shares her potentially hard-to-swallow perspective that all online tests are open-book and open-note—whether or not you intend them to be. Students are resourceful people, and there is simply no way to enforce compliance. Online proctoring is neither an equity-focused nor a particularly effective solution. Starting from a place of suspicion (the antithesis of trust; see Unit 4) strains the faculty-student relationship and results in hardship for neurodivergent students and those with a wide range of physical and learning disabilities. In addition, many Black students experience discrimination in online proctored exams, often being forced to undertake postural contortions, move the light source, and expend a tremendous amount of mental energy—which could be better used on taking the exam itself—just to get the proctoring software to recognize their facial features.[39]

Online tests are not the only concern regarding student honesty; plagiarism continues to be a problem with the increase of paper mills such as Research Papers Online, one of many websites that sells existing or customized writing assignments to students, ostensibly as a model or example, which students may submit as their own work. In addition, as Susan Blum writes, our approaches to promoting academic integrity are often limited or ineffectual, missing key components such as teaching students why we value it and, in the case of avoiding plagiarism, exactly how to carry it out.[40] Policing honesty just doesn't work.

Instead, we suggest creating assessments that promote integrity, following the recommendations and guidelines we've discussed, as well as lowering the stakes of assessments. The latter might entail breaking major exams into multiple smaller tests or increasing the number and decreasing the length and weight of written assignments. Further reduce the temptation to engage in dishonest behavior by permitting students to retake tests or revise and resubmit papers and projects, or by empowering students to drop their lowest test score from their final grade. If your context permits, you can foster enhanced interest and engagement by inviting students to choose their preferred format for demonstrating their learning (such as giving them the option of submitting an infographic, traditional paper, or slide deck for a learning task)—this is UDL in action. These ideas, paired with your intentional creation of authentic, meaningful, and purposeful projects, papers, and tests, can help students choose ethical academic behavior over dishonesty—and reap the corresponding learning gains.

Take Extra Transparency Steps Online

Transparency applies to every design decision and every interaction online. More intentional effort is required for faculty to overcome the inherent distance, the often-confusing layout of online environments, and students' general inability to get real-time answers to their questions. As Valencia College professor of graphic and interactive design Meg Curtiss put it, "You can qualify things more easily in person," whereas online, "students aren't able to ask questions as readily—or don't—therefore, clarity/transparency is paramount to success and to outcomes being reached."[41] Tiffany Howard and colleagues' research on the use of transparency in online courses found that "when utilized in the online classroom, transparent teaching methods can help mitigate some of the challenges that are associated with online instruction. The findings suggest that the performance of students in online courses that use transparent teaching methods is comparable to the performance of students in the traditional classroom setting."[42]

Nudge Online Students to Engage with Instructions

Providing explicitly clear guidance for assessments in online courses is essential yet insufficient. In Flower's experience, both in her own online classes and in hearing from countless frustrated online instructors, it often feels like students don't attend to the helpful guidance we write or record. Recall that many online students choose this modality because it allows them to pursue a postsecondary credential alongside managing other responsibilities in their busy and complex lives. As we discussed in Unit 1, the perceived value of classwork may compete with other worthwhile demands on their time. For this reason, online students may not avail themselves of our clarifying and helpful materials. That's why we suggest providing intentional support that nudges students into making time to read or watch our instructions and explanations. How?

Here are a few approaches: (1) provide written instructions clarifying the assignment's purpose, task, and criteria, and include intentional visual design elements to break up the text and make it easier to read and process; (2) record informal mini-videos to explain the purpose, tasks, and criteria; (3) host an optional synchronous meeting to go over each assignment and answer any questions (be sure to record and post the meeting for students who could not attend); and (4) create an anonymous discussion forum where students can post questions about each assignment or about the class more broadly—and normalize the use of it through frequent messaging about its availability and usefulness.

To add a layer of accountability, you can require students to take a short quiz or send in a written or recorded reflection stating what they gained from the written and/or recorded guidance, or how it is shaping their thinking, their plan, and so on. For ease of grading, and to center the focus on learning rather than points and grades, short reflections such as these can be assessed as complete/incomplete. When you use the rubric tool in the LMS, reviewing and assigning credit takes mere seconds.

Updating Your Grading System

Given the significant impacts of grades on students, we describe several ways to make your grading more equitable and want to point out that the approaches below complement and strengthen one another, so it's best to use more than one:

- *Increase the weight of assessments as the term progresses.* This strategy aligns with Feldman's pillar of accuracy.[43] Averaging assessment scores over time privileges learning quickly, whereas adding value to more recent performance better represents level of mastery.

- *Focus grade calculations on assessments aligned with course learning objectives.* This way, students' grades will better reflect their learning. At the same time, you'll minimize the introduction of bias from incorporating elements such as participation or timeliness.

- *Offer retakes and redos with writing assessments and projects, and/or with exams.* This approach aligns well with the goals of ungrading. Feldman promotes redos as a way to motivate students to learn from mistakes, and for us to improve the accuracy of our course grades. What does this look like in practice?

  » For written assignments and projects: When asking students to revise a written assessment based on your feedback (and/or that of a peer or other reader), guide students in engaging with the feedback and making decisions about how to enhance their work.

  » For in-person tests: What might an exam retake entail? Based on his own teaching experience, coauthor Bryan Dewsbury attests to the effectiveness of offering two-stage exams. Basically, two-stage exams offer students a second attempt at taking an exam after they have individually completed it. The second attempt, completed in groups, gives students a chance to discuss their responses and understandings with—and therefore learn from—their peers. Two-stage exams also help with test anxiety.[44] (Incidentally, Michelle Miller recommends two-stage exams as a way for faculty to "dip our toes" in ungrading.[45])

  » For online tests: Another option for allowing students to learn material while improving test scores is to allow multiple attempts at online tests. This works well in large and small classes alike. You can enhance the learning opportunity by embedding hints and reminders within the quiz itself; most LMSs allow you to enter feedback for an incorrect response so that students get your specific comment when they get a question wrong. Use this impactful moment, when you likely have students' full attention, to guide them to review certain pages in the textbook, or to rewatch the mini-lecture video starting at a specific time, to find the correct answer.

    While it can take time to embed this just-in-time support, this is a tangible way of keeping equity front and center in your online teaching. If you think about it, when you share comments for incorrect answers you are, in fact, *teaching* your students through your prewritten pointers for success. Plus, once you've developed these pieces of feedback, they'll carry over when you copy the course from one term to the next, so you and your students benefit from this powerful opportunity every time you teach that course.

One final idea for allowing rewrites and test corrections on paper or online: along with having students revise or retake the entire test or resubmit previously missed questions, ask them to explain where they went wrong and/or what they'll do differently next time. This is a powerful chance for students to reflect on their approach and understanding, a metacognitive strategy that can advance equitable outcomes. Through a setting or a manual process in your LMS, you can choose when to reveal students' grades on a test or assignment—for example, after they submit a metacognitive reflection on how they studied and how they think they did on the assessment.

Put Your Online Grade Book to Work

At most colleges, every course comes equipped with a corresponding online space in your school's LMS—for example Canvas, D2L, or Blackboard—even if it's an in-person class. And your online space comes equipped with a powerful tool for advancing equity: the grade book. With equity firmly in view, you can deliberately set up your grade book to accomplish two goals: (1) implement inclusive grading practices such as dropping the lowest test score and (2) ensure students can accurately gauge their progress and grade standing at any time during the term.

The first goal supports your ability to reduce student anxiety and shift students' attention to learning instead of grades. In addition to automating the dropping of the lowest test score, you can set up the grade book to automatically show which students earned less than 70 percent on a quiz, for example, so you can send a personalized email reminding them about your optional review session or reach out to the tutoring center.

The second goal aligns with our focus on transparency as a key equity-focused strategy. Make sure you've made grades visible to students—in some LMSs, this is a setting that may default to "hidden." And create an overall grading scheme that makes it simple for students to check and understand what their grade is at any given time. For example, a points-based system rather than a percentage-based system may make more intuitive sense to your students.

Because the LMS grade book is technologically powerful and complex, and because it's such an impactful tool for equity, carve out time to set it up correctly. Seek assistance from your local instructional designer, technologist, or LMS help-desk hero, and review local and LMS-provided tutorials for step-by-step walkthroughs. Don't neglect this important step for your class, regardless of modality. You can promote—or hinder—equitable outcomes based on your effective use (or lack thereof) of this powerful tool.

- *Reduce the stakes of major assessments.* As Jack and Sathy explain, "When a single exam or a paper carries a lot of weight, you risk letting that one experience or day wreak havoc on a student's grade. You can downplay high-stakes work by: (1) allowing students to drop one or two of their worst scores on exams, assignments, or quizzes; (2) letting students replace an earlier score with a cumulative final grade; and (3) replacing some of the weight of high-stakes work with smaller, more frequent assessments."[46] To uphold the validity of your grades, it's essential that these lower-stakes assignments are carefully designed in relation to your learning objectives.

- *Talk to your students about grades and their impact.* Remember, some students will view any unsuccessful grade as evidence that they do not belong or cannot succeed. But as you know, there are many other factors that impact a student's grade. These include the student's own academic behaviors and their earlier schooling and social situations. They also include elements of our own teaching approaches, such as the effectiveness of our pretesting learning opportunities and test design.

  Timing is key with this strategy; you'll want to talk to students (whether in person, via email, or in an online video or post) about what grades do and don't mean as close as possible to the moment you share an assessment grade with them. Such a conversation should also identify specifics of their preparation strategies and even elements in that process where there was lack of clarity from you, the instructor. This type of conversation allows you to offer specific guidance that will help students attain a better score next time, and it can provide you with feedback that will help you design a cleaner formative process before you give major exams. Further, as Lisa Nunn suggests, normalize academic challenge:[47] connect students to college tutoring and other resources and encourage (perhaps even incentivize) out-of-class study groups; you can even help to form these groups according to students' schedule availability, for example, with a simple Google Sheet. Finally, offer to support students individually, too.

Keep in mind that an unsuccessful grade in your class may mean that a student is no longer eligible for their desired program or area of study or won't be a competitive applicant for a position or undergraduate or graduate program. If you know of options for grade forgiveness or course retakes that could change this trajectory, you should definitely share these with students. Overall, students deserve our candor and compassion. We may not be able to immediately change the larger systems and structures that cause inequitable outcomes, but we can empathize with students and let them know we believe in their capacity, even when it is not reflected in their grades.

- *Maintain high expectations.* In Unit 1 we discussed the centrality of rigor to equity. Here, we offer a quick reminder that our commitment to equity does not mean all students will earn good grades in our classes. Giving a high grade to every student regardless of performance would be a disservice to students, our institutions, and the many others who rely on the understanding that successful grades are signals of earned knowledge and abilities. Yet without lowering expectations or giving out meaningless A grades, equity-minded instructors provide support through intentional course design and grading approaches, daily teaching interactions with students (see Section Two), and the kind of supportive coaching we've described.

HOW CAN I GET STARTED?

The following suggestions are intended to prompt implementation ideas for classes in all disciplines and enrollment sizes. Because assessment and grading practices do not differ widely by course modality, we've focused primarily on ideas to get you started in any class mode.

For Any Class

- Implement one strategy recommended in this unit to reduce assessment-related pressure on students. (Keep in mind, making multiple changes at once may overwhelm you and create less-than-desirable learning conditions for your students.) Consider starting with one of the following changes:

  » Allow students to drop their lowest test or quiz score.

  » Implement two-stage exams: students take an exam the first time by themselves, then work in groups to retake the same exam for added points.

  » Lower the stakes of students' first major assessment grade.

- To enhance purpose and authenticity in your assessments, add connections to issues within the context of your discipline that are personally meaningful to your students. When designing test questions, discussion prompts, and paper or project prompts, consider topics students have expressed interest in, such as the following:

  » climate change

  » global or local health crises

  » historic or current public figures who are important to students' culture or community or who serve as personal or professional role models for students

  » local natural disasters

  » police killings of unarmed victims

  » local, state, or national political developments

- To increase transparency in your assessments, record and post an informal three-to-five-minute video in which you provide tips for success and describe common pitfalls and how to avoid them.

- Offer choice, choice, choice—wherever possible. Let students choose a topic and/or an artifact that allows them to either play to existing strengths when showcasing learning or to develop a new skill they're interested in, for example infographic or mobile app creation.

- Add an additional formative quiz before each major exam, and if the quizzes are given online, allow students multiple attempts.

3

WELCOME AND SUPPORT STUDENTS

Design an Inclusive Syllabus and Online Course

Carefully constructed syllabi and online courses provide students with a road map for learning and communicate both our respect for them and our desire to see them succeed.

Although few of us may know the term *syllabus* derives from the Greek word for book label, faculty tend to have strong opinions about the document. From the meme-status "It's on the syllabus" sentiment to frustrations with required statements and policies, the syllabus is ubiquitous for faculty. As it relates to teaching and learning, the syllabus can be said to enact one's theory of teaching.[1] It also includes core pedagogical features such as learning objectives and assessments and can serve as a learning guide for students. Meanwhile, scholars and practitioners of inclusive teaching have identified the syllabus as an important tool through which faculty can advance equity. They describe syllabus refinement as an important and concrete step that faculty can take to turn their inclusive commitments into action.

The syllabus is often the locus of institutional requirements, whether regarding the use of a syllabus template or the inclusion of specific testing policies, academic integrity statements, and procedures for students with disabilities. Some institutions provide templates for instructors to use partly for the purpose of ensuring their requirements are met. In this way, the document represents a "relatively unexamined battleground" between institutional expectations and faculty members' preferences and commitments, suggest James Dyer and colleagues.[2] Their analysis uses the example of language expectations to demonstrate that equity-minded faculty may want to "uphold students' rich cultural and linguistic experiences" yet can be constrained by their college's requirements on language norms. Later, we'll revisit their study and suggestions, and we'll also provide recommendations for faculty who are expected to use an existing syllabus or online course.

In the case of fully online courses, we find significant parallels between the influence of the course syllabus on student learning and that of the design of an asynchronous online course. Indeed, we argue that an online course's design can conceivably impact students' ability to persist, learn, and succeed even more than a syllabus for an in-person class, because students must immerse themselves in the online environment every time they go to class. An in-person classroom can promote or hinder learning through structures and features such as the size of the room or lecture hall, visibility of projection screens and whiteboards, quality of the audio in the room, the mobility (or not) of furniture such as student desks and chairs, and so on. Online courses have corresponding features: the strengths and limitations of platforms such as Canvas, D2L, or Blackboard; the way the course has been organized given the available structures; the placement of module materials and activities; and the availability of navigational guidance (such as, "Click the link below to access the assignment instructions and submission area"). Each feature can serve to foster—or restrict—students' ability to progress without causing them to waste precious cognitive resources on the logistics of completing coursework.

Unlike a physical classroom, an online course contains all instructional materials, activities, assessments, policies, and, typically, interaction with other students and with you, the instructor. How well the online course has been designed therefore has a significant impact on student learning and success. And in our combined decades of experience teaching online and supporting online educators, we've found that many dedicated and well-meaning online faculty members simply haven't been offered the adequate time and professional development they need to accurately discern whether their course design—either provided or self-created—advances equity. Also, as can be the case with syllabi, your college or department may mandate your use of an institutionally or departmentally approved online course. There may be elements of this predetermined content, including course materials, activities, assessments, layout, navigation, and support structures (such as embedded links to the library or tutoring office), that align to greater or lesser extent with your equity-minded values, perspectives, and goals.

Because online courses present these unique challenges, in this unit we will devote specialized consideration to equity-focused online course design recommendations in addition to our review of the research and practical suggestions related to course syllabi. (We'll provide even more guidance on how online course design can facilitate effective learning in Section Two, focused on day-to-day teaching.) This unit begins with a brief overview of research on the syllabus and inclusive syllabi because this guiding document sets the tone for classes in all modalities. We will then describe the final stage of L. Dee Fink's course design model: putting it all together, including the identification of course materials, with focused considerations for asynchronous online course design. The closing segment of this unit offers suggestions for each primary syllabus section—from the office hour listing to the course schedule—as well as for overall tone.

What Does the Research Say about the Syllabus?

As authors William Germano and Kit Nicholls describe in *Syllabus: The Remarkable, Unremarkable Document That Changes Everything*, syllabi served mostly as tables of contents from the Enlightenment through the middle of the twentieth century. Meanwhile, in religious circles, they consisted mostly of condemned practices and opinions. Germano and Nicholls recognize that today's course syllabi play varied roles: "For most of us who teach, the syllabus is not only document but rule book, canvas, and plan, and perhaps most of all a model for imagining a sphere of operations for a course's ideas."[3] Other common functions include establishing an early point of contact and connection between student and instructor, helping set the tone for the course, describing your beliefs about education, acquainting students with course logistics, and describing student responsibilities for successful coursework.[4]

Michael Palmer, director of the Center for Teaching Excellence at the University of Virginia and professor of chemistry, has studied the impact of the course syllabus on students. His research team advocates for syllabi that serve primarily as tools that support student learning. They contrast *learning-focused syllabi* with *content-focused* ones, suggesting that the latter "have become increasingly authoritative and rule-infested to the detriment of student learning."[5] A learning-focused calculus syllabus might, for instance, describe how the course will approach the learning of calculus and why calculus matters, whereas a content-focused version may only list the calculus subtopics to be covered, dates, and deadlines. Content- and learning-focused syllabi differ even in syllabus areas that may appear neutral, like the course description. In the examples shown in figure 3.1, note the differences in tone, level of formality, and clarity for students on what to expect and why the course is relevant.

Ken Bain, in *What the Best College Teachers Do*, likewise stresses the centrality of learning to the course syllabus. Bain finds that the best college syllabi, which he terms *promising syllabi*, accomplish the following:

1. Make a promise to students about what they can expect to gain during the term as a result of the class
2. Describe the course activities designed to fulfill this promise

3. Begin a conversation about "how the instructor and the students would understand the nature and progress of the [students'] learning"[6]

Content-Focused Syllabus for History 1000: US History since 1865

Course overview

This course emphasizes the major political, social, economic, and intellectual developments in the nation from the Civil War to the present and aims to challenge students to critically analyze these developments. The course also examines how events and developments that occurred prior to 1865 influenced the nation's evolution after the Civil War. The course will cover such topics as Reconstruction, the New Deal, the Great Depression, the Atomic Age, the Cold War, and the 1960s. Due to the constraints of the semester, the 1970s–80s will only be covered generally, while the 1990s–today will not be covered.

Learning-Focused Syllabus for History 1000: US History since 1865

A bit about the course

You've probably studied US history before, exploring the major themes, events, and people who have shaped this country. In your other history courses, you may have learned certain historical information and then been required to write clear, evidence-based arguments about the past. We will do that, but I expect you will find this course to be different in useful and challenging ways.

Together we will explore how and why individuals chose to act—or not to act—in response to the local, national, and global forces that have shaped the United States since 1865. For example, how did Americans respond to the US acquiring and using the atomic bomb? And how were they affected by the twentieth-century tech boom? Historians call this approach *social history*, a major trend in historical analysis over the past few decades. This focus on the lives of ordinary (and not so ordinary) people can help you deeply understand the past. It also might prompt you to reflect on how and why you choose to act (or not to act) in response to the local, national, and global forces shaping our world now.

To allow you to experience doing what historians do, you will get to contribute to an oral history project. This project, developed in partnership with a local community organization, will encourage you to ask some big questions about how to do historical research and historical meaning as well as to explore the relationship between personal/local stories and national ones.

FIGURE 3.1   Content- vs. Learning-Focused Syllabus Course Overview

Source: Michael S. Palmer, Lindsay B. Wheeler, and Itiya Aneece, "Does the Document Matter? The Evolving Role of Syllabi in Higher Education," Change: The Magazine of Higher Learning *48, no. 4 (July/August 2016): 38, https://www.csun.edu/sites/default/files/Syllabus%20Perceptions%20 -%20Palmer%20%28FINAL%29.pdf.*

Bain's third point is essential to equity-minded teaching, which, as we've described, commits to an ongoing, relationship-rich dialogue with students about their learning and development.

How are learning-focused syllabi developed, and what else do they include? Palmer and colleagues' overview aligns well with the guidance on inclusive teaching in this guide. In addition to being developed using research-based practices like backward design, they write, "learning-focused syllabi make clear what 'you [the student] will do' and what 'we [the class, including the instructor] will do' throughout the semester." They add that learning-focused syllabi have the following characteristics:

- engaging, question-driven course descriptions
- long-ranging, multifaceted learning goals
- clear, measurable learning objectives
- robust and transparent assessment and activity descriptions
- detailed course schedules—ideally, framed in "beautiful questions"
- a focus on student success
- an inviting, approachable, and motivating tone[7]

Later in this unit, we'll provide concrete suggestions on how to incorporate most of these criteria into your own syllabus.

Whether you find the idea of a learning-focused syllabus intriguing or inspiring, you may be wondering at this point if the syllabus really matters and whether improving one or more of your syllabi is worth your while. On the one hand, we don't want to overstate its impact; it's only one document. And in a study of students' syllabus preferences, students counsel us to be realistic about what any one document can accomplish.[8] They expect to be motivated and engaged in the class via interactions with you and with the course content, *not* on the basis of this one document.

On the other hand, research has demonstrated that the syllabus influences student learning and success in a few ways. For one, it shapes students' perceptions of both the course and the instructor—including how accessible the instructor is and how motivated they are to teach the course.[9] According to Palmer and colleagues' research, the type of syllabus matters too: students had significantly more positive perceptions of learning-focused syllabi, and of the learning-focused course and instructor.[10] Other studies have found that the syllabus informs important student decisions, such as whether to seek assistance when academic difficulties arise.[11] Similarly, Rebecca A. Glazier and Heidi Skurat Harris's research on student retention in fully online courses found that minor changes to an online course has considerable impact on students' perceptions of the course and instructor, and on their intent to complete the course.[12]

Pause to Consider

- When your students read the first page of your course syllabus or scroll through your online course, what impression do you want them to have? What do you want to make sure they don't miss about the class, or about you?

- Where in your syllabus do you think your students will see themselves?

The Inclusive Syllabus: Essential in All Modes

Scholars of inclusive and equity-minded pedagogy have likewise studied the course syllabus, viewing it as an important tool for advancing equity. Former University of Minnesota professor of writing and literature Terry Collins, for instance, suggests a direct relationship between the inclusive syllabus and students' sense of inclusion in college. Recalling his journey as a first-generation college student, Collins reminds us that higher education is a distinct culture, one with rules and expectations often invisible to students. These cultural elements frequently signal to students, particularly those from minoritized groups, that they do not belong—which can contribute to their withdrawal from college (see Unit 5 on belonging). Through inclusive syllabi, Collins argues, we can begin to "make explicit the befuddling mores, assumptions, work habits, background knowledge, key terms, or other markers of the academic subculture too often left implicit, inaccessible to outsiders"—thereby "establish[ing] an assumption of inclusion" for all students and improving their odds of success.[13]

Online teaching expert Michelle Pacansky-Brock echoes many of Collins's sentiments regarding how the syllabus influences students' sense of belonging in all classes. She explains the psychological mechanisms through which syllabi can compromise students' ability to learn:

> *The deficit-based language, academic jargon, lists of what not to do, and fear-evoking policies contained in a syllabus serve as microaggressions that can exacerbate stereotype threat, belongingness uncertainty, and imposter syndrome—social psychological phenomena that take up a student's mental bandwidth that is needed for learning to occur.*[14]

Yet Pacansky-Brock also affirms that syllabi can have the exact opposite impact on students, not only signaling students' inclusion but also helping them to feel safe in their identities and motivating them to learn.

Many other equity scholars echo Collins's and Pacansky-Brock's sentiments and have developed a number of tools to support the development of inclusive syllabi. A notable example includes the Social Justice Syllabus Design Tool developed by Sherria D. Taylor, professor of family studies at San Francisco State University, and colleagues.[15] Another robust resource is "Rethinking the Course Syllabus" by Montclair State University psychology professor Milton Fuentes and colleagues, which includes both general and psychology-specific guidance.[16]

How can changes to your syllabus help you advance equity? Here are four ways that have been underscored in research:

- *By showcasing your course's relevance.* As described in Unit 1, relevance is central to motivation and learning, and it serves to validate students. The course description, course learning objectives, primary assessments, and course materials sections are key syllabus areas in which to showcase the relevance of your course to students' identities, experiences, lives, and goals.

- *By humanizing you.* Although the faculty-student relationship is one of the strongest predictors of student learning and success, students are often intimidated by faculty. Your syllabus can begin to convey to your students that you're a real person committed to their success.

- *By emphasizing student success.* When your syllabus is "built on the principle of full disclosure of the terms of success,"[17] you signal to students that their success is important to you. For students who worry they may not be successful in college (or in your particular course), your syllabus can offer an affirming counternarrative, a set of assurances that you know they can succeed and look forward to helping them achieve course success.

- *By signaling that equity matters to you.* Whether conveyed via course content, a learning objective, an assignment, or a stand-alone equity statement, a tangible commitment to equity stated in your syllabus can help you begin to establish trust with and motivate your students from minoritized backgrounds.

Final Stages of Course Design and Syllabus Upgrades

In the previous units, we described steps one to three of L. Dee Fink's course design process, which together entail analyzing your course context, developing or updating your course learning objectives, and identifying assessments aligned with these objectives. As depicted in the three-column course map, these steps are mapped onto the left-hand and middle columns. In Fink's model, the right-hand column describes the learning activities, step four in his approach.[18] Since Section Two is dedicated to equity-minded day-to-day teaching, this section only touches briefly on learning activities, focusing instead on the relationship among the course elements and an additional course feature central to equity and relevance: your instructional materials. We'll then walk you through each common section of the course syllabus, providing concrete suggestions for updating each.

Although Fink's model calls for a three-column map, we suggest adding a fourth column, to the right of the learning activities (see the Appendix)—this one will be labeled "Technology Considerations." Since tech is ubiquitous in all classes, online and off, and since, when implemented effectively, it represents a powerful tool for advancing equitable learning, we encourage you to consider the following questions as part of the course-planning process:

1. What technology is available to support students' ability to interact with, practice, and apply new concepts and skills? Does the availability of a tech tool imply we should or must incorporate it into our classes?

2. Is the potential tech tool aligned with the other major course elements (learning objectives, assessments, and learning activities)? Or would it detract from the otherwise well-aligned components?

3. Who would I be excluding by using this technology? Whose data would I be sharing, and with whom, if I were to use this tool?

Deliberate reflection on these questions, perhaps in consultation with your local instructional designer, can help prevent the common mistake of adding tech for tech's sake, which can then lead to "edutainment"—a potentially fun and engaging experience that does not actually progress learning. Worse, adding unnecessary technology can raise barriers for individual learners based on their identities, abilities, access to technology including reliable internet, and life circumstances. For instance, and in mindful consideration of individual learner variability according to UDL principles, today's students are likely to be juggling work and family obligations in addition to school. Adding needless tech-mediated activities may interfere with their ability to succeed.

> ## Pause to Consider
>
> - For each technological tool you are currently using or considering using, how does it align to your learning objectives? How can you tell if it's "working"?
>
> - How might you find out if some of your students experience challenges accessing the tool(s)?

However, technology also offers powerful opportunities to advance equity through the intentional application of learning-science-based practices, as Michelle Miller has written.[19] So it would be a mistake not to implement tech-enabled solutions out of an abundance of caution. In the list of questions we just posed, the first one invites us to reflect on both course modality and readily available technology resources. Do course activities take place primarily in your LMS? In Zoom? In a physical setting such as a lab or clinic? Wherever it may be, what technology is available to you in that environment, and in your LMS as well? Is there a pedagogically sound reason to implement it? Next, we check to ensure that the incorporation of technology will not derail otherwise sound, aligned course design. Finally, online teaching experts encourage us to carefully consider the accessibility and the privacy of tech tools: Are apps usable by students relying on screen readers or keyboard access? Does a "fun" or even learning-promoting app or website require a separate log-in? Which companies will now have access to students' demographic data? Careful reflection on these kinds of questions helps us avoid inadvertently designing for *inequity* by the selection and requirement of tech. One generally safe bet is to stick with the functionality available in your LMS, which has been tested for accessibility, is supported by your school's IT department, and is contained within the "walled garden" of your institutional data management policies.

Step 4: Identify Your Main Learning Activities and Tie It All Together

The key question at hand in step four of Fink's process is, "What are the primary ways students will practice the learning goals and receive feedback?" Fink uses the term *learning activities* to refer to the activities students will do in and out of class, or in each online module, to prepare to successfully complete your primary assessments and therefore make progress toward or master your course learning objectives. (You might think of them as classwork and homework.) His general guidance is to expand our toolkits beyond lectures and discussions, and he directs faculty to various kinds of active learning, including opportunities for student reflection, case studies, simulations, and so on.[20] (See Unit 2 for detailed suggestions.) One of Fink's key ideas at this stage of course design is that the integrity and quality of your course depend largely on the alignment among its various parts, including the key elements of course design introduced in Units 1 and 2:

- the context of your course
- your long-term goals for your students
- the corresponding learning objectives
- the major assessments
- the learning activities

We would add an additional element: the technology with which you teach. These course elements should reflect and reinforce one another, maximizing the probability that your long-term aspirations for your students will be realized. The four-column course map helps us view all of these elements in one place and test their alignment and complementarity.

An Equity-Focused Way to Select Your Course Materials

The selection or updating of course materials also happens at this stage of course design. Students have been telling us for decades that our course readings and other materials speak volumes about our commitment to equity and the extent to which they feel they belong in our classrooms. As a reminder, one of the key findings of Stephen Quaye and Shaun Harper's extensive study was that high-achieving Black students supplemented their formal course materials with culturally relevant books and essays. Quaye and Harper also describe the impact of including limited scholarly perspectives in our courses: "When students are exposed only to white, dominant perspectives, they come to believe that viewpoints from other racial and ethnic groups are trivial and lack value, intellectual worth, and scholarly credibility."[21] Others have argued that the diversity of the authors of course readings "supports students who may otherwise feel invisible."[22] It is thus essential that we take the time to not only include but also draw students' attention to diverse perspectives in our course materials.

English professor Allison Parker encourages us to look closely at our selections, even when they include people of color. "Often, either texts about people who are othered are told from a White person's perspective or they tell the same stories about slavery, racism, oppression, violence, poverty, urban settings, and injustice," she explains, which plays into and can reinforce stereotypes. Parker suggests that we seek out "counterstories," perspectives and experiences that counter and thereby ask us to question the validity of dominant stereotypes.[23]

Before searching for new or supplemental instructional materials, ask yourself these questions:

- Whose perspectives are represented in your primary texts/readings?
- What are the identities of the authors and editors? (You can find bios and visible markers of identity via a Google search.)
- When minoritized identities are referenced in the readings, how are they portrayed? For instance, are they depicted in ways that reinforce deficit or stereotypes? Are any of their values or strengths included?

Based on what you learn from this reflection and analysis, you might take one or more of these actions: request review copies of alternative textbooks and courseware designed with attention to equity and inclusion; identify new readings from current scholarship in your field, which tends to represent more diverse perspectives than older research does; and/or use materials from popular culture as primary texts (like Brian Mooney did with Kendrick Lamar lyrics, as we saw in the previous unit).

A commitment to equity also requires considering the cost of each instructional material you require students to purchase. More faculty have begun to rely on open educational resources (OER) at least in part because of their very clear cost savings for students. OER is part of a broader landscape of open education (OE), a more general movement rethinking who owns information, codifies it, and makes it available for users. On the one hand, concerns have been raised about OER content quality, the accessibility of materials (from a student disability perspective), and the loss of student and faculty access to supplemental resources (such as online quizzes and test banks). On the other hand, the open license structure of OER has allowed for a rapid improvement of quality and adaptability, even accessibility, in a relatively short time. It also allows faculty to edit these resources in ways that make sense for a specific course.

Therefore, as you develop your equity-minded course, consider the following: Are there low- or no-cost OER options available that meet the needs of your course? Do the OER materials allow you and your students to engage in the process of knowledge construction and remixing? Will your students, and you, use enough of each resource and its associated materials to warrant the purchase?

Ways to Update Each of Your Primary Syllabus Sections

In the following pages, we'll walk through a set of common syllabus sections and offer our best thinking on how to make each of them more equity-minded. But first, if you're able to do so, you might consider the overall format of your syllabus. Pacansky-Brock developed what she calls the "liquid syllabus," which she defines as "an accessible, public website that incorporates a brief, friendly welcome video and course information written in welcoming, student-centered language."[24] Recognizing that many minoritized students are more likely to have smartphones than laptops, her proposed liquid syllabus, with easy-to-view pages and videos, increases access for those who may be least likely to have home computers.[25] (You can access her free self-paced Canvas course for a step-by-step guide to creating your own liquid syllabus at https://ccconlineed .instructure.com/courses/6771.)

Syllabus Headers. Key heading information includes the syllabus title, information about you, and your office hours. Here are three updates to consider:

- *Revise the document title.* After all, "syllabus" is not exactly intuitive or descriptive. Some scholars encourage us to consider a more meaningful term such as "Learning Guide," to signal the emphasis on learning and on supporting students.

- *Rename office hours.* Faculty have begun renaming office hours, too. Bryan found out some of his students thought the name "office hours" meant that was the time professors were in their offices getting their work done, so he renamed them "student hours." Other faculty call them "connection hours" or "meet and greets." Share with students the kinds of questions or requests they can bring to office hours to help them succeed in your course, and you might also let them know if/how they can connect with you outside of the established hours. A scheduling app like Calendly can make it easy for students to schedule meetings with you and will save you time coordinating schedules.

- *Introduce yourself.* In addition to listing your name and title, consider what else you could tell students about yourself that would help them see you as a real person. This might include your pronouns, something personal (like a hobby or fun fact), and perhaps even a photo—or in the case of a digital syllabus, a link to a quick introductory video. By including this introduction, you'll begin to humanize yourself, laying the groundwork for trust and making it more likely students will reach out to you.

    Terry Collins suggests noting how you want students to address you—as in, "Please call me _____."[26] Here, we acknowledge that preferences vary and may depend on your identities. For instance, many faculty (and especially women) of color ask students to refer to them as "Doctor" or "Professor." This request is often in response to the fact that, as Chavella Pittman and Thomas Tobin have written, "Students—especially white males—are already more likely to challenge the authority, expertise, and teaching skill of instructors who fall into underrepresented categories of the professoriate by virtue of their race, gender, sexual orientation, ability, religion, and so on."[27] We respect whatever decisions you make and are suggesting here that you let students know up-front how they should address you (vs. hoping they get it right). In figure 3.2, you'll see that in Valencia College professor of psychology Melonie Sexton's General Psychology syllabus the "About Your Instructor" section includes several of the suggestions we've just discussed.

Course Description. The course description is your first chance to get students excited about the course content. Instead of relying on a canned catalog description, we suggest that you:

- *Add a better header.* As with the "syllabus" and "office hours" headings, you can get creative with headings for the "course description" part of your syllabus. In the syllabus for University of Virginia biomedical engineering professor Dr. Brian Helmke's class on biotransport, he uses the question "Why should you care about Biotransport?" as a heading for what would commonly be called his course description. Meanwhile, Florida International University literature professor Heather Blatt labels her course description "Why take this course?" (See figure 3.3 for both professors' full course descriptions.)

About Your Instructor

Professor:

Melonie W. Sexton, PhD

Please call me:

Dr./Prof. Sexton (pronouns: she/her/hers)

Ask me about:

Being a professor. Maintaining a work/life balance. Becoming a psychology major. Getting into and going to graduate school. Doing psychological research. Anything about the class. Being a first-generation college student.

Email:

msexton@valenciacollege.edu

Phone:

407-983-2929

Student Hours:

Mon.–Thur.: 10am–11am via Zoom
Mon.–Thur.: 1pm–2pm via Zoom
Friday by appointment

If these times do not work for you and your schedule, please contact me to make an appointment.

FIGURE 3.2 "About Your Instructor" Page Sample

Source: Melonie Sexton.

- *Use questions to prompt student curiosity.* In addition to the question in his header, Dr. Helmke includes questions in the description itself to pique students' interest.

- *Foreground relevance.* Notice that both Dr. Helmke and Dr. Blatt address relevance head-on in their course descriptions; the questions that serve as headers acknowledge explicitly that students may not think the course matters or may not know how or why it does. And the descriptions focused on relevance signal that Helmke and Blatt know relevance is foundational to their students' success.

Dr. Brian Helmke's Biotransport Class

Why should you care about Biotransport?

How can you deliver a drug to kill tumors without killing the patient? How can you harness nanotechnology to design inexpensive kits to diagnose diseases in low-resource countries? How do new blood vessels grow? These are examples of "grand challenges" faced by practicing biomedical engineers that require us to design mathematical and experimental approaches for predicting, measuring, and interpreting flow phenomena quantitatively. In this course, you will combine your knowledge of applied mathematics and human physiology from the molecule to cell to whole-body-length scales to begin exploring how to answer grand-challenge questions such as these.

Dr. Heather Blatt's Medieval Literature Class

Why take this course?

Have you ever seen a movie, TV show, or TV episode that contained medieval or fantasy-medieval elements? From *Lord of the Rings* and *Game of Thrones* to Disney's *Mulan* to the recently released film *The Northman*, pop culture over the last seventy years has frequently turned to the Middle Ages for storytelling and inspiration. But we also use the Middle Ages for other purposes. We describe what we dislike or think ought not to be part of ourselves and our cultures as "medieval"; we say that we need to "get medieval" on COVID-19, or that Rafael Nadal "got medieval" on his rivals, or that, in invading Ukraine, Russia used "ruthless tactics more in line with medieval times than the twenty-first century." Why do we keep returning to the Middle Ages? What stories about the Middle Ages do we tell ourselves today? This class takes as its focus modern re-imaginings of medieval literature and culture to better understand how we construct ourselves and our societies by contrasting ourselves with a largely fictionalized version of the past.

FIGURE 3.3   Two Sample Learning-Centered Course Descriptions

Sources: Brian Helmke and Heather Blatt.

Learning Objectives. As described in Unit 1, course learning objectives are a key feature of the syllabus and are foundational to equity-minded teaching. In addition to enhancing their relevance and rigor in some of the ways suggested earlier, you might try the following:

- *Rename this section (too).* For instance, some faculty frame the learning objectives section as "What will you get out of this course?" or "How will this course help you succeed?"

- *Add a preface.* Consider adding language just above the objectives themselves that provides a high-level summary of the goals. Here's an example from Dr. Helmke's Biotransport course syllabus:

  > *Grand challenges are fundamental questions in biotransport with broad applications to science, engineering, and human health. This course will help you acquire a conceptual and practical framework that you can apply to solve complex grand challenges in your future research, engineering practice, or clinical practice. By the end of the course, you will be able to answer the following questions:*
  >
  > 1. *How do I use math to figure out how, why, and where stuff flows in the body?*
  >
  > 2. *Some equations in physics and engineering are easy, like F = ma. When and how can I use simple common-sense equations for flows in my complicated biology models or medical device designs?*
  >
  > 3. *I've taken classes like calculus and cell biology, but I don't know what those classes have to do with each other. How do I put stuff from other classes together to solve real-world biology problems or to design medical devices?*
  >
  > 4. *Can I use equations and answers that I found using Google and Wikipedia to solve homework problems and to do engineering design?*
  >
  > 5. *How do I use equations and answers from this class to solve problems in research and medicine next year in my Senior Capstone Project or after I graduate?*[28]

  Dr. Helmke's objectives exemplify the equity-minded practices of foregrounding relevance and using accessible, jargon-free language.

What If I'm Required to Use a Standard Syllabus or Syllabus Section?

If your institution requires that you use a standardized syllabus or syllabus section, identify your sphere of influence—that is, where you have the ability and authority to use ideas from this part of the guide. See Unit 1 for ideas on how to work with required learning objectives. Milton Fuentes and colleagues advise that if you are required to use the catalog description of your course, consider adding a "My Course Description" section before or after it, using that space to foreground relevance and motivate students.[29]

If you are asked to use the full syllabus as-is, identify opportunities during your class sessions or within your learning management system to implement equity-minded syllabus practices. For instance, infuse relevance, transparency, and course success into your first-day lesson plan and/or introductory course module or welcome video.

Grading Scheme. Whereas Unit 2 summarized the research on grading practices and their impact, and offered equity-minded suggestions for updating your grading system, our focus here is on how students engage with the grading section of your syllabus. Many of us know from experience that students focus intently (sometimes exclusively) on the grading scheme section. It's often less apparent to us that the grading section plays a symbolic role: it implicitly tells students which features of the course are most important and which ones they should spend the most time on. As Rebecca Cox explains, "The grading procedures in each class exert a huge influence on everyone's approach to the coursework," even for the "highly motivated, most self-confident and academically accomplished students." She adds that grades and grading criteria elicit a great deal of anxiety from students and that they view instructors as the ones who "control" grades.[30] Our advice?

- *Check (and, if necessary, lower) the stakes.* If your current scheme includes only a handful of assessments, each of which carries a lot of weight in students' grades, see Unit 2 for information about the impact of high-stakes grading on students and for ideas on how to lower the stakes.

- *Incorporate one or more equity-based grading practices.* Ideally, your syllabus would feature opportunities to improve one's grade, such as retakes and revisions. Or consider offering students the opportunity to earn additional points by submitting a written or recorded reflection on what steps they took to prepare for an assessment, and what they plan to do differently to show improved achievement for the next one.

- *Verify alignment with your priorities.* Students should see a strong connection between the tasks that carry the most weight and the course learning objectives.

- *Avoid fancy algorithms and empower students to monitor their progress.* Your syllabus should clearly state how grades will be determined and how students can compute their own grade during the term. Students should never experience an unhappy surprise when it comes to their course grade. Their grade reflects their work, and as such, they are entitled to monitor this information as they regulate and adjust their learning strategies (see the "Put Your Online Grade Book to Work" box in Unit 2 for advice on using your LMS grade center).

Major Assignments/Assessments. As with the grading section of the syllabus, the part that describes your major assignments/assessments is a focal point of student attention and often a source of anxiety. In addition to the substantive improvements to the assignments/assessments themselves recommended in Unit 2, we suggest these syllabus refinements:

- *Guide students with your heading.* In Dr. Helmke's Biotransport syllabus, this section is titled "How will you and I evaluate your progress?" This question communicates to students (1) that the assessments have a purpose: to evaluate progress toward the course learning objectives, and importantly, (2) that Dr. Helmke sees evaluating progress as a shared responsibility between student and professor.

- *Check assignment descriptions for authenticity, transparency, relevance, and choice.* Reviewing our discussions about these topics in Units 1 and 2 should help you with this process.

- *Verify alignment.* As with the grading scheme, your syllabus should clearly describe how the assessments align with the course learning objectives.

Policies and Rules. It may seem odd or unnecessary to examine one's course policies through the lens of equity. As Virginia Commonwealth University social psychologist Kim Case writes, "We tend to think of course policies as neutral and impacting students across all backgrounds in the same way."[31] Yet she adds that policies often result in disparities that fall along social identity groups. Considering these potential disparities, we recommend the following updates to ensure equitable course policies:

- *Check for accuracy.* In "Transforming Your Syllabus with an Equity Mindset," her blog post on the Intentional College Teaching website, Bridget Arend prompts us to make sure the policy descriptions, as written, reflect our actual policies.[32] It's important that policy statements accurately reflect your policy because "privileged students tend to ask; marginalized students tend not to ask," Arend affirms. For instance, in the case of late work, she encourages us to be clear and honest about whether extensions are possible. Since "it is a privilege in itself to ask for an exception to the rule," Arend advises us to examine our syllabus policies regarding late work and appeals to the policy.

- *Be deliberate with deadlines.* Matthew R. Johnson, professor of higher education in the Department of Educational Leadership at Central Michigan University, reflected on his own ability to meet deadlines during the pandemic and how much he appreciated the grace extended to him by his colleagues and editors.[33] "College students deserve that same grace and understanding when they have trouble meeting your deadlines for course assignments," he writes—and he's offered three alternatives:

  » Set target dates instead of firm due dates.
  » Have a "consequence free" late policy on one or more of your assignments (e.g., if an assignment is fewer than five days late, it will be considered as submitted on time).
  » Offer incentives for early submissions (e.g., five extra points for an assignment submitted five days early, four extra points if it's four days early, and so on).

  Another idea is to nudge students toward meeting deadlines while offering some flexibility in case of need: coauthor Flower Darby gives students a limited number of "Oops" tokens, alternatively known as "NQA"—no questions asked—passes, to use when they have to miss a deadline. The fact that students don't have to share personal information about why they need extra time reinforces trust (see Unit 4), affirms their value as members of a learning community, and respects their privacy. Please note that we're not suggesting you eliminate deadlines altogether. Actually, students have told us that, in an effort to provide flexibility, the instructors for some of their classes (including online classes) have given them no or very few deadlines.

This strategy, though perhaps well-intentioned, lowers the time-sensitivity of that coursework and potentially does a disservice to students who are leading complex lives and need firm dates to plan around. It can also make it extremely difficult for you as a busy faculty member.

Students' response to increased flexibility can also vary based on the faculty member identity, report Pittman and Tobin. In their courses, they used nearly identical due-date policies (which included a grace period and tokens for limited extensions). Pittman (who identifies as a Black female) found that her students constantly requested extensions, even beyond the built-in flexibility, sometimes using aggressive and entitled language. In contrast, Tobin (who identifies as "a white, male instructor with gray hair," which he acknowledges "ticks a lot of boxes signaling 'dominant culture'") found that only five of his students even used the built-in flexibility.[34] It may be necessary to strike a balance between offering flexibility and establishing boundaries.

- *Provide a rationale per policy.* This is one of Arend's suggestions.[35] She echoes Collins's point that inclusive syllabi make students feel included by demystifying and clarifying our academic norms and expectations. Rationales for course policies likewise demonstrate respect for students. For instance, if you do not accept drafts past a certain date—and that is so students can benefit from your feedback to improve their paper or help with a subsequent assignment—adding this explanation to your late policy will show students the deadline is meant to support their success.

- *Look at language expectations.* As Dyer and colleagues point out, many of the language expectations in college syllabi suggest to students, including our linguistically diverse students, that their ways of writing and communicating are inadequate or inappropriate in college. References to "Standard Written English" are common, for instance, suggesting that there is only one approved and appropriate version of English and by extension that students' non-standard varieties of English and other languages are not relevant or welcome in the class. Consider using what Dyer and colleagues call an "additive approach to language education."[36] Rather than asking students to leave their ways of communicating outside of the course, invite them to add or continue adding college-level academic language to their toolkits. When she taught first-year writing, Isis included a version of the Conference on College Composition and Communication's statement "Students' Right to Their Own Language" in her syllabus, encouraged students to use non-English languages when conducting research, and even piloted a bilingual (English/Spanish) version of the class.[37]

- *Adjust the tone*. More than other sections of the syllabus, the policy section, with its lists and descriptions, can take on a legalistic or contractual tone, one that cannot only be off-putting to students but also suggest an antagonistic student-professor relationship, like you're on opposing sides versus partners in learning. The upcoming suggestions regarding tone will thus be especially helpful when updating your policies.

Course Materials/Readings. We described the impact of course materials both in Unit 1 and in earlier sections of this unit. So that your syllabus itself shows students that diverse perspectives matter to you and that they are represented in the course content or in the identities of the authors you will be reading, consider these updates:

- *Check for representation.* Refer to our earlier discussions on representation in this unit and section for guidance as you are making this update.

- *Bring the authors to life.* In addition to descriptive titles of books, articles, and other learning resources, a digital version of your syllabus could include hyperlinks to author biographies.

- *Support informed purchasing and accessibility.* In this area of your syllabus you'll also want to specify if any of the materials are optional, whether they may be available online or on reserve at the library, and/or if students can use older editions of the text.

Be Honest About Diversity—and Ask for Help!

If you have difficulty finding diverse materials, consider following the lead of Monica Linden, professor of neuroscience at Brown University, and be open and honest with your students about what accounts for the (relative) omission in your syllabus—and ask for them to partner with you in adding diversity to your course.[38] Linden's example illustrates both of these ideas, as she originally wrote the following statement in collaboration with a former student, Krisha Aghi. She also reached out to former students to make sure that the language she had chosen was, in her words, inclusive and would resonate with students.

> *In an ideal world, science would be objective. However, much of science is subjective and is historically built on a small subset of privileged voices. I acknowledge that the readings for this course, including the course reader. . . . were authored by white men. Furthermore, the course often focuses on historically important neuroscience experiments which were mostly conducted by white men. Recent edits to the course reader were undertaken by both myself and some students who do not identify as white men. . . . Integrating a diverse set of experiences is important for a more comprehensive understanding of science. Please contact me (in person or electronically) or submit anonymous feedback if you have any suggestions to improve the quality of the course materials.*

Schedule. As with policy statements, the course schedule may seem inherently objective and thus irrelevant or unimportant to equity-minded teaching. Collins explains, however, that the *level of detail* of our course schedules—and *when* we share the schedule with students—impacts their success.[39]

- *Aim to be comprehensive.* Many faculty try to build flexibility and imprecision into the course schedule so they can be responsive to what happens during the term. And it's true that this responsiveness can bring opportunities for students to shape the course, make connections to their lives, and so on. At the same time, college students are increasingly like the urban commuter students Collins taught, ones who "work nearly full time, who have young children, whose lives take them away from campus for the majority of their days and nights." Therefore, "success in our challenging courses often depends on their capacity to plan ahead, to schedule precisely, and to manage competing demands." Students thus benefit tremendously from "getting as much information as they can as soon as they can get it."

- *Help students plan ahead, especially online.* Given the complexity of the lives of students who choose online courses and programs, it is particularly important that all deadlines are communicated up front. Better yet, in line with UDL guidance related to supporting students' executive function and planning, provide time estimates for readings, videos, and other activities (this applies to in-person courses, too). Finally, consider making all modules, assignments, and materials available in "read-only" mode so that students can plan around work and family schedules. Content and assignment availability enables students to plan ahead, yet the "read-only" setting allows you to maintain the benefit of your intentionally created course cadence and interactions.

- *Avoid conflicts with key religious events.* Check multifaith calendars to ensure that due dates are not scheduled on important holidays (or at least to identify when the holidays take place). Many of our academic calendars privilege Christian religions and celebrations.

- *Scan for how diversity appears.* Review your course calendar for topics of equity, diversity, or justice, and likewise examine your visuals for images that represent people of diverse racial and ethnic backgrounds as well as other intersectional identities. Are diverse topics and images infused throughout your course or included only once or twice? As Fuentes and colleagues indicate, many of us may be inclined to add a reading or two about diversity.[40] However, the risk in doing so is that the addition may appear to be **tokenism**.

tokenism: The practice of making only a symbolic effort to do something.

Stand-Alone Diversity Statements. The preceding ideas demonstrate that you can make your syllabus more inclusive in practically every section. In addition, some faculty—in fact, some entire departments and institutions—have begun including what are commonly known as syllabus "diversity statements." You may recall that two of the ways your syllabus can advance more equitable outcomes are by humanizing yourself and communicating to students that you value equity. A diversity statement can do both; it is an opportune place to describe your personal and professional commitments to equity. How?

- *Describe why equity matters to you.* As the most equitable course policy section includes a rationale for each policy, the best diversity statements will tell students *why* inclusion matters to you. The departmental statement in the "Two Sample Diversity and Inclusion Statements" box below celebrates the department's conviction that diversity, equity, and inclusivity are "the foundation for a diversity of perspectives that enrich" all facets of the field. In her statement, Dr. Linden also lets students know that she values diversity "for a more comprehensive understanding of science" and because she strives to cultivate an environment in which all students can succeed.

- *Make a specific connection to your discipline or a course objective.* Another strength of Dr. Linden's statement is its connection to her discipline, which adds depth and credibility. Many disciplinary organizations have crafted statements you can adapt or use as inspiration for your own. For instance, the field of composition and rhetoric has long affirmed students' right to their own patterns and varieties of language. The official statement of the Conference on College Composition and Communication (CCCC) indicates that "language scholars long ago denied that the myth of a standard American dialect has any validity." It goes on to explain:

  > *The claim that any one dialect is unacceptable amounts to an attempt of one social group to exert its dominance over another. Such a claim leads to false advice for speakers and writers, and immoral advice for humans. A nation proud of its diverse heritage and its cultural and racial variety will preserve its heritage of dialects. We affirm strongly that teachers must have the experiences and training that will enable them to respect diversity and uphold the right of students to their own language.*[41]

  Drawing on these ideas, many writing faculty include statements in their syllabus that affirm students' rights to their own languages. As noted previously, Isis not only lets students know that she values and respects their languages, but she also invites them in the syllabus to use their multilingual skills to conduct research, write essay drafts, and even submit assignments in languages other than English.

- *Freewrite to generate ideas.* To craft a diversity statement, you may start by reflecting on the following questions from the Harriet W. Sheridan Center for Teaching and Learning at Brown University:[42]

» What are your discipline's conventions and assumptions? How might students with varying backgrounds respond to them?

» What role does your respect for and engagement with diversity in the classroom play in your personal teaching philosophy?

» What do you want your students to know about your expectations regarding creating and maintaining a classroom space where differences are respected and valued?

The Sheridan Center website also includes several sample statements.

Two Sample Diversity and Inclusion Statements

Adapted from the University of Washington's Sociology Department Diversity Statement

The Department of Sociology at the University of Washington values diversity, equality, and inclusivity in our community. We define diversity broadly, as differences in social categories like race, ethnicity, religion, gender, sexuality, socio-economic status, nationality and citizenship, veteran and parental status, body size, ability, age and experience. We believe these social differences are the foundation for a diversity of perspectives that enrich our classrooms, our professional lives, and our research.

Excerpt from Dr. Monica Linden, professor of neuroscience at Brown University

I would like to create a learning environment for my students that supports a diversity of thoughts, perspectives, and experiences, and honors your identities (including race, gender, class, sexuality, religion, ability, etc.). To help accomplish this:

• If you have a name and/or set of pronouns that differ from those that appear in your official Brown records, please let me know!

• If you feel like your performance in the class is being impacted by your experiences outside of class, please don't hesitate to come and talk with me. I want to be a resource for you. Remember that you can also submit anonymous feedback (which will lead to me making a general announcement to the class, if necessary, to address your concerns). If you prefer to speak with someone outside of the course, the associate dean of the College for Diversity Programs is an excellent resource.

- I (like many people) am still in the process of learning about diverse perspectives and identities. If something was said in class (by anyone) that made you feel uncomfortable, please talk to me about it. (Again, anonymous feedback is always an option.)

- As a participant in course discussions, you should also strive to honor the diversity of your classmates.

College Resources. This section of your syllabus is an opportunity to inform students about resources and offices at your college they may not know about—and to encourage engagement and help-seeking for both academic and nonacademic reasons. Check your syllabus for the following resources and add any you may have missed:

- tutoring and writing support
- counseling services (including anonymous hotlines)
- student accessibility support
- library support
- advising resources
- career development resources
- financial wellness support (the Financial Aid Office or general financial planning and budgeting resources)
- identity-specific offices such as multicultural or Black male centers
- student clubs and organizations
- food pantries and clothing supply closets

Overall Tone. Some studies on the impact of the course syllabus on students have focused specifically on the tone of the syllabus. Richard Harnish and K. Robert Bridges, for instance, find that students perceived the instructor to be more warm, more approachable, and more motivated to teach the course when they found the syllabus tone to be friendly. The researchers add that in fully online courses, particularly asynchronous ones, students and faculty may never "meet"—so impressions of faculty members based on syllabus tone may impact students' perceptions even more.[43]

From the perspective of equity, as Maxine T. Roberts writes, "language that is pleasant and welcoming" can be "particularly important in courses where students face academic difficulty."[44] Sherria D. Taylor points out that an inconsistency between our commitment to inclusion and our syllabus' inaccessible language can have a negative impact on students: "If the syllabus for a course is intended to be grounded in social justice but is written in the traditional content-focused style, it sends a mixed message to students and may inadvertently promote values of hierarchy and individualism."[45]

Here are a few specific suggestions for ensuring that the language of your syllabus reflects your commitment to equity:

- Avoid jargon—where necessary, include a synonym or brief description.
- Use the first-person voice (*I* or *we*; *me* or *us*).
- Consider replacing "command" verbs such as *must, will,* and *should* with ones that imply more choice and negotiation, such as *can* and *may.*

Warm Up Your Online Tone, Too

Although the Harnish and Bridges study referenced here focuses only on the tone of written syllabus materials, their recommendations apply equally well to the tone of written elements in asynchronous online classes. Currently, most online class components are made up of text: headings, menu items, instructions, rubrics, and others, are all presented in written format. It can be easy to fall into an impersonal, even robotic, voice when writing these materials, and this tendency may be exacerbated in online course templates, which are intentionally designed to be used by multiple instructors.

Earlier in this unit we reviewed the findings of Glazier and Harris, which show that minimal changes to syllabus and online course content, to make the writing sound more like a real person and less like a machine, have a positive impact on learner engagement. A 2017 study by Marcia Dixson and colleagues found that using emojis and friendly and approachable language to warm up the tone of online materials similarly enhanced student engagement.[46] These strategies build rapport, help to establish trust (see Unit 4), and reduce the distance online. Given these relational benefits, attending to warm written (and recorded!) online communications is a key equity-minded practice.

Equity-Minded Design Considerations for Online (and Online-Enhanced) Courses

While the syllabus takes on an important guiding role in all class modalities, additional design considerations may play an even more important part in asynchronous online courses. For this reason, and given most instructors' relative lack of experience in online learning spaces (as compared to our decades' worth of experience as students and educators in person), we recommend that you embrace theoretical frameworks and evidence-based tools to support your online course design. That is to say, in comparison with in-person instruction, which has taken place for millennia, teaching and learning in online environments is in its infancy. Theory and practical guidance can help you create the best experience possible for the students in your online courses.

In earlier units, we introduced Universal Design for Learning (UDL). This framework takes on special significance when supporting individuals learning in online and hybrid courses, because of the especially-for-online access considerations regarding both technology and students' variable life circumstances. UDL guidelines inform the recommendations we will offer here and in Section Two, where we'll describe in more detail the frameworks and rubrics we introduce here.

We'll also explore the Community of Inquiry (CoI) framework, which was proposed in 2000 and based on the research of Randy Garrison and his colleagues.[47] This team of researchers wanted to understand what goes into effective and engaging asynchronous online classes, and what prevents them from feeling like electronic correspondence courses. Widely tested and refined in the two decades since its proposal, this theoretical approach "represents a process of creating a deep and meaningful. . . learning experience through the development of three interdependent elements—social, cognitive and teaching presence."[48] The CoI framework invites us to attend to social and instructional interactions online, as well as to interactions with course content and materials. In Units 6 and 7, you'll find specific guidance on how this interaction plays out in day-to-day online teaching.

In addition to the seminal UDL and CoI theoretical frameworks, online faculty can draw on important design guidance and support in the form of established course design rubrics. As noted earlier in this guide, the Quality Matters (QM) Rubric and the Online Learning Consortium (OLC) OSCQR Course Design Review Scorecard offer a systematic review process based on a robust body of literature about what supports effective student engagement and learning in online courses.[49] Your institution may have a local rubric derived from either or both of these. As noted in Unit 1, we recognize that some scholars are raising concerns about the validity of these rubrics. These conversations are in an early stage relative to the length of time these rubrics have been in use. While we plan to monitor and engage in such conversations, at the time of this guide's publication it is the case that the rubrics we mention here are widely available and used, and can be a helpful tool for equity-minded online instructors.

Finally, and importantly for equity-focused online faculty and course designers, the more recent Peralta Equity Rubric offers a specific—and not previously articulated—lens for course design that advances equitable learning experiences and outcomes.[50] The rubric was created and is maintained by a team of educators including online teaching expert Kevin Kelly and faculty members from the Peralta Community College District in California, and it too is grounded in a solid research base. This equity-focused rubric invites instructors and course designers to include assignments and activities that lead students to explore the benefits of valuing diversity or to connect with others both in and out of the class (such as with local community members). The Peralta Equity Rubric development team has created and shared an open-access Canvas course to support the use and implementation of the rubric, complete with examples and instructor spotlights to illustrate rubric recommendations and bring them to life.[51] As is the case with the QM Rubric and the OLC OSCQR Course Design Review Scorecard, the Peralta Equity Rubric was specifically designed to support online classes, but it walks equity-minded faculty through considerations that apply in all class modes.

Based on the foundation of these frameworks and rubrics, what follows are a few specific getting-started and navigational solutions for asynchronous classes. Section Two will provide additional guidance and examples in terms of how these ideas play out in daily teaching practice.

Online Navigational Support: Help Students Focus on Learning, Not Finding Materials

A significant challenge for students in asynchronous classes is that online environments aren't always intuitive or easy to navigate. Flower has heard from countless students that Canvas is confusing, or that their (well-meaning) instructors have organized class materials in hard-to-find ways, or that they can't see their grades or comments. Such difficulties present a barrier to students' ability to locate required activities and can even contribute to higher attrition rates in asynchronous courses. Imagine if you walked into your classroom and none of the furniture and teaching tools you regularly use (as in, desks, chairs, the lectern, whiteboards, and screens) were where you expected them to be. Now imagine you're the student facing that level of disorganization. It can feel frustrating, off-putting, and demotivating, to say the least. Yet we know that no one sets out to intentionally confuse online students, and we can do much to preserve students' limited cognitive resources for the work of learning, not finding.

Further, online classes require people to effectively regulate their own learning, a complex skill that our students may still be developing. These challenges may be exacerbated for marginalized students, who, while bringing a much-needed diverse array of experiences, abilities, and perspectives into our institutions and classes, may have experienced opportunity gaps in their previous education. Although perfectly capable of the work we require, some of our students may not have had the chance to develop executive functioning and self-regulation skills such as setting goals for their learning, planning and carrying out strategies to achieve their goals (such as time and task management and prioritization), monitoring their progress, and adjusting their approach as needed to facilitate their success. Asynchronous learning requires more autonomy and independence. To meet these challenges and promote equitable outcomes, consider the following design recommendations to better guide students through the course and its modules.

First, determine whether you are organizing the course yourself or using a preset college or departmental course structure, often called a template. Using such a template may feel constraining, but think about it like the furniture in a classroom. It's just a group of structural elements to help online students learn and succeed, and these templates are typically created by instructional designers and other online teaching and learning experts. So, if one is available to you, you may want to take advantage of it. One more benefit: these templates often come populated with links to student success resources like the library, tutoring center, disability resources, and counseling offices. Embedding these links directly into the online course structure makes it easy for students to access helpful, up-to-date resources, and can increase their sense of belonging, too.

If the organizational structure is up to you, consult with an instructional designer (ID), and choose a system that supports students' flow through the course. LMSs make it possible to organize modules, folders, materials, activities, and assessments in varying ways. While this may seem advantageous, too much flexibility in this regard raises barriers, especially since (in the absence of a required template) students may be navigating four or five different online course structures in one term—and more, if they're also using publisher courseware or online materials. A standard recommendation is to organize modules in a chronological order, rather than in a system that groups materials by type.

For example, each module should include everything students need to proceed through the module, including links to readings, videos, publisher materials, quizzes, assignments, and discussion forums, organized in the order you want students to complete them (more details on this strategy are in Unit 6). A common mistake is to put all the videos in one online folder and all the quizzes in another, for instance. While this organization makes sense in other contexts, in an online class it results in students spending time and attention looking for the things they're supposed to be working on. This time and attention is better spent on engaging in the activities themselves. The most effective online courses smooth the way before students, making it as easy as possible for them to locate and dive into learning tasks. Recruit a colleague or an ID to click through your course and see if it is easy to navigate, and ask them to tell you if and where they get stuck.

Once the course's structure is established, help students know what to expect and how to start classwork. Make sure you have a course introduction page, and that you intentionally introduce yourself, too. Glazier and Harris found that including a photo of yourself helps to build rapport,[52] an equity-minded strategy we'll explore in Section Two when we turn our attention to belonging and trust. If you prefer not to show your face online, we encourage you to interrogate your reasons; after all, your students see you when you teach in person, and connecting with you as a person is even more important for your online students. However, we know there are valid reasons not to post identifying images. Alternatives include a picture of you in which your face is obscured, say, you on a mountain bike on a favorite trail, or a representative image such as a landscape or pet.

In your welcome or introduction page or folder, provide written or recorded guidance to help students feel at ease and confident about what to do to get started. For example, post an overview video that highlights the main goals of the class, provides a screen-capture tour of the course, and helps students know what to expect. Consider creating a "course at a glance" page that lists each week's readings, videos, and assignments in a table format to provide an easily accessible road map (you'll find an example of this table in Unit 6). In line with UDL, you may want to provide this feature as both a page in the course and a printable PDF (and if you do so, it's important to plan accordingly when updating due dates, for example, from term to term). At the beginning of each module, include a module introduction along with a list of module goals. This can be a short piece of text including two to four sentences and/or bullet points or a brief, informal captioned video of one to three minutes—or both.

One challenge with asynchronous online courses is that they can feel very linear and very transactional. Each module may appear to be a list of things to do, with little explanation about the purpose of activities, how concepts and tasks relate to and build upon each other, or other forms of guidance and "connective tissue" that you may so easily provide in the physical classroom.

You can add such guidance and make such connections explicit simply by adding a sentence or two in writing or captioned video/audio between elements in the module. For example, add an introduction to a reading above the link to the reading, or add a chapter introduction above the instructions to read, say, chapter 3 of the textbook. In this introduction, provide an overview, background, or context to help students know what to expect—a key strategy that helps learners harness attention and maximize focus and their subsequent memory of information in the reading. Better yet, include a few guiding questions, for points or not, to help focus students' attention on key concepts in the reading. Above or as part of the reading quiz instructions, add a few lines such as, "Now that you've completed the assigned reading, check your recall of important facts. This will help you build a foundation for this week's discussion and project." Ideally, this message will be followed by logistical instructions about how long students have to take the quiz, whether they have multiple attempts, and so on. Find a balance between providing short snippets to explain why you're asking students to do things and an overwhelming amount of explanatory text or video that will add to students' workload. You can be both concise and supportive.

Providing these kinds of introductions, overviews, and explanations in each module and between module tasks helps to replicate what a syllabus, and your daily interactions in the classroom, can do in the best of circumstances. Even better than the fleeting interactions in in-person classes, these short guiding elements stay in front of the students as they work their way through each online module.

Intentionally Design for Connections, Interactions, and Community

A critically important equity strategy for online courses is to build features and opportunities that promote interaction among classmates in order to extend belonging to everyone and to foster trust in you, the instructor, and other students. This approach is central to the Community of Inquiry (CoI), the theoretical framework introduced previously, that invites us to leverage three interdependent elements—social presence, cognitive presence, and teaching presence—for online student learning and success. Before we dive deeper into course design for connection, we'll provide a quick overview of the presences in CoI.

By *social presence*, we mean interactions among the people in an online class. Without consistent, engaging interactions with others, online classes can feel like a list of to-do items to check. These are hardly conditions that foster deep and transformational learning, hence the importance of online classes that prioritize learning with and from the other people in the class. *Teaching presence* gets at this idea. Rather than expecting online students to teach themselves, or to walk themselves through class content, equity-minded online instructors actively facilitate learning by engaging with students through, for example, discussions, assignment feedback, announcements, and individual phone calls or small group meetings. And students teach each other, too, often in discussion forums and collaborative group projects—an important reminder that each person in our class brings cultural wealth, capabilities, and perspectives that strengthen and enhance the learning experience for everyone. Finally, *cognitive presence*, in simplest terms, is the thought work that goes into planning, teaching, and learning online—both yours and your students'. What have you offered to help students acquire competency of new concepts, skills, and information? What learning tasks and assessments will students undertake to acquire and demonstrate their learning? These questions inform the development of the cognitive presence online.

These three elements, or presences, occur in person as well, but the CoI framework helps us to center the social and teaching presences in online environments, which can feel cold and unwelcoming. All three ingredients are necessary to foster online conditions in which deep learning can occur, according to Garrison and countless other online teaching experts.[53] However, despite the recognition that CoI has earned, it still remains that many online students report feeling isolated and out of touch with their instructor and classmates. At least one likely reason online students feel this way is that in person, we frequently experience spontaneous connections—for example, asking a neighbor for a piece of notebook paper. Research conducted in 2020 showed that the lack of such spontaneous interactions in Zoom classes led to decreased student motivation and increased feelings of loneliness and isolation, neither of which promote student mental well-being (or our own, for that matter). The point is, there is very little that is spontaneous about connections in asynchronous courses, and they don't happen by accident. We have to intentionally plan opportunities for students to interact with and build relationships with others in the class.

We'll explore this in much more detail in Units 6 and 7, where we look at what day-to-day community-building looks like online. For now, here are a few course design strategies that will lay the foundation for effective engagement during the term.

- *Find varied ways to demonstrate your availability.* Students frequently tell us that their number-one challenge in online courses is their perception that their professor isn't readily available to them (at least not in the same way as when they see you in person and can linger after class to ask a quick question). Yet, as the instructor, you get to set the tone in your online class. Establish the groundwork for robust, purposeful interactions with your students by humanizing yourself in the course materials they'll find when they first click into class. For example, an "all about me" video or slideshow makes a world of difference in helping students recognize you're a real person.

- *Design discussion prompts that stimulate robust conversation online.* Determine your pedagogical purpose for discussion prompts, a mainstay of online courses. Do you want students to practice scholarly writing? If so, require an academic tone and credible citations. If your primary purpose is to replicate less formal classroom discussions, a formal tone and full citations may not be necessary. After all, you don't require students to verbalize a correctly formatted citation every time they answer your question in class—right?

- *Consider adding purely social and relational activities to your course.* Many online classes feature an Introduction forum, where students post some information about themselves and their academic and personal interests. But often, the interactions on a personal level end there. If we struggle to get students to engage in online discussions, as a common example, it could be because it feels weird for them to talk with people they hardly know. As a solution, add a feature like "Question of the Week" or asynchronous getting-to-know-you activities such as those found at Equity Unbound,[54] in which you ask students to answer and interact with topics that aren't class-related. Make these fun, get students laughing if you can, and participate in such activities yourself. The goal is to help everyone in the class feel that they belong and that they are in a vibrant community. Take some module time and space to foster relationships. It will make the online learning experience in your course more equitable (and it'll likely make you enjoy and find more fulfillment in your online teaching, too).

Bottom line, engagement comes before learning. Students have to *want* to be in class in order to learn. Can you say, in all honesty, that your online students want to be in class? Do you? Designing relational activities and course features will help to establish a trusting environment in which students know they're a valued member of the group. This type of environment is a key feature of an equity-focused online class, and as an added (and important!) benefit, it will likely result in greater engagement and enjoyment online.

As we wrap up this section of the guide, we hope you've taken us up on some of our recommendations and are now heading to the day-to-day teaching section with a strong foundation for more equitable teaching that includes enhanced learning objectives, updated assessments, a more equitable grading scheme, an inclusive syllabus, and especially for asynchronous online courses, a design that reflects your commitment to equity. Next, we'll focus on helping you connect with your students and promote connections among them in order to foster trust and a sense of belonging. We'll also help you set up structures that facilitate and integrate inclusion.

HOW CAN I GET STARTED?

For Any Class

- Introduce students to your syllabus and explain its purpose, what you included and why, and how you hope they'll use it to support their course success.

- During class or asynchronously, annotate the syllabus in a Google Doc or an app such as Hypothes.is or Perusall.[55] Annotating the syllabus invites learners to dig into this often-overlooked document, ask clarifying questions, and otherwise benefit from your efforts to infuse equity throughout.[56] These tools make it possible to facilitate this activity in real time during a class session or on students' own time—whatever best serves your purpose and works within your context.

- Engage your students in a discussion of the syllabus as if it were a chapter in the course textbook, as James Dyer and colleagues suggest. In this way, students don't see it so much as a "list of rules etched into a stone tablet, but rather as a document whose understanding is to be collaboratively constructed by the classroom community."[57]

For In-Person Classes

- While it's not ideal to devote the entire first class session to the syllabus (see Section Two for first-day suggestions), make sure to show students the parts of the document that are focused on their success and talk about how you've designed the syllabus as a tool for them, and if equity is visible in the form of an equity statement or is infused another way, point this out.

- Ask students to complete a syllabus scavenger hunt, challenging them to find elements you want to make sure they know where to locate or commit to memory, or a syllabus quiz, explaining that you want to make sure they're familiar with the tool because it will help them succeed.

For Asynchronous Online Classes

- Record a video in which you describe how your syllabus supports equity and how online students should use it as a tool for their success.

- Create a syllabus quiz or agreement, highlighting learners' responsibilities and promoting active reading and engagement with the tool. This can be in the form of an auto-graded quiz that either asks students questions about information contained in the syllabus or provides a list of statements ("I will request a deadline extension in advance of the due date whenever possible") to which students answer "true" in a true/false manner.

- Assign a syllabus reflection, asking students to share, in written or recorded form, their goals for learning, questions about the syllabus, and so on.

For Synchronous Online Classes

- Similar to what you would do in an in-person class, talk through important parts of the syllabus and highlight how the tool has been designed for equity and supports student success.

- Use breakout groups for a group syllabus scavenger hunt and a small-group discussion or goal-setting session. For example, students could discuss questions that you provide ("What are you most excited about reading/learning/doing in this class?") or set two goals for their learning in your class, then give each other feedback to strengthen their individual goals.

- On an anonymous Padlet, ask students to post questions or concerns about the syllabus, or to share things they're most excited to learn about in the course, for example.

SECTION TWO

INCLUSIVE DAY-TO-DAY TEACHING

"There is no teaching without learning."

—Paulo Freire

Inclusive day-to-day teaching practices and decisions are as important as equity-focused course design, perhaps more so. We can plan and prepare, yet at the start of each academic term, we are entrusted with a new set of students who have a new mix of identities, aspirations, background knowledge, abilities, and so on. It's up to us, as equity-minded faculty, to get to know them and assume some responsibility for their social and academic growth—growth that will differ for each student. As we'll discuss in this section, everyday teaching strategies are most effective when they focus on both *promoting* student growth and *understanding* as clearly as possible where students are on their respective pathways. Teaching expert Stephen Brookfield puts it this way: "The most important knowledge that skillful teachers need to do good work is a constant awareness of how students are experiencing their learning and perceiving teachers' actions."[1]

Faculty striving to advance more equitable outcomes use a variety of approaches to monitor and sustain inclusion throughout students' learning experiences. These include ways to welcome students and get to know them, validate their abilities, demystify our expectations of them, and help them learn deeply. Unit 4 describes strategies for building and maintaining *trust*, the foundation upon which we can champion students' growth and development. These strategies are especially important for online classes, where the absence of physical proximity makes trust harder to establish and maintain. Unit 5 focuses on the impact of students' *sense of belonging* and the ways in which you can cultivate a learning environment where students feel they belong, matter, and can thrive. Unit 6 outlines how to intentionally *structure* class meetings, online modules, and individual activities in order to promote equitable outcomes. Section Two concludes with a one-of-a-kind Unit 7, consisting of two case studies that illustrate what it looks like when the practices described throughout the guide come together in the day-to-day work of teaching.

4

RELATIONSHIPS
Earn and Maintain Students' Trust

Distrust can compromise learning, yet faculty can earn and deepen students' trust by getting to know their students, demonstrating care for them, and trusting them.

Most faculty can recall building relationships with students that endured long after the course had concluded. And many, if not most, of us perceive ourselves as welcoming individuals whose commitment to student learning and success is not only genuine but also self-evident and tangible. So it can be hard to imagine that students don't always perceive things the way we do and that many of them—especially minoritized students and those who are first in their families to attend college—initially view faculty with suspicion and even fear.

The way students perceive us matters a great deal because, as Peter Felten and Leo Lambert stress in *Relationship-Rich Education: How Human Connections Drive Success in College*, relationships are the single most important factor in college education.[2] Equity scholars have long emphasized the need for faculty to cultivate trusting relationships with students. Laura Rendón reminds us that, in the 1980s and 90s, feminist teaching and learning theorists introduced models of connected teaching focused on "building relationships among faculty and students" and on creating "learning communities."[3] Meanwhile, in *Culturally Responsive Teaching and the Brain*, Zaretta Hammond explains the neuroscientific finding that the need to be connected to others is wired into the human brain; it's a survival instinct. When we are alone or fail to have positive relationships, our brains become preoccupied with scanning our environment for threats—a process scientists call *neuroception*.[4] This process can hinder our ability to focus and learn.

Trust, in turn, is key to effective relationships. Stephen M. R. Covey calls trust "the most effective way of relating to and working with others" and "one of the most powerful forms of motivation and inspiration."[5] In teaching, trust is the basis for all else, allowing us to challenge students because they know we have their best interest at heart and will therefore support them. In the case of equity-minded teaching, we can't take trust for granted. Many students from historically marginalized backgrounds join our institutions in a state of distrust based on their experiences with prior schooling and both direct and indirect interactions with large bureaucracies like colleges and universities. Schools may have been sites where these students were disciplined for minor infractions, while their families or loved ones may have had trouble navigating governmental regulations and agencies, including our justice system. Aspects of our identities such as race and gender can also make it more difficult for students to trust us.

Fortunately, scholars have also found that trust is key to advancing more equitable outcomes. Hammond calls it the "secret weapon" of the culturally responsive teacher.[6] Plus, building trust is not as elusive as you might think. There are concrete steps you can take to earn and maintain your students' trust. In this unit, we'll first distill research in this area, including how trust plays a role in democracy, how to establish trust among teachers and students, how our identities relate to trust, and how trust manifests itself in fully online courses. Then, we'll suggest three approaches to building and maintaining your students' trust, starting with ways to get to know your students and help them get to know *you*.

What Does the Research Say about Relationships and Trust?

Research on relationships in teaching and learning is extensive,[7] but one finding exemplifies the impact of faculty-student relationships. When Gallup asked more than seventy-five thousand college graduates to reflect on their campus experiences, they found that alumni who felt strongly that one of their professors "cared about them as a person" were more engaged in their work and experienced higher levels of overall well-being. That's right: not only were relationships with faculty important while these individuals were enrolled in college, but they also had a *long-term* impact on alumni wellness. Unfortunately, only 27 percent of college graduates indicated that they had a professor who cared about them as a person.[8] This disconnect between students' *perception* of care and what we know is faculty members' deep commitment to students raises several important questions: Why might students not notice or believe that we care for them as people? Are there patterns in the types of students with whom we *are* connecting deeply? (Perhaps we connect with those who aspire to earn advanced degrees in our fields, those who attend office hours, and/or those with whom we share similar identities, backgrounds, or hobbies.)

Pause to Consider

- Picture two to three students with whom you've stayed connected long after the end of the course. Do you notice any patterns in these students' identities or aspirations?

- What does it take for someone to earn your trust?

- How do you earn your online students' trust? For instance, how can they tell that you're "there"—that you're present in the course and ready to support them?

Research on equity-minded teaching likewise emphasizes the importance of relationships. Here are a few examples we'd like to highlight: Geneva Gay, pioneer of culturally responsive pedagogy, affirms that "positive relationships exemplified as 'caring' are one of the major pillars" of inclusive practice.[9] Hammond calls relationships "the on-ramp to learning,"[10] adding that they "are as important as the curriculum."[11] She urges us to begin our culturally responsive practice by establishing meaningful relationships, or "learning partnerships," with students.[12] Coauthor Bryan Dewsbury describes his "deep teaching" model for the STEM classroom as a pedagogy predicated on relationships.[13] Last, but certainly not least, the late bell hooks wrote that her approach to teaching centers on loving relationships with her students, ones characterized by "care, commitment, knowledge, responsibility, respect, and trust."[14] In Unit 9, we describe a study of undergraduates that likewise concluded that students, regardless of their institutional type, discipline, or course modality, seek above all else a well-rounded education grounded in meaningful relationships.[15]

Regarding the connection between teaching and trust, Stephen Brookfield calls trust "the affective glue binding educational relationships together."[16] Psychology professor Stephen Chew and his colleagues identify trust as a key element of a successful student mindset. Their definition of trust is "students' willingness to take risks based on their judgment that the teacher is committed to student success."[17] Implicit in this definition are two key ideas: that trust allows students to take risks and that trust requires showing students that we're committed to their success.[18] To help elucidate the former idea, scientists indicate that the brain seeks to minimize uncertainty and social threat, so the safer one feels the more risks one takes.[19] Thus, when students trust their instructors, they are able to negotiate with the uncertainty that comes with taking risks to learn.

In an article coauthored with educational developer William Cerbin, Chew clarifies that student trust consists of three components: competence, integrity, and beneficence. *Competence* means showing students that we know not just how to teach our disciplinary content and skills but also how to help them learn and succeed.[20] Equity experts Estela Bensimon and Lindsey Malcolm reinforce this idea, reminding us that expert knowledge in our profession is essential but insufficient when it comes to advancing racial equity.[21] The latter requires humility, inquiry, and the willingness to expand our teaching toolkits with equity-minded practices like the ones we discuss in this guide. *Integrity* means acting truthfully, consistently, and with respect. Brookfield calls it "congruence between words and actions, between what you say you will do and what you actually do," and he warns us that "nothing destroys students' trust in teachers more quickly than seeing teachers espouse one set of principles or commitments . . . and then behave in ways that contradict these."[22] *Beneficence* means demonstrating clearly with our actions (such as course and assignment design, feedback, and class activities) that we have the students' best interests in mind and will support them. "That doesn't mean that the assignments will be easy, but that they will be worthwhile in terms of student growth and learning," explains Chew.[23]

Scholars consistently describe the positive impact of trust on students. In their study, Chew and colleagues asked students to read four scenarios, each one representing a different level of trust. In the high-trust scenario, the professor gives everyone an equal opportunity to succeed and always returns assignments in a timely manner, for instance, while in the low-trust scenario, the professor picks favorites and teaches in a way that makes the material hard to understand. After reading each scenario, students were asked questions related to their feeling of trust and their willingness to work hard in the class and to complete difficult assignments. The researchers found that trust in the teacher improves students' willingness to give their best effort and take on more challenging assignments.[24] Hammond puts it this way: "When students trust that we have their best interests at heart, they give us permission to push them to higher levels of achievement."[25] Brookfield echoes this point by describing the consequences of student mistrust. When students don't trust us, he writes, "they are unwilling to submit themselves to the perilous uncertainties of new learning. They avoid risk. They keep their most deeply felt concerns private. They view with cynical reserve the exhortations and instructions of new teachers."[26] Brookfield reminds us that learning is risky, as it often elicits vulnerability and doubt, and that mistrust can lead students to distance themselves from us and be suspicious about our intentions.

Why Am I Reluctant to Cultivate Relationships with My Students?

Many faculty feel uneasy about the general idea of establishing relationships with their students. One likely reason is that higher education has traditionally been characterized by competition (as in grading on a curve, class rankings, and faculty rewards structures). Rendón contends that in order to teach in new ways, we must first examine a set of agreements that is "firmly entrenched in the academic culture of the academy." In addition to "competition," the academy has privileged "separatism," she writes. This includes the tenet that "faculty should keep a distance between themselves and students" and that faculty outreach to students is a form of coddling.[27] If you hold some or all of these beliefs, we respect them. Indeed, your own deeply held cultural values may have shaped your thinking about them. But we also ask that you interrogate your beliefs a bit (where did they come from?), reflect on the role of relationships with teachers during your own experiences as a student, and consider trying out one of the strategies described in this unit. Remember that it's okay to start small, perhaps by implementing one new practice that will move you a little closer to more relational teaching.

To grasp the centrality of trust to equity-minded teaching, it helps to zoom out a bit. Remember that a key goal of our educational system is to prepare students for engaged participation in democracy. As scholars write, trust is "a vital precondition for overall social cohesion and vibrant, engaged citizenship within a well-functioning and thriving democracy."[28] In the United States, higher levels of education have historically been associated with increased civic engagement; individuals least likely to be civically engaged include racial and ethnic minorities, the children of parents with less formal education, and individuals living in poorer neighborhoods. By definition, our minoritized students and their communities have experienced underrepresentation and subordination in U.S. social institutions. In our equity-minded classrooms, we can provide students with an opportunity to practice trust building, not solely in service of content-related goals but also to promote and prepare students for full participation in democracy. This participation, in turn, will enrich our democracy itself.

Brazilian philosopher and educator Paulo Freire captured this sentiment directly in his book *Pedagogy of the Oppressed*. In his proposed approach, called critical pedagogy, teachers help students free themselves from the constraints of their circumstances through the power of critical conscious-ness.[29] Gloria Ladson-Billings's model of culturally relevant teaching, intro-duced in Unit 1, likewise emphasized that students should develop a critical/sociopolitical consciousness.[30] Freire further expands our understanding of trust: at the core of his critical pedagogy is dialogue, dialogue based on "intense faith in the inherent capabilities of all people to name their realities and to transform them." He writes, "Faith in people is an a priori requirement for dialogue; the 'dialogical person' believes in others even before he meets them face to face."[31] Here, faith is synonymous with trust, which becomes not only something equity-minded faculty seek to earn from our students but also something we must extend to them, a *means* of demonstrating our respect and belief in them, and of earning their trust.

Who Trusts Whom?

Research demonstrates that we are inclined to associate with and trust people who are most like us, including those who share our gender, race, class, age, sexuality, and ability. In essence, our brains assume we are safe with certain people based on our similarities. In contrast, "out-group trust" refers to how much we trust those outside our immediate group affiliations.[32] One study con-ducted in 2020 after the outbreak of COVID-19 identified considerable trust gaps by race, age, marital status, and income.[33] Specifically, while 61 percent of White study participants felt most people could be trusted, fewer Black (36%) and Hispanic/Latino (29%) participants shared similar beliefs. The researchers suggest that minoritized individuals feel more vulnerable in the United States and are thus reticent to extend trust.

With respect to the trust levels of college students in particular, Kevin Fosnacht and Shannon Calderone studied more than eight thousand under-graduates enrolled at twenty-nine U.S. colleges and universities, seeking to understand whether and how trust levels vary for different groups of under-graduate students and across different geographies. Using data from the 2020 administration of the National Survey of Student Engagement (NSSE), they find that "white students demonstrated higher trust levels across nearly all trust dimensions than Black, Latino, multiracial, and the catch-all 'another' student groups." The authors pose several hypotheses for this distinction in trust: lim-ited faculty and leadership diversity, campus racial conflict, and racial battle fatigue (the sheer exhaustion minoritized individuals can feel). They encourage institutions to "recapture important yet historically marginalized constituen-cies' trust" in order to convince them we "have their best interests in mind."[34]

David Yeager, of the University of Texas at Austin, is a leading researcher of student trust. In describing the context for their study of middle school stu-dents' levels of trust in their school, Yeager and his colleagues help us under-stand students' developmental process of trust-building. They explain that for adolescents, learning whom to trust is "a key developmental challenge."[35]

Students of color are often reluctant to trust our institutions and, in turn, us as faculty, based on experiences such as mistreatment by authorities and the police, low teacher expectations, and inconsistent disciplinary referrals. With these student experiences in mind, Yeager and his colleagues clarify that mistrust among students is not only understandable but a "natural adaptation."

The researchers add that trust in school settings is even more challenging given the racial divide among teachers and students in the United States. In higher education, three-quarters of full-time college faculty identify as White, whereas only half (51%) of the 16.6 million undergraduate students enrolled in fall 2019 identified as White.[36] Yeager and colleagues conclude that we're swimming against the tide: "The [very] demographics of most American schools may act as an affordance of mistrust."[37] Importantly, it is not the differences in identities themselves that create challenges with trust; it's the fact that our students' "perceptions and ways of making meaning vary from one another and from the instructor," as Margery Ginsberg and Raymond Wlodkowski explain.[38] As we mentioned in this section's introduction, each of us brings our cultures, beliefs, values, privileges, and biases into our teaching, and these intersect with our students' cultures, beliefs, values, privileges, and biases.

What's at stake? Yeager and colleagues describe how students experience a chain event of mistrust and its costs:

> When students have lost trust, they may be deprived of the benefits of engaging with an institution, such as positive relationships, access to resources and opportunities for advancement, and avoidance of punishment. Thus, racial and ethnic minority youth may be twice harmed by institutional injustices: They both receive the lion's share of the initial punishment, and then may be required to psychologically adapt, through a loss of trust, in a way that prevents them from profiting from instruction and relationships.[39]

Recognizing how students' earlier educational experiences influence their willingness to trust us is key to becoming truly equity-minded faculty. Particularly when teaching minoritized students, we must strive not only to earn their trust but also to do our part to help them regain trust in schooling and in educational settings. This process takes time, patience, and intentionality. We may not be able to fundamentally undo the harm many of our students experienced before they arrived at our institutions, but we have an opportunity to pivot, to show them that trust is possible.

Earning and Restoring Trust

We turn now from research on the importance of and challenges with cultivating trust to research that can inform our teaching. One key finding is that trust is not a fixed state; we can absolutely succeed in earning and maintaining it.

How? Hammond distills her guidance into one word: caring. "Caring is the way that we generate the trust that builds relationships," she affirms.[40] The most powerful way to demonstrate our care for students, she adds, is to actively listen to them, and to give our full attention to both their words and their non-verbal communication. Hammond adds that another way to demonstrate care is to hold students to high standards while offering them new intellectual challenges (see Unit 1 on rigor). In 1990, Brookfield outlined a set of steps we can take to build trust with students. He advises us to, in addition to making sure our words and actions are congruent, be explicit about our organizing vision (as in the transparency we described in Unit 2), be ready to admit our errors, and avoid playing favorites.[41]

One of the most comprehensive and helpful studies we've found on earning and maintaining students' trust was conducted by Peter Demerath and his colleagues in an urban high school. They studied educators who had been nominated by students for helping them develop a sense of agency and academic aspirations for the future. The researchers found that, for the students taught by these educators, the biggest barriers to academic success and college aspirations were internal—that is, for varied reasons, students expected that things would not work out for them. Notably, many of the teachers they examined were effective in supporting students across racial and ethnic lines. As the researchers learned how these teachers helped students overcome their limited self-expectations, "the biggest surprise . . . was how much time, thought, and effort these teachers put into compelling students to trust them."[42]

Drawing on this study, Demerath and colleagues developed a 2022 article titled "A Grounded Model of How Educators Earn Students' Trust in a High Performing U.S. Urban High School," in which they illustrate six dimensions of trust. They frame their model using a set of unspoken questions they found students instinctively ask themselves when they first meet their instructors, what the authors call a process of *mutual discernment*. In essence, when we engage in this process we check each other out to explore "the possibilities of entering into learning partnerships."[43] Demerath's full model is in the Appendix, and we encourage you to take a few minutes to review it. For now, we isolate in table 4.1 students' unspoken questions regarding trust, and we include some of the steps faculty can take to earn and maintain trust.

Although each of these questions and trust-earning behaviors can go a long way in cultivating trust, we want to pause and again highlight the role of "care." When students ask themselves, "How much do they know and care about me?" they are thinking both about themselves as individuals and about their communities—which may include their local community, racial or ethnic community, or another kind of community. Thus, one important way to demonstrate care and concern is to stay informed of significant, impactful events such as hate crimes or mass shootings. In most cases, it can be meaningful to your students when

TABLE 4.1   Responding to Students' Unspoken Questions about Trust

Students' Unspoken Queries about Us	Behaviors That Earn Trust
Why are they here?	Let students know what motivates you to teach.
How much do they know and care about me?	Make the effort to get to know your students and their backgrounds.
How much do they respect me?	Avoid unnecessary criticism and trust students with knowledge of your nonfaculty life.
How real are they? Do they know who they are in relation to me?	Demonstrate self-awareness, particularly relating to your identity (e.g., acknowledging the parts of your identity that have resulted in privilege), and look for common ground (as in gender, socioeconomic background, learning experience).
Do they know how to help me learn?	Share accounts of your prior students' learning, discuss effective study habits, and explain why—that is, be transparent about how you have designed the class to ensure students learn, how assessments and activities connect to the course learning goals, and so on.
How close are they willing to get to me? What are they willing to do to help me learn?	Be patient, available, and express that you care about the whole student, not just their academic success.

Source: Adapted from Peter Demerath et al., "A Grounded Model of How Educators Earn Students' Trust in a High Performing U.S. Urban High School," Urban Review *54, no. 5 (December 2022): Fig. 1, https://doi.org/10.1007/s11256-022-00635-4.*

you acknowledge that these incidents may be affecting them; create space for discussion and offer flexibility in deadlines, when possible; and let them know about available resources (such as counseling). Authentically expressing concern helps build and maintain trust.

The Power of Wise Feedback

Education researchers like Demerath and his colleagues have become increasingly interested in studying trust between students and educators, and each of their studies features strategies we can use or adapt in our teaching.[44] One important subset of this research is based on the use of what are called **wise interventions**. Erving Goffman coined the term *wise* in the 1960s in his

wise interventions: Brief, precise strategies based on psychological theories that aim to improve personal and social outcomes.

analysis of social stigma. Yeager and colleagues explain that "to be 'wise' is the act of seeing stigmatized individuals in their full humanity, which enables an openness and honesty when one interacts with them." They go on to state that "wise" strategies, in turn, "convey to students that they will be neither treated nor judged in light of a negative stereotype but will instead be respected and treated as a valuable individual."[45] How do "wise" teachers and faculty build trust with and motivate minoritized students? In short, they combine high standards with high levels of care for students' well-being. The terms *warm demanders* and *compassionate disciplinarians* have been used to describe wise educators.[46]

Many empirically tested wise interventions exist. In some examples, students are asked to affirm their values, are taught about a **growth mindset** of intelligence, and are helped to develop a sense of belonging (the subject of Unit 5).[47] We focus here on a few studies that employ a specific wise intervention known as **wise feedback**. By *feedback*, we mean "information given to students about their performance that guides future behavior."[48] Feedback is essential to equity-minded teaching given students' heightened vulnerability when receiving feedback, and the fact that focused feedback promotes the greatest learning gains.[49] The stakes are high for students when they receive our feedback. These moments can either promote a trusting relationship or result in student mistrust and disengagement. In fact, Yeager and colleagues describe *wise feedback* as a way to break "the cycle of mistrust" across the racial divide.[50]

In 1999, psychologists Geoffrey Cohen, Claude Steele, and Lee Ross conducted a seminal study of wise feedback. They examined the response of Black and White students to critical feedback on a writing assignment. Two types of feedback were provided: a straightforward description of what to improve and an example of wise feedback. The latter contains two distinguishing elements: (1) an indication that the evaluator (in our case, you, the faculty member) has high standards and (2) an expression of confidence that the student has the capacity to reach those standards. Cohen and colleagues found that wise feedback increased Black college students' motivation and reduced their sense that the evaluator was biased.[51] In a daily diary study, Black students who reported experiencing both high expectations and feelings of personal care were the most likely to report that they trusted their teacher—regardless of the teacher's racial and ethnic group.[52]

Earlier, we introduced the study by David Yeager and his colleagues of middle schoolers and its depiction of a chain event of mistrust in the lives of many adolescents. Surveys indicated that the Black students were more aware of racial bias in school disciplinary decisions, and as this awareness grew they lost trust in school, leading to a large trust gap between these students and their educators by seventh grade. The researchers in this study employed a wise intervention: a single handwritten note including both criteria for wise

growth mindset: The understanding that qualities like intelligence are malleable, not fixed traits, and that success comes from effort.

wise feedback: Feedback that indicates that the evaluator has high standards and expresses confidence that the learner has the capacity to reach those standards.

feedback—conveying high expectations and confidence that students could meet those expectations—from the students' seventh-grade social studies teacher was attached to an essay they had written. Yeager and colleagues saw both immediate and long-term results: The proportion of Black students who revised their critiqued essays a week later increased from 17 percent to 72 percent. (We can hear the collective gasp of all faculty who assign writing revisions.) About two months later, the wise-feedback strategy effectively halted what had become a trend of declining trust for the Black students. Students who had received the "wise note" were assigned fewer disciplinary infractions after the study and, nearly six years later, they were more likely to attend a four-year college.

Pause to Consider

- Did a teacher or professor ever give you wise feedback? How did you respond, or how do you think you would have responded?

- What are the main types of feedback you provide to your students, and how "wise" would you say they are?

Why do wise strategies "work"? Yeager and colleagues explain that their power is in conveying to students "that they will be neither treated nor judged in light of a negative stereotype but will instead be respected as an individual."[53] At the same time, the authors are careful not to oversimplify or suggest that any one intervention is a magic wand: "Truly 'wise' educators do not simply append notes to essays and end their interventions there," they write. "Instead, they continually send the message that their students are capable, valued, and respected, weaving it into the culture of the classroom."[54]

On Cultivating Trust Online

If we apply Yeager and colleagues' research findings to online learning contexts, we'll understand that "continually" sending messages about students' capabilities, value, and our respect for them requires that online faculty engage "continually" with students. Although this may seem self-evident, asynchronous online classes (still) suffer from a reputation of being like a slow cooker: set and forget. Many online instructors inaccurately believe that because a great deal of work went into creating class materials, activities, and assessments before the first day of class, they don't need to do much once the class begins to facilitate this work. Faculty have told us their online course "runs itself" after they finish updating the syllabus, due dates, and so on. This sentiment likely accounts for a widespread perception among students that their online instructors are absent and unavailable to answer questions, give feedback, or otherwise provide guidance. The level of instructor involvement can make or break online students' experience. Research has long shown that students' sense that their online instructor is present, actively involved, and available to help them succeed plays a major role in student learning and persistence online.[55] In fact, Shanna Smith Jaggars and Di Wu find that interpersonal interaction among faculty and students—for which, of course, active presence is required—is the most important factor in online student success.[56]

As an illustration, consider an experience coauthor Flower Darby had while attending an online teaching conference in 2019. In one highly impactful session, conference organizers hosted a panel consisting of community college students from all walks of life. To investigate a hunch she had, Flower went to the mic and asked the students how they know their online teacher cares about them. She was stunned by the response. One student pulled the mic toward her and said, "When my online instructor replies to my email, I feel like I *actually* matter." All the other student panelists nodded in agreement. The unspoken message was clear: most of the time, online students feel like they *don't* matter to their instructors. Flower admits that, at some points in the past, she was guilty of not really seeing her online students as real people; rather, she saw them as names on a screen or tasks on a grading to-do list. In practice, this meant she was not as responsive as students needed her to be, inadvertently communicating a lack of concern for them—even though, like you, she has always had a genuine commitment to supporting students' learning.

To overcome this challenge, and to help us build relationships with online students as real people who matter to us, it's our responsibility to create equity-focused asynchronous courses that have been intentionally designed to prioritize interactions among faculty and students and among students with each other. Recall the Community of Inquiry (CoI) framework introduced earlier in this guide that describes three factors key to effective virtual learning environments: cognitive, teaching, and social presences. To foster and sustain trust online, it's critically important to focus on the teaching and social presences. In doing so, we actively plan for and engage in relational opportunities (see Unit 3 for design suggestions and Unit 7 for what this looks like day to day). Student trust is much harder to earn in the slow-cooker online course model.

Building on the importance of relationships, and drawing on numerous studies of how care relates to learning, author Harriet Schwartz argues that caring closes the distance online and strengthens all-important connections among instructors and students. Schwartz is a professor of psychology and counseling at Antioch University and the author of *Connected Teaching: Relationship, Power, and Mattering in Higher Education*.[57] In an eloquent blog post published on April 2, 2020, written just days after the unprecedented COVID-19 pandemic caused a pivot to emergency remote instruction, Schwartz shared this sentiment with her fellow faculty:

> *As we engage with students remotely, we construct learning spaces (synchronous and asynchronous), and then through each interaction, we create small moments of big possibility. Every communication has the potential to say: "I see you," "I care," and "you matter." And we are connected, even from afar.*[58]

Schwartz reminds us that small interactions in online environments can have a big impact. When students feel that connection, they feel cared for. These feelings of connection and care build trust.

In our efforts to demonstrate caring as we foster and sustain relationships online, it's also important to consider what we communicate (possibly inadvertently) regarding our time. When students feel like we are not available to them, or not invested in their learning, their perception of not mattering erodes trust. Recent research on student engagement online recommends that faculty consider two common habits related to time. First, examine the amount of time that elapses between receiving an email and replying to that email, for example, or how long it takes you to return an assignment with feedback. Second, think about what you (inadvertently) communicate through the apparent amount of time you spend "looking at" online students and interacting with them.[59] For example, writing a class announcement that includes explicit encouragement in addition to course-related reminders shows students you spent some additional time crafting that message to promote their well-being (e.g., "Hi everyone, you've come so far in this class! You're really working hard, and I appreciate that. This week, remember . . . "). Another way to demonstrate time spent with students is to add a brief personal note to assignment comments instead of a terse comment or no comment at all. These and similar ideas can help online students feel that we're spending time with them, which fosters trust-filled relationships as students feel cared for, seen, and supported.

Trusting Our Online Students

Key ways to earn students' trust are to trust them and to *demonstrate* that we trust them. Yet, as we acknowledged in Unit 2, many faculty think their students will cheat when completing assessments online, particularly as this practice has become more prevalent.[60] As you might imagine, starting from a place of suspicion can instantly erode trust. Online proctoring solutions not only embody mistrust but also symbolize a form of policing and surveillance that can make students feel unsafe. We recognize that in some cases faculty are required to rely on proctoring, as when mandated by accrediting or professional agencies. In all other cases, we recommend the "Design for Integrity" ideas in Unit 2, some of which are briefly summarized here:

- Knowing that it is neither possible nor advisable to police online students, consider all online tests and quizzes open-book and open-note, and design them accordingly.

- Write test questions that aren't easily "Googleable": create questions that require critical thinking and analysis, or ask students to explain why a phenomenon happens or how they arrived at their solution. To streamline grading time, consider a mix of auto-graded multiple-choice types of questions and a few short-answer questions that require manual grading. If you minimize the number of manually graded questions, you can still foster integrity while not creating an overwhelming grading burden.

- Since each quiz and test is both an act of learning and an assessment of learning (see Unit 2), lower the stakes of each. Low-stakes assignments have been shown to increase academic honesty.

- Take advantage of the "multiple attempts" feature in auto-graded quizzes. For example, create "mastery quizzes" that require students to earn 100 percent before they can proceed to the next task in the module. Offer unlimited attempts to do so.[61]

- Instead of thinking about how to prevent cheating, create online activities and assessments that promote academic integrity, ones that explain the value of the task you're asking students to do. Studies of plagiarism have shown, for instance, that students often fail to effectively cite their sources because they don't understand the value of citations in academia.[62]

Building and Maintaining Trust

First, we want to point out that many of the suggestions in Units 1–3 are inherently helpful in earning students' trust. To mention a few, crafting a syllabus as described in Unit 3 fosters trust by communicating to your students that you are in their corner and want them to succeed. Transparency (discussed in Unit 2) is also critical to maintaining and deepening students' trust. It's a powerful way to respond to students' questions, as identified by Demerath and colleagues: Do they know how to help me learn? Do they have my back? As coauthor Mays Imad explains, a focus on creating and maintaining trust can mitigate the adverse effects of uncertainty and help students find meaning and connections in your class. You can accomplish these goals by articulating how each assignment relates to the objectives of the course, as well as spelling out the steps required to complete each assignment and how it will be evaluated.[63] Since clarity, transparency, and reliability foster trust, you may want to revisit the ideas and resources shared earlier. Similarly, table 4.1, "Responding to Students' Unspoken Questions about Trust," includes many suggestions for earning and deepening students' trust, so if you haven't had a chance to review it carefully, consider revisiting it too.

One overall approach to earning and maintaining students' trust is to assign them tasks and responsibilities that are traditionally viewed as yours and yours alone. English professor Jane Tompkins describes an occasion when she ran out of time to prepare her course in the way she had done previously, with an emphasis on what *she* would say and do. So she experimented with one of her peers' teaching methods and made her students responsible for presenting the material to the class and facilitating discussion.[64] Upon reflection, Tompkins realized that her prior approach to teaching boiled down to the performance of her expertise, such that it replicated "power relations currently in force," in contrast to what she wanted to see changed in the world: students becoming invested in their own learning and developing expertise of their own, which is exactly what happened when she made this change. Whether you find opportunities for your students to present content, facilitate discussion, co-create course policies, submit test questions, grade their own work (see Unit 2 on ungrading), or take on another part of the faculty role, you will implicitly be communicating that you trust them.

Following are three concrete suggestions for establishing and maintaining student trust. We hope you'll use the first two at the very start of the term, as this timing is key to their effectiveness. As Michelle Pacansky-Brock describes for online courses, weeks 0–1 of any teaching term are a "high-opportunity zone." She explains that "feelings of social isolation can worsen when students learn at a distance from their peers and instructor. To lower this barrier, human-ized online courses incorporate kindness cues of social inclusion . . . [during] the week prior to the start of instruction and the first week of a class."[65] We have found this to be true in all modalities. After these two introductory strat-egies, we suggest ways to "wisen-up" your feedback.

1. Get to Know Your Students (Even before Day 1)

No student walks or clicks into the first day or module of class as a completely blank slate. Each student arrives as an amalgamation of experiences, all of which shape how they engage in the course. Yet most of us know very little about our students' prior experiences when they enroll in our courses. Thus, we (unknow-ingly) rely on our assumptions, including assumptions about their knowledge and abilities—which makes it difficult to earn their trust. As the students in the study by Demerath and colleagues wondered, "How much do [teachers] know and care about me?"[66] Knowing students goes hand in hand with caring. We suggest getting to know students at two levels: personal and social.

These two pre-class activities can help you learn about your students' unique stories:

- *First-day info sheets.* Developed by Tess Killpack and Laverne Melón, this strategy consists of sending out a survey designed to capture identity-related information typically not captured by other data collection mechanisms (like pronouns and access to Wi-Fi at home) and to give students a chance to describe their strengths.[67] Though qualitative, the open-response questions are relatively short, allowing you to get a more detailed sense of who is in your class. These info sheets also come in handy when you are meeting with students individually, as you can easily check the sheet to refresh your memory on what's important to the student and reference these insights during your discussion.

    A similar option is the "Who's in Class?" form developed by Tracie Addy and colleagues (see Appendix). They recommend that it be used after a couple of class sessions or the equivalent of online course facilitation, to make it more likely that students will respond honestly and substantively. The form is also meant to be administered anonymously and is accompanied by an Instructor Planning Form to help faculty determine what course modifications to make as a result of students' responses.[68]

- *This I Believe.* The second option is a reflection essay created by the National Public Radio (NPR) program *This I Believe.*[69] A publicly funded oral history project, it provides an almost perfect prompt to help us begin to establish rapport with students and earn their trust. On this NPR program, guests read aloud essays they have written, all of which begin with the words "I believe." Authors are limited to an essay of no more than five hundred words or one page, roughly the equivalent of three minutes of speaking time, in which they "describe the values that shape their deepest passions." Faculty have adapted this exercise using the prompt found at http://thisibelieve.org. Notice that the nature of the prompt aligns with the wise interventions discussed previously, in that students are being asked to state and affirm values as they pertain to the things they identify with the most. Given the personal nature of the essays, it's best not to ask students to read them aloud and to assure them of confidentiality.

We suggest assigning this essay on or near the first day of class—and setting aside ample time for yourself to read them carefully. Reading these essays will humanize your class roster in powerful ways. Certainly, in very high-enrollment courses, finding time to read every single one may not be possible, but even reading a sample from as many students as possible will shed light on the depth and complexity of your students' lives, on their humanity. After reading them, it is practically impossible to view the classroom as a set of student ID numbers or to view online students as to-do items on a grading list, for example. Bryan, who has been giving this assignment ever since he began teaching, says he is amazed every semester at the ways in which students reflect on this prompt and how open they are in sharing their value system.

Bryan shares an example of an insight that can be gleaned from these essays and used to support students' success: You may notice students' concerns about succeeding in your course that suggest a **fixed mindset**, as in "I'm not really a math/science person." This may lead you to incorporate a mini-lesson on growth mindsets early in the term, or to discuss growth mindsets with individual students when they attend office (student) hours.[70]

fixed mindset: The belief that qualities like intelligence are static and that success comes from talent, not effort.

Next, take the time to learn about your students at a broader level. As with the previous exercises, it's ideal to do at least some of this work prior to the start of the term, although you can certainly expand on your knowledge over time. Consider the following:

- What do you know or what can you learn about students' high school contexts and experiences?

- Where were your students raised? And what do you know or can you learn about the social context and history of these locations?

With respect to the latter questions, you might come to find, for instance, that a large proportion of students are from redlined neighborhoods, ones that still exhibit the consequences of a racial segregation policy that was enacted almost a century ago. These consequences include depressed real estate values, under-resourced K–12 institutions, and even reduced access to high-speed internet. This in no way suggests that students from these communities are any less capable, but years of being exposed to significantly fewer resources reduces the opportunities available for them to shine. If you know your students come from this background, you may choose to build in low-stakes opportunities early in the term so they can be successful and demonstrate to themselves that they are absolutely college material.

When trying to understand students' backgrounds, it can be extremely helpful to spend time with scholarship that has detailed the ways in which students' social experience differs in time and space within the United States. As Anna Ortiz and Lori Patton explain in *Why Aren't We There Yet: Taking Personal Responsibility for Creating an Inclusive Campus*, learning more about the history and contemporary situation of a group (whether racial, ethnic, socioeconomic, etc.) is helpful "not only in reversing noninclusive values but in building a knowledge base necessary for multicultural competence."[71] Having this enhanced knowledge communicates that you care, which, as mentioned earlier, is a key way to earn and sustain trust. More specifically, Patrick Turner and Efren Miranda Zepeda recommend that when working with male students of color we seek to learn about "tribal cultures, masculinity, social justice, and other historical and current challenges that Black and Brown males have encountered over the last [several] years."[72] In table 4.2, we provide a list of classic works that will get you started in your research, and we include key insights from each.

TABLE 4.2   Suggested Books for Expanding Your Equity-Minded Knowledge Base

Author(s)	Book	Relevance
Elizabeth Armstrong and Laura T. Hamilton	*Paying for the Party: How College Maintains Inequality* (2013)	In this book, sociologists conduct an ethnography that documents the impact of the college social structure on students with privilege and on those from rural, impoverished communities.

Sara Goldrick-Rab	*Paying the Price: College Costs, Financial Aid, and the Betrayal of the American Dream* (2016)	This is perhaps the most detailed account to date of how the financial-aid system differentially impacts students seeking a college education.
Alex Kotlowitz	*There Are No Children Here: The Story of Two Boys Growing Up in the Other America* (1991)	An extremely personal account of two young boys growing up in Chicago, IL. Useful for empathizing with the day-to-day experiences of those with extreme lack of means.
Jonathan Kozol	*Savage Inequalities: Children in America's Schools* (1991)	The author describes the wildly different experiences that students have depending on the K–12 schools into which they matriculate.
Bettina L. Love	*We Want to Do More Than Survive: Abolitionist Teaching and the Pursuit of Educational Freedom* (2019)	Love paints a vivid picture of what it means to work in solidarity with communities of color.
Sarah Smarsh	*Heartland: A Memoir of Working Hard and Being Broke in the Richest Country on Earth* (2018)	This account describes the everyday experience of growing up poor in the American Midwest. The author also touches on the impact of "being broke" on her matriculation into higher education.
Beverly Daniel Tatum	*Why Are All the Black Kids Sitting Together in the Cafeteria? And Other Conversations about Race* (2017)	The author addresses the psychology of belonging and in so doing describes behaviors that students may engage in to ensure their personal sense of belonging.
Keeanga-Yamahtta Taylor	*Race for Profit: How Banks and the Real Estate Industry Undermined Black Homeownership* (2019)	The author extends previous scholarship on redlining and shows, with astonishing detail, its impact on minoritized communities.

2. Help Students Get to Know *You*

Several of the questions in Demerath's model (table 4.1) reinforce the importance of humanizing ourselves. When students wonder, "Why are you here? How much do you respect me? Do you know who you are in relation to me?" they are essentially saying they cannot trust us until they know us. Hammond concurs. She identifies, in addition to caring and authentic listening, a set of strategies she calls "trust generators"—most of which entail ways to help students get to know us.[73]

Enacting some of Hammond's trust generators is especially important in asynchronous online classes, and in synchronous online ones, too. Students who are enrolled in asynchronous classes repeatedly share that they think their instructor isn't real, which certainly indicates that they don't feel like they know us, let alone trust us. Existing systems and structures that surround the current state of online courses contribute to this overall student perception that online teachers aren't real (such as the format and appearance of LMSs and the general lack of adequate preparation for and support of online teaching in higher education today, despite the good work of scholars and organizations). In other words, you—the caring, passionate educator who is reading this guide—are not to blame. However, there is much we can do in our asynchronous online classes to help students overcome that perception, and we can do so in ways that are both authentic and protective of our work-life balance, too. And while synchronous classes can facilitate better real-time interactions and can lead to students knowing more about us as people, students still tell us they struggle to overcome the distance over Zoom.

Because we will each differ in our comfort levels, you'll need to determine what you're comfortable sharing with students and how to share it with them. And if, based on your identities, your cultural values, or your personal and professional preferences, you're hesitant to share much at all, consider the question Flower has posed to faculty: "Is there a *little* more you can do? Within your comfort and safety zones, is there a *little bit* more about yourself and your personality you could be willing to share?" In our commitment to advancing equity, tolerating a bit of discomfort and vulnerability can powerfully aid our efforts to realize more equitable outcomes for our students.

Here are three of Hammond's trust generators, with one quick idea for online implementation, given the added importance of building trust online:

- *Selective vulnerability* means being explicit about the imperfections that likely dotted our academic journeys or otherwise exhibiting some level of humanness. Admitting that our journey to the classroom was not necessarily paved with a perfect GPA gives solace to students as they navigate struggles of their own. In online classes, this vulnerability could look like your mini-videos not being perfectly polished or produced.

- *Familiarity* comes with repeated interaction. To this end, create as many opportunities as possible to engage students, especially one-on-one or in small groups. (For more information on student hours, see Unit 3.) Serendipitous encounters on campus or in unexpected settings are also opportunities to increase familiarity. When teaching online, structure interactions with students because those serendipitous encounters are unlikely to happen. One way of doing so could be using an informal app, such as Discord, Slack, or WhatsApp, to facilitate spontaneous conversation.[74]

- Finding *similarities of interests* can also build trust. Casual conversation about the non-job aspects of your life creates opportunities to identify interests you share with your students. In your online classes, consider posting photos from your weekend hike or of your dog doing something silly. Students love seeing you as a real person with a life outside the LMS.

3. Wisen-Up Your Feedback

First, if the terms *feedback* and *grades* are synonymous in your teaching, we implore you to branch out and, at the very least, have a discussion with your students about what you're gleaning from their grades. For instance, you might summarize the class's performance by describing the topics or types of questions in which they excelled, as well as areas in which many students experienced challenges. In general, it's helpful to talk to your students about the feedback process and how you intend for your feedback to support their learning and success. You might also ask yourself, "How well does a grade clarify for my students how their performance compares to the target goal, and how well does it guide their future behavior?" Knowing that many students are equating their academic competence and belonging with their grades in your class (as we will describe in Unit 5), what can you reasonably do to upgrade your feedback processes?

If providing students with individualized verbal and written feedback is already part of your practice, or if you want to add this mode of feedback to your toolkit, here are a few ways to "wisen" things up:

- Include both parts of the wise feedback strategy: (1) an indication that you have high standards and (2) your confidence that each student has the capacity to reach those standards.

- Take care not to inadvertently attribute student performance to their innate intelligence or ability (as in "You're a natural!" or "You're such a great writer!"). These sentiments reinforce fixed mindsets about learning. Instead, praise student effort and use of study strategies.

- Offer specific suggestions. This recommendation goes hand in hand with the previous item. Common tropes such as "study harder" or "put in more effort" don't help students identify or address why they came short of the learning objectives. These sayings also disrespect students by implying they didn't study enough or exert adequate effort. Research suggests it's more likely students have not yet developed the kinds of study behaviors that are most effective in college.[75]

- Invite students' feedback, so that guidance is not flowing only in one direction. (See Unit 9 for ways to gather student feedback.) Along the same lines, stay open to interpreting students' assessment scores and progress as feedback on your course and teaching. For instance, students' performance on an exam can be as much a reflection of our own exam-writing and pedagogical approaches as it is about students' preparation strategies.

- When teaching a fully online course, deliver your feedback message in voice or video, as this type of communication can include verbal or nonverbal cues and minimize misinterpretation, suggest online teaching experts such as Michelle Pacansky-Brock.

HOW CAN I GET STARTED?

For Any Class

- If possible, obtain a roster of the students who you will be teaching. If this is not an option, request information from your institution on characteristics of the incoming class of students. Use this knowledge to get an early understanding of your students' social histories.

- At the start of your first class or in a welcome video, let your students know what motivates you to teach and what you love most about teaching, and describe how you've designed the class to support their learning and success.

- Tell students the *why* behind your course structure and assignments.

- Before giving students any feedback (whether as a grade, in writing, or verbally), describe the value of feedback to learning, your high standards, and your belief in their ability to succeed. If you know from previous courses that students in your class tend to be successful, you might share this with your current class, too.

- Provide feedback on all assessment types early and with specific suggestions that represent changeable behaviors students can act on.

- Choose one book, podcast, or area of scholarship that you will personally engage in during the semester to consistently enhance your understanding of the diverse histories that your students bring to the course experience.

For In-Person Classes

- During the first class session, resist the temptation to review the syllabus (or at least delay the review for a bit). Instead, use the time to (1) humanize yourself, perhaps sharing parts of your identity that have resulted in privilege or challenge, and (2) inform students what you know or have learned about them. Even if you haven't used a tool to learn about the specific students in the class, you might share observations based on a previous class. The point is to convey that you prioritize getting to know your students—and letting them get to know you.

- Consider doing an "Ask Six Questions" exercise on Day 1 of the semester. Project a list of six questions on the screen and ask for three volunteers to come forward, sit in front of the class, and answer them. You may want to aim for a mix of surface-level and deeper-level questions to, for example, reveal and affirm values. After the three volunteers have each had a turn, answer each question yourself, and consider inviting additional questions from the class. Sharing more about who you are, and intentionally being selectively vulnerable, does much to build trust. Broward College professor Rudy Jean-Bart asks the following six questions:

» "Why are you here?" (to uncover motivations and goals)

» "If this were your last day on earth, who would miss you the most and why?"

» "What is something you would like to accomplish that you haven't yet?"

» "Tell me about something that you found challenging that you were able to overcome." (to extend belonging and help students see that others have overcome obstacles and they can too)

» "Who inspires you the most and why?"

» "I want to make the world a better place. Do you mind helping me with that?"

Jean-Bart then invites students to ask him any six questions they want, to build trust and community.[76]

For Asynchronous Online Classes

- Use your LMS to send out a simple, low-effort "get-to-know-you" survey, such as first-day info sheets, in order to get some nonobvious information about your students. This survey should be disseminated on or just before the first day of class.

- After grading or reviewing an assignment, post a feedback video that celebrates what students did exceptionally well and that mentions an area where you noticed a learning gap and will help them improve.

For Synchronous Online Classes

- Use the "waterfall" format in a Zoom poll to invite each student to share something about themselves with their new classmates and with you. In the waterfall format everyone types at the same time, but no one presses "enter" until you say "go." This way, the chat comments all appear at the same time, like a waterfall. Make sure you include yours too, and give students a chance to learn about one another and about you.

5

BELONGING
Validate Students' Presence and Abilities

Cultivating safe learning environments and affirming students' strengths can offset their uncertainty about belonging and keep them engaged and enrolled.

Earlier in this guide, we shared Linda Nilson's troubling observation that many students believe "they do not *belong* in this strange culture of higher education, and any poor or mediocre grades they get 'prove' it."[1] But what does belonging have to do with equity? What does it mean for students to believe that they belong? What factors influence their belonging? Why does belonging matter? And how can we as faculty influence students' sense of belonging? This unit explores these questions, and more.

As Tracie Addy and colleagues point out, when faculty are asked to define inclusive teaching and describe what it looks like in practice, fostering a sense of belonging emerges as a key theme.[2] Inclusion and belonging have become virtually inextricable. Belonging is the fundamental human need to be affiliated with and accepted by a group, the "desire for interpersonal attachments."[3] It is often traced back to psychologist Abraham Maslow's theory of human motivation, in which Maslow isolates "belongingness" as one of our basic needs. In the 1990s, social psychologists Roy Baumeister and Mark Leary suggested that "the desire to belong is a deeply rooted human motivation that, underpinned by our ancestral origins, permeates our thoughts, feelings, and behaviors."[4] Maya Angelou expresses this sentiment and its universality as, "I long, as does every human being, to be at home wherever I find myself." Knowing that belonging is a fundamental *human* (not just student) need helps explain why it has been linked to important outcomes like student retention and student learning.

Research has consistently shown that minoritized students are less likely to report feeling a **sense of belonging**, particularly when they are attending

sense of belonging: The feeling of acceptance and support that comes with knowing that one is part of a group. In an academic setting, it refers to a student's feeling of acceptance, inclusion, support, and respect in a learning environment.

Predominantly White Institutions. In fact, the construct of college students' sense of belonging was introduced in the 1990s, when scholars were examining the experiences of college students of color and seeking to understand why the retention and graduation rates for these students were lower than those of their White peers. Extensive research has been conducted ever since, deepening our understanding of what it means to belong and even generating types of belonging (description to follow).

Although several definitions have been articulated, college students' sense of belonging generally refers to the feeling of acceptance and support that comes with knowing that one is part of a group. Terrell Strayhorn, a leading scholar of college student belonging, defines it as "a student's perceived social support on campus, a feeling or sensation of connectedness, the experience of mattering or being cared about, accepted, respected, valued by, and important to the group (e.g., campus community) or others on campus (e.g., faculty, peers)."[5] Human development and family studies scholars Annemarie Vaccaro and Barbara Newman sought to understand how students themselves define belonging and how these descriptions vary across students' identities.[6] Based on their analyses of two rounds of in-depth interviews, belonging entails *being comfortable* and *fitting in* for all students in the study. However, minoritized students indicated that for them, belonging also requires *safety*, *respect*, and *the ability to be their authentic selves*.

belonging uncertainty:
The state in which individuals are *uncertain* of the quality of their social bonds.

Two related terms—**belonging uncertainty** and group membership—help to clarify the impact of not feeling that one belongs. *Belonging uncertainty* describes the state in which individuals are *uncertain* of the quality of their social bonds. Gregory Walton and Geoffrey Cohen suggest that "in academic and professional settings, members of socially stigmatized groups are more uncertain of the quality of their social bonds and thus more sensitive to issues of social belonging." They call this state *belonging uncertainty* and suggest that it contributes to racial disparities in achievement.[7] This definition echoes some of the earliest studies of belonging, in which limited or lacking belongingness was identified as a key reason that students from minoritized groups left college without securing a degree. The term *group membership*, in turn, reminds us that for each social group, there are various (often invisible) rules at play that define the features and requirements for membership. Although learning how to navigate new norms is a common part of the transition to college for all students, minoritized students can experience far more than uncertainty about their belonging when they encounter social groups in college and are not accepted. They can feel like full impostors who will eventually be found out. Not only is this **impostor syndrome** mentally and physically taxing but it also robs the student of the sociocognitive bandwidth needed to be fully present in the course.

impostor syndrome:
The sense that one is an impostor or fake, which makes it difficult to believe that one deserves or has earned success.

What does all of this information about student belonging have to do with us as faculty? Can we really help students overcome impostor syndrome?

Thankfully, several recent studies have examined students' sense of belonging in ways that relate to faculty and our teaching, offering a variety of practical ways for each of us to shape our courses and interactions with students to promote belonging. As with previous units, this one begins with a preview of the research, both in general and as it relates to teaching. It then provides strategies for cultivating course environments in which students feel that they belong, matter, and can thrive.

Pause to Consider

- How would you describe your own sense of belonging in your department? In your college/university?

- What might account for your perceived sense of belonging, and what could you do to help yourself and/or a peer feel a stronger sense of belonging?

What Does the Research Say about Belonging?

This research overview consists of four general areas: first, historical and social factors that offer context for students' sense of belonging; second, key factors in college that impact students' sense of belonging; third, research on why belonging matters (that is, its impact on key outcomes such as learning and retention); and fourth, factors associated with our role as faculty that contribute to students' sense of belonging.

The Historical and Social Context for Belonging in Higher Education

The history of students' access to higher education provides an important backdrop for student belonging. As historians have described, the demographic makeup of U.S. college campuses has largely mirrored broader social struggles with equity and civil rights. Institutions of higher education were largely created and attended by White males, and for much of the institutions' existence, access was outright denied to students of all other identities.[8] This practice began to change only during the last century, such that today, Black and Latinx students are still underrepresented in U.S. colleges and universities relative to their population. Additionally, when some students of color begin their college experiences, it may be the first time they are in predominantly White environments and/or interacting with individuals whose identities differ from theirs. How could this be?

Despite the current overall diversity of the U.S. population, many people reside in ethnic and ideological silos. Pursuing higher education is often the first real opportunity some students have to fully engage with difference. To be fair, this is, all things considered, a positive thing and a powerful argument for the transformative potential of a college education. Psychology professor Jeffrey Arnett, in his theory of emerging adulthood, identifies the years spent in higher education as a time when students are most open to change, possess malleable ideologies, and are actively exploring their identity and sense of self.[9] Nonetheless, many students lack experiences with diversity and enroll in settings where they see relatively few individuals who share their identities. Most U.S. colleges and universities are predominantly White,[10] and as mentioned earlier, although student populations have become more diverse, nearly three-quarters of full-time college faculty identify as White.[11]

In their study of belonging uncertainty, Walton and Cohen provide additional examples of contextual factors that prompt minoritized students to question whether they belong:

> *When Black Americans, Latino Americans, and Native Americans look at schools and workplaces in the United States, they see places in which members of their group are numerically under-represented (especially in positions of authority), encounter overt and subtle forms of prejudice, and receive lower grades and salaries. They see same-race peers who feel alienated on college campuses and who are cut off from the "insider" contacts and social capital that White students enjoy.*[12]

They add that "belonging uncertainty can prove especially pernicious" because students can't quite pinpoint a "culprit" (as in someone who is plausibly racist). Instead, students may take stock of their environments, noticing who is in positions of authority, what policies are in place, how they feel, and so on—and simply conclude "that 'people like me do not belong here.'"[13] The authors rightly recognize that overt discrimination has become less frequent, yet they emphasize that it is important to acknowledge it persists.[14] Discriminatory and outright racist incidents reinforce the dominance of one set of identities and make students from marginalized backgrounds feel physically unsafe. As noted previously, minoritized students consider safety inextricable from belonging.

More frequently, however, students of color experience what are known as **racial microaggressions**, or "everyday, subtle, intentional—and oftentimes unintentional—interactions or behaviors that communicate some sort of bias toward historically marginalized groups."[15] Each of these interactions or behaviors signals to some students that they are in a space where they do not belong. Several vivid examples are featured in the Purdue University student-created documentary *What It's Like*.[16] In the video, a Black male student majoring in math describes two microaggressions he experienced on a regular basis: (1) surprise/disbelief when he told his peers that he was a math major. "Black people do math?" he was often asked, and (2) incidents reflecting the assumption he wasn't good at math. The latter incidents played out like this: At the

racial microaggression:
A brief incident, act, or remark that discriminates against or insults someone based on their race.

start of his math classes, in which he was typically the only Black student, he tried to encourage his peers to get together to do the homework and study for exams. Nine times out of ten, no one took him up on the offer, avoiding him altogether until the first test scores were announced. When the other students realized how well he had performed, they were suddenly eager to form a study group with him. Although his professors were likely unaware of this recurring microaggression, this example raises several important questions for us: (1) How might we inadvertently reinforce microaggressions about our students' general abilities or abilities in a specific discipline? (2) How could authentic validations of our students' abilities help minimize the microaggressions they experience? (3) What kinds of classroom and module structures could have alleviated the challenges this student experienced? (See Unit 6.)

The phenomenon known as **stereotype threat** also helps demonstrate how social factors shape students' experiences. In the late 1980s, Claude Steele was invited to the University of Michigan to help develop an academic support program for students of color. As he reviewed the data and saw that Black students—even those with the highest SAT scores—consistently earned lower grades, Steele rejected the possibility that these students' grades reflected their innate ability or intelligence. When he talked with students, he heard time and again that Black students didn't feel they belonged—and he wondered how this lack of belonging could relate to their academic performance. Eventually, he formulated the theory of *stereotype threat*, which in essence, describes the phenomenon in which our performance becomes worse when we risk confirming a negative stereotype about one of our identities (including our race, gender, or age). For instance, older adults may worry about conforming to the stereotype that they have weaker memories, which in turn, could result in them performing poorly on a memory test.

In the original study, Steele and NYU professor Joshua Aronson studied African American students who were asked to answer difficult verbal questions.[17] When the students were told that the test measured verbal ability, they scored considerably lower than their White peers. Yet when the task was framed as a problem-solving exercise that did not measure intellectual ability, that gap disappeared. This seminal research suggested that negative societal stereotypes can impede students' performance. In their analysis of twenty years' worth of research, Charlotte Pennington and colleagues summarize *how* stereotype threat has been shown to impact performance: "Experiences of stereotype threat may increase individuals' feelings of anxiety, negative thinking and mind-wandering which deplete the working memory resources required for successful task execution."[18] These studies show us that, rather than focusing exclusively on the learning or assessment itself, students in our classes spend mental energy worrying about whether they're going to confirm a stereotype about one of their identities. Since the 1990s, scholars have also developed a number of strategies we can adapt in our teaching, like the wise interventions featured in Unit 4, and several others we'll share later in this unit.[19]

stereotype threat: The phenomenon in which our performance becomes worse when we risk confirming a negative stereotype about one of our identities (including our race, gender, or age).

The College Context for Belonging

Both the college environment as a whole and the **campus climate** have been examined at length in relation to students' sense of belonging. In their foundational study on the belonging experiences of nearly three hundred students, for instance, Sylvia Hurtado and Deborah Carter tested a model that examined how much Latinx students' background characteristics and experiences in their first and second years of college contribute to the students' sense of belonging in year three.[20] They found two factors strongly associated with Latinx students' sense of belonging: discussions of course content with other students outside class and membership in religious and social-community organizations. Meanwhile, not surprisingly, perceptions of a hostile racial climate were found to have a direct negative effect on these students' sense of belonging. Many other scholars have confirmed the role of campus climate in the development of a positive sense of belonging among students of color.[21]

In her text *College Belonging: How First-Generation Students Navigate Campus Life,* Lisa Nunn provides an additional reason *belonging* warrants our attention. She reminds us that "belonging is something that communities provide for individuals; it is not something individuals can garner for themselves."[22] Thus, it is on us to leverage the power of our teaching and regular interactions with students to help them develop a sense of belonging in our classes and institutions. Nunn examined this broad college context for belonging in her study of first-generation college students, using open-ended discussions that (as in Vaccaro and Newman's work) invited students to define belonging in their own terms. Based on students' responses, Nunn formulated three categories of belonging:

1. Social belonging, which means feeling that you "matter to the group, that you are valued for who you are and what you bring" (15).
2. Campus-community belonging, which means feeling that you matter more broadly at the institution.
3. Academic belonging, when you feel like "an accepted member of the academic community" (66).

Nunn asked a student named Grayson, who identifies as Latino and White, to describe what belonging means to him, and he referenced all three types: "Being comfortable in different settings across campus [*campus-community belonging*]. Being comfortable in my classes . . . [*academic belonging*], [a]nd also having a group of friends who is accepting of you, how you are, and enjoys hanging out with you genuinely [*social belonging*]" (10).

One of Nunn's most significant findings is that social belonging does not necessarily equate with or lead to a broader sense of belonging in the institution. Several students in her study—particularly first-generation students and students of color—said they felt well-connected to groups that gave them "social belonging" yet felt "adrift, out of place, or 'alone' when navigating wider campus life" (26). This finding demonstrates that we can't take for granted that the students we teach feel a sense of belonging at our institutions simply because they seem to have a friend or friend group, or vice versa. Nunn also found that students' social belonging shifts over time, in both directions, reminding us that it's malleable. In the following section on faculty-facing factors that impact belonging, we revisit Nunn's insights regarding *academic belonging* and how we can influence it in our teaching.

Patrick Turner and Efren Miranda Zepeda sought to identify specific factors that fostered an atmosphere of belonging for men of color in a Predominantly White Institution.[23] The title of their article, "Welcoming Ain't Belonging," highlights one of their main findings. Students in the study noticed and appreciated efforts by college employees to make them feel welcome, but they made it clear that being welcomed did not make them feel that they belonged. In one student's words, "I think it is open and welcoming, but I wouldn't say that I belong. They treat you differently." Similarly, in Vaccaro and Newman's research, minoritized students "viewed the campus as an environment where they regularly felt judged and treated differently and a place where they could not always be their authentic selves."[24]

Turner and Miranda Zepeda urge college faculty and staff to move past "minor gestures of short-lived acts of welcome and civility" to actions that "translate into deep, long-lasting and enduring relationships that demonstrate a commitment to the person and promote a sense of shared experience and solidarity."[25] The students in their study identified two additional changes their college leadership could make that would strengthen their sense of belonging: (1) substantive cultural representation and celebrations, which would foster pride and build community, and (2) efforts to build cultural competence among faculty and staff, as they experienced many microaggressions that reflected a lack of understanding of their backgrounds.

One last set of factors with a strong correlation to students' sense of belonging is their diversity experiences: negative interactions with diverse peers can interfere with the establishment of a sense of belonging for students of color, whereas affirmative diversity experiences contribute to a positive sense of belonging.[26]

Pause to Consider

- Can you be your authentic self within your department? At your institution broadly? Why or why not?

- Would your students say they could be their authentic selves in your course or in your institution? Why or why not?

How Does Belonging Impact Students?

As mentioned previously, the construct of *sense of belonging* first emerged as a hypothesis about student retention—specifically, that limited or lacking belongingness helped explain relatively low graduation rates among students from minoritized groups. Leslie Hausmann and her colleagues tested this hypothesis empirically with a sample of 254 Black and 291 White students at a Predominantly White Institution. After asking students about their intentions to persist or stay enrolled in college (a common stand-in outcome for student retention), they found that all students who reported a greater sense of belonging had stronger intent to persist.[27]

Other scholars have related sense of belonging to student learning. For instance, in their analysis of the role of affect in learning, biology education researchers Gloriana Trujillo and Kimberly Tanner highlight belonging as a key contributor to student learning. They isolate three of the ways researchers have described the impact of sense of belonging on student learning: academic motivation, academic achievement, and overall well-being. Specifically, regarding motivation, students' sense of an academic activity's relevance is correlated with their sense of belonging (see Unit 1). Belonging has predicted final semester grades and GPA; in terms of well-being, students' sense of connectedness was found to correlate to the avoidance of "risky behaviors" in the areas of violence, substance use, and sexuality.[28] The authors also synthesize research on students' sense of belonging within an academic subcommunity (such as biology, physics, or STEM). A key point here is that students' sense of belonging can be context specific. For example, a student can feel a general sense of belonging in their college yet at the same time feel they do *not* belong in the college's scientific community. This particular set of experiences has been linked to difficulties in diversifying STEM fields and professions.

From Belonging to Mattering

As belonging research has matured, some scholars have called into question its ubiquity and noticed its limitations. Karen Gravett and Rola Ajjawi, for instance, prompt us to consider "the experiences of those students who may not wish to, or who cannot, belong."[29] Alison Cook-Sather and colleagues explore "whether the concept of *mattering* might more effectively capture the practical benefits of belonging for practitioners and scholars without the serious limitations of that construct as well as push us to question and change the existing institutional structures that perpetuate inequities." They describe mattering, in its simplest terms, as "our belief, whether right or wrong, that we matter to someone else." Unlike the construct of belonging, they write, "mattering makes space for individuals to be recognized and valued as individuals with distinct identities and contributions to make to the community . . . including changing it."[30]

In her book *We Want to Do More Than Survive: Abolitionist Teaching and the Pursuit of Educational Freedom*, Bettina Love argues that mattering is essential to truly equity-minded key teaching. However, she poignantly describes the contextual factors that make it difficult for some students to believe that they matter to us: "For dark people, the very basic idea of mattering is sometimes hard to conceptualize when your country finds you disposable. . . . How do you matter to a country that is at once obsessed with and dismissive about how it kills you? . . . How do you matter to a country that measures your knowledge against a 'gap' it created?"[31] It's clear from Love's questions that it will not always be easy to prove to students how much they matter to us. We are hopeful that the ideas in this guide (perhaps especially in Unit 4 on earning and sustaining students' trust) will help.

Faculty-Facing Factors That Impact Belonging

We shift now from the elements of the broader college context that influence belonging to factors we're calling "faculty facing"—the ones *we* can influence via our teaching. One way to picture the impact of classroom and online experiences on belonging is to remember that when students begin a new course, there are two conversations taking place: The first is loud and explicit, with clear navigational cues provided by syllabi, online course design and navigational text, in-class explanations, and online or in-person interactions between students and instructors. The second conversation is unspoken, directed by nonverbal messages, the tone of our written words, internalized histories, and interpretations of the explicit communications. This unspoken dialogue might include the identities of their fellow students and professor, how we respond to students' questions or comments, and what we share about ourselves. It is largely in this second, less tangible conversation that students determine whether and how much they feel that they belong in the learning environment.

Susan Ambrose and colleagues refer to this second conversation as the course climate, "the intellectual, social, emotional, and physical [and we would add virtual] environments in which our students learn."[32] They also remind us that one of the primary levers we have to increase student motivation is the "supportive nature of the environment," which we can influence via faculty-student interaction, substantive peer interaction, and the range of perspectives represented in the course content and materials. Motivation researchers Margery Ginsberg and Raymond Wlodkowski, who were introduced in Unit 1, reinforce the deep tie among course climate, motivation, and the experiences of students of color. Recall that in their model of culturally responsive teaching one of the four conditions for optimizing student motivation is *establishing inclusion*, defined as "creating a learning atmosphere in which we feel respected by and connected to one another."[33] They also offer us five practical norms to promote inclusion in any learning setting:

1. "Course work emphasizes the human purpose of what is being learned and its relationship to the learners' personal experiences and contemporary situations" (77).

2. "Teachers use a **constructivist approach** to create knowledge" (78).

3. "Collaboration and cooperation are the expected ways of proceeding and learning" (80).

4. "Course perspectives assume a nonblameful and realistically hopeful view of people and their capacity to change" (83).

5. "There is equitable treatment of all learners with an invitation to point out behaviors, practices, and policies that discriminate" (88).

constructivist approach: An approach to learning based on the premise that individuals actively construct or make their own knowledge.

Like some of the researchers mentioned earlier, John M. Braxton and his colleagues were interested in the relationship between belonging and retention. However, they zeroed in on how teaching practices—and active learning, in particular—impact belonging and retention.[34] Their study was based on the premise that students' college class experiences are more closely tied to persistence than higher ed scholars have realized. They hypothesized the college classroom influences students' social connections, commitment to their institution, and whether or not they persist and graduate.[35] Braxton and colleagues found that two indicators of active learning—class discussions and higher-order thinking activities—influence students' social integration,[36] prompting us to consider incorporating or expanding our use of discussions, as well as to examine the level of intellectual challenge represented in our coursework (see Unit 1 on rigor).

Walton and Cohen's research on belonging uncertainty also has important implications for faculty. The researchers found that when students were led to believe that they might have few friends in a discipline (in their study, computer science), White students were unaffected. Black students, however, displayed a drop in their sense of belonging and potential. Conversely, Black students increased their engagement in achievement behavior (e.g., time spent studying) and improved their GPA when they were led to believe that doubts about belonging in school "were unique neither to them nor to members of their racial group, but rather were common to all students regardless of race" and told that these doubts lessen with time.[37] Walton and Cohen conclude that Black students viewed their hardship as evidence of their limited potential to fit and succeed in an academic setting. They also showed that we can change this narrative by reminding students that belonging uncertainty is common among *all* students and tends to lessen over time.

Implicit in Walton and Cohen's work is that students' sense of their academic abilities is related to their sense of belonging. This finding complements what Nunn refers to as academic competence and **academic belonging**. Indeed, many students in her study frequently used their GPA as an academic belonging indicator. Basically, "good grades validate their capabilities."[38] Other students looked at class averages to measure their own academic belonging. They figured that if others were struggling too, their relatively low grade could signal something about the class or instruction versus their academic competence. Conversely, being among the few students who were unsuccessful would signal they did not belong in that academic course. Students also noted that faculty played a crucial role in their academic competence: "Students feel encouraged by professors who make them feel seen and who acknowledge their efforts; they take this as a sign of their academic worth, regardless of the outcome."[39] They're looking to us, the academic experts and representatives of academia, to validate their presence and intellectual capacities.

> **academic belonging:** When students feel like full members of an academic community.

Competence also features prominently in the scholarship of equity-minded teaching experts. Ginsberg and Wlodkowski explain that "the desire to be competent—effective at what we value, extends across all cultures."[40] One of the four conditions in their model is thus *engendering competence*, described as "creating or affirming an understanding that students have effectively learned something they value and perceive as authentic to their real world." As indicated in Unit 2, Ginsberg and Wlodkowski contend that "teacher assessment, more than any other action, validates student competence,"[41] so we encourage you to revisit the suggestions in that unit for designing more equitable assessments, as well as those in Unit 4 about providing students with wise feedback.

Academic competence is also reminiscent of Laura Rendón's theory of validation. Rendón explains that academic validation occurs when individuals actively assist students to "trust their innate capacity to learn and to acquire confidence in being a college student."[42] Sylvia Hurtado, Adriana Alvarado, and Chelsea Guillermo-Wann's study suggests that "validation from faculty in and out of the classroom may contribute to sense of belonging."[43] What does academic validation look like in practice? First, it means taking the initiative to establish contact with students versus waiting for students to come to you. Then, it involves using every opportunity to show students that they bring innumerable strengths to college and your course and that they absolutely belong and can succeed.

What Do We Know about Belonging in Fully Online Courses?

Much of the research in the previous pages transcends modality. For instance, the association students make between their feeling of academic competence and their sense of belonging is as true online as it is in a fully in-person course. However, online educators and scholars have long emphasized the need to be intentional in developing social connections and a sense of community in online courses, recognizing that these are essential to student learning and unlikely to happen organically in an online setting. Recall that in the Community of Inquiry (CoI) framework, **social presence** describes learners' ability to project their personal characteristics into the community of inquiry, thereby presenting themselves as "real people." This description is consistent with the experience of minoritized students in the studies discussed previously who equated belonging with the ability to be their true selves. CoI guides online instructors to consider how they are developing a community that supports learning through students' interactions with content and assignments, their instructor, and each other. (See Unit 7 for day-to-day online teaching ideas on how to build such a community.)

We have often heard from online faculty and students alike that some online students don't want all this interaction. The argument goes that students who choose asynchronous online courses and programs lead busy and complex lives, as we've noted elsewhere. Their lack of interest in interacting with other people in the class likely indicates that they don't perceive a need to belong in order to succeed. Indeed, some online students perceive required interactions in discussion forums and small groups as busy work, or worse, barriers to their success. For this reason, we encourage you to reflect carefully on two issues: (1) the pedagogical purpose of community-building course activities such as discussion forums and (2) the research on the importance of belonging and mattering (concepts that apply equally online as they do in person). If indeed you can articulate a well-aligned purpose for class interactions, using the steps we outline in Unit 1, then we encourage you to keep them in your online class. And since we know that online learners often feel isolated and disconnected, it can be especially important to incorporate opportunities for community-building, as we explore in Unit 4. So, although your online students might resist it, if you have a pedagogically sound purpose for discussions, group work, and the like, we encourage you to message both the purpose and the importance of these exchanges in an effort to increase transparency (see Unit 2), and to give students ample time to complete the collaborative work.

One part of our practice that can affect students' sense of belonging and is more salient in online teaching is how we communicate with students, particularly in writing. When so much of our relationship with students is mediated by text, it's important that we be extremely attentive to our tone, level of formality, use of jargon, and so on. When possible—and especially when providing critical feedback or when the stakes are high for a message—complement the written word with a video or audio recording, being mindful to infuse warmth, support, and encouragement into your voice. That way, students will benefit from your nonverbal communication and recognize you're there to support them.

Creating Contexts of Belonging

We'll start with a straightforward suggestion: If you do nothing else to help your students realize that you absolutely think they belong and will support them, tell them so. State clearly from the start that they unequivocally belong, that you're glad they're in your class, and that you'll advocate for them. That direct communication will immediately alleviate some of the uncertainty and anxiety most of them feel on Day 1. Coauthor Mays Imad has started doing this in her syllabus, with an opening line that reads: "Welcome brilliant minds! I am so glad you decided to register for _____. This course is going to be amazing because you're part of this awesome learning community." Following are four additional approaches to cultivating learning environments in which all students feel they belong.

1. Tell Students Your Belonging Story

This strategy comes to us from the College Transition Collaborative (CTC), an organization that aims to create higher education learning environments that foster equitable student outcomes by bridging research and practice. In their toolkit for faculty, the CTC recommends that faculty share their "belonging story" with students—basically, that we tell our students a short story about a challenge we encountered in our academic or professional career that made us worry about whether or how much we belonged. To help us identify possible stories to share, the CTC lists a few common experiences that might trigger belonging uncertainty which can be used as topics, as we've adapted here:

- "academic difficulties or concerns that one's skills or knowledge are not on par with those of peers (these relate to *academic belonging*)
- being numerically underrepresented on campus or in class, based on identity group
- difficulty making connections with professors
- not understanding how to navigate university systems
- trouble making friends, or finding a community of peers
- financial strain making it harder to socialize"[44]

In terms of the best timing for sharing your belonging story, we agree with the CTC's suggestion that the first day or early in the term is best, as "students may be wondering if they or people like them can succeed in the course."[45]

And feel free to share additional belonging stories throughout the term, ideally in relation to something students are or may be experiencing (like a poor grade on an assessment).

The organization recommends the following steps and components for crafting your belonging story:

1. "Briefly describe an experience that evoked belonging uncertainty.

2. Acknowledge belonging concerns as real and valid.

3. Communicate that it is common to question one's belonging when facing challenges.

4. Describe how belonging improved over time, with the . . . use of steps to build relationships and ties to the campus community."[46]

If you're teaching an asynchronous online course, you can create a brief video of yourself sharing your belonging story, and consider pairing it with a short reflection assignment (written or recorded) in which students respond to your story and begin to explore their own perceptions of belonging in an online learning environment.

2. Ask Students to Work in Diverse, Interdependent Groups

If we seem to be recommending generic "group work" as an approach to cultivating belonging, please give us a chance to differentiate. Here, we're thinking of the kind of community and group learning that Saundra McGuire describes in her book *Teach Students How to Learn*. Our goal, she writes, is to create "a community of scholars where students hold each other accountable and genuinely care about each other's successes and failures."[47] Recall that students who reported having positive experiences with diverse peers were more likely to feel that they belonged.[48] Ginsberg and Wlodkowski point out that collaborative and cooperative learning is key to establishing inclusion. They cite research indicating that collaborative learning is especially effective when teaching minoritized students, working adult students, students who commute, and students who are re-entering college.[49]

What should you ask students to do in groups? Review your course learning goals and identify the most challenging one(s). Otherwise, students won't be motivated to collaborate; instead, they may resent you for "forcing" them to work in groups. Creating small, concise group activities that can be completed in one online module or one class session is one way to foster belongingness through intentionally structured diverse groups. Or you can create projects that take place over several weeks or most of the semester, as long-term or permanent groups can go a long way toward creating a sense of community. Either way, to foster student engagement, build in relational getting-to-know-you tasks as well as other structures such as guidance on how to work together (see Unit 7), clear expectations regarding tasks and timing, progress checks, and so on. These structures are all helpful for establishing trust among students and for guiding their interdependent learning in support of each other. (For more on adding structure, see Unit 6; for more on fostering trust, see Unit 4.)

Recall, too, the Community of Inquiry emphasis on building community.[50] This is an important consideration in online classes, which can feel isolating and demotivating for students who may be experiencing low belongingness online. At the same time, it can be more difficult for students taking asynchronous online courses to complete short- or long-term assignments in groups. After all, they may have opted for the most flexible of modalities to account for the complexity of their nonacademic lives. Asking them to work in pairs may be a more reasonable expectation, and you can still intentionally create diverse twosomes. In that asynchronous context, we encourage you to think critically about whether meetings in real time are necessary, or whether students can communicate and work together fully asynchronously. Invite student pairs to decide on a preferred communication method, such as texting, Instagram chat, or other channels. Set up their tasks using collaborative spaces such as Google Docs, Sheets, or Slides, and more creative spaces such as Padlet. None of these spaces requires working together in real time, which reflects a core advantage of asynchronous online classes and also prepares students for tomorrow's workplace, in which asynchronous collaborative work is likely to increase.

In a synchronous online class, consider setting aside a full class session or fraction thereof for students to meet in breakout rooms to discuss the week's material, collectively answer focused questions in a Google Doc, and/or work on a collaborative assignment (again, think short term—as in, to be completed that day—as well as longer term). You can also provide some synchronous class time to help students connect regarding individual tasks and timelines (this is helpful for both online and in-person classes with synchronous meetings).

Our main suggestions here, however, are that you focus on forming diverse groups and that you develop group assignments or activities that truly make students dependent on one another, what Ginsberg and Wlodkowski call **positive interdependence**. Forming diverse groups is easier if you've administered a survey to learn more about your students (see Unit 4). If you're not comfortable forming the groups based on limited information (such as students' visible identities), consider using an online tool (like the random grouping tool and setting available in most LMSs, or a web-based system like CATME.org). Organizing groups yourself will minimize the impact of students opting to group themselves with friends or students who appear to be similar. Positive interdependence means "learners perceive that they are linked

positive interdependence: The success of one individual depending on the success of another individual or a group.

with groupmates in a way that they cannot succeed unless their groupmates do (and vice versa) or they must coordinate their efforts with the efforts of their partners to complete a task."[51] In other words, the success of one student depends on the success of the group. Table 5.1 describes four approaches to creating positive interdependence with examples for each, from Carnegie Mellon's Eberly Center for Teaching Excellence and Educational Innovation.

TABLE 5.1   Strategies for Creating Interdependence in Group Work

Strategy	Example
Ensure projects are sufficiently complex so that students must draw on one another's knowledge and skills.	In one course on game design, group assignments require students to create playable games that incorporate technical (e.g., programming) and design skills. To complete the assignment successfully, students from different disciplines must draw on one another's strengths.
Create shared goals that can be met only through collaborations.	In one engineering course, teams compete against one another to design a boat by applying engineering principles and working within budgetary and material constraints. (Boats are assessed on various dimensions such as stability and speed.) The fun and intensity of a public competition encourage the team to work closely together to create the best design possible.
Limit resources to compel students to share critical information and materials.	In a short-term project for an architectural design course, the instructor provides student groups with a set of materials (e.g., tape, cardboard, string) and assigns them the task of building a structure that conforms to particular design parameters using only these materials. Because students have limited resources, they cannot divide tasks and must strategize and work together.
Assign roles within the group that will help facilitate collaboration.	For a semester-long research project in a history course, the instructor assigns students distinct roles within their groups: one student is responsible for initiating and sustaining communication with the rest of the group, another for coordinating schedules and organizing meetings, another for recording ideas generated and decisions made at meetings, and a fourth for keeping the group on task when deadlines are approaching. The instructor rotates students through these roles, so that they each get practice performing every function.

Source: Adapted from Eberly Center for Teaching Excellence and Educational Innovation, "What Are Best Practices for Designing Group Projects?," Carnegie Mellon University, https://www.cmu.edu/teaching/designteach/design/instructionalstrategies/groupprojects/design.html.

3. Ask Students to Wrap an Assessment

We use the term *wrap* here to refer to the best-known version of this strategy, the exam wrapper—basically, a metacognitive activity students complete after an exam. A sort of exam "postmortem" that assists students to learn from their mistakes, an exam wrapper exercise helps them to build mastery and strengthens their knowledge foundation for the succeeding concepts that will build on it.[52] As this activity relates to belonging, it's a way to engender academic competence.

Exam wrappers take various forms, but the most fruitful ones ask students to do two things: (1) Review their test and examine the items they answered incorrectly. As they do so, students should be asked to determine the correct answer and be able to explain why it is the right response. They should also look for patterns in their errors—for instance, whether their mistakes reflect carelessness, miscalculations, misreading the question, and so on. Students also need to identify what major concepts they had trouble with so they can go back and fill in the gaps in their learning. (2) Reflect on how they prepared for the exam. How much time did they invest? What did studying involve—reading the material, outlining, reviewing notes, answering practice questions? (Often, we find that less successful students merely read over their notes repeatedly, rather than grappling with sample questions.) If their strategies didn't work, how do they plan to prepare next time? What can they do to improve their performance next time around? As students work to answer these questions, we encourage you to offer suggestions, as most students don't have a repertoire of study habits from which to choose.

If you can require students to complete the exam wrapper, they will benefit greatly from the opportunities for deeper learning. As Ginsberg and Wlodkowski explain, "As students become more aware of their individual metacognitive processes, they are able to more deliberately access strategies that stimulate internal questions and self-monitoring, both of which are associated with intrinsic motivation and learning."[53] Some faculty don't record the exam grade until the wrapper is completed, some use wrappers as in-class assignments or module reflections, and some administer a second exam on the same material after a week or so and then average the two grades.

In the case of writing assignments and projects, students can "wrap" the assessment after you have evaluated it. And the same two parts apply. Reflection questions might include, What specific changes would you make to the assignment/project in response to the feedback provided? Knowing what you now know, what would you have done differently when completing this assignment/project? As with exam wrappers, we encourage you to offer suggestions during a writing assessment wrapper. It's ideal (and most equitable) to give students the opportunity to revise after the wrapper and improve their grade or earn points.

4. Explicitly Assess Belonging

If you find yourself wondering whether and to what extent your students feel like they belong, you're not alone. But don't just guess—you can ask your students! It may seem odd to assess anything other than your students' attainment or progress toward your course learning objectives, but if a truly inclusive educational experience is meant to foster both intellectual and social growth, it's important for your assessment practices to include both components. You can use qualitative or quantitative methods, or both. If you need guidance as you develop your assessment, refer to figure 5.1, which includes the Classroom Belonging Survey questions from the Panorama Student Survey developed by a team of researchers at the Harvard Graduate School of Education under the direction of Dr. Hunter Gehlbach.[54] The survey was designed to measure how much students feel that they are valued members of the classroom community. As with any survey, you'll want to ensure student responses are anonymous,

---

1. How well do people in your class understand you as a person?

___Do not understand at all   ___Understand quite a bit

___Understand a little   ___Completely understand

___Understand somewhat

2. How connected do you feel to the professor in this class?

___Not at all connected   ___Quite connected

___Slightly connected   ___Extremely connected

___Somewhat connected

3. How much respect do students in this class show you?

___No respect at all   ___Quite a bit of respect

___A little bit of respect   ___A tremendous amount of respect

___Some respect

4. How much do you matter to others in this class?

___Do not matter at all   ___Matter quite a bit

___Matter a little bit   ___Matter a tremendous amount

___Matter somewhat

5. Overall, how much do you feel like you belong in this class?

___Do not belong at all   ___Belong quite a bit

___Belong a little bit   ___Completely belong

___Belong somewhat

FIGURE 5.1   Classroom Belonging Survey

Source: Hunter Gehlbach, User Guide: Panorama Student Survey *(Boston: Panorama Education, 2015), https://www.panoramaed.com/panorama-student-survey.*

let students know why you're asking and how you will use the information gathered, and then summarize key findings and explain what you plan to do in response.

While surveys can be very useful, qualitative approaches to assessing belonging are sometimes more useful because of their ability to capture nuance. One example is an end-of-semester reflection assignment. Walton and Cohen, for instance, asked experiment participants to engage in a two-part reflection exercise: First, the participants read a brief narrative about how students of all identities tend to experience adversity as they adjust to college, as well as brief reflections written by supposed graduating seniors with the same message of initial struggle and eventual success. Then, they were asked to write an essay in which they compared their own experiences to those in the narrative and reflection texts, and they were told that their materials would be used to help advise future first-year students on how to successfully navigate their first semester.[55] The study demonstrated that the simple act of reflecting in this way resulted in not only an increased GPA but also gains in self-reported health and well-being for Black students. You can easily replicate this study in your class, perhaps by writing your own narrative with a message tailored to the class or discipline. In addition to the benefits the students will gain from reading your narrative and reflecting about their experiences, their essays will help you better understand how your students navigated your course and the extent to which they felt they belonged. You might also consider keeping the students' essays to share anonymously with future classes.

HOW CAN I GET STARTED?

For Any Class

- Mention on the first day or in a welcome video that doubts and concerns about belonging are common for all students and tend to decrease over time. You could add details about what you've planned in the course to help with your students' sense of belonging.

- Try this activity from the Mindset Kit, created by the Project for Education Research That Scales, a research center in the psychology department at Stanford University: "Think about the students in your class. Is there a student you can think of who might have belonging concerns? How might those concerns affect that student? Write 2-3 sentences from that student's perspective."[56]

- After returning students' first assessment or reporting their grades on the first exam, tell students about a time you were not academically successful.

For In-Person Classes

- Set aside class time for students to begin "wrapping" a major assessment (see our discussion about wrappers earlier in this unit). This demonstrates that you value the exercise.

- Around midterm, invite someone you trust to have a discussion with your students about the class, when you are not present. They might ask students questions from the Classroom Belonging Survey in figure 5.1. Once this person has reported the students' feedback to you, work with a colleague or a member of your institution's center for teaching, asking them to help you determine the degree to which you're meeting your belonging goals.

For Asynchronous Online Classes

- To help students feel seen and to communicate that each of them matters to you, use the tools in your LMS to send an individualized message to each student early in the term acknowledging their efforts on an assignment.

- Humanize your homepage: "Ensure your students are greeted with a clear, friendly homepage when they arrive in your course. Include a visual banner, a brief video that welcomes and tells them how to proceed, and a clear 'start here' button that links to the first module," suggests Michelle Pacansky-Brock.[57]

For Synchronous Online Classes

- Scan the Zoom room periodically. Watch for verbal and nonverbal responses to the course environment. Withdrawn eyes, apologetic answers (e.g., "I'm sorry this might be wrong but . . . "), and unwillingness to contribute (or turn on a camera) might indicate a level of social discomfort. To help address this, redouble your relational efforts. For example, if your class size permits, admit each student individually from the waiting room, exchanging a brief greeting ("How's your day going so far?") to strengthen contact and extend relentless welcome online.

- Use a poll-group-repoll strategy as an abbreviated version of interdependence. Launch a poll and ask students to respond to a question for which you expect varied responses. Then, ask students to discuss their responses in a small group. Launch the poll again to see if any responses have changed. Conclude the activity with a whole-class discussion focused on changes in students' answers.

6

STRUCTURE
Plan Ahead to Support Student Learning and Success

Highly structured and active classes and modules help students learn and succeed, and help faculty implement and assess their equity-minded practices.

If you've had a hard time imagining how to incorporate the ideas shared so far into your day-to-day teaching, this unit should help. What do we mean by *structure,* and how does it relate to equity-minded teaching? We introduced one form of structure earlier in the guide, in Section One: the backward design method of designing a course. You'll recall that L. Dee Fink's systematic approach to designing courses entails aligning the key parts of your course: the learning goals, assessments, and learning activities. In this unit, we describe how adding structure to your day-to-day teaching is a similar process. The course segments will vary based on what kind of course you're teaching. In a face-to-face course, you may be structuring a whole class session or an activity, whereas in an asynchronous online course, you may be structuring an online module or a learning activity within a module.

Because the term *structure* may be new to you in relation to teaching, we'll start with a specific illustration of how structured course elements affect student success. This example is from a 2011 study by education researchers Scott Freeman, David Haak, and Mary Pat Wenderoth.[1] They tested the hypothesis that highly structured course designs can lower failure rates in an introductory biology course, relative to low-structure course designs based on lecturing and a few high-stakes assessments. Freeman and the team found that failure rates were lower in a moderately structured course design and were dramatically lower in a highly structured course design. What made the highly structured course *highly structured* was the use of reading quizzes and/or extensive in-class active learning activities and weekly practice exams. In this unit, we expand on Freeman and colleagues' use of the term *structure* to also include the careful alignment of course components, the detailed planning of a class session and activity, and the design of online modules.

Adding structure to our teaching practice supports student learning and equitable outcomes for several reasons: First, as Viji Sathy and Kelly Hogan put it, "too little structure leaves too many students behind."[2] Our colleges and universities abound with invisible ink—expectations and rules that (as fish might say about water) we as faculty simply don't see. The structural enhancements we describe in this unit make expectations and guidance more explicit to students, just as *transparency* does for assessment design (see Unit 2). More structured courses make it less likely that students disproportionately benefit from or are penalized by their varied levels of "college knowledge." Second, structure helps us advance more equitable outcomes by requiring us to pay extra attention to our learning objectives and how they relate to the activities we assign, making it more likely that students learn. Finally, attending to structure can help us implement and assess the impact of our equity-minded strategies, including evaluating how these strategies affect students' sense of belonging and their levels of trust.

While high structure is important in all modalities, it's critical in asynchronous online classes, so in this unit you'll find ample guidance on structuring online courses. As we've noted elsewhere, students taking an asynchronous online course must be able to navigate course materials, motivate themselves, organize their time and tasks, and engage in many other self-regulating behaviors. Since we're generally not able to answer their questions in real time, it's important for the structure of the course itself to be easily navigable and supportive.

To illustrate this point, consider a course consultation that coauthor Flower Darby gave several years ago. A well-meaning professor was new to online teaching and had been offered no support in developing his first online course, so he asked Flower for feedback. When she clicked into the class, she was alarmed to discover that the entire course was one gigantic page. Everything was located on the main landing page: the syllabus, readings, videos, quizzes, assignments, and more. Getting to anything required extensive scrolling, and it was difficult to see how any single element of the course fit into the bigger picture. While Flower recognized that the professor was not to blame, as he'd never seen a good online course or learned how to design one, she also experienced tremendous empathy for his students, who would likely flounder in such an unstructured environment.

On the other hand, sometimes online courses can be confusingly or overly structured. Whether we create the online course or use a template course, the location of items and the relationship among them often seem intuitive to us, but when students enter our courses, alone, it's not always clear to them what's where or why. In this way, the structure and flow of online courses can exacerbate inequity. If students are already experiencing a low sense of belonging, for instance, they may interpret their difficulty navigating an online course as confirmation that college is, in fact, not for them.

We begin this unit with a brief distillation of research on course structure and turn quickly to a high-level "Putting the Research to Work" section dedicated to equity-focused instructional design and lesson/module planning for both in-person and online courses. Then, we feature another "Putting the Research to Work" segment that includes a set of practical recommendations, proposing four equity-minded ways to add structure and support to your day-to-day teaching.

What Does the Research Say about Structure?

In general, educational research is unanimous that highly structured courses, from the top-level organization down to individual class sessions and online modules, are beneficial to student learning and success. And as we've noted, structure supports more equitable outcomes for several reasons. In her book *Sentipensante (Sensing/Thinking) Pedagogy*, Laura Rendón contends that equity-minded faculty use highly structured teaching practices to keep students engaged and to cultivate trust.[3] In equity-minded teaching, structure is not simply about content-related course planning; it also entails surveying students, having one-on-one conversations, and maintaining a highly tuned radar so we can understand the social experiences impacting our students. In this way, our structured teaching practices convey to students our continued investment in their intellectual and social development.

At its core, increased structure in our courses is about intentionality. Equity-focused instructors take time to think about what will best facilitate learning for our students in our institutional context. Then we build into our in-person and online classes the course elements and activities that will help students learn, retain, and apply course concepts and skills. As we have pointed out throughout this guide, what's important to do in person can be even more important to do online, to combat students' sense of isolation and distance. Education nonprofit CAST (online at CAST.org), the research organization that created the Universal Design for Learning (UDL) framework and guidelines, specifies that adding structure in asynchronous online classes is essential because "**executive functioning** processes are particularly critical" online, given that "students are required to be far more autonomous."[4] Many tools can help us identify online student supports. For example, based on the Community of Inquiry (CoI) framework, the Quality Matters (QM) Rubric that we refer to in Unit 1 encourages us to ensure that we include opportunities for students to interact with course materials, with us, and with each other. Further, CAST provides suggestions for promoting executive functioning online so we can help students manage their time, tasks, and otherwise regulate their learning. (It's worth noting that some students fare better in asynchronous online courses than in person: some neurodivergent or introverted students prefer the quieter environment with more time to reflect and process, for instance. However, many students struggle with the lack of real-time guidance

executive functioning: A set of mental processes and skills that we use to manage our daily lives, including working memory, flexible thinking, and self-control.

that otherwise takes place in person, which is why CAST encourages online instructors to provide supports for autonomy, among other things.)

Increasing structure in our courses can also be a powerful way to advance equity because we'll be more likely to implement equity-minded and inclusive strategies. For example, a few times during a semester we can give students a preplanned survey that asks about trust or belonging, like the ones we suggest in Units 4 and 5. If we intentionally include equity-minded activities such as these on the course schedule, they become woven into the fabric of our courses and day-to-day teaching, versus optional approaches we may or may not remember to incorporate. Finally, for busy students with complex lives, the time they devote to our courses—whether in person or online—is precious. Attending to structure ensures that we are using students' time respectfully and in service of their learning and success.

Education researchers (particularly from STEM disciplines) stress that course structure is central to inclusive teaching. In her article "Structure Matters," STEM education researcher Kimberly D. Tanner echoes the conviction that course structure is central to advancing equitable student outcomes. In essence, she argues that course structure is the set of mechanisms via which the key ideas introduced earlier—like relevance and belonging—reach all students, who can then reap the benefits. "Without attention to the structure of classroom interactions," she writes, "what can often ensue is a wonderfully designed biology lesson that can be accessed by only a small subset of students in a classroom."[5]

Sathy and Hogan describe what's at stake when faculty provide limited structure.[6] They ask us to imagine a student in a discussion-based class who has a great deal to contribute but is uncomfortable jumping in or raising her hand. In this example, what's missing or inadequate is a framework for the class discussion or alternative structured opportunities for the student to participate in other ways (as in pair work, independent writing, or an anonymous poll). Her peers miss out on her insights, and if participation factors into the course grade, the student misses out too. In another of their examples, the limited structure is in the form of a grading scheme in which the course grade is computed based exclusively on two papers and one exam (see Unit 2 for a discussion on grading). The challenge here is not only that the pared-down grading structure makes the stakes very high for each assessment but also that the class doesn't include low-stakes opportunities through which students can practice the analysis and application required for success.

With an explicit focus on equitable outcomes, Sarah Eddy and Kelly Hogan's study "Getting Under the Hood: How and for Whom Does Increasing Course Structure Work?" sheds light on how increased course structure affects the experiences of minoritized students.[7] They observed the same course during three terms of what they called "low" structure and three terms of "moderate" structure and then compared student performance at each level of structure.

The level of structure was based on how frequently the faculty member implemented three pedagogical strategies: guided reading questions, preparatory homework, and an in-class activity. In the highly structured class, for instance, students completed at least one graded preparation assignment and one graded review assignment per week, and students talked for more than 40 percent of class time. Interestingly, the most positive benefits were seen in the "moderate-structure" course: performance increased for all student populations, and it did so disproportionately for Black students. There was a noticeable impact on two distinct so-called achievement gaps: the Black-White gap visible in the low-structure version of the course was cut in half in the moderate-structure version, and the gap seen for first-generation students was closed altogether. This considerable progress toward equity confirms that we simply cannot afford *not* to pay close attention to structure.

Foundational Structures and Key Strategies

We hope the research summary we've just shared has inspired you to reflect on the structures that are already part of your course design and recognize opportunities to add or enhance student support. In general, the practitioners involved in the research have identified a set of tools and practices through which we can add structure to our courses. We'll briefly describe five of those we consider foundational to equity-minded teaching: alignment, active learning strategies, sequencing, scaffolds, and time considerations, including recommendations for effectively engaging students in all class modalities.

Alignment

Architectural design and construction provide one way to think about adding structure to our courses. Just as building a house starts with an overall blueprint and extends down to the careful alignment of lumber and other building materials, structuring a course begins with the alignment of learning goals and activities and extends into the planning of individual tasks or assignments a student completes. In Unit 1, we walked you through Fink's research-based course design process and described his emphasis on the interrelationship among your course learning objectives, primary assessments, and learning activities. Linda Nilson and Ludwika Goodson echo this guidance in their book *Online Teaching at Its Best*. They explain that "aligning all parts of your course will help your students achieve your intended learning outcomes and make a positive impression."[8]

Other than referencing the four-column Course Planning Map (see the Appendix), how else can you tell if your course elements are aligned? You should be able to take any assessment, assignment, or course activity and match it up to a course outcome, suggest Nilson and Goodson. In short, "All of the learning activities in your course should be organized around your course outcomes so that you have no inconsistencies in what you teach, how you teach, and what you assess."[9] Recall that the Online Learning Consortium (OLC) and Quality Matters (QM) course design rubrics, while not perfect, provide systematic guidance to help you align online course elements as well—indeed, the systematic approach of these rubrics is one of their strengths.

It might feel like busy work to match up learning objectives to learning activities and assignments, particularly if learning objectives were set by your department. But mapping out those connections, however obvious they might seem to you, can help your students see the connections and can help you identify weak spots in your structure. Perhaps you'll see that your existing course offers many opportunities for students to master one learning objective, but you'll realize that for another objective students can rely only on the course reading and have no opportunity to apply this knowledge. The careful alignment of course outcomes, assessments, and learning activities also sets the stage for the other structural enhancements we describe in this unit.

Finally, aligning course elements can and should be an iterative process, just as we might describe the writing process. Coauthors Isis Artze-Vega and Flower Darby both have extensive experience in teaching composition courses. They know that writing teachers commonly advise students to go back and reread the introduction and thesis statement after an entire draft paper exists, to make sure what was said in the introduction matches what was actually written—and, if not, the student must revise the first paragraph. The same advice holds true for aligning course elements. Because we describe these steps in a sequential order, the process can feel linear: Complete step 1. Check. Move on to step 2. But as you proceed in (re)designing your course, it's important and necessary to circle back to check alignment in earlier steps.

Active Learning Strategies and Practice

Although it's beyond the scope of this guide to describe at length the research on active learning, suffice it to say that the research is clear. In *Learner-Centered Teaching*, Terry Doyle sums up the findings this way: "The one who does the work does the learning."[10] And he reminds us that as faculty we're often the ones doing the work (and thus the learning)—as can be true in fully lecture-based courses. Scott Freeman and colleagues' meta-analysis is often cited as the most definitive evidence to date that active learning is effective. The comprehensive study supports active learning as the preferred, empirically validated teaching practice in regular classrooms.[11]

In the study mentioned at the start of this unit, Freeman, Haak, and Wenderoth examined the impact of active learning on course success. They asked themselves, "How can we reduce failure rates in STEM courses, without reducing rigor?"[12] They hypothesized that the use of intensive active learning, in concert with frequent formative assessment, would lower course failure rates. We would call this a highly structured approach, given the addition of active learning exercises and the frequency with which they were used.

Importantly, Freeman and colleagues took great care in selecting the daily and weekly active learning exercises used in the study, aiming to provide "constant practice with the analytical skills required to do well on exams."[13] The researchers' decisions were thereby guided by the question that frames step four of Fink's model (introduced in Unit 2): What will your students *do* in and out of class, or in each online module, to prepare to successfully complete your primary assessments and therefore make progress toward your course learning objectives?[14] Freeman and colleagues found that failure rates were lower in a moderately structured course and dramatically lower in a highly structured course. The authors indicate that these results support the use of active learning to "make students more skilled learners and help bridge the gap between poorly prepared students and their better-prepared peers."[15] Importantly, to the question of rigor, they found no evidence that points earned by students when completing active learning exercises inflate grades or reduce the impact of exams on final grades.

Additional research has demonstrated that active learning narrows performance gaps among students of varied identities,[16] and it suggests that a combination of active learning and inclusive practices can powerfully improve student success. Why might this be? Elli Theobald and colleagues propose what they call the "heads-and-hearts hypothesis." Here, *heads* refers to a specific kind of active learning known as **deliberate practice**. The researchers explain that "meaningful reductions in achievement gaps only occur when course designs combine deliberate practice with inclusive teaching."[17] They define deliberate practice as emphasizing the following:

deliberate practice:
A form of practice that consists of structured activities designed to improve performance over time on a specific competency or domain.

1. Extensive and highly focused efforts geared toward improving performance—meaning that students work hard on relevant tasks
2. Scaffolded exercises designed to address specific deficits in understanding or skills
3. Immediate feedback
4. Repetition

The *hearts* part of the hypothesis relates to the use of inclusive practices, which in this case are "treating students with dignity and respect, communicating confidence in students' ability to meet high standards, and demonstrating a genuine interest in students' intellectual and personal growth and success"[18]—all of which are foregrounded in this guide.

The "heads-and-hearts hypothesis" also applies to the study by coauthor Bryan Dewsbury and colleagues, which we mentioned in the Introduction to this guide. Recall that in the introductory biology course featured in the study, using inclusive and active pedagogies not only resulted in more short-term gains in equitable student learning and success but also resulted in improved success in the subsequent biology course.[19] Specific active learning strategies included pre-class assignments, group assignments, and formative assessments, in contrast to the mostly lecture-based sections that constituted the control group in the study. Regarding the overall structure of the course examined in the study (Bryan's biology class), Bryan describes it as semi-flipped. The term **flipped classroom** generally denotes courses in which students read materials and watch lecture videos prior to attending class. Then, in class, students engage in

flipped classroom:
A teaching approach that "flips" the model of in-person lecturing and out-of-class problem-solving. Students complete readings or watch videos *prior* to class, so that they can engage in problem-solving, discussions, and so on during the class session itself, while the professor and their peers are there to support their learning.

hands-on practice activities and exercises so that they don't have to struggle to complete challenging homework or solve complex problems by themselves at home. Bryan describes his teaching as "semi" flipped because he also incorporates mini-lectures during class meetings. Although the study did not untangle the impact of the active pedagogies relative to that of Bryan's many other inclusive practices, the benefits to students that Bryan has observed validate previous studies. Particularly effective are those involving a combination of active learning and equity-focused practices.

Along similar lines, Andrew Phuong and colleagues developed and studied a highly structured approach they call "Adaptive Equity-Oriented Pedagogy." It incorporates elements of both active and justice-oriented instruction, as well as distinctive features like gaming and the collection of data during each class session.[20] Study participants of all identities who were students in the course using the adaptive, equity-oriented pedagogy had considerably higher scores on the final assessment, and qualitative analyses indicated that these students had higher levels of course engagement, were more motivated, and reported feeling reduced stereotype threat.

On Active Learning Online

Active learning is just as important online as it is in person. On one hand, every task in an asynchronous class could be considered active learning: taking quizzes, writing papers, and posting in discussion forums all constitute things students *do* to earn course credit. On the other hand, online classes can sometimes feel quite passive—as in, do the bare minimum: complete the reading, watch a video, and do as few discussion posts as possible. So it's important to carefully identify what we are asking students to do, and to ensure the work is purposeful and rigorous. The good news is that when teaching online, we benefit from the many different opportunities built into our LMSs to deeply engage students. As Flower writes, "LMSs [may] leave a lot to be desired in terms of welcoming and supporting students, but they do have a particular strength: these platforms feature tools and technologies that foster effective time on task."[21]

Flower recommends that, when determining which active learning strategies and tools to use, we first explore the LMS options. These include features that allow students to practice applying new concepts, to try solving problems, and to interact with information—get their hands on it, work with it—and then demonstrate their learning. She continues:

> Our LMS allows us to create activities and assessments that take
> advantage of the affordances of technology. . . . Will students solve
> homework sets? Take weekly mastery quizzes? Engage in lab
> simulations? Process new concepts in online discussions? Annotate

texts with their peers? Create video presentations to explain why a phenomenon does what it does? The technology in our online classes helps students work with material in meaningful ways that will lead to deeper, more durable learning.[22]

In short, we can use the LMS to structure online activities that help students spend meaningful time on task. For additional ideas about effectively using technology for active learning, see Stephen M. Kosslyn's book *Active Learning Online*.[23] In this short yet research-based guide, Kosslyn reviews how and why active learning works and offers dozens of examples, ranging from simple to creative, of how to structure activities in online environments—and these ideas are useful to enhance in-person classes, too!

Sequencing and Scaffolding for Support

Scholars also provide guidance on two related kinds of structure: sequencing and scaffolding. *Sequencing* describes how we arrange learning activities and assessments during a term or semester. We sometimes model our course schedules on the organization of the textbook, arrange topics chronologically, or simply order things the way our colleagues do. Yet, for students, a key part of retaining knowledge relates to how we as instructors organize information,[24] including the connections we make among content and competencies. By attending to the sequence of items or subcomponents in our course, including our assessments, we gain a powerful opportunity to help students learn more deeply.

Fink refers to the process of sequencing as the development of an "instructional strategy" and explains that by arranging or sequencing a set of learning activities, "the energy for learning increases and accumulates as students go through the sequence." Thus, our role as faculty, according to Fink, is to do the following:

> Set up some activities that (a) get students ready or prepared for later work, (b) give them opportunities to practice—with prompt feedback— doing whatever it is you want them to learn to do, (c) assess the quality of their performance, and (d) allow them to reflect on their learning.[25]

These four elements—preparation, practice, assessment (with feedback), and reflection—can guide your design of an individual class session or online module.

Relatedly, the concept of *scaffolding* our instruction might conjure up images of construction sites. However, scaffolding also refers to a teaching technique and a kind of structure that can help students bridge the gap between their current levels of knowledge or skill and the levels we want them to attain.

In principle, the use of scaffolds in teaching is not unlike their use in construction: just as construction workers need temporary support structures during the initial phases of building, our students often need support as they begin to learn a new or complex concept or skill. Barak Rosenshine and Carla Meister define scaffolds as "forms of support provided by the teacher . . . to help students bridge the gap between their current abilities and the intended goal."[26] (Recall that as faculty, we're aiming to challenge students; see Unit 1 on rigor.) Rosenshine and Meister add that although scaffolds are nimble and can be used in a variety of teaching contexts, they are "particularly useful, and often indispensable, for teaching higher-level cognitive strategies." In addition to helping students learn the material or enhance a particular skill, scaffolding can also help you cultivate a supportive learning environment because it demonstrates to your students that you are willing to serve as a guide, mentor, or coach—as opposed to simply a disciplinary expert.

To help faculty picture what his approach to sequencing and scaffolding looks like when teaching an in-person course, Fink created a diagram that helps us outline in-class and out-of-class activities (see figure 6.1). Filling in the blanks within the diagram prompts us to identify the learning activity for each in-class and out-of-class block of time. The aim is to create a sequence of activities that build on each other in a scaffolded approach. This method applies to a range of modalities, including flipped, blended/hybrid, and synchronous online classes. In all of these modes, the principle remains the same: intentionally plan activities for students to complete on their own outside of

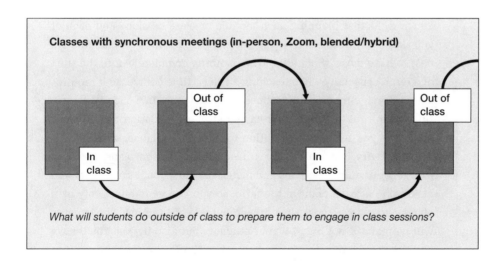

FIGURE 6.1 Template for Creating an Instructional Strategy

Source: Adapted from L. Dee Fink, Creating Significant Learning Experiences: An Integrated Approach to Designing College Courses *(San Francisco: Jossey-Bass, 2003), 139.*

class meetings, with the goal that they come to class ready to engage in active learning exercises that you have purposefully created to prompt higher-order thinking.

Having students who are ready for class is not the only benefit of carefully designed homework. As Sarah Eddy and Kelly Hogan write, one of the significant benefits of assigning structured out-of-class study time is that it results in students distributing their practice more evenly throughout the course (vs. cramming prior to an exam), which is known to be a more effective method for learning.[27] It can also provide students with a model for doing homework in other courses where they may be instructed to simply read a certain number of chapters or pages.

Bryan finds Fink's in- and out-of-class template useful for mapping carefully constructed learning outcomes onto his everyday course schedule. He also relies on the diagram when determining how to improve his class. For example, if he realizes that a particular topic needs more formative assessments (like low-stake quizzes or writing assignments), examining the diagram helps him identify where to provide those additional opportunities, and which other activities will be adjusted as a result.

Sequencing and Scaffolding Sound Like Too Much Work! Why Are They Worth My Time and Effort?

You're right that planning each module or class session—and each of your key class/online activities—takes a good amount of time. And it's best to have most (if not all) of the planning complete before the start of a term, especially when teaching a fully online course, so it requires a considerable up-front investment of your time. But once you carefully plan a full course, you'll have a strong foundation to refine the next time you teach it. In addition to a robust syllabus, you'll have a set of activity instructions for students, daily lesson plans, and/or a robust set of online modules and materials. Plus, you'll know what you need to do at each point in the term, so you can more effectively plan ahead and manage your time, in and outside of teaching. The benefits will be realized not only by your students but also by *you*. You'll have additional time during the term to get to know your students and to provide them with valuable feedback, and more. And if you teach the class again, as many of us do, you and your future students will reap the benefits of this careful, intentional planning for, potentially, years to come.

The principles of intentional sequencing and scaffolding represented by Fink's in- and out-of-class template still apply in asynchronous online courses, but in a different manner (see figure 6.2). Rather than thinking about what students will do on their own time and what they will do during class meetings, it's helpful to think of each asynchronous course module as consisting of two broadly defined elements: (1) opportunities for students to independently interact with course materials, such as engaging in readings and completing quizzes, and (2) activities students complete with classmates and with you, such as discussions, small-group projects, and one-to-one meetings or phone calls with you. The key to creating effective online modules is to achieve a balance of both elements, deliberately sequencing them to maximize engagement and build on each other in the same scaffolded approach we recommend for in-person classes.

To illustrate how to sequence and structure online modules in order to maximize engagement and learning, we'll briefly examine Flower's graduate online course, Technological Fluency and Leadership. The course is organized into four modules of two weeks each. Each module features the following elements, and they appear in this order:

- First, students find a brief written overview of the module's overarching concept, supported by a video mini-lecture.

- Next are links to popular/current media news and opinion pieces (articles, blogs, or YouTube or TED Talk videos) relevant to the topic, with a variety of workplace contexts.

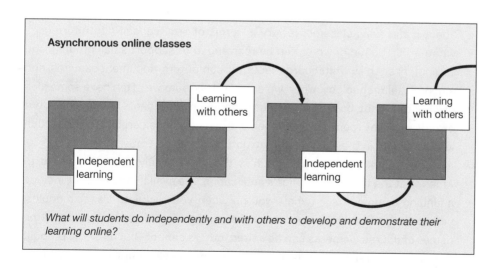

Asynchronous online classes

Learning with others

Learning with others

Independent learning

Independent learning

What will students do independently and with others to develop and demonstrate their learning online?

FIGURE 6.2 Template for Creating an Instructional Strategy, Adapted for Online Module Design

Source: Adapted from L. Dee Fink, Creating Significant Learning Experiences: An Integrated Approach to Designing College Courses *(San Francisco: Jossey-Bass, 2003), 139.*

- For each concept, students select from these resources and/or find their own based on interests and goals.

- Then, in discussions, they report back to their classmates about what they read or watched, and they continue to engage in discussions throughout the module (which Flower structured based on staggered due dates for initial and reply posts). Each student individually reflects on their overall learning in each module, both from what they read and watched and from what their classmates shared in discussions.

- Throughout the course, students apply and demonstrate their learning by completing three projects, which are associated with modules 2, 3, and 4 (module 1 is focused heavily on course orientation and getting-to-know-you activities).

Using this modified diagram has helped us as faculty members, and it should help you, too: you can methodically identify where and how your course learning outcomes map onto daily and weekly activities in your online modules, and you can add or adjust activities accordingly.

Working with the LMS Structure

One way online courses differ significantly from in-person ones is the degree to which learning spaces in the LMS are preset by categories, structures, and labels that are hardwired into the environment and cannot be changed. Think about it this way: classrooms vary in terms of size, capacity, furniture (e.g., whether it's bolted down or can be rearranged to support small groups), and equipment such as whiteboards, lecterns, computers, document cameras, and audio/visual technology. When we enter a classroom we often have some idea of what to expect, based on previous experience as students and teachers, but exactly what the room looks and feels like can vary considerably. There is much less variability in the existing infrastructure of today's LMSs.

For example, in Canvas, which is the most widely used LMS in North America at the time of this guide's publication, the available structures include a landing or home page (where you go when you click into class), modules, pages, discussions, assignments, quizzes, and group workspaces. Some of the names of course elements can be edited; others cannot—but all of the prebuilt structures are relatively inflexible. Because online elements are presented in such a linear way (e.g., the "modules view" presents a list of materials and tasks from the top of the page to the bottom), and given the importance of sequencing and scaffolding discussed previously, the order in which course elements appear is important.

Take, for instance, the first online class Flower taught, one she inherited (as you may have experienced). In the LMS, the course featured quiz and assignment links buried in a series of nested folders, making these required assessments difficult to find. As another example, Flower recently spoke with a first-year college student who shared that in her kinesiology Canvas space, items appeared out of order. The student said that a video lecture with an associated quiz due two weeks later appeared closer to the top of the page than the video lecture with the quiz due that week. One instructor Flower worked with placed assignments in the announcements area, which made sense to her, but was likely not as clear to her students.

So, the relative inflexibility of predetermined LMS structures necessarily adds a kind of default structure to online modules. This can work to our and our students' advantage to greater or lesser extent. The rather linear look and feel of most LMSs implies that students should do the tasks in the order in which they appear, starting from the top of the page. However, what makes sense in your own head may not translate to your students. Therefore, when considering the flow of online courses and modules, it's important to take the student's perspective and consider whether items are organized logically (better yet, ask for a review from a faculty colleague, instructional designer, or current or former student).

Because organization that seems obvious to us can be confusing to students, in *Online Teaching at Its Best*, Nilson and Goodson stress the importance not only of carefully structuring online courses but also of clearly communicating this structure to students. "Explicit organization and clearly labeled segments reduce student anxiety, help students better understand the learning process, and facilitate their time management," they explain.[28] Clear communication about course structure is necessary in all modalities and is especially important online. So consider creating a short (less than five minutes) screencast video tour of your online course, showing students where they can find module materials and activities. Then, to triple-check that students can easily locate course elements, you might even consider administering a version of the "syllabus quiz" at the start of the term that asks students about where to find things in the LMS. In this way, you can identify any misconceptions or incomplete understandings early and provide clarity and guidance.

A simple yet powerful way to clearly communicate to students your online course structure is to develop a "course at a glance" table. You can create this table within a page in your LMS, add a link to the table in a Google Doc (which allows for easier editing if you have a valid reason to change due dates to benefit students), or it can be a PDF attachment. Choose whatever format is most accessible for your students and will best facilitate its effective use. The purpose of this table is to prevent hidden surprises (such as those hard-to-find nested assessments in Flower's first online class) and to ensure students know exactly what is expected of them (refer to Unit 2 on transparency). The table should feature all due dates, list major and minor activities and assessments, and provide a clear sense of what's needed to be successful in your course. See table 6.1 for an example of the first three weeks of class, and notice the consistent and predictable scheduling of required tasks and activities.

TABLE 6.1   Sample "Course at a Glance" Table

Module	Task / Activity (listed in the approximate order these should be completed)	Due Date (everything is due by 11:59 p.m. on the date listed)
Module 1 (Orientation) Mon. 8/29–Sun. 9/4	Watch welcome video	
	Access and read syllabus	
	Submit any questions in the Course Q&A discussion forum	
	Take the syllabus quiz	Tues. 8/30
	Post your introduction in the Introductions discussion	Tues. 8/30
	Submit the Getting to Know You survey	Thurs. 9/1
	Submit the My Learning Goals reflection assignment	Sat. 9/3
	Reply to at least three classmates in the Introductions discussion	Sun. 9/4 (sooner is always better!)
Module 2 (name topic here) Mon. 9/5–Sun. 9/11	Readings and Videos • Chapter 1 in the textbook • Mini-lecture videos (three total, five minutes each) • Select one of the five available linked articles	Before taking the quiz
	Take reading and mini-lecture quiz (multiple attempts allowed)	Tues. 9/6
	Submit initial discussion post	Tues. 9/6
	Submit module mini-project	Thurs. 9/8
	Submit completed module note-taking guide	Sat. 9/10
	Reply to at least three classmates in the Module 2 discussion	Sun. 9/11
	Submit Key Takeaways assignment for Module 2	Sun. 9/11

Module 3 (name topic here) Mon. 9/12–Sun. 9/18	Readings and Videos • Chapter 2 in the textbook • Mini-lecture videos (three total, five minutes each) • Read and annotate the provided article	Before taking the quiz
	Take reading and mini-lecture quiz (multiple attempts allowed)	Tues. 9/13
	Submit initial discussion post	Tues. 9/13
	Submit Paper 1	Thurs. 9/15
	Submit completed module note-taking guide	Sat. 9/17
	Reply to at least three classmates in the Module 3 discussion	Sun. 9/18
	Submit Key Takeaways assignment for Module 3	Sun. 9/18

Structuring Time

Time considerations are critically important for equity-focused instruction. As noted previously, when we're intentional about how we think about and structure time in our courses, we demonstrate respect for our students' valuable time and work to ensure the time they spend on classwork most effectively advances their learning. Both of these practices foster trust. In this section, we'll address learning time more broadly, then turn our attention to considerations specific to courses with synchronous meetings (whether in person or in Zoom).

It's important to strike a balance between overloading students with work and not providing enough structured activities. Your college or university likely has a policy to help you gauge how much time students should spend on coursework in class and out of class, or how many hours they should spend in total each week (which also works for asynchronous classes). For example, at Flower's institution, the Board of Regents sets an expectation that students will complete two hours of classwork for every hour they spend in class. And as we've mentioned, to advance equitable outcomes, you should create activities that space out and reinforce learning, such as reading quizzes or practice exercises. Wake Forest University has created a course workload estimator that guides you through a comprehensive process to estimate how much time your planned activities will take per week.[29]

Further, two considerations can help us think strategically about how to intentionally plan courses with synchronous meetings. First, how can students best benefit from limited time with you, the expert, in the (physical or Zoom) room? What in-class activities will enable you to model disciplinary thinking or help students explore, practice, and interact with complex concepts and skills—while you are there to answer questions and provide feedback in the moment?

Second, which activities are best facilitated by readily available asynchronous online technologies, and which are best suited for in-person or Zoom rooms, where you can get students together to collaborate and learn from each other in real time? For example, we can use auto-graded quizzes in or through the LMS to help students recall foundational concepts or to hold them accountable for doing the reading. Think of such tools as formative—facilitating assessment *as* learning in addition to assessment *of* learning. Offering multiple attempts on a quiz, and encouraging students to review information on questions they missed before reattempting the quiz, enables students to immerse themselves in the reading and thereby learn concepts more deeply. In this example, we're leveraging what the LMS does well, asynchronously, in order to prepare students for in-class application, problem-solving, and collaboration with each other and with you.

Help! I'm Still Not Confident about My Online Class Structure. Where Can I Get More Support?

If you're like most faculty members, you have a wealth of experience in physical classrooms (both as a student and as a teacher). Based on your experiences, you may have an intuitive sense of what well-structured in-person classes look like. This sense is likely much less developed for online classes, however. Most professors today have not had the same experience in online learning spaces as they have had in person, again, both as a student and as a teacher. So it isn't surprising if you feel confused about how to add structure to an online course.

In this guide, we provide course and unit design considerations, but it's beyond our scope to go into depth regarding the equity-minded instructional design of online courses. For more on equity-minded instructional design in general, see two collections that were new at time of publication, *Toward a Critical Instructional Design* and *Designing for Care*.[30] Meanwhile, if you're looking for additional support related to adding structure online, here are a few ideas and resources to consider, depending on your available time:

- First and foremost, reach out to your local instructional designer, who most likely works in your digital learning faculty support office. Instructional designers bring a wealth of evidence and expertise to help you evaluate your course design and identify places to add structure. Whether you engage with them in a workshop they offer, a one-time individual consultation, or an ongoing conversation, these folks can be powerful partners in developing your equity-focused course design and teaching.

- Consult online resources such as the OLC Quality Scorecard, freely available and designed to help you systematically review your online course for areas to add structure.[31] Though not perfect, quality rubrics such as this scorecard can be a good place to start if you're new(er) to online course design and teaching practices.

- Nilson and Goodson's *Online Teaching at Its Best* provides comprehensive guidance and robust research support that can improve any online (and in-person) course.

- The K. Patricia Cross Academy (a free and highly robust online library of evidence-based teaching techniques for all modalities) offers a resource called "5 Tips for Engaging Online Course Design."[32] If you've got limited time, this could be a great place to start.

Specific Structural Strategies for Advancing Equitable Outcomes

Researchers have demonstrated that students benefit from structured courses, class sessions, and modules. And we imagine that as you read about the five tools and practices we've just shared, you thought of several implications for your own teaching. Because the number of options can be overwhelming, we'll now suggest four specific ways to leverage the power of structure in order to advance more equitable student outcomes.

1. Try Using a Lesson or Module Template

In Courses with a Synchronous Component (In-Person, Zoom, Hybrid)

Stiliana Milkova, of University of Michigan's Center for Research on Learning and Teaching, breaks down the lesson planning process for a fully in-person (or Zoom) course into a series of steps:

1. Outline learning objectives for the class session.
2. Develop an introduction.
3. Plan the specific learning activities.
4. Determine how you will check for understanding.
5. Draft a conclusion (and ideally, a preview of what comes next).
6. Work on timing each of these.[33]

In the first step, outlining the learning objectives for the class session, Milkova recommends ranking the objectives in terms of their importance. In the second step, developing an introduction, she encourages us to try to ascertain students' prior knowledge of the topic and then begin the lesson by stimulating students' interest. Next, in the third step, which is the learning activities part of your lesson plan, identify what *you* will do during the class session (e.g., explain, describe, or demonstrate) and what *students* will do to practice and receive feedback on their progress toward the course objectives (i.e., decide which active learning strategies you'll use). She also echoes the UDL guidance that students should represent their knowledge in multiple ways: verbally, written, illustrated, and so on.

Next, in step four, we check whether and how much students are learning. Perhaps we ask students to respond to a question in writing or complete a brief quiz. To the extent possible, these formative assessments should resemble your summative assessments, giving students practice with both the content/

competency and the format. In the fifth step, drafting a conclusion or preview, it's helpful to either summarize or ask students to summarize the lesson. (Student summaries can also serve as a check for understanding.) Previewing the next lesson reinforces the relationship among concepts or sections of the class. Finally, in the sixth step, you work on a realistic timeline, estimating how much time each of the activities will take the students to complete.

What would a completed lesson plan look like? Fancy formatting is optional. A lesson plan can be as simple as the one shown in table 6.2, in which we illustrate

TABLE 6.2 A Validation Lesson

Learning Objectives
- Normalize belonging uncertainty
- Validate students' strengths

	Description	Time
Introduction	Let students know that you're not only interested in how much they learn (your discipline). You're also invested in their broader academic success—and in their overall wellness. To that end, you know how common it is for students to feel they don't quite belong in college (or in a particular class or discipline)—and to wonder if they "have what it takes" to be successful.	2 min.
Learning Activities	I will - tell my belonging story (see Unit 5), helping to humanize myself and communicate how common it is for students to question their belonging - list a few of the strengths I brought to college, ones that aren't typically considered college success skills Students will - ask me questions about my story - privately reflect on their own sense of belonging and list a few of their strengths by freewriting for four minutes	10 min.
Check for Understanding	Invite students to ask you additional questions, share something they noticed while freewriting, and/or list some of the strengths they bring to college and/or this particular class.	5 min.
Conclusion and Preview	Validate that each student brings innumerable strengths to college and your course, that they absolutely belong and can succeed, and that it's a priority of yours to ensure they feel a sense of belonging in your class. Explain that you will be administering an anonymous survey on belonging at the course midpoint and later at the end of the term.	3 min.

how you might design a stand-alone twenty-minute lesson on belonging to use in any class with a synchronous element.

In Asynchronous Online Courses

As described previously, each module in an asynchronous course typically consists of two elements: opportunities for students to independently interact with materials and activities (such as readings, videos, quizzes, and assignments) and activities to complete with other students and with you (such as discussions and small group projects). Here, we describe the module template Flower used to create her asynchronous online course, Technological Fluency and Leadership (CCHE 590). Each module includes the following elements, intentionally sequenced for optimal and scaffolded learning:

- *An introduction to the module.* In Flower's case, this introduction is a mini-video lecture in which she is talking directly to the camera or voicing over presentation slides. In line with UDL principles, these videos are captioned, include a text bullet-point summary of main points, and are generally three to six minutes long. This element also includes two to four learning goals (or objectives) for the module.

- *Content.* Because making choices is empowering, Flower includes a selection of readings from which students can choose. Her students can select five items from a predetermined set of online articles and YouTube videos on the module's topics (e.g., how to evaluate technology for effective implementation in team and personal settings). She also allows students to identify outside readings and videos that are more relevant to their lived experiences, goals, and interests. Students may conduct their own online search to explore a topic of their choosing in depth.

- *Formative assessment.* The "Check Your Understanding" quizzes in Flower's class help her hold students accountable for engaging with the preset class materials and the guidance she has provided.

- *Links to key activities.* Flower includes links to the class's weekly discussion, the assignment area where students submit module projects, and the "Lifelong Learning Log" (more on this to come). These links are embedded in the module to make it easier for students to navigate to those places and engage in activities as they're working through the module. The key principle is to make sure students aren't wasting precious time trying to figure out where they're supposed to go to do their work.

- *Summative assessment.* The "Module Questions" assignment in Flower's class represents and upholds her high standards for a graduate-level course. Students write approximately five to eight pages in each module, documenting their engagement with the videos and readings they have completed. (Because students can choose their own adventure, so to speak, a standard test or quiz would be impossible and would not reflect the level of work Flower expects in a graduate course.)

- *Weekly discussion forums.* Weekly discussion forums are the backbone of Flower's CCHE 590, because, as mentioned in Unit 5, peer-to-peer connections build community and increase students' sense of belonging.

- *Module commentary and guidance.* Throughout the course, Flower provides short written guidance to explain how module elements connect with and relate to each other. This practice is critically important. Based on over fifteen years' experience teaching, reviewing, and consulting on asynchronous classes, Flower has concluded that this kind of guidance—this "connective tissue," as one of her primary mentors calls it—is often missing. The result is a module experience that feels transactional, like a to-do list. So before various elements of the module (within reason, so as not to frustrate and overwhelm students), she adds blurbs of one to two sentences. For example, the blurb at the beginning of a module would read, "In this module we'll focus on the life cycle of technology . . . " or "As you work through these materials, ask yourself how what you're learning can help you become a more effective leader. . . . " Before a link to the discussion forum, the blurb would read, "Now that you've completed the readings and videos, let's discuss how these concepts apply at work and at home."

- *Reflection opportunity.* The remaining feature of each module is what Flower calls the Lifelong Learning Log. This is a weekly journal-type activity that encourages reflection and application, and is another way to enhance relevance in this course.

Notice that, like the lesson plan structure, this module template outlines learning objectives, has an introduction, and includes learning activities and mechanisms that check for understanding. For each module, Flower follows the same basic sequence, yet she includes some variety within the structure because, as much as our brains crave structure, we are also wired for novelty.[34] The variety Flower provides might be in the form of two or three additional two-minute videos to illustrate a concept, for example.

If you teach a hybrid course that's partially in person and partially online, use both sets of ideas we've suggested: the lesson plan format to design the in-person component, and the online module elements to make the most of the time students spend learning independently within the LMS. Many faculty who teach hybrid courses have found it helpful to modify Fink's in- and out-of-class template to cultivate the relationship between the in-person and out-of-class components.

2. Add Structure to Existing Activities

This approach entails taking a learning activity you are already using—such as group work, individual writing, or class discussion—and upgrading it by adding specific guidelines, making the activity more likely to reap its intended learning goals. We'll focus on small-group discussions as a concrete example because, particularly in large classes, they can be an excellent learning activity. Sathy and Hogan recognize that these smaller discussions can feel safer to students and can give more students practice engaging with the question or task (vs. the small number of students who raise their hand and respond in a whole-class discussion). "Yet this technique is not as inclusive as it could be," they warn, "if you leave it to chance that the teams will function well (low structure)."[35] Thankfully, Sathy and Hogan provide excellent guidance for adding structure to small-group discussion:

- *Assign and rotate roles.* Students who are at ease in class discussion have a tendency to take over. By assigning and rotating roles, such as reporter, skeptic, or facilitator, you increase the structure and level the playing field a bit so all students have an opportunity to participate.

- *Take time to teach students how to participate in small groups.* Be explicit with students about some of the "rules," such as exchanging names before they get started and putting away their cell phones or laptops.

- *Provide clear instructions on a screen or worksheet.* We've observed many faculty members giving a single oral prompt, but that leaves behind students who have hearing loss, who have learning differences, or who simply need to be reminded about the task at hand.

- *Assign a task to make groups accountable for their work.* For example, have groups submit ideas via a worksheet or a shared online document.

Flower also shares guidance for online discussions. Informed by the Community of Inquiry framework and learning science, she explains that her use of structured online discussions reflects her conviction that people learn from each other in myriad formal and informal ways. Although asynchronous online discussions aren't perfect (they can be stilted, weird, and inauthentic), she still sees them as absolutely necessary in most online classes. How does she structure them? By giving students clear guidelines and carefully worded questions, and by clarifying the role she will play in the discussion. Here are some of the specific principles Flower applies to online discussions:

- *Asking nuanced questions, thought-provoking questions, and multiple questions in each forum.* To promote effective discussion, questions have to be "discussable"—not too black-and-white. Students can respond to one or more as they like.

- *Not requiring scholarly citations* (though you might have a valid reason for doing so). Flower's goal is to replicate in-person discussion, and since she doesn't require each student to spout out a formal citation every time they say something in person, she doesn't require it online, either. This helps to create a more conversational tone, which encourages a trusting and inclusive learning environment.

- *Leaning heavily toward video discussions.* Although Flower uses both written and video discussions, she now uses mostly video discussions to parallel classroom discussions. Since her class focuses on effectively using technology, video-based discussions align pedagogically too. Depending on the topic's context, she gives students the option to write or record their posts in line with UDL guidelines. Other times, and because using technology well is the main focus of the class, she requires recorded videos. Canvas makes it easy to record video posts, and FlipGrid, while not a perfect tool, is fun, easy to use, and in Flower's experience, facilitates the most informal and conversational recordings. Although students often tell her they're nervous about video discussions at first, she consistently explains that their videos don't have to be polished or perfectly executed. (By the end of the term they typically tell her the video discussions were the best part of the class.)
  A word about equity and camera use: seeing each other's faces and surroundings goes a long way to building community and increasing belonging and trust, qualities that are often lacking in asynchronous classes. However, requiring the use of cameras in asynchronous or Zoom classes can lower students' sense of belonging and cause them to feel

excluded—not part of the group—if they don't have a video camera or if there are valid or cultural reasons not to display their face or surroundings. Therefore Flower does not require camera use, although she strongly encourages students to show their faces, just as they would in an in-person class and because video communication is an increasingly important workplace strategy. Consider carefully your camera policy, and consider cocreating this policy with your students, inviting them to partner with you in a trust-building exercise.

With respect to asking specific questions and providing detailed guidance for class discussions, Flower has provided the actual prompt she uses in her course's Module 1:

Interact on Module 1's topics. Address one or more of the following questions (you can choose what you're interested in talking about), or come up with your own topic related to Module 1. Aim for at least 175 words if you're posting a written response, or two minutes if you're recording a video.

- *What qualities do you think workplace or educational leaders need to be successful? Do you have a plan to develop these yourself?*

- *Of the article selections, which did you find particularly interesting? Explain.*

- *What was left out of the overview and foundations module? Can you think of something that should have been included?*

- *What else are you thinking about, related to Module 1 concepts and materials?*

Reply to at least three classmates in a supportive and substantive way that furthers the conversation. We're in this together, so let's respect and value other people's ideas and input. See the Course Schedule document for initial and reply-post deadlines. Sooner is always better. Thanks!

As equity-minded faculty, we craft learning activities that, like the two previous discussion examples, are well structured. We also take responsibility for student learning and use every opportunity to notice and respond to student progress. To read about Bryan's and Flower's roles in these discussions during the semester (including how many student discussion posts Flower responds to), see the case studies in Unit 7.

3. Scaffold Something Sticky

Sticky is not a technical term; rather, it's one we're using to describe a course concept or competency that students struggle with. If you've taught your course before, you may already have a sense of where students get stuck. Or perhaps you want to focus on what's known as a **threshold concept** in your discipline, one that "represents a transformed way of understanding, or interpreting, or viewing something without which the learner cannot progress."[36] Other faculty use mechanisms to identify in real time what's unclear or posing challenges. For instance, Bryan requires that his students spend out-of-class time engaging with new course content. He also requires them to post their questions about the content in an online forum that closes the evening before class. These questions show him what concepts are "sticky," and he updates his plans for the next class session to help students get "unstuck."

How does Bryan get students unstuck? His classroom strategies include a mini-lecture on the concept with built-in opportunities for students to self-assess their understanding. Sometimes, he describes an applied example via a case study or problem set. Often, he relies on students to teach the sticky concepts to one another. By building a process that identifies where students are getting stuck and then devoting class time to helping students bridge the gap between their current level of understanding and the intended one, Bryan is, in essence, scaffolding.

Scaffolds can take many other forms. One common version you might try consists of four steps: First, the instructor explains or models the task. Next, the whole class works on an example together. Third, students work in pairs or groups to practice the skill or discuss the topic. Finally, the individual student is given the opportunity to practice and, ideally, receive feedback. The key purpose of scaffolding is for students to begin learning the concept or task with support and detailed guidance; then, as they develop expertise in the area, they can be asked to complete tasks of similar cognitive complexity with less support.

To scaffold a sticky concept asynchronously, refer to the deliberate module structure Flower described previously, which is inherently a form of scaffolding because it helps students proceed step-by-step through the course without requiring you to be available at all times. Here are three other ways to scaffold challenging tasks online.

Leverage Technology for Immediate Feedback. Feedback on student attempts is critical for learning, and the sooner students receive feedback, the sooner they can act on it. In all modalities, but perhaps especially in asynchronous online courses, we can take advantage of built-in features like the auto-graded quiz tool. With some effort up front you can embed targeted feedback into the responses students see based on whether they answered correctly. Setting these quizzes to allow multiple attempts enables students to learn from mistakes, deepen their

> **threshold concept:**
> A core concept that tends to be conceptually challenging for students yet key to them truly understanding a subject.

learning, and recover valuable points (see Unit 2 on equitable grading). Similarly, work backward from a major assessment so that students have opportunities to, for example, submit concept maps, annotated bibliographies, and early drafts, with ample time to get your feedback before the final product is due.[37]

Schedule a Focused Synchronous Opportunity. If you know a concept is particularly challenging for your online students, consider offering an optional synchronous meeting to engage in a live Q&A (which you record and post for students who couldn't attend). Such meetings can truly lead to those "aha" moments we experience in the classroom. Consider offering these sessions after business hours or on weekends, to demonstrate that you know your asynchronous students are likely working and juggling other important commitments. You might send your students a Doodle poll to identify a day and time that works best for the group (and, again, post a video for later review).

Scaffold the Technology Itself. For some students, using technology for class work can be overwhelming, even technologies that we might think are easy and very intuitive. For example, in early 2021 Flower spoke with a college student who said she and her friends didn't know how to use Zoom at first and wished their professors had provided an orientation after the pandemic caused an abrupt shift to emergency remote teaching. Flower then realized her own daughters had to be shown how to attach a document to an email, and even how and where to save documents to their computers.

We should not expect students to enter our online spaces prepared to use academic and productivity software effectively. Supportive first-week activities that help overcome this sticky point include the following: asking students to submit a simple, low-stakes assignment such as a Word document with one sentence that says, "I have reviewed the activities in the orientation module, and I'm clear about how to get started in the class"; asking students to send you an equally simple course message to demonstrate that they know how to contact you; and taking a syllabus quiz that functions to both orient students to the quiz-taking process and increase accountability for syllabus content. And you can take this technology practice a step further: if your class uses specialized software such as SPSS, or if your students will prepare a video presentation at the end of the term, provide easy, low-stakes tasks that allow students to practice the specialized technology and develop increased self-efficacy. This reduces student anxiety and promotes more equitable learning.

4. Schedule an Intervention (and/or a Shout-Out)

Even if you set a welcoming tone and cultivate trust in an inclusive learning environment, you can't take for granted that students are learning and poised to succeed in your class. Rather than waiting to address a problem like a poor exam grade or limited engagement in class or online activities, equity-minded faculty carefully monitor student progress. Observe both social and cognitive growth—and intervene or celebrate progress early, so that students can either recover (before missing too many points) or be reassured and motivated to keep doing what they're doing. By *scheduling* an intervention or shout-out, we mean deliberately setting aside a moment early in the term during which you will check on students' progress, celebrate their achievements to date, and help any struggling students identify what's causing their challenge and what they will do differently in the subsequent weeks. In the spirit of transparency, you might even include this scheduled check-in on students' course schedule on your syllabus.

Technology can help you identify students who would benefit from a shout-out or intervention. Fortunately, most LMSs include features that can make it easier to check on student progress and reach out to individuals. The information you need is often in the grade center of the LMS. On Canvas, for example, a feature called Message Students Who is included in the contextual menu at the top of each grade center column. Faculty enter performance or submission-related criteria (e.g., "earned 95% or more on a quiz," "haven't yet submitted an assignment that was due 1 day ago") and send a message to students either recognizing their achievement or inviting them to visit tutoring or office (student) hours. Such structured interventions do not necessarily rely on sophisticated technology, however. In Bryan's class, he schedules an "intervention week," typically during the third week of class. (He describes it in Unit 7.)

One last point regarding structure and its benefits to you: Most faculty find that by planning ahead and creating materials to use during the term, they can take better care of themselves, even during the busiest of times. We insist that you be vigilant about your own wellness and emotional sustenance. If the implementation of one of our suggestions were to compromise your emotional or mental health, it would cease to be equity-minded.

HOW CAN I GET STARTED?

For Any Class

- Choose one homework assignment you assign regularly and describe to your students—in writing, orally, and/or in a video—the steps you would take to complete it.

- Identify two points in the term when you'll check your grade sheets or LMS grade center to find out which of your students are struggling. Put those dates on your calendar and then, when the time comes, send those students a note to let them know you noticed and to provide suggestions (including that they meet with you).

- Practice telling students how one of the homework assignments or in-class activities aligns with and helps them work toward one of the course learning objectives.

For In-Person Classes

- Select one class session you've facilitated before that didn't go well, or as well as you would've liked. Use the lesson plan format to brainstorm ideas to improve it.

- Try out one of Sathy and Hogan's suggestions introduced earlier to add structure to a class discussion (i.e., clarifying roles, providing instructions, and building in accountability).

- Add an active learning activity to give students practice with a difficult concept or competency during one of your lectures.

For Asynchronous Online Classes

- Within each module, add quick guidance before and between online elements so students understand the pedagogical purpose of your intentional sequencing and scaffolding of materials and activities.

- Create a "course at a glance" table (see table 6.1).

For Synchronous Online Classes

- Before sending students out into break-out rooms, assign them to roles (e.g., timekeeper, facilitator, reporter), and ask them to produce something together to bring back to the whole class.

7

AN INSIDE LOOK
Examples of an Equity-Minded Online Class and In-Person Classroom

As described in the Introduction, we structured this guide in three segments to replicate the flow of teaching a college course. Section One proposed an equity-minded approach to designing or refining a course before the term, and the previous units of Section Two dove into what happens while you're teaching the class. In Section Three, we will propose what equity-minded faculty do after the term has ended. But before proceeding to those important suggestions, we want to help you picture what faculty committed to equity actually do on a day-to-day basis. To that end, this unit looks very different from all the other units in the guide. There's no "What Does the Research Say?" section, and we don't end with ideas for getting started.

Instead, this entire unit consists of two extended case studies, enabling us to offer a behind-the-scenes view of the day-to-day teaching practices of two of the coauthors, Flower Darby and Bryan Dewsbury, teaching two distinct courses: a small asynchronous graduate-level online course and a large introductory in-person course. Although the case studies do not (and, of course, could not) describe everything either Flower or Bryan does in their teaching, they provide much more specificity than other parts of the guide. We've included these specific examples because faculty have told us time and time again that it's difficult to picture how to implement inclusive teaching. To truly bring these case studies to life, each author has written them in first person.

Flower's case study is based on her extensive online teaching experience as well as her work in instructional design and educational development, and it reflects that she's learned a lot from other compassionate and enthusiastic online instructors. The study highlights one online asynchronous course, CCHE 590: Technological Fluency and Leadership, a course Flower created for a large public regional comprehensive university. The study also includes examples and stories drawn from previous online courses she has taught, designed, consulted on, and been inspired by. We chose to highlight asynchronous online teaching instead of Zoom or hybrid teaching because it looks significantly different than in-person teaching. By weaving together this range of examples and stories (from both faculty and students), Flower demonstrates what she learned through research and experience. She also shows how she took that learning into account to build and teach CCHE 590 in a focused effort to implement evidence-based practices in online course design and teaching. (Spoiler alert: She connects with and interacts with her online students—a lot.)

Meanwhile, Bryan's case study features BIO 101, a large-enrollment introductory biology course he has taught at multiple institutions. Like Flower's online teaching practices, Bryan's approach to inclusive teaching has evolved considerably since his initial experiences teaching an honors section of introductory biology as a graduate student. And a great deal of his growth as an instructor has been informed by deep partnership with faculty and staff colleagues, opportunities to learn with and from faculty from across the country, and importantly, his students: both those who have enrolled in his class over the years and those who support his teaching directly by serving as undergraduate learning assistants and graduate teaching assistants.

You'll find brief references to the equity-focused planning and design that went into each of these classes, but the focus in these case studies is on what the instructors actually *do* when teaching a class. We hope these concrete examples will help you imagine what you can do next week or next semester to advance equity in your own classes. We also hope that reading them prompts you to seek out other ways to pull back the curtain and see other examples of equity-minded teaching in action. Perhaps you can take turns with a colleague to visit one another's class, or ask a peer to enroll you as a guest in their online course. Finally, although these examples come from two very different course contexts, and one may be more familiar to you or more similar to your teaching context, we encourage you to read *both* with an open and inquisitive mind. We hope you will find inspiration in each to make small changes to your teaching, no matter your institutional, disciplinary, and modality contexts.

How Do I, Flower Darby, Teach My Asynchronous Online Class?

A Few Considerations before I Start

Before I describe this class and my daily practices to advance equity online, it's important to acknowledge a few things in brief. First, I didn't always teach online in this way; what follows is an evolution of much that took place by trial and error in my earlier years of online teaching. Second, I am on my own personal equity journey. Through various life and professional experiences, I've committed to progressing toward equity-focused teaching and to helping others do the same (hence, humbly and gratefully accepting the invitation to coauthor this guide). This case study is not a perfect example; it is an honest account of a work in progress. At the end of my case study I'll share what I would add, change, and do differently to further advance equity in this and future online classes.

Third, and of critical importance: the approach I describe may feel overwhelming to some of you, especially if you're new to the idea of prioritizing interactions with online students. (You can't be blamed for feeling this way; many instructors, through no fault of their own, begin teaching online with inadequate preparation and support.) Let me be clear: self-care is most important, and so is advocacy for systemic change. You'll find these two themes throughout this guide; let me unpack them a bit in the context of my case study.

Just as you may not have had adequate preparation to teach effective and equity-minded online courses, your departmental and institutional leadership may not have had adequate preparation for administering online courses and programs. In my experience, there is a widespread belief that online enrollments are financially beneficial. There is also a widespread lack of recognition of the time and energy it takes to teach well online. So, a special reminder here: As we state elsewhere in this guide, if any practice we describe depletes you or otherwise detracts from your holistic well-being, don't implement it. And don't feel you need to make lots of changes all at once. Small steps enable long-term progress on your equity journey, and the practices I describe in the following pages result from fifteen years of online teaching and a combined total of twenty-six years teaching college courses. Give yourself grace to make incremental changes as you proceed along your personal teaching journey. While doing so, collaborate with your colleagues near and far to advocate for broader recognition of the time and effort it takes to teach well. All of us need a community to support us and whom we can support. Meaningful change won't happen unless we are all pulling in the same direction.

With that, let's dive into what a typical online teaching semester looks like for me.

Right before the Semester Begins

My Technological Fluency and Leadership online class is about how to use technology well in the workplace and in life in general. It's the evolution of what used to be an Educational Technology class. With appropriate committee approval, I expanded the curriculum beyond teaching with technology to apply in every workplace setting, because about 50 percent of students taking this class aren't teachers and never will be. After extensive revision, the focus is on the intentional selection and use of technology no matter where you work (think: mobile apps, productivity software like Microsoft Office or Google Suite, video conferencing systems like Zoom, specialized software such as project management websites, *and* classroom and online tech to support teaching and learning). And because tech pervades our everyday life, I further expanded the focus to include purposeful integration of solutions-oriented technology in home life and in community engagement (like in volunteering roles) as well.

The course is a requirement for a few different master's of education programs and an elective option for many other master's programs at this university. As such, it attracts a wide range of students, most of whom are working professionals, parents, engaged community members, and generally very busy people. Students in this class are usually seeking career change or advancement. It's a small class, capped at twenty-five, and I've gotten to know hundreds of students over the seven years I've taught it. Many students tell me they fear this class and feel like they'll be out of their league when it comes to technology. I believe that while this fear is misguided—we discuss everyday tech; it's not a computer science or coding class—the fear is real. It's real for my students, and I know fear and anxiety shut down learning, so I intentionally address it up front.

I work hard to both normalize and mitigate the anxiety that many students feel even before Day 1. One week prior to the first day of class, I email students, sending them the syllabus and a two-minute video. In this recorded greeting, I talk directly to—and make strong eye contact with—the camera (this helps students feel that I am looking at them, so they feel *seen*, which is very important in equity-focused courses). I make a deliberate effort to express warmth, friendliness, enthusiasm for the course and semester ahead, encouragement, authenticity, and approachability. In this way I begin working to reduce student anxiety, establish trust, extend belonging, and invite relationships even before we start.

In my welcome email, I also extend a sincere invitation to reach out with any questions, and lately I've started including my personal phone number so students can call or text if they prefer. These early approaches are based on two of Michelle Pacansky-Brock's recommendations.[1] First, take advantage of the "high opportunity engagement zone" in the run-up to the class start date, during which time online students may experience high anxiety about what their class experience will be like and about what their instructor will be like. Second, invite students to use their cell phones to engage with class materials and with you. Students of color may have consistent access to their smartphones but be less likely than their White peers to have easy access to a laptop, Pacansky-Brock argues, so empowering students to engage on their phones can be a practical way to level the playing field in classes of all modalities.

Worried about a potential flood of reply emails and texts? That hasn't been my experience, nor that of psychologist and teaching with technology scholar Michelle Miller.[2] Rather, this welcome email and the invitation to text set the tone for a caring, relationship-based online learning experience that helps to set students' minds at ease.

In addition to the initial welcome email, I do a few other quick but important things to help my students feel like I am present with them in the room as soon as they click into class for the first time. Let me explain. When students first click into an asynchronous online class, it can feel lonely. It's like walking into an empty classroom with the lights off and a stack of syllabi left on the table.[3] Anxious students may feel unwelcome and unsupported by the very nature of an asynchronous class. To counter these feelings, I complete a few tasks in class so students feel like I'm there with them (even though I'm probably not at the exact moment they are):

- **I post my video introduction in the "Introductions" discussion forum.** I want my greeting to be there as soon as students log in, and I model the kind of relational approach I want students to take. In the "Introductions" forum, I prompt students to post one of their own. My prompts have varied over the years, but they all feature an invitation to students to share something about themselves—academically, professionally, and if desired, something about themselves personally, including their pronouns and their preferred name—to help build connections among the people in the class. Because my goal is to model and encourage authenticity in our newly forming online community, I never post the same introduction twice. One semester, in a moment when I was feeling particularly playful, I posted two pics from my smartphone library: one photo of me making a silly expression in a selfie I snapped for my childhood best friend, and one photo of my daughter, eight months old when I took it, making the *exact same* expression (except looking much cuter, of course). I'd never posted anything quite so goofy before, but I felt inspired to do so that time. The result? I've never seen such a lively and real response from my online students. They followed my lead and posted silly pics of their pets, creative Halloween costumes, and many other personality-revealing things—which laid a strong foundation of trust, belonging, and inclusivity in our class community. More on this foundation later in the case study, but for now I'll say that posting these silly pictures is an example of the efforts I make to help my online students get to know me.

- **I write or record an announcement (new and unique every semester) that is prescheduled to go out on the morning of the first day of class.** Yes, I've already sent a welcome email and video, and I've already posted my introduction in our forum. But I would rather over-communicate than under-communicate, to combat feelings of isolation and uncertainty experienced by online students. I write (or record) this announcement, like all of my communications, with a deliberate effort to be enthusiastic, warm, and encouraging—and to provide helpful information. Like I do with my introduction post, I create a fresh announcement every semester. Students can smell a canned response a mile off. One even told me he disregards obviously canned assignment comments like he does a phishing email. Plus, I'm a different person every time I get ready to teach. Right? You wouldn't read from a script on Day 1 in your in-person class, would you? You may follow an established lesson plan or list of talking points, but you also flex in the moment and improvise and respond to the people in front of you. I suggest you do the same online.

- **I triple-check my course at a glance table, assignment due dates, that I have the correct syllabus linked or uploaded, and other logistical and technical details.** Do I therefore have a perfectly accurate, updated, functioning online course? Nope. It's almost impossible to achieve that level of perfection, given how much material appears in writing and via links in a well-developed online class. But I sure do try. And I tell my students they'll earn extra-credit points (and public praise) when (not if) they find typos, inaccurate dates, broken links, or other errors and notify me so I can correct them. (See Unit 6 for more about course setup.)

- **I review my "About Me" course page (you may have an "All About Me" video) to update photos or text as needed.** Focusing on relationships is a key part of my online teaching practice. Helping my students get to know me as a real person is a critical first step. Since I'm a different person every time I teach a class, even one I've taught before, I take a few minutes to update my "About Flower Darby" biography (which includes professional information and personal components such as information about my family and my hobbies) and the photos on the page (including a professional headshot and also casual pictures of me in settings that convey things about who I am as a person).

- **I review my "Getting to Know You" survey to make sure I still like the existing questions and add or replace questions as needed.** This survey asks students for basic demographic information and invites students to share other things about themselves that take the relationship to a slightly deeper level, as recommended in Unit 4. For example, I've asked students if there's anything they're concerned about with this class, which shows that I care about them and also helps me respond empathetically if challenges arise. One semester a student told me she was seven months pregnant and had enrolled in my eight-week class thinking she'd be able to finish before the baby arrived. But the previous week her doctor had told her she may have to go on bed rest, so she worried about how this situation might play out. Knowing this information in advance helped me reassure her that I'd work with her to facilitate her completion of the class, and sure enough, she did so just fine. I also ask my students values affirmation questions such as what strengths they're bringing to the group, what challenge they have overcome, or what accomplishment they're particularly proud of. These types of questions, to which answers are never required, can help students feel confident in their ability to succeed.

- **I open the entire course in read-only mode a few days ahead of the actual start date.** (Your IT help desk may be able to do this for you, too.) Giving students access to get into the course and nose around, to see what to expect and how to plan their time, can be an impactful way to build trust and extend belonging. Talk about transparency and alleviating anxiety! Students can't do anything before Day 1—they don't post an introduction, take a quiz, or otherwise start the class. At this point the course is truly read-only, and all modules are open in that state. Opinions vary on whether to open all modules before a term begins, but I firmly believe that doing so is an inclusive practice, given how complex students' lives are. Note: opening the course in this way requires that I am ready for class *before* the start date, which has often been a stretch for me. But it's a compassionate and effective way to demonstrate pedagogical care for students and thereby build trust. So I make every effort to provide early access.

- **I go into my calendar and block off abundant time for interacting with students during the first day and week of class.** I'll explain in the upcoming "During a Regular Week" section more about my weekly cadence for class interaction, but for now, I'll share that I frontload lots of time for my online students in Week 1, reprioritizing and postponing other standing commitments and tasks in order to do so. It's important to me to start off strong and to foster trust in a meaningful way through my presence and interactions in class. So I intentionally protect time in Week 1, and especially on Day 1, to do so.

Having done everything I can before Day 1 to "greet students at the door," I feel satisfied that students will experience welcome and feel valued the minute they click into class.

On Day 1

Because I deliberately arranged my schedule to have extra time for my new students, I now spend that time productively, forming connections and building relationships, both of which are key to establishing trust and extending belonging. I want my students to know that I'm actively engaged and ready to be with them—more, that I *want* to be with them. Students have told me repeatedly (and have expressed on social media) that online teachers aren't real; these students include my own daughters, who felt this way after their mixed experiences taking asynchronous online classes during COVID-19. So I show up—a lot. To demonstrate that I'm real and I'm here and I'm engaged. And that I like them. And I want them to succeed.

On Day 1, I log into class as soon as I reasonably can, sometimes even at 6:30 a.m. while having coffee—at least to check if anyone is in there yet, posting their introduction or a question in the "Questions About the Class or Assignments" forum. I even like to look at who has logged in (there's a record you can see in varying locations depending on what LMS you're teaching in). I continue to log in frequently throughout the day. I reply to every single student's introduction. To be clear, I do not continue this practice of replying to every student in subsequent discussions. But doing so here is a way of "looking" directly at students, at seeing them, so I make sure every person gets an individualized response.[4]

In my Tech Fluency class, because it's about effectively using technology at work, I ask my students to record a video introducing themselves. I used to require them to show their faces, but after one student belatedly confided in me that she posted a photo and a written introduction instead of the video because of temporary markings on her face, I stopped requiring this. I still highly encourage it; even pre-pandemic I felt that becoming more comfortable on video is an important competency for today's workplace (for example, for job interviews and meetings). But students can opt out with a short explanation they provide to me before they post. (For more on camera use in online classes, see Unit 6.)

I also reply to emails, as well as to texts or calls, throughout the day. I answer any questions in the Q&A forum. Although I step away to do other regular daily tasks, I keep going in all day long to demonstrate my presence. (Side note: this involves publicly visible activity such as discussion posts and announcements in addition to private communications such as email or assignment comments.[5])

On Day 3

On Day 3, I specifically check to see who *hasn't* logged in yet. I reach out to each student to encourage them to do so if they plan to take the class so they don't fall behind, and to let me know if they're having challenges or if they have any questions. Though it sounds like reaching out takes a lot of time, it truly doesn't. I write an individual email to each person who hasn't yet logged in (it's typically a tiny fraction of the class, maybe two or three students). I address the email to them personally, making sure to spell their name correctly, then paste the rest of the email text and send the message. Students who received this email have told me they feel cared for, and certainly a personal message from the instructor is highly motivating to students.

Note: addressing students by name is an important practice to help students feel seen in asynchronous classes. Names are a key part of our identities. And it's critically important to spell them correctly (and to pronounce them correctly if you're recording feedback or meeting by phone or Zoom). My student Flor told me it really makes her mad and that she feels marginalized when professors call her Flora: "That's not my name," she told me. "There's only four letters. Why can't they get it right?" Using a tool like namecoach.com, which allows people to record themselves pronouncing their name, can help establish an inclusive environment and foster trust and belonging.

During a Regular Week (after Week 1)

I work hard to be in class and visibly engaged a lot in Week 1, but that's not sustainable for the entire course. In a typical week, here's what I do:

- **I log in on multiple days** to post publicly (discussion replies and announcements) and correspond individually with students (email and assignment feedback). The number of days I log in depends on the length of the session. In an eight-week session, logging in to class around four days per week feels sufficient. We faculty have to remember to protect our time and boundaries so we can meaningfully engage with students. But when I teach this class in a four-week session, I try to log in six days per week because of how condensed and fast-paced the course is. No matter the duration, I always log in on one weekend day, usually Saturday. Online students tend to do a lot of classwork on weekends. Me showing up on that day is respectful of their commitment to succeed despite their busy lives.

- **I aim to reply to email within one business day**, on the same day when possible. I aim to return assignments with feedback within two to four weekdays, depending on the length of the session. And I tell my students these things in my syllabus and in announcements to strengthen this message, because it's important to me that my students know that I'm here for them and when I'm available. I tell them that I'm generally not online after 6 p.m. and that I protect Sundays for my family. If I happen to respond during a time I've said I'm offline, that's a bonus, but my students know that if they email me Saturday evening it will be Monday morning before they hear back from me, thus adding transparency in my availability and communication.

- **If at all possible, I respond in the moment to texts I get on my personal phone.** It's important to protect my boundaries, but I also know that my quick answer will enable my student to make progress during the time they've set aside for classwork. Students are truly so grateful, and it prevents a backlog of email, as Michelle Miller has also pointed out, so it feels both compassionate and efficient.[6]

- **I engage in quick and informal communications** in varying forms, again, to demonstrate to my students that I'm there and I'm thinking about them. I love recording very informal smartphone videos and, over time, have developed a level of comfort with just how casual these can be. One online teacher I know records ninety-second video announcements while filling up her car with gas. Another greets her students from the trail where she's walking her dog. Another records herself when she goes to a Día de los Muertos festival, for example, showing her students displays of sugar skulls. The point? Take your students with you. Let them into your life a bit, where you feel comfortable and safe doing so. Reduce the distance online. Help them see you as a real person. As online teaching scholar Karen Costa has written, online students don't expect Hollywood-level video production.[7] They want to see *you*—the same way they would if in your in-person class. Let them see you, or, if you have valid reasons for minimizing images of yourself, let them learn more about who you are as a person. My introverted husband Tim, for example, shares photos of tabletop war-game miniatures he's assembled and painted, rather than always putting his face in front of his students.

One other way I engage informally and in the moment is by creating a Discord server: a private space in an app where invited members can post text, voice, and video chats. Other instructors use a Slack channel to accomplish the same goal. Educational developer Maha Bali calls such online spaces the third place, an informal place to hang out with students and where they can connect with each other.[8] I like the ease of group communication on my phone or laptop, but I've also learned that adding a tech tool that requires a separate account or log-in can raise barriers for some students and present data security and privacy concerns, so I think carefully about using an external app. In a class like Tech Fluency, however, it may be somewhat justifiable since our focus is on the use of tech to solve problems (in this case, the lack of real-time interaction in asynchronous classes).

- **I let my students see the real me—a lot.** Throughout the class (and from before Day 1, in my welcome email and video greeting) I do many different things to help my students get to know me, as we discuss in Unit 4. I write announcements and discussion posts in my "real-person" (not distant or authoritative instructor) voice. I post silly pictures of my cats. I post before and after pics of home projects that take me offline for a few days (which I announce in advance). During COVID, I told my students that I was struggling with the severe illness and eventual death of the man I consider to be my second father. I tell my students when my daughter's health crisis is eating into the time I usually grade, as well as my plan for catching up on grading. In short, I tell (and show) my students a lot about my life—not everything, but a lot more than I did earlier in my online teaching career. As an example, I used to record formal mini-videos, dressed professionally, seated in my campus office, and generally looking pulled together and authoritative. I still record videos like these, but now I'm much more comfortable recording videos when I'm not so pulled together, like when I'm grading papers on my treadmill desk and want to share general feedback with my students—they see me red-faced, sweaty, and authentic.

I do all these things, including helping my students get to know the real me, because interacting with and communicating with my online students is top priority. This is where I do what we recommend in Units 4 and 5: that is, extend belonging, form relationships, and foster trust. As part of this commitment, I am very transparent with my students about when I need to be absent from class for a few days, informing them that something has come up (I choose to share varying levels of detail depending on the circumstances—this works for both planned and unplanned absences) and when I will be back in class and available for them. When we acknowledge that we are only human and that life happens for us too, students feel more trusting that we'll be empathetic when they need flexibility.

- **I model authenticity** to build trust in my own video discussions and announcements, being very transparent and posting a video with foibles or tongue-trips or when I've lost my thought for a moment (after which I'll typically make a goofy expression and pick up where I left off). In one case a student posted her introduction video even though halfway through her cat had knocked over the plant behind her. I publicly praised her for bringing her genuine self—and this helps everyone relax and feel more at ease both with each other and with technology, thereby accomplishing two pedagogically driven goals at once.

- **I stay in the weekly discussions with my students.** Although I don't reply to every student, I do reply, ideally on at least three to five separate days. Some practitioners argue that the instructor can dominate or shut down the conversation, so they shouldn't post at all, but I disagree. After all, would you launch a classroom discussion and then turn around and walk out the door? No. I stay in the discussion, posting strategically where I can make the most impact—for example, by asking guiding questions, praising contributions, taking advantage of teachable moments that arise, gently pushing students for more, or suggesting additional resources. In fact, I tell my students that if they see me posting in the discussion, they should read or watch it, because that's me teaching. I also rotate who I respond to in each module. I keep track on a simple piece of paper that stays on my desk while class is in session. Other instructors I know use a spreadsheet to ensure they reply to every student on a rotating basis. This kind of intentionality characterizes equity-focused online teaching. Like the use of a rubric to minimize subjectivity in grading (see Unit 2), using a tool helps ensure that are we consistently and fairly responding to each student.

- **I use a simple version of Linda Nilson's specifications grading** to streamline grading of discussions and to reduce students' focus on and anxiety about grades.[9] All discussions in CCHE 590 are eligible to earn all five points or zero points based on whether the post meets my detailed specifications for success. A simple one-row rubric allows me to evaluate and grade points extremely quickly—and I add a quick personal comment in addition to clicking the appropriate rubric column.

Toward the end of the class, students routinely tell me this class has been their most engaging one to date. Engagement precedes learning, so keeping online students engaged is a major focus of my equity-focused online teaching practice.

Last but by no means least, I maintain a Change Log throughout the duration of the class. I find that while teaching—based on interactions I have with my students, materials, and assignments—I can identify improvements I want to make next time. But it's hard to remember what those were once the class has ended and I have time to reflect on possible changes. My Change Log helps me gather and record data while teaching so that I can go back and reflect on it after the semester, in line with our recommendations in Unit 9.

Before the First Project

Because online students can feel challenged by the inability to raise a hand in a physical class or stay after class to ask a question, I go to great lengths, both in the course design and in my teaching, to set them up for success. I do this especially on the first major project because they don't know what to expect. CCHE 590 has three medium-sized projects instead of one cumulative or final assessment. Performing poorly on the first one won't sink students' grade, because in keeping with the equity-minded grading principles in Unit 2, weekly discussions (low-stakes assessments that also encourage exploration of, interaction with, and application of course concepts) are worth an equal percentage of the final grade. But still, students experience anxiety in direct relationship to the weight of an assessment, so to alleviate that and foster deep learning, I TILT my instructions (refer to Unit 2), recording videos to explain the purpose and task of the assignment—and how to succeed. As the project due date approaches, I make an extra effort to quickly respond to student questions or hop on a call if needed. It's amazing how much can be accomplished in a five-minute call, and as I mentioned earlier, since this quick clarification often results in better student work, it both shows compassion and saves me time when grading.

In short, my goal is to do everything I can to equip students for success as they approach the first graded assessment worth a significant percentage of their final grade.

After the First Project

As we mentioned in Unit 2, the unique moment following the first major assessment represents a specific opportunity to engage with students based on their performance. Steps I take when evaluating and working with students in this moment:

- **Devoting adequate time to truly read or watch students' submissions.** Online students frequently tell me that they feel like their instructors don't even look at their work, likely because of obviously canned comments with no attention to the individual student, which contributes to online students' feelings of not being seen and not mattering in class.

- **Taking time to provide feedback in supportive ways.** I praise strengths and offer suggestions for what they can do better next time. I write or record comments with a deliberate focus on coming across as a real person, someone who genuinely cares about their success. This helps to sustain trust, which as we noted in Unit 4, is critically important online.

- **Reminding students** (either the whole class by sending an announcement or an individual student in private feedback) that they can use one of their three Oops Tokens to revise and resubmit, no questions asked (other instructors call these NQA passes). This is another element of Nilson's specifications grading, and it allows me to hold students to the highest standards while also offering flexibility and empathy. As discussed in Unit 2, grading schemes and policies that encourage students to learn from mistakes and resubmit work are equity-focused. Offering Oops Tokens is my application of this principle.

As we saw in Unit 3, compassionate and equity-focused grading schemes and practices demonstrate care for the whole person. And because of their prior educational experiences, it's likely that our students may be hyper-focused on their performance as reflected in the grade we assign. (Recall from Unit 4 that students told us grades signal their *academic* belonging, which impacts their broader sense of belonging.) Taking the time to offer feedback and support that are both considerate and helpful is a key way to respect our students' sensitivity and validate their belonging at this pivotal moment.

Approaching the Finish Line and Requests for Deadline Extensions

Because I know that students who choose online courses and programs often do so because of the flexibility of the asynchronous modality, I anticipate requests for deadline extensions at any point of the semester. These requests may increase as we near the end of the course. To account for individual learner variability as well as the complexity of students' lives, I carefully think through and explicitly state my late-work policy. I include this policy in the syllabus, and I remind students about it through written and recorded announcements when we're almost to the end of the semester.

Although I used to be firm on deadlines, permitting no exceptions, I've softened on this point as I've progressed on my equity journey. On the other hand, it does not serve my students well to have too much flexibility, as I learned in fall of 2021 when I announced that all deadlines came with an automatic five-day grace period. Many students floundered with that approach, falling further and further behind as a likely result of my possibly too-empathetic policy. Structure with some flexibility, and explicitly stated flexibility, provides the most supportive and equity-focused approach, as other teaching and learning scholars have reminded us. So I have deadlines; I have wiggle room in the form of the three Oops Tokens students get, to be used for deadline extensions or resubmissions; and I have accountability and reward built in, as well. If students don't use any Oops Tokens, they receive extra credit—my way of encouraging them to meet deadlines if possible.

This combination of deadlines and limited opportunities to submit work late promotes learning and progression yet recognizes that life happens. Offering these options right up front does three things. First, it demonstrates to students that I'm a real person and I see them as real people living complicated lives—again, building trust and belonging. Second, it accords a degree of privacy and respect to students: the Oops Tokens mean that I don't need to get into personal details when life circumstances conspire against students' ability to progress in class. Third, it acknowledges that even asking for a deadline extension is a privilege, so I normalize the opportunity to request extensions when needed. Finally, there are always exceptions, so I've become willing to talk with students about unusual requests. I much prefer talking by phone rather than by email about their circumstances. Because we can communicate in rich and nuanced ways when speaking, using tone of voice in addition to words, I can relate more effectively with my students that way. Further, a phone call is simpler relative to Zoom. To protect my time and boundaries as an act of self-care, I reserve phone calls for individual cases to determine what additional scheduling or other accommodation I can manage. Sometimes I can't reconcile the request with my principles—see the following section about activities that take place after the semester ends, for example. But in general I find this blend of structure, accountability, and flexibility best supports equitable learning outcomes in my asynchronous classes.

After the Semester Ends

Wrapping up an online class is not vastly different than an in-person one, but I have noticed in my online classes more requests to submit work after the official last day. Once, for example, I received an email from a student who never logged into class—not one time while class was in session, despite multiple check-ins from me. Two days after the term ended, he asked for the opportunity to complete all work in one week. I wrestled with this request, trying to decide whether accommodating him was equity-minded, because holding our students up to our standards is also an equity-focused practice. Eventually I declined. Other times, based on varying circumstances, I've extended more grace and accepted work after the last day. These requests don't tend to happen when I teach in person, leading me to believe that fully online students' lives really are more complex, yet I truly want my students to achieve equitable outcomes. A delicate balance must be struck, sometimes on a case-by-case basis.

Otherwise, once an online class concludes, I enact strategies of the kind you will find in Units 8 and 9, so the following list is something of a preview. Here are several things I do after the semester concludes:

- Review any late work I agreed to accept.
- Respond to individual emailed questions.
- Calculate grades and submit them using the official process.
- Send an announcement to students once final grades are posted and available in class (this typically happens before they'll see them in official registrar systems).
- Reflect on my personal sense of what went well and what I can do to foster more equitable outcomes, making appropriate notes and listing tasks in my Change Log—I maintain the log in a Word document throughout the semester and revisit it once the class has ended.
- Review my student evaluation of teaching results, applying the ideas we describe in Unit 8 to use this data source.
- Engage in overarching critical reflection, asking myself what I learned in this class from these students, and how I might therefore better support my future students in future classes.

This list appears in roughly sequential order, but of course these activities take place in less linear ways, too. I've found that, for me, seeing the bigger picture and practicing more effective critical reflection happen through two channels: (1) mind-wandering when doing something else (like working on chores or walking around campus) and (2) conversations with my best instructional designer and online teaching colleague, my husband, and with the students closest to me, my three teenage daughters (all of whom took online classes during COVID-19).

Flower's Concluding Thoughts

Though I came to many of the teaching practices described previously simply because they seemed like good pedagogy, I've since realized many are indeed equity-focused strategies—and this course is still a work in progress. Having worked on this guide, I now see how I could enhance relevance and culturally responsive elements in the course. For example, I would add materials and assignments that prompt students to explore sites of inequity in topics related to technology based on the work of leading scholars in this area. Such topics might include digital redlining, which describes restrictions on access to technology and websites experienced in some communities; how online proctoring software disadvantages students of color, neurodiverse students, and students with physical and learning disabilities; inequitable allocation of technological infrastructure and funding in various communities; practices that perpetuate injustice in the software engineering and development; and surveillance capitalism, to name a few.

I would also add a few course components to share power with students, amplify student voice, and more explicitly assess students' sense of belonging in my class. I would administer a belonging survey and reflect on students' submissions both in the moment and when planning my next class. I love coauthor Mays Imad's simple yet powerful question (which we write about in Unit 8): "What am I (or others in the class) doing that is making you feel excluded?" I would incorporate this question in an anonymous one-question survey. To prepare students, I'd record a short video that explains the importance of helping everyone feel included and welcome in class, then provide a link to a survey with that one, powerful question. I'd reflect in the moment, share back to the class what changes I intend to make in my own communication or practices, and invite students to help me be accountable to this commitment to do things differently. I'd adjust the class the next time I teach it to incorporate what I learned by talking with and hearing from my students (even asynchronously). This and other revisions to both the course and my practice may advance me on my equity journey and support equitable outcomes for my students, too. Would I do all of these things at once? Maybe not, as I seek to follow our "small teaching" advice to start small. But I would keep track of these adjustments in my Change Log and systematically alter my approach step by step.

How Do I, Bryan Dewsbury, Teach My Large, In-Person Class?

A Few Considerations before I Start

Like many people in the sciences, I was advised against spending any real time on teaching when I was a graduate student. It was the grace afforded to me by the mostly first-generation college students I taught in one of my first classes as a TA that ushered in my love of teaching. Since then, I have considered myself to be on a delightfully never-ending journey. What that means is that I never consider myself to be a perfect equity-minded instructor, nor do I think of my course as the perfectly designed equity-minded course. I approach my course design with humility, staying attuned to what the collected data surrounding the course are telling me is working for the students and what is not. Over the years, I have had to learn some tough lessons pertaining to implicit biases I held.

I have also come to realize that teaching has more in common with UPS than most of us would imagine. Let me explain: If you ask most people what the primary function of the United Parcel Service (UPS) is, they will likely say "to deliver packages." After all, the word *parcel* is in the company name. Plus, most of us probably picture brown vans operated by people dressed in brown clothing transporting cardboard boxes (also brown) to a building's front door. However, UPS might be more accurately described as a logistics company, whose main function is to optimize supply chain complexities in order to move goods and services from sites of production to consumers. A significant percentage of the company's bandwidth goes into solving this optimization challenge.

While teaching a college class differs considerably from delivering parcels, our time and human bandwidth are equally constrained. Therefore, I have learned how to pay careful attention to optimizing my limited time and resources to make my equity-minded teaching work. In the following case study, I provide specific examples of the considerations I make when teaching a large introductory biology course. My goal is to show how context informs the decisions I make about course content, structure, approach, and delivery. I describe my practice not as a blueprint plan to be replicated verbatim but rather as a process, the finer points of which you can adapt for your unique environment. In the spirit of open pedagogy, my approaches and specific techniques are open to be remixed and reused for your own context. I consider all of my approaches a work in progress in that I am always looking for ways to make each and every aspect of the course more beautiful and equity-minded—and I invite you to join me in this ongoing experiment. The course I describe was taught at my most recent institution (I moved in 2021). I continue to teach the same course at my new one, but I reflect here on seven years of implementing equity-minded practices.

Right before the Semester Begins

My section of this introductory biology course is relatively highly enrolled (155 students), with the majority of students coming directly from high school. Most of the students are biology or life science majors, with a very small percentage taking the course for a general education science requirement. The institution is a large, public, research university in the northeastern United States. Most of the students who attend the university matriculate from northeastern U.S. regions, with about half of the student body matriculating from the same state the institution is in. About 75 percent of the students identify as White, 11 percent as Black, and 12 percent as Hispanic, with the remainder either identifying as Asian, Native American, two or more races, or choosing not to report their ethnicity. My introductory biology classroom largely follows this same demographic spread.

The course is the first in a two-semester sequence of introductory biology. The first semester (which this case study describes) focuses on molecular biology, cell biology, and a brief overview of anatomy and physiology. The second semester focuses on ecology and evolutionary biology. Students who are in the two-semester sequence must attain a C or above (considered a productive grade) to be allowed to take the second course in the sequence. The course is taught in a traditionally structured sloping lecture hall that encourages permanent front-facing during class, but as I will describe, I use several strategies to encourage and maintain interactivity.

Another important contextual point is that I don't usually teach alone. I have the privilege of hiring both a graduate-student teaching assistant (TA) and undergraduates, students who have previously taken the course and serve as learning assistants (known as LAs).[10] In a typical term, I work with four LAs and one TA. As I'll describe later, each of these wonderful individuals plays an important role in ensuring that the pedagogy in the course constantly attends to equity-mindedness. Many high-enrollment courses use graduate TAs in ways similar to how I described the LA model, yet my TA plays a distinctive role. Given the LA model and because the TA is available to support me for only five hours per week, my TA focuses on course management and grading and has little interaction with students. In this model, the TA is a data manager who understands the inner workings of the LMS and/or courseware so that the various forms of assessments, activities, and feedback mechanisms are clear and unambiguous for the student navigating the platform. An added benefit for me is that, at any given moment, the TA can let me know how a given student is doing not just in general terms but also in relation to specific topics and learning objectives.

Because I have taught the class before, taken notes on where students are getting stuck, and collected data on student success, **I research alternative ways to introduce my students to the most challenging course topics**. Common sources for new ideas include the National Center of Case Study Teaching in Science (NCCSTS) and the Science Education Resource Center

(SERC) at Carleton College.[11] Sometimes, ideas for new approaches come from colleagues who have disciplinary expertise in the topic area or who teach that particular topic as an elective upper-division course. Either way, in response to suggestions or new ideas, I spend several days reconfiguring learning outcomes, activities, and assessments for that topic and soliciting advice from previous (and upcoming) learning assistants on how they viewed the learning experience associated with that topic when they were students.

For example (and without getting too deep into the gritty details), the topic of *meiosis* can be challenging to teach. The meanings of certain labels like *chromosomes* and *chromosomal pairs* are not always obvious to students. The students' responses on some of the exams suggest that I may not have been successful in getting them to understand the differences between the terms. Before the semester begins, I spend time identifying new ways to have the meiosis conversation without confusing them. In other words, while I accept that students can always be more effective with their study strategies, I also assume some of the responsibility in my pedagogy, particularly on tricky topics.

I also use this time to reflect on and make changes to the affective components of the course—that is, how students feel and develop during their time in my class. In this context, I use data from end-of-semester reflections, student evaluations of teaching, and feedback from the learning assistants to try to understand how effective I was in creating a sense of community in the previous iteration of the course. My learning assistants are crucial in this process because they can often identify things that are happening nearer to the students' individual experience that I may not as quickly perceive, even in an active learning dynamic course. During this time, difficult conversations and reflections are necessary because it is possible that my well-intentioned approaches didn't work as planned. I use this opportunity to think carefully about how I gave students feedback, how I attended to representation in the curriculum, how I constructed and supported difficult dialogues, and the extent to which my teaching took into account students' outside-of-classroom realities.

In addition, I take the following specific steps to improve my course:

- **I fine-tune my day-to-day course plans.** As a result of the pre-term reflection I've described, I often decide to change student (office) hours times, adjust group work and peer feedback processes, and/or restructure the intervention week (more on that to come). Once I determine which parts of the class to revise, I take the time to identify the corresponding changes in the in- and out-of-class template I use for day-to-day planning (see figure 6.1). For example, if I realize that a particular topic needs more formative assessments (like low-stake quizzes or writing assignments), then examining the template helps me identify where and when to provide students with the additional opportunities, and which other activities I'll need to adjust as a result.

As a case in point, students tend to struggle a bit with the physics topics like thermodynamics that we discuss to help understand biological systems. If I realize that such a topic needs more attention, I will invest in a different explanation approach and give students more time to write answers to questions on the subject.

I call this stage *semi-finalization* because it is important to me not to make the final course plan too inflexible, since what I learn about the students closer to the course's beginning, and during its evolution, must allow for some flexibility in how the course unfolds. What I find useful in this scenario is to have a few options available for each learning activity and assessment, so that if conditions on the ground require different approaches, I have options available.

- **I compile students' exam schedules by talking to other instructors.** It is useful for me to have a sense of the summative exam schedule of other courses, notably other STEM courses. Though taking summative assessments will be a relatively expected part of the students' college experience, lack of communication between instructors can result in students having multiple high-stakes exams on the same Friday. Assuming that the assessments' purpose is to gather information about cognitive progress and not to evaluate the students' response to extreme conditions, I find it well worth the effort to coordinate with my colleagues in chemistry, mathematics, and other disciplines to ensure that the students' overall assessment schedule allows them reasonable time to prepare for their exams.

- **I double-check external support structures to ensure they are available and functional.** Several students every semester require disability-related accommodations, and the institution has specially designated offices to provide those accommodations. These may include, but are not necessarily limited to, extra time on exams, taking exams in separate spaces, and allowing for note takers in the classroom. Liaising with these offices includes knowing things like (1) the deadline to research rooms for separate exams, (2) a revisiting of the procedure for exam drop-off and pick-up, and (3) general conversations on best strategies for ensuring the course's material and technology are accessibility compliant. Classroom technology should also be double-checked to ensure that it is UDL compliant.

- **I check the curriculum for alignment and excess content.** Although I have carefully designed the class such that the learning objectives, assessments, and activities are aligned, I still take the time to review the fidelity between what I ask of students outside of the classroom in preparation for the classroom experience, the stated learning outcomes of the course, and the realities of the students' lives on the ground. For STEM disciplines, the learning outcomes are sometimes dictated by an a priori agreed-upon textbook, whose sequence of content and comprehensive coverage can bias the instructor into a similar extent of coverage.[12] Here again I ask myself the question, "What is it students really need to be able to do at this level?" The answer to this question often directs me to further limit myself to only subsections of textbook chapters.

  For example, cellular respiration is commonly covered in Introductory Biology. The splitting of glucose (sugar) molecules, which through several subsequent steps results in the energy molecules we use, is very complicated. Most comprehensive textbooks are highly detailed, indicating the name and structure of each enzyme and intermediate compound until the energy is produced. While these details are quite cool, at the introductory level I deem it more important that the students understand how energy changes in form from ingestion of a food substance to fuel the body is able to use for "work." Getting lost in the weeds of enzyme names strikes me as both time consuming and maybe unnecessary for this stage. The majors will get into details in upper-division classes, and the nonmajors do not need all of the minor details to understand the importance of cellular respiration.

- **I closely examine (and re-examine) the classroom's physical infrastructure.** The physical infrastructure of the teaching environment is typically what instructors have the least control over and is often dictated by resource availability on a given campus. Large active learning classrooms are still rare (and expensive to build), so many of us are still working with sloping theater-style seating with furniture that usually is static. During this pre-course period I spend time physically assessing the room without students present. What is the state of the furniture? If small groups will be used, how will they be configured given the physical layout of the room? What is the state of the classroom media? Do laptops connect seamlessly? Is a direct connection necessary, or can wireless work? What technology is there for voice projection? Is a lapel mic handy, or does one need to be rooted to a lectern? I like to use a lapel mic even though I am a naturally loud speaker. Students who may have hearing challenges benefit from the clarity and voice projection offered when I'm mic'd. These are all questions worth knowing the answer to before the first day of class, so where possible, I physically visit the space to begin envisioning what the actual day-to-today classroom experience might be.

Additionally, I use this pre-course time as an opportunity to work on my oratory and voice projection. Certainly, with the rise of active learning pedagogies, the notion of the professor lecturing for extended periods of time has come into disrepute. However, the dialogic model of education still requires significant oral engagement from me, and in this vein, I still pay attention to the ways in which words, style, and nonverbals can uplift and relentlessly message the inclusive atmosphere I aim to create. In some years, I ask colleagues from the theater department to observe me (upon my request) before the semester begins and give me helpful feedback on breathing patterns and speaking style and offer other suggestions on ways in which my social radar can be more fine-tuned to remain connected to my physical audience. Other nonclassroom elements need to be secured as well. I like to hold office hours (which I call "student hours," as we explained in Unit 3) in the basement of one of the student dorms, and therefore, before the semester begins, I ensure access to the lobby, have conversations with the academic mentors assigned to the dorm, and request the approval of the resident director.

- **I examine the digital infrastructure.** I also pay careful attention to the digital infrastructure. Courseware, learning management systems (LMSs), textbook-affiliated software, and other educational tools come in a variety of configurations, not all of which play nicely with each other in a digital environment. From a convenience perspective, it is worth asking the question, "How many different programs am I asking my students to log into and have unique credentials for?" This type of question forces a mindset where one has to decide the digital spaces that are absolutely necessary to serve the equity-minded purposes of the course. Once those decisions are made, similar to what I do in the physical infrastructure, I spend some time logging into the LMS with both a professor and student profile to ensure that the tools required function in the ways I expect them to.

- **I convene the available personnel involved in the course.** Again, I have the privilege of hiring undergraduates who took the course and now serve as learning assistants (LAs) and a graduate-student teaching assistant (TA) to help with grading. Colleagues of mine at different institutions have identified group leaders within the class who often play similar roles to LAs. The key is that, particularly for high-enrollment courses, it is important to identify potential teaching partners. Pre-term, I spend about three hours with my LAs to review the syllabus, course logistics, expectations of the position, an overall picture of what I think the incoming student body will be like, and plans for the LAs' own growth as pedagogues.

- **I carefully explore the roster and other pre-course data.** Working closely with the Office of Institutional Research, I gather data not just on the demographics of incoming students but also on the high schools from which they matriculated, their exposure to science classes while there, and other measures of academic performance. I send students the "This I Believe" reflection prompt and a first-day survey (both described in Unit 4) about a week before classes begin; I tell the students this assignment is due by the end of the first day, clarifying that it is a way for me to get to know who they are beyond simply being a student in my course. The assignment also allows me to gather a variety of more personal information that helps me get to know students on a deeper level, using Tess Killpack and LaVerne Melon's first-day info sheets.

    It's also important to me to know about my students' academic and social backgrounds. Many of my students matriculate into the institution from the capital city of the state where the institution is located. Without infantilizing them by making fixed assumptions about how their experiences might unfold in my class and on campus, I do understand that their primary and secondary education experience, as well as their home community, can impact their psychosocial state when they do arrive to my class. In this case, the neighborhoods still bear the economic consequences of historic redlining, poorly implemented urban renewal policies, and low investments in community infrastructure. To this end, knowing the high schools and communities they came from is useful information because very often their experiences in those communities help explain the different levels of readiness they possess for my course. This does not mean that underpreparedness is assured, but the literature I have read and digested describes how those environments may impede students from coming into my course feeling fully confident of their potential to be successful. For example, some of the communities are ethnically monolithic, meaning that the students' matriculation into college is the first time many of them have experienced a predominantly White environment. This demographic change can trigger feelings of reduced belonging and/or stereotype threat, especially when the ethnic minoritized status is correlated with income level.

On a more practical level, the introductory survey provides helpful information about the amount of experience students have in biology. There is no prerequisite or qualification needed to take introductory biology. Therefore, introductory biology courses include students who have taken Advanced Placement® (AP) Biology as well as students whose only exposure was a general science course in the ninth grade. This scenario requires highly differentiated approaches to inspire and build skills of all whom I have the privilege to teach.

On Day 1

- **I alleviate students' anxiety and validate their presence with carefully constructed messages.** For example, I attended an undergraduate school where the infamous "*look to your left, look to your right; one of you will not be here next year*" speech was given. That ominous warning explicitly suggests that a sizable percentage of students will not make it to sophomore year, but also, in warning the students, it subtly implies that the cause for their departure will be of their own doing. I flip that tradition on its head by radically rephrasing it. I ask students to look to their left and right, and appreciate that the person they are looking at will open a business one day, become a doctor, be their best study partner, be their future roommate, or some other outcome that assumes that they will thrive in the present day. This simple language change can serve to ease the fears of students who might be programmed to see me as a barrier, a problem to be solved, or a gatekeeper for their progress in the discipline. Alongside other affirming language, it sets up a facilitative culture where it is clear that I view my role as supporter of success for *all* of them, not for a select few.

- **I normalize the use of services and supports.** I start by making it clear to the class that the LAs are as knowledgeable on the subject matter as I am, and thus they can trust their LAs' ability to identify misconceptions as they would trust my ability. In this model, some students connect better socially to the course LAs or find their explanation of concepts easier to understand. It does not matter to me if a student learns more from an LA or from me; the point is that they thrive. I also discuss services like tutoring, LA hours, and student hours—again, being careful with my language. In many cases, tutoring is presented as a place you go to if you can't figure out the material on your own. This notion implies that only those who are not up to snuff will seek out tutoring. As a result, using these services can bring a sense of shame and embarrassment, because to use them feels like a tacit admission of one's inadequacy in the subject matter.

    In my reframing on Day 1, I describe the fact that biology is a very technical discipline, which by definition means that students will encounter words and ways of describing things that they are likely not to hear in everyday vernacular. They will also spend time trying to understand and describe things that seem abstract or not easily processed upon first encounter. Therefore, like any new technical area, frequent engagement and repetition are necessary for them to become comfortable enough in the space to then themselves become budding experts. I emphasize that the tutoring service, LA hours, and student hours are simply opportunities for the students to get that additional repetition with guidance and support from people who have more experience than they do in that subject area. This guidance also highlights the role that the LAs, other support staff, and I will play in their learning progression. I also describe the student expectations to help students understand the role they will need to play in their learning.

- **I help establish cultural classroom norms.** To prepare students for effective group work, a significant portion of the first day of class is spent discussing the cultural norms that will guide us. I use a set of guideposts originally written for group discussions where there is some expectation that the conversation will be challenging (see table 7.1). While

TABLE 7.1 Classroom Norms

Guidepost	How to Implement
Be present and welcoming	Be 100 percent present. Set aside the usual distractions of things not done from yesterday or things to do tomorrow. Bring all of yourself to the work. Practice hospitality. We all learn most effectively in welcoming spaces.
Listen deeply to learn	Listen intently to what is said; listen to the feelings beneath the words. Listen to yourself also. Strive to achieve a balance between listening and reflecting, speaking and acting. You will be invited to share in pairs, small groups, and in the larger group. The invitation is exactly that: you will determine the extent to which you want to participate in our discussions and activities.
No fixing	Each of us is here to discover our own truths, to listen to our own inner teacher, to take our own journey. We are not here to help right another's wrongs, to "fix" or "correct" what we perceive as broken or incorrect in another member of the group. Be a community of learners; set aside perfectionism and the fear of "messing up."
Suspend judgment and assumptions and seek understanding	Set aside your judgments. By creating a space between judgments and reactions, we can listen to the other, and to ourselves, more fully, and thus our perspectives, decisions, and actions are more informed. Our assumptions are usually invisible to us, yet they undergird our worldview and thus our decisions and our actions. By identifying our assumptions, we can then set them aside and open our viewpoints to greater possibilities.
Speak your truth and respect the truth of others	Say what is in your heart, trusting that your voice will be heard and your contribution respected. Your truth may be different from, even the opposite of, what another in the circle has said. Speaking your truth is not debating with, correcting, or interpreting what another has said. Own your truth by speaking for yourself, using "I" statements.
Maintain confidentiality	Create a safe space by respecting the confidential nature and content of discussions held in the group. What is said in the group stays here. What is learned in the group leaves here. Everyone gets to tell their own story for themselves.
Respect silence	Silence is a rare gift in our busy world. After you or someone else has spoken, take time to reflect without immediately filling the space with words. Look inward and listen to yourself in the silence.

When things get difficult, turn to wonder	If you find yourself disagreeing with another, becoming judgmental, or shutting down in defense, try turning to wonder: "I wonder what brought her to this place?" "I wonder what my reaction teaches me?" "I wonder what he's feeling now?" You do not have to agree with another's story, but you do have to respect their right to tell their own story.
Trust the group	In the group, all voices are valued equally. All gifts are welcomed and respected. Within each circle is the genesis of renewal and community well-being. The circle can be the instrument for creating a new community narrative for the sake of our children and grandchildren.

Source: Adapted from the Center for Courage and Renewal's Touchstones and the Alluvial Collective, https://alluvialcollective.org/.

not every group conversation in this course is challenging, some will be, and so it is important for us to have an explicit conversation about this early on. We read the guideposts aloud, with different students taking turns to read each one. After the read-aloud, I ask the students to take about thirty seconds to answer the following question: Which of the guideposts do you think you will struggle with the most? After giving students some time for personal reflection, I invite them to share with their group their thoughts. We then do a class-wide sharing-out and make collective decisions to tweak any guideposts that need changing in response. For this exercise, I give the class physical copies of the guideposts *and* post a copy on the LMS, reminding groups to return to it if they need to discuss group dynamics for any reason.

A Typical Class Session

- **To prepare for class, students complete** a carefully chosen reading, an open-book problem set, and a brief open-sourced video lecture (not recorded by me) on the topic, and they enter any "sticky points" they would like further work on in an online forum that is anonymous to their peers. (On the first day of class, I discuss the sticky-points entry to give students a sense of what they'll typically enter as points of confusion and how I will handle them in the classroom.) Every student is required to enter a sticky point before class. If students are not confused by anything, then they enter that they understood the material fully. This semi-flipped approach (described in Unit 6) allows for the in-person portion of the experience to focus only on student misconceptions.

I encourage students to complete the pre-class work and am transparent with them about the intentions of this model. I tell them that not everything they read or watch will be rediscussed in class. Therefore, there will be material that appears on assessments that they engaged with outside of class but did not reappear in a class activity. It thus behooves students to be clear on articulating the elements of the material that don't resonate well. Because so much depends on their ability to describe the "sticky points," I dedicate time in the early days of the course to teaching them how to do this.

- **To prepare for class, I check the forum** in which students enter their sticky points (which "closes" the day before class in the mid to late evening). I do a quick content analysis to identify common themes, gleaning the things that students are still struggling with conceptually. Since I meet regularly with the LAs, I also hear their observations about where students may need more assistance. In response, I choose activities from my experience navigating these conceptual misunderstandings to help students during the face-to-face portion. Sometimes the concept might require me to provide a different type of explanation, interrupted by frequent opportunities for students to self-assess their understanding. Sometimes going through an applied example via a case study or problem set brings the point home more effectively.

- **The start of class** often includes a surprise quiz or a brief session where I address some of the sticky points that were raised in the forum. The quizzes are unannounced to ensure that the pre-class videos and readings are done.

- **Peer-to-peer learning** is a common element of my classes, as many times students are each other's best teacher. For instance, I often use an "each one teach one" approach. Here, a willing student will explain something specific to the class, for example, how messenger RNA is processed in order for it to leave the nucleus. Note that it is important for students to have a decent comfort level in the course for this particular approach. Messenger RNA is usually discussed in the second month, which means that most students are comfortable enough at this point to volunteer an explanation. This comfort building begins with guideposting (described previously) but is maintained by ensuring that the class's agreed-upon cultural norms are respected. The class is given a few minutes to discuss the topic in groups and identify both the strengths and the areas of improvement in the response provided by the student. The student will take the feedback and offer a refined response.

Other times, I use a comparable approach using the software Eli Review.[13] Students are given a question prompt similar to what they might see on a summative exam and asked to write their answers on their computer. I am able to switch their answers anonymously so that their peers can give them feedback. (Note that I give students clear directions on how to give good, respectful, and useful feedback.) I then switch back the answers so that students can improve their responses.

- **Checking in.** Students' physical presence allows me to attend to nonverbal cues, visualizing the ways in which body language and facial expressions might be indicative of students' comfort level with the material, sense of belonging in the class, and even their out-of-classroom responsibilities. From my introductory survey, I know how many students are working a job and for how many hours per week. Depending on their job, students can display signs of fatigue from their shift at work. Many of my students live at home and are often caring for relatives or younger siblings. Their body energy levels sometimes indicate that they were attending to family responsibilities in addition to preparing for class. Seeing that makes me create a mental note that perhaps today is not a day I call on that student, or expect full engagement, but that I should connect with them afterwards to talk about scheduling and balancing all aspects of their lives. I would also ensure in my physical engagement with students that my body language does not spotlight their lethargy in any way. At the same time, I may choose to increase small-group interaction or longer breaks before asking for responses to questions. Even though my class is held in a sloping lecture hall, I am a mover. And since I am usually wearing a microphone, I can just as easily communicate with the whole class while pacing at the front of the room as I can seated comfortably in the middle rows and fielding questions after having checked in with a peer group. Learning assistants are also spread out around the room such that the students in each quadrant of the classroom feel physically close to at least one of us.

Assessments and Grading

My Grading Scheme. Because I believe introductory biology is more about *introductory* than *biology*, I set up assessments to reflect my sense that students need a bit of a psychological on-ramp before their excellence begins to shine. Each summative exam is worth 15 percent of the grade (there are four exams). The other 40 percent of the course credit is dispersed among several things. Even if a student struggles mightily on one exam, their final grade is salvageable. The exam weighting is, however, high enough that it allows for a meaningful discussion with students that encourages them to adjust their practices when necessary.

My Main Assessments. Since the course is large, it would be reasonable for me to rely mostly on multiple-choice exams. But instead, because a key goal of my course is to help students cultivate the skills associated with clearly articulating complex scientific concepts, most of my assessments require written short-answer responses. This means I must devote considerable time to helping students develop this ability in writing. It also means, of course, that summative exams can be time-consuming to grade. Each student produces ten to fifteen short-answer responses per assessment. As mentioned earlier, a key area of support that the graduate TA provides is in grading. My TA and I share this responsibility by using qualitative coding methods. In short, we co-create a codebook (a rubric, of sorts) that we use to evaluate student responses until our assessments closely approximate one another (in technical terms, until we have an inter-rater reliability of at least 85 percent). The codebook allows for faster grading because the expectations are clear for what each response should entail.

The last (ungraded) question on the summative exam asks students to predict their score. The idea is that if you have confidence in your knowledge, theoretically your prediction should be closer to your actual grade. After grading, I plot the relationship between the actual scores and the predicted scores along with the R-squared value (an indication of the strength of correlation). During intervention-week meetings (described next), students and I discuss why the difference between the predicted and the actual exists, and how we might go about closing that gap. In other words, how does one know that they know something?

Intervention Week

In Unit 6, we suggested scheduling an intervention or shout-out as a structural change that supports student success. In my class, I typically schedule an intervention week during the third week of class. By this time, students have completed several quizzes, one summative exam, a major group assignment, and several formative learning activities (like the active learning strategies described in Unit 6). I look at the bottom 30 percent (on average) of my roster and email requests for individual meetings. Before each meeting, I examine the entire spread of the student's point distribution, and since I have tagged individual assessment questions based on their complexity (using Bloom's hierarchy, discussed in Unit 1), I identify where their cognitive struggles lie. I also revisit their first-day info sheet as well as their "I Believe" reflection. This preparation sets me up to have a personal, individualized, and informed conversation with students, seeking to better understand their experiences in the course, how they are engaging in the prework and in-class activities, and their test-prep practices. Importantly, I also ask them for suggestions on how I can support them further or differently so that they can be more successful in the course.

Beyond Biology

I devote time during class to help students connect the course experience to the broader infrastructure of the campus. Here, I invite friends and colleagues from tutoring services; Early Alert, a special office that deals with extraordinary circumstances; affinity student groups; mental health services; and others to speak briefly (usually five minutes) about what their office or group does and how it can be helpful for the students' navigation of the course and the campus in general. This equity-minded approach is important for a couple reasons. For students without the capital to understand how campuses, particularly large-enrollment ones, are laid out, navigation can be an overwhelming proposition. The "if we build it they will come" mentality serves only those with the knowledge of how those services are organized and maximized for their benefit. "Beyond Biology" is also a series of in-class opportunities to demystify for students parts of the institution that are there to support their holistic success. Mental health services, in particular, are important to leverage because stigma still exists around students self-reporting and seeking help in this regard. Allowing campus professionals to use class time to discuss their roles also brings a level of normalcy to discussing these issues and increases the likelihood that students will use them.

At the End of the Course

I review all available data. A key feature of equity-minded teaching is the recognition that all stakeholders in the dialogic process are on a growth journey (the subject of Section Three). From my standpoint, students' social and intellectual growth is the overall goal of the experience, and therefore I examine multiple data sources to determine the degree to which this growth occurred:

1. I use grade data disaggregated to see if traditional racial and ethnic categories were statistically correlated with course outcome.

2. I conduct item analysis of assessment questions on which students performed poorly and revisit the reliability and validity of the question.

3. I carefully read the students' final reflections, entitled "Letter to a Future First-Year Student." In this reflection, students write a one-page (no more than five hundred words) piece of advice to a hypothetical future first-year student on how to successfully navigate college, based on the student's own experience with success and challenges. In so doing, the students clearly articulate the elements of the course and other aspects of campus that have allowed them to see what they need to be doing to be successful. Their course reflections are instrumental in showing me how aspects of the course that were designed for this specific purpose were effective (or not) in achieving their purpose.

4. I carefully read the university-mandated official student evaluations, paying special attention to the open responses where students tend to elaborate more on the relational aspects of the course.

5. I consult with my LAs and graduate-student TA on areas of the course they felt could improve.

All of these conversations and subsequent reflection time allow for a very comprehensive evaluation of how the course implementation worked from a variety of angles. This evaluation allows me to identify the things I can improve on when I work on course upgrades in the upcoming summer.

I reflect again on course logistics and my overall wellness. As noted in my comparison to UPS, the course logistics need to be constantly fine-tuned for all the equity-minded approaches, activities, and outcomes to occur. This is important not only for the efficiency of the pedagogical operation itself but also for my own wellness. I seek to ensure that I am mindful of the personal time needed for the nonteaching aspects of my life (including family life). Therefore, I also reflect on the quality of my course operations, asking such questions as: How much time did it take me / the LAs / the TA to complete x task? Might a technological tool help streamline y? I gather feedback on this from these individuals, as I want to make sure neither the LAs nor the TA are overtaxed or overworked. With these reflections and data in hand, I am well positioned to continuously improve the design of the equity-minded experience and my students' corresponding outcomes.

Bryan's Concluding Thoughts

The implementation of equity-minded practices is shaped by varied contextual factors. That context includes the instructor. I am six feet tall with a naturally loud voice and (at least in public) a charismatic extroverted persona. I am aware of the ways in which these features endear me to many of the social-based techniques described here. In my faculty development practice, I am mindful of instructors whose identities predispose them to negative biases because of their sex, personality style, and ethnicity (as documented in Unit 8). In this vein, I message to instructors, and to you, our readers, that equity-minded approaches do not require you to create whole new personalities; rather, these approaches are more authentic and thus more effective when implemented within the demeanor in which you are most comfortable.

Philosophically speaking, teaching introductory biology is a privilege. Not many opportunities exist to welcome students into the beauty of a discipline and show them the ways in which this discipline is there for them to shape. Your course may exist in a different part of the curriculum, but it is still worth considering the opportunities present for you to either create or sustain students' interest in identifying with the discipline. I wish you the best as you design your own, unique equity-minded experiences for your students. And now, this concludes the first-person case study, and with that, we invite you to continue to Section Three.

SECTION THREE

LEARNING THROUGH CRITICAL REFLECTION

"Teachers must be actively committed to a process of self-actualization that promotes their own well-being if they are to teach in a manner that empowers students."

—bell hooks

The previous sections of this guide focused on what you might do before the term begins and during the term to support more equitable outcomes. One salient question remains: How will you know if these inclusive approaches are working and positively influencing your students' learning and success? Gathering and reflecting on evidence that responds to this question is key to equity-minded teaching. Recall from the Introduction that one of the distinguishing features of equity (in contrast to similar constructs like diversity and inclusion) is its emphasis on outcomes. Our good intentions and use of equity-minded practices can make a difference, but they fall short if we do not take the time to monitor the impact of our teaching on student learning and success.

This section of the guide is meant to support your practice of critical self-reflection, as well as your gathering and processing of evidence throughout but especially at the end of the term, when you may have a bit more time. By **reflection**, we mean an intentional process whereby we examine and evaluate ourselves, our perspectives, our attitudes, our experiences, and the journey of our own learning. In *The Courage to Teach*, educational theorist Parker

reflection:
An intentional process whereby we examine and evaluate ourselves, our perspectives, our attitudes, our experiences, and the journey of our own learning.

Palmer reminds us that teaching is a human activity and that "we teach who we are."[1] That is, we don't teach in a vacuum. We don't isolate our identities, experiences, and biases and leave them outside the classes. We, like our students, bring all of ourselves into our courses. Such a commitment may also cause you to feel drained at the end of another busy semester, so we encourage you to take the time to rest and replenish yourself before trying out any of the suggestions in this section. As we noted earlier, your wellness is foundational: *you* matter!

The overarching equity-focused idea underlying this section is that teaching is a dynamic and two-way human endeavor. Yes, we read and enact evidence-informed teaching practices. At the same time, we recognize that teaching and learning cannot be standardized. No class or group of students will be the same, and no two students are alike. Thus, using our personal reflections, examining available data about our students and seeking our students' input and insights will help us attain more equitable outcomes. The power of this work is directly correlated with our own openness to learning with and about our students—and ourselves. This willingness to learn is central to our personal journey toward becoming more connected, equity-minded instructors.

This section consists of two units: Unit 8 prompts your personal reflection and synthesizes the research concerning traditional student evaluations of teaching, typically referred to as SETs. Given their wide use across institutional types and availability to most instructors, SETs represent an important data source. While acknowledging and addressing the potential bias and common misuse of such data, the unit offers suggestions on how you can nonetheless use SET outcomes to improve student learning and success. Given the importance of more nuanced student feedback, Unit 9 offers alternative ways of gathering this input, continuing to reflect on your practice, and identifying refinements to make the next time you teach.

8

REFLECTION
Take the Time to Look Inward and Engage with Student Ratings Data

Identifying the impact of our teaching requires meaningful personal reflection and deep engagement with student perspectives, including data collected regularly in the form of student course ratings.

Teaching scholar Maryellen Weimer describes self-reflection as a process of self-discovery, of "coming to know ourselves as teachers," and views it as central to faculty growth and change.[2] She recommends a three-part process distilled in the questions, "Who am I, and what can I become, as a teacher and in the classroom?": (1) taking detailed stock of what we do when we teach, (2) exploring *why* we do each of those things, and (3) making discoveries about our instructional identity. Even though the act of reflecting requires us to pause—and even at times look backward—the purpose is not to ruminate but rather to learn and gain insight so we can move forward in an authentic and meaningful way. When we develop a natural disposition to pause and reflect, we can also develop the propensity to have a deeper, more empathic understanding of the lived experiences of others. In the context of equity-minded teaching, acquiring these characteristics means we are not only open to—but actually committed to—regularly learning from and with students, using varied forms of data and evidence.

Lindsay Malcolm-Piqueux and Estela Bensimon, both affiliated with the University of Southern California's Center for Urban Education (CUE), affirm that engaging with evidence about teaching and learning is key to equity-minded practice because "data can help practitioners to truly understand the nature of problematic inequalities in outcomes."[3] For college faculty, no data source is more readily available than student evaluations of teaching (**SETs**), sometimes referred to as student ratings of teaching. Likewise, there are few topics

SETs: Student evaluations of teaching.

more controversial with faculty members than SETs and their use and potential abuse.

Recent headlines tell part of the story: "New Study Could Be Another Nail in the Coffin for the Validity of Student Evaluations of Teaching"; "In Defense (Sort of) of Student Evaluations of Teaching"; "Student Course Evaluations Get an 'F.'"[4] Meanwhile, academic organizations have released warnings about overreliance on student evaluations,[5] and arguments have been made that SETs hurt not only teachers but also students, by helping produce "passive, even contemptuous students who undermine the spirit of the class and lower its quality for everyone."[6] We recognize that the fallibility of SETs and the misuse of their data can negatively impact you as a faculty member. We also know the extent of this impact will likely vary based on such factors as your identities, type of faculty position, institution, and so on.

Why, then, have we devoted considerable space to SETs in a guide on equity-minded teaching? Whether we like them or not, SETs are the most widely used way in which colleges and universities gather evidence about student experiences. And, as the title of a *Chronicle of Higher Education* article makes clear, "Student Evaluations: Feared, Loathed, and Not Going Anywhere," they endure (for most of us).[7] Because SETs are so widely used and are part of most institutions' set policy and routine, administered automatically, their results also tend to be readily available and accessible to instructors. Most importantly, as Tony Knight and Art Pearl write, educational equity increases when students have a voice regarding course pedagogies.[8] On many, if not most, campuses, SETs are the only systematic opportunity for students to share their voices.

Although we wish institutions weren't so reliant on SETs for student feedback, we find encouragement and inspiration in faculty efforts to gather their own input. You'll read about some of these approaches in Unit 9, where we outline varied ways to gather student feedback. Here, we contend that, despite their many shortcomings, SETs are an important source of data about your students' experiences in your class. Our goal in this unit is thus to suggest how to learn from both your personal reflections and your SET results. We'll distill key findings from research on SETs, including studies on their potential biases, and explore some of the nuances of their faults to help you put your results into context. The research summary might also help you minimize SETs' negative influence, not only on your own professional success but also on that of your colleagues with whom you may collaborate, or whom you might mentor or evaluate. Following the research discussion, we'll share specific recommendations for equity-minded reflection and engagement with SET data, plus we'll demonstrate how to identify steps for improvement based on what you uncover in this analysis.

What Does the Research Say about Student Course Evaluations?

Research on SETs reveals a ton, actually. As early as 1987, higher education scholars noted that student evaluation of teaching was one of the topics most emphasized in American educational research.[9] First, what do scholars tell us about why SETs are so widely used? Typically, SETs are used for two sometimes conflicting purposes: a formative purpose—to provide you, the instructor, with feedback to improve your teaching—and a summative one—to provide colleagues and administrators with data to inform decisions about reappointment, promotion, and tenure. Yet this single survey instrument is now often asked to serve even more varied roles for even more varied individuals: at institutions where the results are made available to students, SET data can help students in course selections. They also inform research on instruction in higher education.[10] Additionally, a well-designed SET has the potential to prompt students' own critical reflection on their engagement with learning, what they have learned, and on their own contributions to the class. Perhaps most importantly—and often overlooked in the controversy surrounding the validity of SET data—is the point we've made previously: these recurring surveys provide a mechanism via which students can have their voices heard and their experiences in class recognized. In fact, SETs originated as a way for students to share their experiences in the classroom.[11]

Help! My Job Depends on My Student Ratings

For faculty who are not in a tenured or tenure-track role—whether in annual contracts or part-time positions—SET data may determine whether your contract is renewed or you are assigned classes to teach. If you're unsure how your institution uses SET data, we strongly advise you to ask. By distilling some of the research, we seek to inform and empower you to minimize the data's negative consequences. In addition to the ideas in this unit, we'd offer three recommendations to all faculty who have a lot at stake and/or are anxious about their SET results: (1) work closely with your supervisor when making changes to your practice, (2) use the SET questions to survey your students a few weeks into the term, and (3) monitor your results carefully.

Because supervisors make and/or support personnel decisions, it's helpful to let them know what adjustments you plan to make and why. Coauthor Isis Artze-Vega used the last two strategies when she was a new faculty member, knowing that a great deal depended on her student responses. At the midpoint of every term, she surveyed her students using the exact questions from her university's SETs form. She discussed the results with her classes and identified refinements she could make long before her students received and completed the official SETs. Whether because of these adjustments or the message to students that their voices mattered, students consistently provided higher ratings in the official SETs.

Isis also plotted her results on a graph and monitored changes over time. This graph was helpful when her program director pointed out a low student response on a question; she was able to show that, over time, her ratings scores for all of the SET questions had consistently increased, and she was able to describe how she planned to respond to the data.

The SETs debate has primarily centered on the summative purpose of SETs, that is, institutions' use of evaluation results, sometimes exclusively, in making decisions about faculty reappointment, promotion, and tenure. This singular focus on SET results likely explains why, for over forty years, researchers have questioned the use of SETs as a reliable measure of teaching effectiveness on the grounds that such ratings are biased by variables such as gender, race, and even academic discipline.[12] Many faculty and scholars from across disciplines have been compelled to study these surveys because they're a recurring, consequential part of their professional life.

Given the intensity of this debate, we want to state directly that we find the usage of SET data for summative decision making both problematic and inequitable. Teaching is a multifaceted and complex endeavor, such that teaching effectiveness cannot be reduced to any one data source. Instead, we concur with scholars and practitioners who argue for comprehensive teaching evaluation that uses multiple sources of data and perspectives. For instance, Justin Esarey and Natalie Valdes's SETs analysis concludes that "evaluating instruction using multiple imperfect measures, including but not limited to SETs, can produce a fairer and more useful result compared to using SETs alone."[13] These multiple measures ideally include the perspectives of faculty themselves, and that of their peers and of their students, all in alignment with an institutionally defined vision or framework of teaching excellence.

For the aims of this guide and research overview, however, we shift our attention away from the use of SET data for administrative decision-making. Instead, we focus on how each of us, as faculty, can engage with and learn from our students' responses. Unpacking the results of SETs research, much of which reexamines previous studies, can be complex—almost as complex as the many factors that seem to influence the results of the SETs themselves.

We therefore organize our research summary into two parts: (1) studies on the relationship between SET data and student learning and success, and (2) the most recent research on the topic of bias in SETs, including suggestions for how such bias can be mitigated and strategies for using such feedback ethically and effectively. Our brief summary of studies of bias in SETs isolates the variables of instructor gender, race, and ethnicity, as well as other confounding factors.[14]

Pause to Consider

- What are some of the main reasons or motivations for you to make changes to your courses year over year (policy changes, student data/feedback, program assessment, professional development, etc.)?

- Which of the questions in your institution's SETs survey are most meaningful to you, and why?

Do SETs Give Us Insight into "Teaching Effectiveness" and Student Learning?

Educational theorists Thomas Angelo and Patricia Cross explain that when someone asks, "Are student ratings valid?" what they're really asking is "Are students really good judges of effective teaching?"[15] Our response, after engaging with the research, is yes and no. Yes, of course, students can provide us with great insights into their educational experiences that can be essential to improving our teaching. Michael Scriven, an expert in evaluation, writes that "students are the most frequent observers of many facets of teaching and learning and their collective opinions as witnesses can provide useful information, particularly when they are asked to observe specific behaviors or materials."[16] Weimer concurs: "[Students] are there for the course from start to finish; their experience is first-hand and fresh. They can say better than anyone else whether the course design and teacher actions motivated and expedited their learning."[17]

Data about this front-row-seat experience may be even more important in online classes for at least two reasons: (1) Students may have even fewer opportunities to describe their experiences. And (2) in asynchronous courses, most faculty lack access to the nonverbal feedback we rely on from students in in-person courses: their body language, the tone of their responses, where they sit, and so on.

Then again, as Scriven notes, students' opinions can be useful "particularly when they are asked to observe specific behaviors or materials." In other words, the quality of the data we gather depends considerably on the questions we ask in our SET surveys. Too often, SET questions focus on students' evaluation of the instructor, not on their own experiences in the instructor's class. For instance, in their SETs study, business professors Karen Loveland and John Loveland identify ten factors commonly measured by traditional student evaluation forms, including criteria such as the instructor's knowledge of the subject, communication skills, enthusiasm, organization and preparation, timeliness of feedback, and fairness in grading. Almost all of these factors focus on a faculty member's teaching and knowledge, which are only tangentially related to the student's own learning and their experiences of being in that class.[18]

This disconnect between the questions we pose to students in SETs and students' direct experiences suggests that a key challenge associated with SETs validity is the implication that students are "evaluating" faculty and their teaching. Students may or may not be able to judge the effectiveness of a teacher, or even assess their own learning. Recognizing that student *evaluations* of teaching is a misnomer, institutions like Florida International University rebranded their SETs as SPOTs: student perceptions of teaching surveys. This new wording makes it clearer to all parties involved that the data represent student views and perceptions, not their *evaluations* of teaching effectiveness, a much more complex task.

Turning to the relationship between SET results and learning, political science professors Rebecca Kreitzer and Jennie Sweet-Cushman's extensive meta-analysis of bias in SETs leads them to affirm that "Student Evaluations of Teaching (SETs) have low or no correlation with learning," and as such, "are poor metrics of student learning and are, at best, imperfect measures of instructor performance."[19] Although older studies had identified a correlation, Bob Uttl, Carmela White, and Daniela Wong Gonzalez's recent meta-analysis of teaching effectiveness reanalyzes the data and finds no significant correlations between SET ratings and learning.[20]

Bias Affects SET Results

The most recent critiques of SETs focus on the evaluations' inherent bias, particularly related to the personal or social identity of the instructor. Kreitzer and Sweet-Cushman, after reviewing more than one hundred articles on bias, state that there is little doubt that women and other historically marginalized groups face "significant biases in standard evaluations of teaching."[21] In addition, the effect of gender is conditional on a host of other factors, such as discipline, course characteristics, gender expectations, and the students' political disposition, as well as the instructor's sexual orientation, accent, and so on. Here, we synthesize findings associated with gender, race, and ethnicity, and a few additional factors (including course modality).

Sources of Bias: Gender. The research leaves little doubt that most SETs are subject to gender bias, and some critics suggest that such bias "can be large enough to cause more effective instructors to get lower SET than less effective instructors."[22] Study after study demonstrates "a multitude of ways that men benefit from evaluation, while women do not fare as positively."[23] Bias has also been identified in relation to how instructors "perform" their gender and meet students' gender expectations. For example, in a comprehensive study of qualitative comments in SETs, researcher Sophie Adams and her colleagues argue that "student evaluations of teaching seem to measure conformity with gendered expectations rather than teaching quality, with particularly negative effects for women."[24] They conclude "that male-identified teachers are more likely to receive positive evaluations than female-identified teachers, with the 'male effect' being particularly strong in particular disciplines—greatest in the natural sciences, lowest in the humanities, with the social sciences being mixed—and stronger amongst male students."[25] Meanwhile, Kreitzer and Sweet-Cushman synthesize a variety of specific ways in which students' perceptions of male- versus female-identified faculty differ:

> *Disparate research demonstrates that men are perceived as more accurate in their teaching, have higher levels of education, are less sexist, more enthusiastic, competent, organized, professional, effective, easier to understand, prompt in providing feedback, and are less-harshly penalized for being tough graders.*[26]

This varied list suggests that for many students, the image of the "college professor" continues to be male.

Sources of Bias: Race and Ethnicity. Compared to the number of studies on SETs and gender, there are significantly fewer studies on bias in SETs related to the perceived race and ethnicity of the faculty member, but most of the research suggests that such bias exists. Using student feedback from RateMyProfessor.com from twenty-five of the top liberal arts colleges, Langdon Reid finds that in areas related to overall quality, helpfulness, and clarity, faculty perceived to be from racially minoritized groups—particularly Black and Asian—were evaluated more negatively than those perceived to be White faculty. Minoritized faculty, however, were rated "easier" than White faculty. Reid does not find a strong gender effect but notes that "Black male faculty were rated more negatively than other faculty."[27]

In another study, Mara Aruguete and colleagues examine the effects of race and clothing style on student evaluations and find that students—both Black and White—rated Black professors less favorably than White professors. Students also had more trust in Black professors who dressed more formally, whereas they had more trust in White professors who dressed more casually. The researchers suggest that Black professors have to "exert more personal effort to attain the favorable evaluations that seem to come more naturally to White professors."[28] Similarly, Kreitzer and Sweet-Cushman conclude that "SETs disproportionately penalize faculty who are already marginalized by their status as minority members of their disciplines."[29] Finally, psychologists Susan Basow, Stephanie Codos, and Julie Martin examined race, gender, student ratings, and learning by showing students an animated lecture given by both male- and female-appearing professors who appeared either White or Black. The students were then given a quiz to evaluate how much attention they had paid to the lecture. The data showed, among other things, that the animated Black "professors" were rated higher than their White counterparts on their hypothetical interactions with students. However, the quiz scores indicated that students who had the White "professors" scored higher, perhaps because the students paid closer attention to the lecture.[30]

Additional Sources of Bias and Variability, Including Course Modality. Kreitzer and Sweet-Cushman's review of research suggests that evaluations are influenced by myriad intersecting factors, including "discipline, student interest, class level, class difficulty, meeting time, and other course-specific characteristics, but not generally instructor quality."[31] Citing gender, discipline, and other factors that affect bias, researchers Anne Boring, Kellie Ottoboni, and Philip B. Stark believe that "it is not possible to adjust for the bias, because it depends on so many factors."[32]

An additional confounding factor is the modality of the course being taught—whether fully online (asynchronous) or in person. The limited research related to online instruction is inconclusive. For example, in 2006, Alfred Rovai and his educational research colleagues found a significant difference between how students evaluated online versus in-person courses.[33] However, in a second study, published a year later in the same journal, Henry Kelly and his coresearchers found that open-ended comments included similar proportions of praising and negative comments in courses taught by the same instructor, one online and one in person. The topics of these comments, however, did differ in proportion between online and in person: comments about online courses focused more on issues of organization and materials, whereas those about in-person courses focused more on the instructor's knowledge.[34]

Professors Loveland and Loveland offer perhaps the most helpful and interesting analysis of potential bias in SETs for online relative to in-person courses. As noted previously, they identify ten general criteria for effective teaching that are common across many SETs, and they argue that the same criteria apply across modalities. They therefore attribute variations in student responses to the influence of the course modality. Loveland and Loveland find that the instructor's writing is more important to students online than in person and influences the evaluation of criteria such as "teaching effectiveness," "knowledge of the subject," and "rapport with students."[35] You may want to refer back to Unit 3, where we explore the literature on warm tone in your syllabus; we also encourage you to use warm tone in your written online class materials (e.g., instructions, mini-text lectures, rubric criteria, discussion prompts, etc.).

At this point, you may be wondering how taking an equity-minded approach to teaching might shift your student ratings results. We want to be candid: although limited data exist, some have suggested that such teaching could, in fact, lead to a decline in SETs.[36] We think it's likely this effect will vary based on the specific changes you make to your practice. For instance, adding transparency to the design of your assignments or being more intentional about your students' sense of belonging could reasonably result in improved SETs, whereas teaching topics related to social justice and other relevant issues could manifest itself in mixed responses from students, especially if you're teaching these topics for the first time.

As with any significant changes to your teaching, it's a good idea to talk to whomever conducts your annual evaluation ahead of time, to let them know how you plan to adjust your teaching and why. In general, if you suspect your SETs will be lower because you are bringing in new practices to the course, we encourage you to be more transparent with your students about your practices (i.e., clarifying to students why you are making a certain change/adjustment, and how you intend for it to help their learning and/or success). Relatedly, consider how you might cultivate a class culture in which student voices are sought and valued consistently, as opposed to only at the end of the term. The ideas in Unit 9 should help!

Starting with Reflection and Engaging with Student Perspectives in SET Data

Before you review your SET results, we encourage you to take a bit of time to conduct your own self-assessment of the term. As we noted before, *your* observations about students' learning and experiences, as well as your learning activities, assessments, and course design decisions, are essential data points. Ask yourself and take some notes on the following questions:

- What do you think went well?
- What do you think could have been improved?
- What do you think your students will say in their evaluations?

You might also consider Weimer's question included earlier in this unit: "Who am I, and what can I become, as a teacher and in the classroom?" In addition, Weimer prompts us to ask ourselves, regarding our teaching decisions, "Why do I do this?" (For instance, "Why do I rely on multiple-choice exams?" Or "Why do I devise my grading system the way I do?") The Pause to Consider questions throughout this guide may also help you reflect on key features of your course. We find Kimberly Tanner's questions, which are designed to foster metacognition in teachers, extremely helpful as tools for self-reflection.[37] The questions include the following:

1. If I were to teach this course again, how would I change it? Why?
2. What might keep me from making these changes?
3. How is my thinking about teaching changing?

And we suggest adding one more: "How is my thinking about learning changing?"

After reflecting, you're ready to read your student evaluations. Because you've taken this time for reflection, you'll have helpful context for students' responses and can identify ways that your perspectives are similar and different—and what might account for the differences. Here are five suggestions for equity-minded engagement with SET results:

1. Examine SET Results Systematically and Holistically

If you accept the premise that we can learn a great deal from the student perspectives gathered via SETs, we suggest that you take additional steps to examine your course data more carefully and systematically than you may be used to doing. The first of these steps is reading your SET data. "It may seem self-evident to say that the first step in learning from a student evaluation is to read one," writes university administrator and *Chronicle of Higher Education* columnist David Perlmutter. "[B]ut what professor has not been tempted to disregard student comments? Or even insist on ignoring them?"[38]

As you read, it's best to look for trends and "scan for red flags."[39] For example, if your institution uses a five-point Likert scale for quantitative student responses, which might range, for instance, "Never / Rarely / Sometimes / Often / Very often," there is little difference between the top (or bottom) two categories. The difference between Often / Very often is marginal, and these categories can be grouped together for the purpose of looking for any potential problems or negative trends. Do a sizable number of students, say four out of twelve or eight out of forty, rate you poorly on organization or returning work on time? Or do they indicate that you are not responsive to questions or requests to meet? Each of these insights may help you identify an area of improvement with respect to equity-minded teaching. For instance, in the latter case, if students perceive you as less welcoming than you had intended, you might take a moment to ask yourself, "Why might that be? What might I be doing that leads them to feel that way? What might I do differently?" This process of reflection may lead you to try some of the recommendations in Units 4 and 5 such as rebranding office hours as "student hours" or trying out a trust generator.

Do the same for qualitative comments. Is there a trend of praise or concern? Why might that be? Do the comments ring true? Are they consistent with your self-assessment? Charlie Blaich and Kathy Wise of the Center of Inquiry at Wabash College advise us faculty to think about clusters of negative comments in student evaluations and feedback as we might a dashboard light on our car: "When it lights up, you know that something is going on; you don't necessarily know what, but it is certainly worth investigating."[40]

Similarly, Angela Linse, in her guide for faculty and administrators on how to interpret and use student ratings data, notes that "small differences in mean (average) ratings are common and not necessarily meaningful." She recommends that faculty focus on the most common ratings and comments—as in, a cluster indicating a similar theme or trend—rather than the rare views, also reminding us that "contradictory comments are not unusual."[41] Also look for trends over time. Linse notes that any anomalies—in both an overall course average and with single raters—should be treated as such. (However, sometimes an anomaly warrants further exploration and leads to important critical self-reflection, as we'll see in coauthor Mays Imad's account of reading a challenging student comment, included under the next heading.)

Finally, to engage in a more explicitly equity-minded review of your SET results, identify which of the questions in your institution's survey reflect key ideas from this guide and your own readings on justice or inclusion. For instance, do any questions ask about students' sense of belonging or how accessible or trustworthy they perceive you to be? Are there questions about the relevance of the class or the clarity of your expectations (transparency) or belonging and respect? If so, you may want to focus in particular on students' responses to these questions, looking to earlier units in this guide for ways to refine your teaching the next time you teach the class.

2. Lean In to Negative Feedback

We recognize that most of us faculty members care deeply about our students' experiences and learning, and that we're human. This means negative or harsh comments can be painful to read. You've likely noticed that even when the majority of comments are positive, one negative or mean comment can become stuck in your mind. Kreitzer and Sweet-Cushman explain that both novelty and negativity bias are at play in this common occurrence: the former causes us to remember anomalous comments, while the latter causes us to remember and be influenced more by negative comments than positive ones. All four guide authors recall fixating on the one or two negative comments in our evaluations, even in the context of overwhelmingly positive feedback.

For example, at the beginning of her career Mays received an evaluation for her general biology course. One student comment included: "She's heartless. She taught the class like it was a graduate course and didn't care about those of us who failed." As you might expect, Mays recalls getting stuck at the "heartless" part and feeling devastated by that characterization. One of her colleagues encouraged her to dismiss that one comment because it was an "outlier." But she couldn't. Mays then shared the comment with another senior colleague whom she looked up to and who told her that "every feedback has truth, and it's a matter of getting to the heart of it." A commitment to equity provides another reason to examine rather than dismiss "outlier" comments: particularly in Predominantly White Institutions, the outliers may very well express the perspectives of our minoritized or otherwise marginalized students—ones who have been not only ignored but also silenced.

How can we as instructors unpack or dig deeper into negative or hurtful comments and try to understand what the student is trying to convey to us? In Mays's case, she set aside the "heartless" part and focused on the rest of the feedback, which did, in fact, speak the truth that she was teaching the course at a much higher academic level than an undergraduate freshman course. "There was a disconnect between my perception of where my students were academically and where they actually were. I didn't spend the time getting to know my audience. I lost those who needed the most help, and worse, I gave them the impression that I didn't care when they failed," Mays says. It was neither fair nor ethical nor equitable to present graduate-level materials to students who were only just learning about the basics of DNA replication, she recognized.

Coauthor Bryan Dewsbury remembers midsemester feedback from a student who was incensed at the amount of active learning used in his course. The student remarked on an anonymous survey that "they paid tuition to be taught, and not to do a bunch of group work." While the feedback stung, it reminded Bryan of the importance of being transparent about his methods at the beginning of the semester. When we are explicit with students about how we've designed our courses, online modules, class sessions, and assessments, the equity-minded approach does not become a version of "eat your vegetables"—a decision from on high. Rather, taking class time or module space to describe why we've made pedagogical decisions that advance students' deep learning demonstrates our commitment to transparency (see Unit 2) and building trust (see Unit 4).

As you work to move past the sting of hurtful comments, keep in mind that you don't have to read your SET results alone. For example, at Connecticut College, the Joy Shechtman Mankoff faculty Center for Teaching & Learning (CTL) sponsors "feedback-reading parties" for early-career faculty. At those events, faculty gather together, often over food and drinks, and simply sit and read their own students' feedback. As part of the event, participants can volunteer to share student comments aloud. Reading—and sharing—comments together not only encourages faculty members to read and "hear" their student feedback but also brings some lightheartedness to the process. The purpose of this activity is to humanize the experience of reading student comments, normalize the wide variety of comments that we receive, celebrate student voices, and have a community that will help us process the messages.

As part of the CTL event, faculty members often share their entire set of comments with another participant, who reads them at the same time. The person reading the feedback looks for red flags or trends in the feedback (as we've previously described). The reader then begins a conversation by asking the person whose feedback they just read, "What did you think about your comments? What stood out?" The reader can then share what they noticed, and ask, "Why might have students felt or experienced _____?" Having a trusted colleague read your feedback may help you keep your student comments in perspective and not focus too much on outlying negative comments; at the same time, it may deter you from quickly writing off potentially valid suggestions or criticisms. Back to Mays: After the experience with the hurtful student comment, she developed a strategy that has helped her make the process of reading SET results less jarring. She now has a trusted colleague—in a nonevaluative position—read her comments and discuss them with her over lunch. Her colleague helps her get beyond the hurtful comments so she can tune in to the students' voices and learn from their insights.

If your schedule or busy life makes it difficult to attend in-person events like the CTL reading parties, and a virtual option is not available, we still encourage you to seek support in this area. Perhaps you could request a mentor from your department chair, or you could ask someone at your local teaching center if they can connect you with a colleague who can support you in this way.

3. Mitigate Bias from the Start

Working to eliminate as much bias as possible from your SETs review process means that the data you receive will be more useful and accurate and that you will be more open to engaging with and acting upon these data. One way to contend with bias is to establish from the start a collaborative relationship with students, one based on trust and the willingness to learn together, an essential part of equitable teaching. Such a relationship enables both you and your students to be invested in the feedback they provide. (See Units 4 and 5 for ideas on how to establish and strengthen collaborative academic relationships with students.)

Another research-informed approach to minimizing bias in SET results is to raise students' awareness about the use of their feedback and their own potential for bias. Political science professor David Peterson and his colleagues note that the negative biases in SETs are likely what are known as implicit or **unconscious biases**, "meaning they are automatically activated, unintentional, and occur below the conscious awareness of the individual."[42] Their recent study offers one model of how to mitigate bias: randomized students in courses were given a "treatment" in the form of a brief introductory paragraph to the questions on the SET, and control students in the same courses were not. The introduction not only discussed the importance student evaluations play in faculty review but also explained that the institution recognized students' unintended biases. Here is the full introductory paragraph (the "treatment" text):

unconscious bias: Also known as "implicit bias," attitudes or stereotypes developed over the course of our lives that affect our actions and decisions in ways we are not aware of.

> *Student evaluations of teaching play an important role in the review of faculty. Your opinions influence the review of instructors that takes place every year. Iowa State University recognizes that student evaluations of teaching are often influenced by students' unconscious . . . biases about the race and gender of the instructor. Women and instructors of color are systematically rated lower in their teaching evaluations than white men, even when there are no actual differences in the instruction or in what students have learned.*
>
> *As you fill out the course evaluation, please keep this in mind and make an effort to resist stereotypes about professors. Focus on your opinions about the content of the course (the assignments, the textbook, the in-class material) and not unrelated matters (the instructor's appearance).*[43]

After implementing this controlled study, the research team found that giving students this introduction made a significant impact on their responses to the SET surveys, concluding that "a simple intervention informing students of their potential for gender biases can have significant effects on the evaluation of female instructors"—as much as 0.5 point on a 5-point scale.

4. Empower Students to Complete SETs—and More Effectively

Another way to make sure that the data you receive are as accurate and helpful as possible is to encourage students to participate in the SETs process, in both your course and others. Students from minoritized backgrounds may feel disempowered by previous educational experiences or lower levels of agency and thus be less likely to complete their course evaluations. When we have poor response rates, we may miss out on different student voices and perspectives altogether—and the students, in turn, are missing out on the opportunity to have their voices heard. Hence, incentivizing and increasing the participation of all students is critical to equity-minded teaching.

Mays encourages student completion by talking to her students about the importance of their evaluations. She tells them explicitly that good teaching is a work in progress, and that teaching is a two-way relationship: just as they are learning, she too is learning about teaching and is growing as an instructor. It can also help to tell students about specific improvements you've made based on your past students' feedback, and to assure them that their feedback will, in turn, improve the course for future students. This information provides students with context for your request(s) for their feedback and lets them know you will value their input when they share it. Online, this kind of communication can be done effectively using informal recorded videos so that students see your facial expressions and hear the variation in your vocal tone. A written announcement or email could also work, but video messages ring more true, so use them when possible.

We can also show students how to provide valuable, actionable SET feedback (e.g., comments that are specific and include examples) and encourage them to make sure their voices are heard by completing the evaluations. Because a low response rate means less data (and lower overall validity of the results), consider incentivizing SETs completion. For instance, you can offer the class incentives to meet a certain percentage of completed feedback forms; for example, if 95 percent of the class fills out the forms, everyone in the class will get bonus points (while ensuring that these points do not skew the validity of grades; see Unit 2).

5. Advocate for Change

Part of becoming an equity-minded faculty member is to "view inequities as problems of practice and feel a personal responsibility to address them."[44] Given the research on the many limitations of SETs and how they are often misused, we encourage you to enlist your colleagues and advocate for change, both in how they are designed and how they are used. (Senior faculty and/or those with tenure should ideally lead the way.) Angela Linse concludes her article on SETs with the reminder that improving the use of SET data can help us avoid "turning the important process of listening to students' voices into a rote activity that has no meaning for the students or faculty."[45] In other words, we have an opportunity to turn the tide and reclaim student feedback as meaningful data. Whether you seek change in the questions asked, the way SETs are administered, or the way the results are used by individual faculty members, departments, and institutions, don't underestimate the impact that faculty—and especially coalitions of faculty—can have on this kind of systemic change.

Reflecting on Results and Identifying Improvements

The richest data we have on our teaching practices are what students experience in our courses, but the value of these data is leveraged only when we reflect and identify steps for improvement. Critical self-reflection for equity-minded teaching requires that we each commit to examining our biases and privileges, which are often related to our own cultural backgrounds or personal histories. Educational theorist Stephen Brookfield developed a strategy for exposing one's assumptions in the teaching process through actively reflecting from four perspective lenses: personal experience, colleagues, students, and scholarship.[46] Comparing our personal reflections to those same reflections viewed through any of the other lenses enables us to examine similarities and contradictions in the way we view the world. Scholars confirm that equity-minded faculty reflect on their identities and lived experiences to establish authentic relationships with students and minimize the impact assumptions and problematic biases may have on them.

For example, coauthor Flower Darby remembers a semester several years ago in which a Black student showed signs of low engagement in her class. At this institution, Black students were few and far between, and upon reflection, she realized that he may have felt a low sense of belonging in her class and perhaps at the university in general. Although it can be painful to dig into uncomfortable experiences such as these, Flower has since thought deeply about what she may have done differently with her course structure, assignments, and daily interactions to be more inclusive and extend belonging more intentionally.

This and other experiences Flower has had when interacting with people of different races and ethnicities have led to intense and repeated examination of identities she holds that are privileged, and opportunities and life chances she's had that racially diverse people may not have had. As a White, cisgender, able-bodied, heterosexual woman, Flower has never experienced discrimination in the form of, for instance, being followed around a retail store. And having a dad with a graduate degree meant that Flower never doubted she would attend and succeed in college—something that marginalized students may not take for granted. However, Flower has had cause to think deeply about her experiences and life chances, and she is working to become the kind of co-conspirator Professor Bettina Love calls for, someone who uses their privilege to fight systemic injustices alongside those who experience oppression.[47] In equity-focused teaching, such critical reflection is essential. We cannot meaningfully progress on our journey toward equity without this kind of "heart work"—an intentional self-scrutiny centered on advancing justice. Attending to systematic, frequent, and genuine critical reflection helps us, at a deeply personal level, authentically transform our teaching and our lives.

To ensure we practice critical reflection when engaging with student feedback, we might ask ourselves questions such as these:

- How do my students' perspectives compare to mine? How might the similarities and differences in our perspectives reflect the similarities and differences in our identities and lived experiences?
- How do I want my students and myself to be changed by the end of this course?
- In five years, when students look back at my course, what do I want them to remember most?
- What points of inequities might I be able to challenge and transform?

Such questions offer us the opportunity not only to improve as teachers but also to grow as human beings. What we do with such opportunities for critical reflection and then action determines whether we perpetuate or challenge the inequities in higher education.

As we suggested previously, one approach to critically considering the feedback you receive is to share it with a trusted colleague and then discuss each other's thoughts about it. You too can offer to read the information that your colleague has gathered. Doing so not only gives you insight into the range of student responses but also helps you both put the feedback in context and take the feedback more seriously—it is harder to discount a trend or theme when another person has also discerned its existence.

Once you have gathered your reflections and the data you want to act upon (in this case SET results), examine the results systematically as suggested previously, take the time to carefully reflect on them, and ideally, enlist your students as partners in more fully understanding the feedback and identifying what kinds of changes would be most helpful. For instance, do the data suggest changes in your instructional materials, online module design, facilitation of discussion, grading practices, and so on? Refer back to the earlier parts of this guide for suggestions on how you might refine your practice the next time you teach. For instance, if student perspectives or success rates suggest that students may not be motivated, perhaps because they do not yet realize the relevance and significance of your course goals, revisit Unit 1 for ideas. Unit 2 can help with matters of grading or assessment, while Unit 3 can help you tweak course policies or how you communicate them to students. For issues of belonging or trust, Units 4 and 5 offer a variety of suggestions, and Unit 6 describes equity-minded refinements to respond to day-to-day challenges.

HOW CAN I GET STARTED?

For Any Class

- Identify one question in your institution's SET that stands out to you as important to equity-minded teaching (whether it's about respect, transparency, trust, etc.). Scan your quantitative results for that question, and then simplify the results by combining the top and the bottom two categories together (e.g., combining always/often or excellent/good into the "top" category, and never/sometimes or poor/fair into the "bottom" category). Draft a quick hypothesis about what might account for that score and one thing you can do differently to try to improve it.

- Share the results of your SETs with a trusted colleague—a peer in your department, an instructional designer or teaching center professional, or an instructor friend who teaches for another college or university—who is either an expert in equity-minded practices or seeking to become one. Ask them what they notice when they look at your SETs through the lens of equity and inclusion.

For In-Person Classes

- Carve out a bit of class time to talk to your students about the SETs process. Tell them how you use the data to improve your practice, how important it is that you hear *all* of their voices, and how your department or institution uses the data to make decisions.

- If possible, give students fifteen or twenty minutes during class to complete their SETs on paper or using a mobile device.

For Asynchronous Online Classes

- List the SETs completion deadline in the appropriate "at a glance" weekly schedule. Prerecord (and preschedule, if your LMS allows) a quick video announcement in which you describe how you use the data to improve your practice, how important it is that you hear *all* students' voices, and how your department or institution uses the data to make decisions.

- In a weekly content-adjacent discussion forum, ask students to reflect on concepts discussed in each module. You could ask them to share their experiences and thereby shape the experiences of future students in the class or program. Be sure to interact in these conversations just as you would in class-focused online discussions.

For Synchronous Online Classes

- Ask students to discuss some of the SET questions in pairs or small breakout groups; this activity will prepare them to craft helpful feedback when they complete the official surveys. Draw their attention to the questions that reflect your commitment to equity-minded practice, such as those regarding trust, your accessibility, and transparency.

- Lead an anonymous collaborative activity using tools like Google Jamboard, Padlet, or a poll or whiteboard in Zoom. Ask students to reflect on their sense of the value of SETs, or ask them how they think instructors use the feedback, how the department or college might use it, and so on.

9

INQUIRY
Gather and Learn from Additional Student Feedback

Equity-minded teaching is a process of inquiry, so gathering focused data on students' experiences is key to identifying the improvements that will make the biggest differences for them.

As we've proposed, critical self-reflection and student feedback are central to equity-minded teaching. Leading equity scholars Tia Brown McNair, Estela Mara Bensimon, and Lindsey Malcolm-Piqueux explain the connection in their text *From Equity Talk to Equity Walk*: equally important to gathering both quantitative and qualitative feedback, they write, is the process of reflecting on the data and using them to take action.[1] The fact that our most readily available data, SET results, are characterized by bias and limited in their connection to learning begs the question: How else can faculty gather student feedback as part of a commitment to more equitable student outcomes? That's where this unit comes in. We offer suggestions on how you might collect additional information beyond SETs and how to respond to what you learn—reflecting the conviction that equity-mindedness is both evidence-based and action-oriented.[2]

This unit offers four general recommendations on additional ways to collect student feedback—from straightforward ones you can easily integrate into your practice to ones that require collaboration and planning. And we indicate which strategies you can implement independently and which would benefit from (or necessitate) collaboration with faculty colleagues, departmental leadership, and/or institutional research staff. The number of options offered is meant to provide you with choices, *not* to suggest that you try out many or most of them. In fact, we caution you not to begin collecting copious amounts of additional data and feedback all at once. Instead, try reviewing all of the options, identifying which strategy best meets your needs, and considering which data/feedback you'll be able to engage with deeply. You'll then be ready to commit to taking a small step each term.

What Does the Research Say about Gathering Student Data and Feedback outside of SETs?

Norwegian scholars Iris Borch and colleagues invite faculty to consider alternative ways to understand the student experience in their classes—and they demonstrate that the process doesn't require a fancy strategy: Talk with students. Listen to them. The authors affirm that "dialogue-based evaluation methods stand out as a promising alternative or supplement to a written student evaluation approach when focusing on students' learning processes."[3] Such a dialogue, for example, might focus on student experiences, both inside and outside of our classrooms, online spaces, labs, and studios. If you're teaching online, engage students asynchronously through email, anonymous surveys, or an anonymous discussion forum. Offer synchronous dialogue opportunities through optional Zoom sessions or one-on-one meetings.

These suggestions are in keeping with the reminder of coauthor Bryan Dewsbury and his colleague Cynthia Brame that "inclusive teaching is most effective when the academic experience is based on relationships and dialogue."[4] Being open to making the educational process a dialogue with and among your students means allowing for your vulnerability and being open to your own learning, which will improve both your teaching and your students' learning. This idea of prioritizing our relationship with our students is featured in recent research on effective teaching. Educational developers and leaders Peter Felten and Leo Lambert, for instance, reaffirm the impact of relationship-rich education, writing that all students—but perhaps especially minoritized students—benefit from experiencing genuine welcome and deep care, being inspired to learn, developing a web of significant relationships, and exploring questions of meaning and purpose.[5] In the book *Learning and Teaching Together: Weaving Indigenous Ways of Knowing into Education*, professor of education Michele T. D. Tanaka reminds us that the "learner-teacher relationship requires the teacher to be very open-minded in terms of what direction the learner might take, and what his or her needs might be."[6] Similarly, Bryan's "Deep Teaching" model of inclusive teaching requires that instructors "authentically listen to the voices of their students." Bryan explains that "creating the space for [student] voices . . . is key to building an empathic relationship," which in turn forms the basis for a course climate and pedagogy that promote effective learning.[7]

In *Inspired College Teaching*, Maryellen Weimer implores us to gather formative feedback outside of the SETs process. She explains that the following traits are characteristic of a feedback-gathering process that is led by faculty:

- The data are relevant in that faculty ask about what *they* want to know.

- Faculty can gather just-in-time feedback, in contrast to waiting until the end of the term.

- The feedback is not as judgmental.

- Student input can be iterative: "connected, circular, and ongoing."

She reminds us that a commitment to improving one's practice means faculty take the reins in the gathering of feedback, in terms of content, timing, and usage; they don't passively rely on their institutions to collect SET data.[8]

Readily Available Data beyond SETs

In addition to the perspectives we have discussed on *why* to engage with student voices, scholars increasingly call our attention to specific sources of data, including ones that, like SETs, may be easy to access. In fact, in *Data Tools*, a publication in their Equity-Minded Inquiry Series, the Center for Urban Education (CUE) begins with the recognition that today's colleges and universities abound with data about students. What is unclear, they acknowledge, "is whether and how these data are used to improve practice in ways that advance success for students generally, and racially minoritized students in particular."[9]

While it may be harder to influence how data are used at the institutional level, there is a lot we *can* do with the data we each collect regularly within the scope of our own classes. For instance, our course records tend to include evidence of our students' progress in our class—their attendance, participation, and grades on individual assignments and major assessments. More subtle cues, such as where a student sits or how often they log into your course LMS, also count as data. Many faculty also have access to their students' distribution of grades, course dropping/withdrawals, and so on. With respect to data on student learning, program learning outcomes results are ubiquitous (as they are required for accreditation) and often underutilized. Although much of this assessment work generates data at the program level (vs. the individual faculty member level), it can still provide you with important insights.

Recent research points to a correlation between student experiences and student learning. This makes sense considering that emotions act as a gateway to learning. If students have a positive experience, that will help enhance their learning. Several data sets focused on student experiences may be available to you. For instance, the National Survey of Student Engagement (NSSE; pronounced "Nessie") focuses on what students report experiencing in their classes and on their campus. The nationally normed NSSE's forty-seven "engagement indicators" include topics such as academic challenge, learning with peers, and experiences with faculty. The survey also includes six "High-Impact Practices" and quantifies students' self-reported experiences with each practice.[10] More than 1,650 colleges and universities have administered the NSSE since 2000, so you may want to find out if NSSE data are available to you at your institution. In turn, the Wabash National Study of Liberal Education, in which forty-nine institutions have participated, focuses on students' development of twelve outcomes associated with liberal arts and general education.[11] In both the NSSE and Wabash studies, the more students report positive experiences with high-impact teaching practices and supportive institutional conditions, the greater their success and learning.[12]

Filling in Your Data Gaps

This section describes several options for gathering and responding to additional data and feedback, so that each of you may find your "next step," one aligned with your priorities, context, and available time to devote to this task. Regardless of which new approach you select, remember that equity-minded faculty treat feedback and data as gifts. They are invaluable resources for critical reflection and improvement. Before you proceed to the remainder of this section and identify ways to gather additional student perspectives and data, we suggest that you pause to reflect on and jot down responses to the following questions.

Pause to Consider

- What do you wonder about the experiences of your students from marginalized backgrounds?

- What's missing from your SET results? What questions do you wish were included?

- What do you wonder about students' learning and success in your course? Have you noticed any patterns in terms of who succeeds?

- What data are available to you to support your equity-minded practice (whether via your institution or from your personal class records)?

Keep your responses to these questions handy while you review the following ideas and determine which (one or two) strategies you will implement the next time you teach.

Four Equity-Minded Ways to Gather, Engage with, and Respond to Data

We have sequenced these in order of complexity (from simple to complex).

1. Ask Your Own Questions, Including Explicitly Equity-Minded Ones

One approach to using data in your quest to become an equity-minded teacher is to supplement your institution's current SET questions. If your college doesn't allow you to adjust or add questions to the official survey, you might use Google Forms or a survey tool available at your college, like Qualtrics. You could also administer the extra survey via your learning management system (like Canvas or Blackboard). In either case, consider asking questions that speak closely to what students experience in your class. The implication from the NSSE and Wabash studies, for instance, is that instead of asking students to "evaluate" teaching, we might ask them to describe their engagement in specific practices known to be associated with learning and success. Consider these three NSSE prompts, for instance:

> *In your experience at your institution during the current school year, about how often have you done each of the following?*
>
> - *Asked questions in class or contributed to class discussions*
>
> - *Included diverse perspectives (different races, religions, genders, political beliefs, etc.) in class discussions or writing assignments*
>
> - *Put together ideas or concepts from different courses when completing assignments or during class discussions*[13]

Given your interest in more equitable student outcomes, it can be extremely helpful to ask questions that specifically address how students perceive your teaching in terms of inclusivity and equity-mindedness. Some institutions have begun helping faculty gather these data, offering us models for this work. The Ohio State University's College of Education and Human Ecology recently piloted a survey titled "Supplemental Evaluations of Inclusive Classroom Instruction," recognizing the importance of inclusive practice and of students' take on the implementation thereof. The seven-item scale in the 2020 pilot includes questions related to instructors' actions regarding the following:

- use of culturally diverse examples in their courses
- privileging of students of the instructor's own culture over students from different cultures
- high expectations for all students regardless of their cultural background
- facilitation of disagreements from students from different cultures

- valuing cultural commonalities and differences
- respect for their own cultural background.[14]

Similarly, Tasha Souza at Boise State University offers a variety of possible items to help equity-minded professors assess how effective they are in creating inclusive learning environments (whether online or in physical spaces).[15] See some samples in the following box. Souza suggests that instructors ask students to explain their answers using specific examples. While not all of the questions may apply to every course you teach, her list provides a good starting point to think about approaches to soliciting equity-minded feedback from students during or outside of the SETs process.

Equity-Focused Survey Items

Following is Souza's list of possible equity-focused survey items that could be added to a course feedback form. Souza breaks the list down into three categories: the course, the instructor, and the student. Questions related to the course vary from accessibility and affordability of materials to course content, including asking students to what extent they agree with the following:

- "The course content included diverse perspectives."

- "This course increased my understanding of systems of inequality based on diverse identities."

- "This course increased my understanding of, and empathy for, the experience of people with identities different from my own."

Possible items that relate to the instructor are most extensive and include statements such as these:

- "The instructor took efforts to create an environment that supports diversity, respects differences, and makes all students feel welcome."

- "The instructor demonstrated respect for individual differences (e.g., disabilities, gender, race, religion, sexual orientation)."

- "The instructor made adjustments to the course to address students' learning needs."

- "The instructor provided opportunities for all students to engage meaningfully with the curriculum and achieve their full potential."

Possible items that focus on the student experience include the following:

- "I felt comfortable sharing my ideas and knowledge in the course."

- "I felt like I belonged in the course due to the instructor's efforts."

- "If I needed help, I felt like the instructor was eager to help me."

The instructor-related questions, which focus on students' impressions of how students in general experienced the course, could easily be tweaked to make them more focused on how each individual student experienced the course (e.g., "The instructor provided opportunities *for me* to engage meaningfully with the curriculum and achieve *my* full potential").

Source: Tasha Souza, Evaluation of Teaching Items in Course Evaluations *(Boise: BUILD, Boise State University, 2022), https://www.boisestate.edu/build/inclusive -excellence-resources/inclusive-resources-evaluation-of-teaching-items-in-course -evaluations/.*

2. Seek a Deeper, Broader Understanding of Your Students' Experiences

Understanding and engaging with the diversity of your students' experiences is a key aspect of equity-minded teaching. And, not surprisingly, research on student experiences is opening up a world of new information about what an effective, equitable, and holistic education might look like. One way this picture is emerging is through what is known as a **phenomenological approach** to understanding students' experience of learning.

Phenomenological studies aim to understand the experience of a situation as it really is.[16] If we apply this methodology to teaching and learning, as done by Amedeo Giorgi, Max van Manen, Kiymet Selvi, Allen J. Heindel, and Amy J. DeWitt,[17] we ask: "How can I understand the meaning of my students' educational experience *as it really is to them*?" To do so, we must engage with each student and seek meaning by immersing ourselves in the experience itself.[18] In other words, it is not enough to ask the students what they experience; we commit to engaging with their "experienced truth," and how that experience *feels* to them, to try to understand its meaning.

Coauthor Mays Imad, for example, conducted a preliminary research study using both qualitative and quantitative approaches to try to understand what matters to her students and how they experience their courses and the institution.[19] The research was prompted by her learning that some of her anatomy

phenomenological approach: A methodology that aims to understand students' experience of learning as it really is.

and physiology second-year students were feeling disenchanted with their educational experience. She recalls a student asking if they could talk about current events in the classroom to try to make sense of the increasing uncertainty of the world. She reasoned that in order to provide a holistic learning experience, it was necessary to understand what mattered to her students in their education. To ensure that she didn't make assumptions, Mays intentionally reflected and deliberated on her own perception of her students' experience and compared it to the students' actual experience. For example, she assumed that her students didn't care to engage with the liberal arts or that they only wanted to get a job.[20] To further her goal, she developed a twenty-item survey in which respondents consider different statements on a four-point Likert scale (1 = Disagree strongly; 4 = Strongly agree). The items generated for the instrument were inspired by her dialogues with and feedback from Pima Community College students enrolled in her biology course and her anatomy and physiology course.

Mays's conversations with her students revealed that the students were feeling bored, unheard, exhausted, and were craving relationships and meaning.[21] Hence, Mays designed a survey with statements to purposefully examine students' perception of their relationship to the following:

- themselves (e.g., "At school, I feel that I matter.")
- their professors (e.g., "I feel empowered by my professors.")
- their peers (e.g., "I feel empowered by my classmates.")
- the community (e.g., "At school, I feel I belong to a community.")
- teaching and learning (e.g., "Social justice and democracy are intertwined with teaching and learning.")
- education (e.g., "I would describe my education as an equal combination of challenge, inspiration, and motivation.")

Her study has now gathered information from more than eight hundred first- and second-year students from Pima Community College (in-person and online STEM and non-STEM majors) and from the University of California San Diego (in-person STEM majors). The key trends in the data included students overwhelmingly feeling "heard" by their professors (more than 50 percent) and that at school they feel that they "matter" (more than 80 percent). Mays's analysis concludes that in order for students to believe they are receiving an education that offers "an equal combination of challenge, inspiration, and motivation," they must also experience the following three elements: (1) a sense of belonging to a community, (2) a sense of empowerment, and (3) a sense of meaning and purpose.

In addition to completing the twenty-item survey, students were asked to describe their optimal learning environment and to finish the following sentences: "I wish my professor knew _____" and "The purpose of higher education is to _____." Mays also conducted focus-group interviews. The following examples are representative responses from students describing their optimal learning environment:

- "[One] factor that I would find helpful in creating an optimal learning environment would be helping the students get to *know each other* for a few minutes when class starts for the semester."

- "[Professors] can create an optimal learning environment by building *relationships* with students and making themselves available to those who need help."

- "I would like to *know more people* I can relate to in the class. If the professor helped facilitate that, it would help me. I can join study groups then."

The common denominator in these examples and in the three elements (belonging/community, empowerment, meaning/purpose) is relationships. In other words, what emerged from both qualitative and quantitative analyses is that students, regardless of their institutional type or course modality, seek a well-rounded education that is grounded in meaningful relationships. Students want to connect not just with their professors but also with their peers and community, the course content, and with themselves. And, while the categories of peers, professor, content/knowledge, community, and self may have some overlap, regardless of the breakdown, one theme becomes crystal clear: according to students, relationships and connections play a central role in their learning and experiences.

Mays's study focused on students in face-to-face settings, but online instructors can benefit in particular from collecting data about how students experience virtual learning environments, which can feel isolating. Using an LMS survey or external tool such as Google Forms, ask your online students questions related to the following four themes: their sense of belonging and community, their feeling of empowerment, their sense of meaning and purpose, and their feeling of experiencing relationships with other students and with you. This exercise may reveal areas in which you can strengthen these aspects online. Refer to Section Two, on belonging, trust, and day-to-day strategies, for more ideas on how to do this.

While these findings are consistent with those of other studies,[22] what was surprising about Mays's research is that when she asked almost two dozen faculty members to predict what students care about in their education, *those four themes did not emerge*. Most of the professors she interviewed predicted that students care mostly about "getting an A," "getting into medical school," or "getting a high-paying job." This disconnect between our assumptions and students' stated priorities could compromise our relationship with students and our ability to support their learning. You may want to follow Mays's lead, use or adapt her methodology, and seek ways to understand your students' experiences more deeply and comprehensively.

3. Gather Feedback from Start to Finish

Rather than waiting until the middle or end of the term, consider soliciting early formative feedback on your teaching and students' experience. Ask your students what might be helping or hindering their learning and/or otherwise affecting their experience in your class. This practice not only gives you the opportunity to address some issues while the course is still running but also helps you become more critically reflective. Seeking early feedback and addressing it transparently with your students demonstrates your genuine commitment to inclusive teaching and offers an opportunity to strengthen your relationship with your students. This practice also models humility, trust, and lifelong learning, and it helps to reduce the distance that can make online learning and success more challenging.

In Section Two, we suggested surveying students to assess their sense of belonging, yet the process can also be more general. You might ask a few basic questions that focus on students' experience and what changes you and the class as a whole can enact to improve the learning experience. Feedback can be ongoing, on the fly, and as simple as a daily or weekly three-minute paper or online survey that asks students to respond to a couple of simple questions:

1. What did you learn in class today or in this module? (Or, What were your greatest insights? What were the most important things we discussed?)

2. What questions or concerns do you still have? (Or, What are your unresolved questions? What are you feeling confused about?)

In person, you can use the papers with students' responses in a variety of ways. You can ask students to pair off and discuss their responses, then debrief as a whole class. In any size class, you can collect them, quickly scan them, and ascertain your students' level of understanding, looking for trends or important questions. You can then begin your next class with reviewing the most important points, answering questions, and clarifying any possible misunderstandings. Or, in a small class, you can respond to students' questions directly on their essays and then return them. However, you do not have to collect them. You can instead ask one or several students to read their responses from the previous class at the beginning of that day's class. Doing so acts as a review of the previous class and again offers the opportunity to clarify any issues. In an online synchronous class, you can engage students in breakout groups and ask them to respond in collaborative spaces such as Google Docs, Google Slides, or Padlet. This activity could also take the form of an anonymous asynchronous discussion board.

Either way, you are opening up lines of communication between yourself and your students, gathering important information about their learning and experiences in your class and with the material.

There are plenty of other approaches to gathering ongoing feedback, both in class and outside of class or online. You could send an email or announcement to your class after the first week and explain that you will be sending a bimonthly one-question anonymous survey to inquire about their learning experience in your class. For example, a few weeks after the start of the semester, Mays invites her students to participate in a one-question survey that is meant to give her a chance to receive and use the feedback that same term. On the survey, she asks: "Is there anything I am doing or not doing that is making you or your classmates feel excluded from our class? If so, please specify, and if you have any suggestions, do share as well." This pointed question is valuable because student exclusion—or the perception of exclusion—affects students' ability to engage, learn, and thrive. Mays states that she not only reads and reflects on the feedback but also shares a summary of it with her students. She thanks them for their insights and, when warranted, addresses how she plans to improve their experience in her courses.

One key moment in the semester when you should consider soliciting additional feedback from your students is at the midway point in the term. Midsemester feedback is a powerful tool that can play a variety of roles in improving your teaching, and it can be gathered informally or formally, typically (although not always) in writing. Michael Reder, the director of the Joy Shechtman Mankoff faculty Center for Teaching & Learning at Connecticut College, uses a simple approach that requires no preparation: Ask your students to take out a blank piece of paper. Then ask them to help you create a simple list of the components of the class. Write these components on a whiteboard or Google Doc, for example. The list might include items such as the following:

- discussion
- small group work
- lectures
- readings
- labs
- problem sets
- case studies
- in-class writing
- informal postings / journals / reading responses
- instruction during labs
- feedback during studio time
- feedback on your writing

Four Equity-Minded Ways to Gather, Engage with, and Respond to Data

- your effort outside of class
- your effort inside of class / during class

When the list is complete, ask your students to create a horizontal graph labeled "not enough" on the left, "just right" in the center, and "too much" on the right, as in figure 9.1.

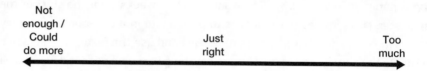

FIGURE 9.1   Template for Student Evaluation of Class Components

Then ask your students to place the different class components on the horizontal axis, according to their assessment of the activities. This exercise can also be done online, synchronously or asynchronously, using a Google Doc laid out with text similar to the illustration in figure 9.1. The labels can even be pre-entered (as they are in figure 9.1), and students can simply cut and paste them in the location in which they desire along the graph.

Because we have found that in each category of activities there are typically a few students at either end of the axis, with a large number in the "just right" middle, this type of feedback can serve as an exercise in norming when you report the results to the class, helping set expectations for the entire class. (For example, "Of the twenty responses, three of you wanted more discussion, two of you wanted less, and fifteen of you thought the amount was just right.") If there are many responses at either end of the spectrum ("too much" or "not enough"), you may want to consider modifying your class in some way.

In addition to, or instead of, the graph exercise, you may want to ask students specific, open-ended questions, such as the following:

- What parts of our course are contributing most to your learning?
- Is there anything you can do to increase your learning or improve your experience?
- Is there anything I, as the instructor, can do to help your learning?
- Do you feel comfortable participating in class? If not, what could change to make you feel more comfortable?
- What can I, your instructor, do to help make your learning journey in this course more meaningful?
- What can you, as a member of this learning community, do to help make your classmates' learning journey in this course more meaningful?

For the midterm survey in asynchronous online courses, you might consider adding a question about a sense of community. For example, "What suggestions do you have for me to strengthen the sense of community in our online class?" The responses to these open-ended questions are often short and can easily be summarized and analyzed. These on-the-fly feedback forms can be used in an in-person class or online (via a Google Form), are quick to compile, and offer you the opportunity to report back to your students during the next class or at the beginning of the next module.

The midsemester check-in process can also be made more formal, giving students more time to think and write about their experiences in the class to date. This can be done in person or using technology. For example, you could send an anonymous midterm evaluation—on Google Forms or another simple survey platform—in which you ask your students to share their feedback about their learning experience thus far in your course.

Regardless of what format or level of formality you choose, begin by explaining to your students the intention behind the exercise and what goals you hope to achieve. For example, you might tell your students that you want to make sure that your perception of their experience in your course matches their actual experience. Then, to better understand their experience, ask your students to give you feedback about a particular part of your course and how it affects them negatively or positively. Remind your students that by giving you feedback, they are contributing to fostering a better learning environment for themselves, their classmates, and future students. Students have told us how much they appreciate this midterm check-in and how powerfully it demonstrates their instructor's concern for their learning and success. It can be a key step in maintaining and deepening students' trust.

Next, take the time to process the feedback on your own. To give your thoughts more structure, you could develop your own rubric: Do you agree or disagree with the student? If you disagree, ask yourself, "Is there any truth in the feedback?" What messages are students trying to convey to you, and what are your points of resistance and why? As with end-of-semester student feedback, use the information you gather from students to compare their experience with your own perception. Do they align? If so, this is wonderful, an indication that you are attuned to your students. If not, why, and how does your perception differ from their experience? What can you do about it?

Finally, report back to students—as soon as possible after they have shared their feedback—what they as a class had to say and how you will respond. For online classes, record a brief video about the feedback and share it with them. As stated earlier, reporting back to students shows that you have read and considered their feedback. It also gives you an opportunity to respond—by way of further explanation, your own suggestions, or with changes you may make in the course. For instance, Mays once received anonymous feedback from one of her students who told her that she often says "you guys" when addressing the class and explained how that made some of the students feel excluded because they don't identify as "guys." Mays responded by taking that comment back to her class, thanking whoever shared the feedback, acknowledging her use of "you guys," and committing to eliminating (or at least minimizing) it from her speech in class. She also asked her students to kindly remind her if it happens again.

Letting students know that you will bring in the feedback along with your reflection and share it with them is especially important if you are teaching an asynchronous online course. It might be tempting for online students to assume that you are seeking feedback only because your department requires it. Don't leave them hanging, wondering what happened to their feedback. Send an email or post an online announcement describing your reflection on their feedback and explaining how you intend to address it. Or consider sharing a three-minute informal video announcement (again, this could be written, but your face and your voice matter, so try recording your reflection if possible).

4. Dive into Disaggregated Student Outcomes Data

This suggestion is last on our list—indicating its relative complexity and ambition compared to our previous recommendations—because it can require partnering with departmental leadership and/or colleagues from the institutional research office. First, we want to explain why disaggregated data are so important to equity-minded teaching and how you might use data already available to you. Disaggregating data essentially means breaking the data down into categories; in education, common categories include students' race, ethnicity, gender, age, and socioeconomic status. When you read about so-called "achievement gaps," those discussions are based on data that have been disaggregated and then compared: for example, comparing graduation rates of students of color to their White peers. Taking the time to disaggregate data is essential in addressing inequities, as Georgia Bauman writes, because it allows us to "see" differences in student outcomes.[23]

The publication *Data Tools*, part of the Equity-Minded Inquiry Series from the Center for Urban Education (CUE), outlines five strategies for analyzing and using disaggregated data.[24] Strategy one is to find course-level indicators or data points—what CUE calls "vital signs"—that are connected to a personal or institutional equity goal. They provide this example:

> **Goal:** *In line with the dean's call to increase Black, Latinx, and Pacific Islander participation in STEM, a math instructor has set the goal of improving the success rates of these students in her college algebra course from 50 to 65 percent—the average course success rate in her department—over the next three years.*
>
> **Vital Signs:** *First- and census-day course enrollment, midterm and final exam grades, all disaggregated by race and ethnicity.*

Benefits and Risks of Data Disaggregation

The Center for Urban Education (CUE) specifies four ways in which disaggregating student outcomes data by race and ethnicity helps advance racial equity:[25]

1. Data disaggregation transforms equity goals from something vague to something measurable.

2. It generates insights, as we discover new patterns in the data.

3. It raises questions and unearths assumptions about student outcomes, as we seek to understand what might account for gaps.

4. It frames racial equity as an ongoing process and as a site of inquiry and learning.

At the same time, a significant risk when disaggregating data is that we reinforce stereotypes about our students and their abilities, or that we do little else after noticing inequities. Tia Brown McNair, Estela Mara Bensimon, and Lindsey Malcolm-Piqueux use the example of a faculty member who notices equity gaps in her students' performance and views the gaps as evidence of her student's deficits. The resulting action (or inaction) differs considerably from that of colleagues who "ask themselves how their own practices create or exacerbate the inequities" revealed in the data.[26] The latter is an essential step in using disaggregated data to advance equity: reflecting on and making sense of the data, and choosing to take responsibility for ensuring more equitable results.

Strategy two is to ensure that the data being monitored are "close to practice"; in other words, the practitioner in question (in our case, faculty) should be able to access the data via their everyday work, which increases the likelihood that the individuals will follow through with the analysis and make changes based on what they find. In the example just presented, the vital signs seem "close to practice" because it seems likely the math faculty would have easy access to the data. However, the instructor may need to partner with a colleague in their institutional research office to disaggregate the data by race and ethnicity.

Strategy three is a process of analysis and sense-making. First, we determine if there are equity gaps associated with student identities, particularly race and ethnicity. Next, we seek to attribute any equity gaps as a dysfunction of policies and practices that may not be working for racially minoritized students. For instance, we might ask, "What is it about my course content and assignments, class policies, communication style, and so on, that better supports White students' learning and success?" Finally, we candidly notice, reflect on, and question our underlying assumptions and biases. Overall, the process pushes each of us to better understand the factors both external to us (institutional policies and practices) and within us (our lived experiences and biases) that may be resulting in our students' inequitable levels of course success.

Strategy four is more tactical in nature. It asks us to translate equity gaps into numbers of students. For instance, the math faculty member mentioned earlier would notice that the equity gaps for her Black, Latinx, and Pacific Islander students represent an average of twenty-four students per year. CUE has found that moving from abstraction to a concrete number can help motivate us to refine our practice and see that our goals are attainable. While closing an intangible equity or opportunity gap may seem out of reach, most of us can imagine supporting the success of twenty-four students.

Strategy five entails articulating specific, time-bound goals. In the example of the math instructor, she has committed to achieving her goal within three years. Setting a time frame helps us stay on track and hold ourselves accountable.

What does setting time-bound goals look like in practice? Informally, you can look at your course records (in your LMS grade center, for instance) for a single semester and consider the following: Who participates and who does not? Is there a trend or pattern in attendance? What about grades for individual assignments? Who shows up for office hours? Who gets Ds or Fs, or withdraws (DFWs)? If you don't have access to students' self-reported identities, your initial disaggregation can be based on students' visible identities (such as their race or gender). These data are admittedly incomplete, but collecting them can still be a helpful first step.

In Mays's case, she noticed a pattern of student performance when she started teaching anatomy and physiology. After the first exam, usually between one and three students dropped her class even before they received their exam grades. So Mays began reaching out to the students who preemptively dropped her course to inquire about what happened. As one student put it, after taking the exam they concluded that "this class is not for me," convinced they wouldn't pass the course. Yet Mays knew that students' fears were not always warranted: several students who had dropped the class in previous terms had earned a B or even higher on the exam.

Mays wanted to see if there was a trend among who was "preemptively dropping," so she worked with her institutional research office to gather data from several semesters and dissect those data. (If you need help retrieving data, your departmental leader can point you in the right direction and/or to an online data request form.) She discovered that those who had dropped were almost always first-generation students from minoritized backgrounds. "Seeing the data from multiple semesters told me that I had work to do. I needed to be more intentional about issues of academic belonging and challenges," says Mays. She started having a conversation with all of her students before they took the first assessment—affirming that the first exam neither defines them nor is an indication that they don't belong in the class. (See Unit 2 for guidance on equitable exam design and discussing grades with students.) The first exam, she tells them, is a data point to let *us*—yes, us: both students and instructor—know what we need to work on.

From this experience Mays learned firsthand the power of obtaining and disaggregating large-scale data. She started asking her colleagues and ultimately the department to investigate who is dropping from their courses and majors. If there is a correlation between those who are dropping or withdrawing and their racial and ethnic backgrounds, what does that tell us and what can we do about it?

Meanwhile, coauthor Bryan Dewsbury disaggregates data as part of his research agenda. Although the following example is not something most of us can do on our own, it illustrates what's possible when we work with departmental and other partners. While teaching at the University of Rhode Island, he and several colleagues (including a member of the teaching and learning team) examined historical student-success rates at the course level in the introductory biology sequence. They found "nagging academic performance gaps between different ethnic groups."[27] In the five years preceding 2014, student performance in both Principles of Biology I and Principles of Biology II followed a mostly similar pattern: White students, in general, earned the highest grades, while Black students earned the lowest.

With these research results in mind, Bryan implemented an inclusive, active approach in the sections he taught, and he monitored the impact. Students in the inclusively taught section of Principles of Biology I were more likely to get an A or B and least likely to earn a DFW grade, the research team reports, adding that "the key difference driving the improved overall performance was the improved outcomes for Black students." And the benefits were seen in students' success in the subsequent course. Students who had taken the inclusively taught section of biology in the first semester followed by an active-learning section of introductory biology in the second semester performed better in 200-level biology courses than students who had not enrolled in either the inclusive or the active-learning sections of Bio I.

Applying CUE's five strategies to Bryan's example, the long-term goal was to contribute to the diversification of STEM professionals by testing the impact of inclusive teaching practices on the course-level success and learning of minoritized students. Vital signs included disaggregated course grades in both the reformed course and the subsequent course. Because Bryan was teaching the course, the data were "close to practice." In terms of analysis and sense-making, the research team grounded its work in the large body of evidence suggesting that both active learning and inclusive practices can effectively improve academic outcomes. They hypothesized that a deeply humane, relational, and active approach to teaching (including a suite of evidence-based methods such as group work, interrupted lectures, and in-class problem solving) would result in more equitable outcomes. What does an improved outcome mean in numbers of students? On average, twenty to thirty-five more self-identified students of color on average per year were successfully continuing with their STEM degree, compared to sections where inclusive practices were not adopted. The study was time-bound, in that the team gave itself five years to implement the inclusive practices and refine their implementation before gathering data and examining the results.

Even after reading these examples, you may be reluctant to request disaggregated data for your students and courses, or unable to do so. If course-level data aren't a possibility, you might consider requesting departmental-level information—such as the demographic profile of majors, DFW rates in courses (the percentage of students who earn a D or F or who withdraw), and grades in courses. Disaggregation by race/ethnicity, first-generation status, gender, and other relevant categories can provide a snapshot of the current state of equity in your department. As you become increasingly aware of your institutional and departmental trends, you can begin to consider how your own individual behaviors and actions might contribute to—or challenge—those trends. And ideally, you'll also join forces with colleagues to engage in the work of attaining more equitable outcomes together.

Taking the Time to Act

As this section has described, there is a world of information and feedback to gather from your students—both within and beyond traditional SETs. This information can help you learn about your individual students, about teaching and learning in general, and about yourself as a teacher. And as we mentioned, more is not necessarily better with respect to data and feedback on your teaching. You can gather a great amount of feedback without it ever being useful—and without improving your teaching, helping your students learn more, or moving you along your journey to become an equity-minded instructor. The key is to reflect on the results and identify improvements you can make, and we hope the ideas in this guide will help you with both of these processes. If you're unsure what changes to try—or what to try first—we encourage you to connect with colleagues, current and former students, teaching and learning center staff, instructional designers, and others at your institution.

HOW CAN I GET STARTED?

For Any Class

- Set aside time after a class session or module to think through Kimberly Tanner's self-reflection questions (see Unit 8). In addition to asking yourself, "How do I think today's class session [or module] went?" ask yourself if you think it went equally well for all of your students, or if you perceived any differences in levels of engagement or understanding for students of varied identities.

- Send students a one- to three-question survey at the midway point of the term to find out how things are going; commit to sharing the results with them, plus tell them the *one* thing you'll do differently during the rest of the term based on their input.

- Determine if there are equity gaps in your students' course success by partnering with a colleague in your institutional research office to view your student success data disaggregated by race and ethnicity.

For In-Person Classes

- Use a few class sessions to gather and take notes on observational data, as an anthropologist might do. Do you notice any patterns in where your students sit, how they interact with one another or with you, and how much they participate in activities?

For Asynchronous Online Classes

- Intentionally create space and opportunities for "listening" to students (even if in asynchronous written form).

- After sending students a one- to three-question survey at the midway point of the term to find out how things are going, post a video in which you thank them, summarize the results, describe the *one* thing you'll do differently during the rest of the term based on their input, and invite them to post on a discussion board what else they suggest you do in response to the feedback provided.

For Synchronous Online Classes

- Use the chat function to ask students which key course features are affecting their experiences in the class (whether the readings, tests, discussions, etc.). Once you've collected those data, use the poll function to ask students to indicate which of the course features they feel are helping them learn, hindering their learning, or not having an impact on their learning.

- If your class is small enough, consider letting students into the Zoom class one by one from the waiting room. Take a moment to check in with each and ask for feedback on the class structure or your teaching.

CONCLUSION

A LEARNING SANCTUARY

If you've read through the guide and made it to this conclusion, you've thoroughly considered course design, teaching, and reflection opportunities. We thank you for persevering to arrive at this point and imagine you may be wondering, "What else could equity-minded teaching possibly entail?" So in this brief conclusion, we'll zoom out from the day-to-day responsibilities of teaching and the cadence of the academic calendar to offer our closing reflections on the beautiful future we can co-create with one another and with our students. We'll share a few examples of the steps we might each take to build—and teach our students to build—a more just world.[1]

Beyond our faculty roles, our disciplinary identities, and even our personal lives, we are each human beings. And as Sylvia Wynter, Jamaican educator, philosopher, and essayist, writes, "Human beings are magical.... Words made flesh, muscle and bone animated by hope and desire, belief materialized in deeds, deeds which crystallize our actualities."[2] She reminds us that in the translation of our hopes and desires into words and actions, there lies infinite potential—including the potential to tell a different story for humanity, one that honors our interdependence and interconnectedness. We share Wynter's vision. We wrote this guide because we believe that those of us who have the privilege of working in higher education can do better—as educators *and* as humans. We wrote this guide because we want to tell and be part of a different story for higher education. The heart of this book is ultimately a quest to cultivate what coauthor Mays Imad calls a learning sanctuary, a space where students are empowered to co-create meaning, purpose, and knowledge. In this space, the path to learning is cloaked with radical hospitality and paved with hope and moral imagination.[3] Here in our conclusion, we invite you to co-create learning sanctuaries with your students.

This line of thinking may puzzle you if you consider higher education an inherently equalizing force, a vehicle for social and economic mobility—in short, if you see higher ed as the solution to societal inequities, not a sector in need of reform. And in many ways, we agree. Earning a college degree continues to confer enormous benefits, financial and otherwise, to students. In addition, our institutions have made considerable progress in improving student learning and success, and in being more inclusive. Yet as economists Sandy Baum and

Michael McPherson write, higher education is both a source of improvement and a "means of reproducing social inequality over generations."[4] They explain that the attainment gaps we see in our colleges and universities mirror social inequities, ones that take their toll long before students arrive in our courses and on our campuses.

A notable example they outline is the racial wealth gap in America. "In 2016, the median White family in the United States had 4.8 times the median wealth of Hispanic families . . . and 6.6 times the median wealth of Black families," write Baum and McPherson—and this gap is "only getting larger."[5] Money isn't the only worthy goal, they acknowledge. However, wealth represents not only how much individuals can consume but also how well they are protected against risks, how they can choose to use their time, and how much agency they have relative to others. In turn, debt accumulation is an example of how inequity can be exacerbated by college participation. As the Institute for College Access and Success (TICAS) explains, the student borrowers who end up defaulting on their loans tend to be the same individuals who faced significant barriers in accessing college and completing their degrees: "The fact that vulnerable students go on to face higher risk of default compounds the inequities in our system."[6]

The correlation of wealth and race in America has a historical basis in enslavement and racism, of course, as Ibram X. Kendi, Khalil Gibran Muhammad, Edward E. Baptist, and so many others have chronicled.[7] And it is important to recognize that although formal enslavement is not part of our contemporary life, the effects of racism endure and affect us all, often in ways that are invisible to us. As sociologist and professor Ruha Benjamin explains, "Racism . . . is a form of theft. Yes, it has justified the theft of land, labor, and life throughout the centuries. But racism also robs us of our relationships, stealing our capacity to trust one another, ripping away the social fabric."[8] Earlier in this guide we explained that social cohesion and trust are core elements of equity-minded teaching, essential to student learning and success. Yet the point here is that each of *us* suffers, too, when inequality and racism deny us the ability to fully connect to our students and to one another.

The history of Black Americans is not only a reminder of hardship and cruelty, however; it also offers us an inspirational precedent for the learning sanctuary we envision. As Jarvis Givens, professor of education and African and African American Studies, writes, Black school teachers in the nineteenth century knew that a key part of their role was "to bring students in the classroom, close the door, and shut the world out," creating an opportunity for students to "reach higher, to think beyond the world that they knew, a world that was not good enough." These courageous teachers insisted that students "deserved tenderness and space to encounter and create beauty, . . . [such that classrooms] were sites for gathering and refuge: realms for teachers and students to model what it truly meant to be in right relationship with one another, opportunities to try on new ways of being in this earthly place."[9] In the learning sanctuaries the teachers created for and with their students, students were temporarily safe, free, and able to be vulnerable and creative—what we want to make possible for all of the students we have the honor of teaching.

What do we, the authors of this guide, see when we envision contemporary learning sanctuaries? Our vision begins outside of our colleges and universities, where we see little to no poverty and comprehensive access to early education. Each member of our society has recognized the futility of and harm caused by divisiveness, and in its place, we have cultivated an ethos and practice of love. In this future, learning is not only an intellectual endeavor but also a spiritual and holistic one. We do not just accept but also truly value different ways of being and knowing. And as students come in and out of our online modules and physical classrooms, they never wonder if they belong because they are our true partners in the work. They are actively engaged in helping us design our courses, teach, evaluate learning, and even more broadly, welcome new students to the institution and help their peers attain academic and personal goals.

Feeling safe, supported, and empowered, students are practicing democratic participation, engaging respectfully with us and with one another on questions of sustainability, globalization, our shared history, and other issues that matter deeply to them. As they practice exercising their student rights, students are reminded that they have agency—that they can absolutely be part of building the compassionate society they seek to inhabit. They freely use their languages and voices, letting us see their authentic selves and, in turn, inspiring us to show more of our authentic selves at work. Cultivating this authenticity requires that the pain that comes with growth and loss—and life—is honored, rather than being pushed aside as inappropriate or inconvenient. When we peek inside classrooms, Zoom rooms, online modules, and email exchanges, we see caring and clear communication facilitated by environments and exchanges that are deeply relational. Technology is effectively deployed to foster connection and to support teaching and learning, and the lines between online and in-person teaching have become blurred. Standardized grading has been replaced by learning- and growth-focused feedback, and external motivators are no longer necessary, as students recognize all the ways in which they are benefiting from and contributing to their education.

The primary outcome of this learning sanctuary for students is, of course, freedom. To be educated is to be freed, freed from being subjected to others' definition of one's reality. As equity-minded faculty, we too are freed. To use bell hooks's words, learning sanctuaries result in "liberating mutuality," where both the professor and their students are co-liberated.[10] Not just free, students are also *empowered* to shape and be shaped by bright futures. They have been equipped with disciplinary content and competencies, as well as the critical thinking, creative problem solving, and interpersonal skills needed to live and flourish in an increasingly uncertain world.

On Building New Systems

With this tapestry of a more beautiful future in mind, you may now wonder if and how any one of us, as individuals, can actually create a learning sanctuary for students. First, we want to clarify that we encourage you to work toward *your* version of a learning sanctuary, which may be markedly different from ours. And yes, we firmly believe that we can each make an important difference.

Generally, people are quick to critique systems, forgetting that they are developed and sustained by individuals. But if systems exist because of individuals, then each of us can create a ripple effect toward the systemic change we wish to see, and collectively, our actions can generate new systems. Teaching, in particular, is an inherently potent catalyst for change: There are inward-facing, day-to-day actions through which we elevate and empower students, and move forward with them. At the same time, we can choose to advocate outwardly— within and outside of our colleges.

How might we turn the tide and create a more beautiful future? Archbishop Desmond Tutu provides some guidance when he speaks to our innate ability to learn with and from each other. He affirms that he "learned to be a human from other human beings," encouraging us to leverage the power of relationality and connections—that is, to engage in our aspirational endeavors in partnership and collaboration.[11] Sylvia Wynter also addresses the question of *how* to advance justice, and she too highlights the role of partnership. She beckons us to "marry *our* thoughts" with the thoughts of those who have historically been silenced.[12] In essence, Wynter asks us to consider, deeply and earnestly, the plight of those who have been marginalized and silenced so we may begin to disrupt cycles of injustice and produce new forms of knowledge.

In terms of specific steps you might take to create learning sanctuaries, we would be remiss not to direct you to the previous units in this guide. The research and guidance on equity-minded teaching we share in the units are intended to result in deep and meaningful learning and academic success, so the practices we recommend are important steps toward this brighter future. To intensify the impact of these practices at your institution or in your discipline, consider sharing this guide or specific insights and practices with colleagues. In doing so, you will be modeling humility and courage, demonstrating that you know there is more you can do for your students. Peer-to-peer connections also have great potential to bring otherwise skeptical colleagues to the equity table. Here are a variety of additional concrete ways to begin cultivating a learning sanctuary:

- *Teach students to value and build a more just society.* Baum and McPherson argue that educating students about inequities in areas such as poverty, access to education, and housing is one of the most important steps institutions can take to help level the playing field.[13] College graduates are more active citizens than people without degrees, and many become politicians, educators, or leaders of industry who can effectuate change. Eboo Patel, in turn, implores us to teach students how to *build*, not simply *critique*, society and systems. "We have enough critics," he points out. "What we need are more builders, more people who know how to create instantiations of a fair, just and inclusive social order."[14] In our courses and assessments, we can give students practice by challenging them to offer equitable solutions to social problems.

- *Promote civic engagement.* In the United States, minoritized individuals, the children of parents with less formal education, and people living in poorer neighborhoods tend to be least civically engaged. Yet some scholars have described civic participation as a proactive means through which youth of color counter adversity.[15] Promoting civic engagement might mean encouraging students to participate in student government, exercise their student rights, complete assessments or assignments connected to local or national agencies or issues, volunteer in their communities, attend a local event, or register to vote. Two helpful resources are the Students Learn Students Vote (SLSV) Coalition (slsvcoalition.org) and Campus Compact (compact.org).

- *Create safe and supported opportunities for students to engage in difficult conversations.* College can be an important time for students to practice and develop the ability to talk productively and respectfully with others who have different views. In addition to the guideposts referenced in coauthor Bryan Dewsbury's case study in Unit 7, helpful tools include the conversation guides developed by the organization Living Room Conversations (livingroomconversations.org). These guides, which cover nearly a hundred topics, lead students step-by-step through discussions that will help them practice communicating across differences while building understanding and relationships.

- *Love your students.* At the core of loving relationships are care, respect, trust, and responsibility. We may not be accustomed to regularly using the term *love* when referring to our students or to teaching, yet this guide's four authors would argue that teaching is an act of love and necessitates love. J. Luke Wood agrees, and he encourages us to love our Black male students, in particular, given that they have been historically denied this virtue.[16] Wood also isolates specific ways we can embed love in our instructional practices: demonstrating excitement for our students' arrival, learning about them with interest, advocating for them, worrying about them, guarding them from others, boasting about them, and investing time in them.

- *Partner with students.* Explicitly seeking out student partnership shows humility, helps you motivate students, and validates students' expertise. Partnership happens when you ask your students to help you refine a course project or identify readings, for example. You can also seek out formal programs at your institution that employ students as partners to faculty (such as a Learning Assistant, Supplemental Instruction, or Students as Consultants of Teaching program).

- *Engage in institutional and departmental change efforts.* Within your department, you could engage colleagues in an analysis of disaggregated course-level data, committing together to make improvements. In Unit 8, we mentioned that you can help to minimize the negative impact of SET data by developing a new survey tool, sharing research on bias, and/or advocating for the use of additional data sources in teaching evaluations. Promoting efforts to include equity-minded teaching practices in incentive and reward structures may be especially powerful, as research by Tracie Addy and colleagues found that faculty often do not prioritize inclusive teaching because they do not see their institutions prioritizing it.[17] Beyond supporting initiatives related to SETs, you might serve on a college-wide committee focused on equity or inclusion, or encourage your institution to support students' holistic wellness, including food security and culturally grounded and accessible mental health support.

- *Model and invite radical empathy.* In her powerful book *Caste*, Isabel Wilkerson advocates for "radical empathy," which she defines as "putting in the work to educate oneself and to listen with a humble heart to understand another's experience from their perspective, not as we imagine we would feel."[18] She invites us to reach across differences of identity and make a connection with a fellow human. In doing so, we not only become more empathetic ourselves but also model to our students the value and process of becoming empathetic.

- *Continue interrogating yourself and practicing humility in discomfort.* As we mentioned in the Introduction, self-reflection on our identities is key to equity-minded teaching. Without reflection, instructional improvements lack authenticity and can have little positive impact. It may be especially helpful to reflect on your experiences of privilege. As literature and writing professor Allison Parker points out, discussions about diversity, equity, and inclusion tend to focus on people of color. The result, she explains, is that our understanding of equity is grounded in students' experiences of discrimination instead of our own experiences of privilege. When we do not recognize the impact of privilege, we inadvertently convey to our students that the challenges they experience come from their own deficiencies, rather than from systems of inequality.[19] Peggy McIntosh provides one helpful set of prompts for self-reflection in "White Privilege: Unpacking the Invisible Knapsack," in which she describes the daily effects of White privilege on her life.[20]

- *Notice and revise unspoken consensus.* In her book *Sentipensante (Sensing/Thinking) Pedagogy,* Laura I. Rendón calls her learning sanctuary an educational "dreamfield," one that is characterized by joy and compassion and that "speaks to who we are as whole human beings—intelligent, social, emotional, and spiritual."[21] To create a more beautiful future, Rendón contends, we must first notice the implicit agreements we have made as educators and how they manifest themselves in our day-to-day teaching. Examples include the agreement of competition over cooperation, the agreement of perfectionism (leaving little room for error), and the agreement of monoculturalism, one that validates Western structures of knowledge. She then empowers us to co-create new agreements. For instance, in place of monoculturalism, we might agree to a multicultural pedagogy and infuse teaching practices used by Native peoples.

We wrote this guide not just for the here and now but also for the future. We are heartened that you have read this work and have undertaken your own journey. At a time of political divisiveness and attacks on education, academic freedom, and even democracy, we recognize that this journey is difficult and at times lonely. And yet, educators like yourself continue to show up for their students and for humanity. Your courage and resolve humble and inspire us—and give us hope. Within the depth of our hearts we hear the echo of your heart's call for a more beautiful story, and we dedicate this guide to each of you.

ACKNOWLEDGMENTS

Writing the *Norton Guide to Equity-Minded Teaching* has been a labor of love and hope. Like many such efforts, it has felt, in turn, exhilarating, exhausting, challenging, humbling, inspiring, and important. This guide would not have reached its finished form without the passion, vision, guidance, critical feedback, and valuable input and care of many individuals.

First, we want to recognize the incredible efforts of the team at W. W. Norton. Editor and Vice President Jon Durbin was the first to reach out to us, inviting us to facilitate a workshop on equity for the editorial team. Ann Shin, Norton's editorial director for educational publishing, then connected us to a Norton working group on educational equity and student success. Discussions with and among this working group led to the idea for this guide, and Justin Cahill, the working group lead, was asked to serve as the project's editor. Justin's commitment to equity, knowledge, conscientiousness, patience, leadership, and collaborative spirit was invaluable at every step of this guide's development. He posed thoughtful questions, cheered us on during the hard parts, nudged gently, and celebrated each milestone with us. We are forever grateful! In turn, senior associate editor Anna Olcott was a patient collaborator and contributor who strengthened the guide with her meticulous eye. Similarly, copyeditor Scarlett Lindsay, proofreader Donna Mulder, project editor Thea Goodrich, and developmental editor Beth Ammerman ensured cohesion and consistency in the content, form, and voice of this guide. Permissions specialist Josh Garvin deftly handled the clearing of text and line art permissions. Jane Searle, director of production, wrangled a demanding schedule with kindness and enthusiasm, while the composition team at MPS Limited came to the rescue by typesetting these pages with dazzling speed and care. Marketing research and strategy managers Michele Dobbins and Julia Hall helped us communicate the guide's vision and distinctive features through the creation of video content and promotional materials.

To ensure that this guide meets the needs of faculty and is informed by faculty perspectives, the Norton team reached out to thirty-one faculty from across the country, and they generously provided feedback at all stages. We want to thank the following faculty for their input:

Mary Abercrombie, Florida Gulf Coast University
Jeremy Adelman, Princeton University
Lisa Armstrong, University of South Florida
Margaret Ayala, DeSales University
Marija Bekafigo, Northern Arizona University
Jessica Best, SUNY Adirondack
Cory Colby, Lone Star College, Tomball

April Ann Fong, Portland Community College

Pat Gehrke, University of South Carolina

Marcella Gemelli, Arizona State University

Anissa M. Graham, University of North Alabama

Julia Hellwege, University of South Dakota

Cathy Ishikawa, California State University, Sacramento

Linda Janke, Anoka-Ramsey Community College

Erica Jones, Northern Arizona University

Rahul Kane, Century College

Sam Kobari, San Diego State University

Mary Kochlefl, Xavier University

Suzanne Long, Monroe Community College

Lucy Malakar, Lorain County Community College

Cheryl Reed, Endicott College

Mary Elizabeth Rogers, Florida Gateway College

Krysti Ryan, College Transition Collaborative

Anna Santucci, University College Cork

Barbara Sarnecka, University of California, Irvine

Chad Sexton, Ocean County College

Evan Shenkin, Western Oregon University

Jeffrey D. Singer, Portland State University

Pam Solberg, Western Technical College

K. Elizabeth Soluri, Cabrillo College

Phillip Tussing, Houston Community College

Jilani Warsi, Queensborough Community College

Umme al-Wazedi, Augustana College

Erin Whitteck, University of Missouri, St. Louis

Russ Wood, Southwest Virginia Community College

Suzanne Young, University of Massachusetts, Lowell

We also thank our colleagues and friends Peter Felten, who provided critical feedback on the guide's proposal, and Susannah McGowan, who skillfully helped us outline and edit a unit that was especially challenging to craft.

In addition to the individuals we've already noted, Flower wishes to thank Isis, Mays, and Bryan, from whom she has learned and whose friendship she values so much. She is truly grateful for the support of various mentors on her equity journey, especially her friend and affinity-group colleague April Peters, and Flower's friends at the American Association of State Colleges and Universities (Melissa Welker, Jacqueline Jones, Robin Ellis, Terry Brown, and more) who rocket-boosted her equity journey through their deep commitment to advancing equity in higher education. Finally, Flower is grateful beyond words for the patient and generous support of her husband, Tim, and their daughters, Emerald, Pixie, and Brit, who freed up precious family time for her to engage fully in this important work; your sacrifice is so very much appreciated.

Bryan wishes to thank his wonderful coauthors, who truly made this a labor of love. He is always indebted to the students he has taught over the years, who have taught him and continue to teach him so much about lived experiences in this complex world. Bryan is especially grateful for his wife, Erica, and sons, Makai and Kenji, whose grace and patience allowed him to help finish this project. Finally, Bryan would like to dedicate this book to his late father, Reverend Sheldon Dewsbury, and his mother, Angela Dewsbury, whose sacrifice and belief allowed him to realize many dreams, including the completion of this project.

Mays wishes to thank Isis for inviting her to join this project and for her leadership throughout. She is grateful for her coauthors' insights, guidance, support, and sense of humor. She would like to thank her colleagues Treya Allen, David Asai, Hilda Ladner, Laura Rendón, Carolyn Sandoval, and Greg Wilson for modeling an unwavering commitment to equity in higher education. Mays is grateful to her family and friends (Nour, Sarah, Maryam, Yaseen, Rula, and Michael) for compassionately pushing her to never give up. She is indebted to her parents, who continue to model impeccable lucidity when it comes to equity and who gave up so much so she can experience a more equitable life. Mays dedicates this work to her students, whose beauty, brilliance, and resolve inspire her to continue to hope, especially on days when hope seems obsolete.

Isis is overwhelmed with gratitude for each of the individuals who contributed to this work; there are far too many to name individually. Bryan, Flower, and Mays each took a leap of faith and made considerable sacrifices to participate in this endeavor, and she thanks them for their trust, insights, candor, kindness, and hard work. This guide honors Isis's students, both those she has taught directly and those who have inspired her through their perseverance and brilliance; the many faculty who have trusted her with their aspirations, fears, and ideas; and her thought partners in a two-decades-long journey in equity-minded practice, notably Melissa Burley, Leslie Richardson, Phillip Carter, Sat Gavassa, Leanne Wells, Erica Caton, Ileana Hernandez, Belkis Cabrera, and Wendi Dew. Isis is especially appreciative of her family's patience and support as she worked through weekends and precious vacations—especially that of her husband, Sinuhe, her greatest champion in work and in life, and her daughters, Kamilah and Delilah, who fill her with optimism for a more just and more loving future.

APPENDIX

SECTION ONE, UNIT 1   **Formulating Significant Learning Objectives**   258

SECTION ONE, UNIT 3   **Course Planning Map**   260

SECTION TWO, UNIT 4   **The Grounded Model: Building Student-Teacher Trust in a "Beating the Odds" U.S. Urban High School**   262

The "Who's in Class?" Form   263

Formulating Significant Learning Objectives

Guiding Questions and Samples from a Developmental Psychology Course

Your long-term aspirations for your students

A year or more after the course concludes, I want and hope that students will _____.

Sample response: "describe key factors, including parents, schools, and society, that account for the individual differences that develop between us; engage civically in policy matters associated with development."

Category of significant learning	Questions to consider	Relevance-enhanced learning objectives *After successfully completing this course, you will:*
Foundational knowledge	• What key information—including key ideas regarding minoritized identities—is important for students to understand and remember in the future? • What key perspectives—including diverse scholarly perspectives—are important for students to understand in this course?	• Describe some of what science can tell us about development, from conception to adolescence, and how those changes are shaped by culture and context. • Describe select theories and findings by diverse influential scientists, both past and present, that help us understand human development.

Application	• What kinds of thinking are important for students to learn?
	  » critical thinking, in which students analyze and evaluate
	  » creative thinking, in which students imagine and create
	  » practical thinking, in which students solve problems and make decisions
	• What important skills do students need to gain?
		• Question whether important development phenomena or research findings are relevant or even applicable across different groups of people.
		
		• Use key developmental ideas to craft questions and hypotheses associated with challenges you see the parents in your families or communities confront.

Integration	• What connections (similarities and interactions) should students recognize and make
	  » among ideas within this course?
	  » among the information, ideas, and perspectives in this course and those in other courses or areas?
	  » among material in this course and the students' own personal, social, and/or work life?
		• Explain how environmental (e.g., income level) and genetic factors interact to shape individual development.
		
		• Notice how key developmental ideas are reflected in current debates about early childhood education.

Human dimension	• What could or should students learn about themselves? • What could or should students learn about understanding others and/or interacting with them?	• Identify some of the factors from your early environment and heredity that may have influenced and will continue to influence your development, particularly the ones that have contributed to your wellness and strengths. • Identify some of the factors from the early environment and heredity of one of your peers from a different cultural background than yours that may have influenced their development (cultural competence).
Caring	• What changes/values do you hope students will adopt? • What feelings do you want them to have about the subject matter?	• Commit to carefully examining policy matters that relate to development (like early childcare) and to becoming sufficiently informed when voting on related policies.

Learning how to learn	• What would you like students to learn about
	  » how to be a successful student in a course like this?
	  » how to learn about this particular subject?
	  » how to become a self-directed learner of this subject (i.e., have a learning agenda of what they need/want to learn and a plan for learning it)?
		• Find reliable sources when developmental questions arise in your life.
		
		• Borrow/adapt some of the methods used by developmental scientists for your own study habits.

Source: Adapted from Robyn L. Kondrad, "Example of a Well-Designed Course in Developmental Psychology" (designed using Fink's model), Design Learning, accessed March 22, 2022, http://www.designlearning.org/wp-content/uploads /2014/04/Kondrad-R.-Submission-Mar.-30.pdf.

Course Planning Map

Consider the following questions and prompts as you fill in the map on the opposite page.

Goals

List each course learning objective in a separate bubble. You may use the wording on your syllabus or your own formulation of the learning goal. For guidance on developing learning goals, review "Step 2. Develop Learning Objectives" in Unit 1.

Assessments

What will students do to demonstrate their learning for this learning goal? Are there multiple assessment options from which students might choose? How will you know if students have achieved this goal?

Materials and Activities

To gain new information or skills, what will students need to read, watch, and do? Are there multiple ways to present or share this information? How will students practice, explore, and interact with the material? Might you offer students options for engaging with practice, application, and problem-solving activities?

Technology and Other Resources

What online activities or apps (homework sets, discussions, publisher-provided activities, apps such as SPSS) will help students learn and retain new information and skills as they progress toward achieving course learning goals? What additional people (guest lecturers, YouTube explainer video hosts) or things (offline activities or materials in the real world) will help students gain competence? Again, consider whether there are options to plan for individual learner variability.

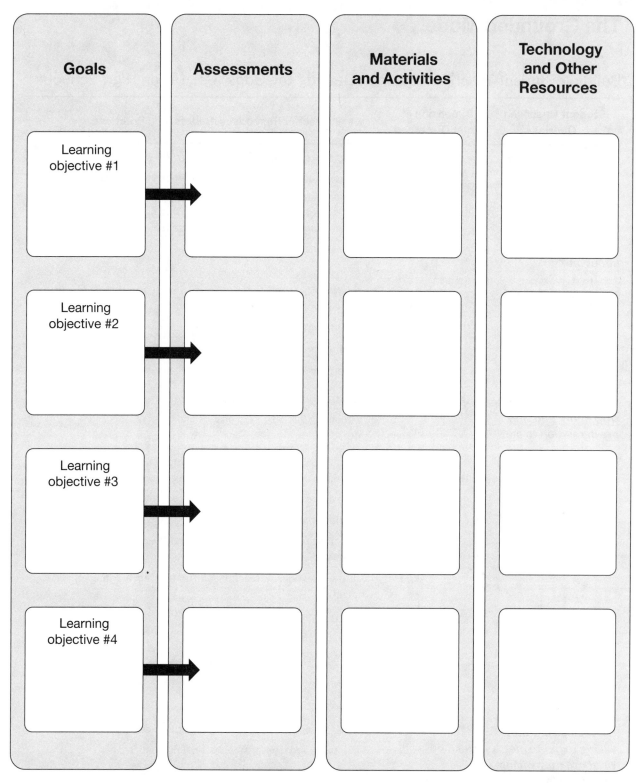

Goals	Assessments	Materials and Activities	Technology and Other Resources
Learning objective #1 →			
Learning objective #2 →			
Learning objective #3 →			
Learning objective #4 →			

Source: Adapted from L. Dee Fink, Creating Significant Learning Experiences: An Integrated Approach to Designing College Courses *(San Francisco: Jossey-Bass, 2003).*

The Grounded Model

Building Student-Teacher Trust in a "Beating the Odds" U.S. Urban High School

Student Unspoken Queries	Dimension of Trust Discerned	Teacher Responses, Beliefs, and Practices
"Why are they here?"	Teacher Motivation	*Trying to make a difference in students' lives* • Common moral purpose: "doing the right thing for kids" • Attitudes towards kids and teaching: "liking kids," "liking their job"
"How much do they know and care about me?"	Teacher Empathy	*Understanding challenges facing students* • Compassionate perspective-taking
"How much do they respect me?"	Teacher Respect for Students	*Optimistic Beliefs in Student Capabilities: Growth Mindset in Everyday Practice* • "Not judging" students: giving them a chance to grow • Avoiding unnecessary criticism: "they're plenty full of that" • Trusting students with knowledge of teachers' out-of-school lives
"How real are they? Do they know who they are in relation to me?"	Teacher Self-Awareness and "Credibility"	*Demonstrating Self-Awareness* • Overcoming divides based on race and class
"Do they know how to help me learn?"	Teacher Professional Ability	*Creating Classroom Belonging, Building Student Academic Engagement, and Practicing Equity Pedagogy* • Creative classroom community and positive affective climate • Engaging students with learning • Drawing on personality, charisma, and "likeability" to "hook" students • Culturally responsive teaching and connecting learning to students' lives • Using play and humor • Mobilizing equity pedagogy • Creating peer learning and leadership opportunities • Allowing for student vibrancy in the inclusive classroom • Providing a "safe space" for students
"How close are they willing to get to me? What are they willing to do to help me?"	Teacher Commitment	*Patience, Proximity, and Willingness to Invest Emotional Labor* • Availability and closeness (emotional proxemics) • Enacting commitment: investing emotional labor

Source: Peter Demerath et al., "A Grounded Model of How Educators Earn Students' Trust in a High Performing U.S. Urban High School," Urban Review 54, no. 5 (December 2022): fig. 1, https://doi.org/10.1007/s11256-022-00635-4.

The "Who's in Class?" Form

Note to instructors: Form is to be distributed via online survey software, not on paper or in PDF form, so as to keep learner identity anonymous within a course.

This form gives you the opportunity to share aspects of your social identity and other attributes that can help your instructor know how to better support overall learning in this course. Please be aware that you are not obligated to complete this form. The information collected will be aggregated, held anonymously, and used to help foster an inclusive and equitable classroom.

Course Name: _____

Instructor's Last Name: _____

Semester (e.g., Spring 2025): _____

Please answer the questions that follow. As a reminder, you are not obligated to answer any of the questions. The goal of this questionnaire is to help me understand who is in class so that I can support your success.

Section I.
Select all that apply.

Yes	No	
☐	☐	I work on or off campus. The number of hours that I work per week is: _____
☐	☐	I play on a varsity athletics team at this institution.
☐	☐	I live off campus. My commute time is: _____
☐	☐	I am over 25 years of age.
☐	☐	I am on active duty or a veteran.

Section II.
Select all that apply.

Yes	No	
☐	☐	I have a mobile device with Wi-Fi capability.
☐	☐	I have a laptop or desktop computer that I can use for classwork.
☐	☐	I am financially capable of purchasing all of the materials needed for this class (e.g., textbooks) without hardship.
☐	☐	I am Pell-eligible, meaning that my family income level allows me to qualify for federal Pell Grants.
☐	☐	I receive other forms of financial aid in significant amounts.

(continued)

Section III.
Select all that apply.

Yes	No

☐ ☐   I have a disability, either invisible or visible. Here is more information that I would like to share about my disability: _____

☐ ☐   Other health concerns that I would like to share are: _____

☐ ☐   I am a "quiet" student, meaning that I reenergize from having time alone.

☐ ☐   I engage in religious or spiritual practices that may impact my ability to attend class. More specifically, I would like to share: _____

☐ ☐   I engage in religious or spiritual practices that may impact my performance in class. More specifically, I would like to share: _____

☐ ☐   I have dependents that I take care of outside of school.

☐ ☐   My preference for class assignments is to complete them by typing rather than handwriting.

☐ ☐   Other factors that may impact my experiences in this class are: _____

Section IV.
Select all that apply.

Yes	No

☐ ☐   I am a first-generation student, i.e., neither of my parents obtained a bachelor's degree at a 4-year institution.

☐ ☐   One of my parents obtained a bachelor's degree at a 4-year institution.

☐ ☐   Both of my parents obtained a bachelor's degree at a 4-year institution.

☐ ☐   I have a sibling who has attended or is currently attending a 4-year institution.

Section V.
Answer the questions below.

My racial/ethnic background is: _____

My gender identity is: _____

My sexuality is: _____

The pronouns I use are: _____

My nationality/country of origin is: _____

English is not my first language. My proficiency level in English is (e.g., beginning/intermediate/advanced for listening/speaking/writing/reading): _____

Source: Excerpted from Tracie Marcella Addy et al., What Inclusive Instructors Do: Principles and Practices for Excellence in College Teaching *(Sterling, VA: Stylus, 2021), Appendix 1: The "Who's in Class?" Form, https://journals.asm.org/action /downloadSupplement?doi=10.1128%2Fjmbe.00183-21&file=jmbe00183-21_supp_1_seq8.pdf.*

NOTES

Introduction

1. Mays Imad, "Integrative Education and Teaching for Wholeness: Creating a Learning Sanctuary" (working paper); Mays Imad, "Trauma-Informed Teaching and Learning," episode 335, November 12, 2020, in *The Teaching in Higher Ed Podcast*, produced and hosted by Bonni Stachowiak, 44:02, https://teachinginhighered.com/podcast/trauma-informed-teaching-and-learning/#transcriptcontainer; Mays Imad, "Leveraging the Neuroscience of Now," June 3, 2020, *Inside Higher Ed*, https://www.insidehighered.com/advice/2020/06/03/seven-recommendations-helping-students-thrive-times-trauma.

2. Bryan Dewsbury et al., "Inclusive and Active Pedagogies Reduce Academic Outcome Gaps and Improve Long-Term Performance," *PLOS One* 17, no. 6 (June 2022), https://journals.plos.org/plosone/article?id=10.1371/journal.pone.0268620.

3. Sat Gavassa et al., "Closing the Achievement Gap in a Large Introductory Course by Balancing Reduced In-Person Contact with Increased Course Structure," *CBE—Life Sciences Education* 18, no. 1 (February 2019), https://doi.org/10.1187/cbe.18-08-0153; Sarah L. Eddy and Kelly A. Hogan, "Getting Under the Hood: How and for Whom Does Increasing Course Structure Work?" *CBE—Life Sciences Education* 13, no. 3 (September 2014): 453–68.

4. Asynchronous courses are those in which students and faculty engage in learning activities at different times; there are no set meeting times. In synchronous online courses, a live instruction component occurs at a set time, often via a tool like Zoom.

5. We use the phrase *teaching via Zoom* in the same way we use *Google a term* or *pass me a Kleenex*—to generally represent teaching in online video conference platforms including Teams, Webex, etc.

6. James M. Lang, *Small Teaching: Everyday Lessons from the Science of Learning* (San Francisco: Jossey-Bass, 2016); Flower Darby and Jim Lang, *Small Teaching Online: Applying Learning Sciences in Online Classes* (San Francisco: Jossey-Bass, 2019).

7. Jane Tomkins, "Pedagogy of the Distressed," *College English* 52, no. 6 (October 1990): 653–60, http://www.jstor.org/stable/378032.

8. Tia B. McNair, Estela M. Bensimon, and Lindsay Malcolm-Piqueux, *From Equity Talk to Equity Walk: Expanding Practitioner Knowledge for Racial Justice in Higher Education* (San Francisco: Jossey-Bass, 2020): 21.

9. Viji Sathy and Kelly A. Hogan, "Want to Reach All of Your Students? Here's How to Make Your Teaching More Inclusive: Advice Guide," *Chronicle of Higher Education*, July 22, 2019, https://www.chronicle.com/article/how-to-make-your-teaching-more-inclusive/.

10. Elaine Seymour and Anne-Barrie Hunter, eds., *Talking about Leaving Revisited: Persistence, Relocation, and Loss in Undergraduate STEM Education* (New York: Springer, 2019): v, https://doi.org/10.1007/978-3-030-25304-2.

11. Jan Arminio, Vasti Torres, and Raechele L. Pope, *Why Aren't We There Yet?: Taking Personal Responsibility for Creating an Inclusive Campus* (Sterling, VA: Stylus, 2012).

12. Available at https://implicit.harvard.edu/implicit/index.jsp.

13. Stephanie Long, "Black People Need Stronger White Allies—Here's How You Can Be One," *Refinery29*, May 27, 2020, https://www.refinery29.com/en-us/2020/05/9841649/allyship-ahmaud-arbery-george-floyd.

14. For the sake of simplicity, we use *hybrid* as a general term to describe classes that exist along the continuum of fully in person on one end and fully asynchronous/synchronous online on the other end. Colleges and universities are beginning to offer an

incredible range of mixed modalities (most often in an admirable effort to offer students increased flexibility and access). *Hybrid* inadequately captures this complexity, yet we intentionally use it as a representative term.

15. Jenae Cohn, "Enhancing the Student Experience" (virtual forum), *Chronicle of Higher Education*, September 21, 2021, https://www.chronicle.com /events/virtual/enhancing-the-student-experience.

16. Doug Lederman, "Detailing Last Fall's Online Enrollment Surge," *Inside Higher Ed,* September 16, 2021, https://www.insidehighered.com/news /2021/09/16/new-data-offer-sense-how-covid -expanded-online-learning; Richard Garrett and Bethany Simunich, "2022 CHLOE 7 Report," ed. Ron Legon and Eric Fredericksen, August 9, 2022, Quality Matters, https://www.qualitymatters.org/index.php /qa-resources/resource-center/articles-resources /CHLOE-7-report-2022.

17. "Executive Functioning in Online Environments," UDL on Campus, accessed October 5, 2022, http:// udloncampus.cast.org/page/teach_executive.

18. Cameron Sublett, "Distant Equity: The Promise and Pitfalls of Online Learning for Students of Color in Higher Education," American Council on Education, November 19, 2020, https://www.equityinhighered .org/resources/ideas-and-insights/distant-equity -the-promise-and-pitfalls-of-online-learning-for -students-of-color-in-higher-education/.

19. Thomas J. Tobin and Kirsten T. Behling, *Reach Everyone, Teach Everyone: Universal Design for Learning in Higher Education* (Morgantown: West Virginia University Press, 2018).

20. D. Randy Garrison, Terry Anderson, and Walter Archer, "Critical Inquiry in a Text-Based Environment: Computer Conferencing in Higher Education," *The Internet and Higher Education* 2, nos. 2–3 (Spring 1999): 87–105, https://doi.org/10.1016/S1096 -7516(00)00016-6.

21. Sylvia Hurtado, Adriana Ruiz Alvarado, and Chelsea Guillermo-Wann, "Creating Inclusive Environments: The Mediating Effect of Faculty and Staff Validation on the Relationship of Discrimination/Bias to Students' Sense of Belonging," *Journal Committed to Social Change on Race and Ethnicity* 1, no. 1 (2015): 73, https://doi.org/10.15763/issn.2642 -2387.2015.1.1.59-81.

Section One Opener and Unit 1

1. Some scholars and practitioners who are working toward dismantling systemic injustices in higher education have raised important concerns about rubrics such as those created by Quality Matters (QM) and the Online Learning Consortium (OLC). For example, in "Quality Theater" (*Toward a Critical Instructional Design*, ed. Jerod Quinn, Martha Burtis, and Surita Jhangiani [Hybrid Pedagogy, 2022], 127–48), Jerod Quinn argues in favor of moving to a "post-rubric" approach based on Self-Determination Theory. At the same time, the QM and OLC rubrics are widely used, widely available, evidence-based, and readily accessible to most instructors. Although they're not perfect, they can still be a helpful tool in the equity-minded instructor's pedagogical toolkit.

2. Mays Imad, "Reimagining STEM Education: Beauty, Wonder, and Connection," *Liberal Education* (Spring 2019), https://www.aacu.org/liberaleducation /articles/reimagining-stem-education.

3. Corbin M. Campbell, Deniece Dortch, and Brian Burt, "Reframing Rigor: A Modern Look at Challenge and Support in Higher Education," *New Directions for Higher Education* 181 (2018): 11–23.

4. Jordynn Jack and Viji Sathy, "It's Time to Cancel the Word 'Rigor,'" *Chronicle of Higher Education*, September 24, 2021, https://www.chronicle.com /article/its-time-to-cancel-the-word-rigor.

5. Susan A. Ambrose et al., *How Learning Works: Seven Research-Based Principles for Smart Teaching*, The Jossey-Bass Higher and Adult Education Series (Chichester, England: Wiley, 2010), 69.

6. Scott G. Paris and Julianne C. Turner, "Situated Motivation," in *Student Motivation, Cognition, and Learning: Essays in Honor of Wilbert J. McKeachie*, ed. Paul R. Pintrich, Donald R. Brown, and Claire Ellen Weinstein (Mahwah, NJ: Lawrence Erlbaum Associates, 1994), 213–37.

7. National Academies of Sciences, Engineering, and Medicine, *How People Learn II: Learners, Contexts, and Cultures* (Washington, DC: The National Academies Press, 2018), https://doi.org /10.17226/24783.

8. Mary Helen Immordino-Yang et al., "Neural Correlates of Admiration and Compassion," *Proceedings of the National Academy of Sciences of the United States of America* 106, no. 19 (2009): 8021–26.

9. National Academies of Sciences, Engineering, and Medicine, *How People Learn II*, 137.

10. David S. Yeager et al., "Boring but Important: A Self-Transcendent Purpose for Learning Fosters Academic Self-Regulation," *Journal of Personality and Social Psychology* 107, no. 4 (2014): 559–80, https://doi.org/10.1037/a0037637.

11. Jeffrey R. Albrecht and Stuart A. Karabenick, "Relevance for Learning and Motivation in Education," *The Journal of Experimental Education* 86, no. 1 (2018): 1–10, https://doi.org/10.1080/00220973.2017.1380593.

12. Jarvis R. Givens, "Fugitive Pedagogy: The Longer Roots of Antiracist Teaching," *The Los Angeles Review of Books*, August 18, 2021, https://lareviewofbooks.org/article/fugitive-pedagogy-the-longer-roots-of-antiracist-teaching/.

13. US Department of Education, NCES, *The Condition of Education 2000* (Washington, DC: US Government Printing Office, 2000), https://files.eric.ed.gov/fulltext/ED437742.pdf.

14. Gloria Ladson-Billings, "Toward a Theory of Culturally Relevant Pedagogy," *American Educational Research Journal* 32, no. 3 (1995): 465–91.

15. Stephen J. Quaye and Shaun R. Harper, "Faculty Accountability for Culturally Inclusive Pedagogy and Curricula," *Liberal Education* (Summer 2007): 32–39, https://files.eric.ed.gov/fulltext/EJ775570.pdf.

16. Luke Wood and Frank Harris, "Employing Equity-Minded & Culturally-Affirming Teaching and Learning Practices in Virtual Learning Communities" (webinar, Center for Organizational Responsibility and Advancement [CORA], March 26, 2020), https://coralearning.org/webinars/.

17. René F. Kizilcec and Andrew J. Saltarelli, "Psychologically Inclusive Design: Cues Impact Women's Participation in STEM Education," in *Proceedings of the 2019 CHI Conference on Human Factors in Computing Systems*, 2019, https://dl.acm.org/doi/abs/10.1145/3290605.3300704.

18. Wood and Harris, "Employing Equity-Minded and Culturally-Affirming Teaching and Learning Practices in Virtual Learning Communities."

19. Margery B. Ginsberg and Raymond J. Wlodkowski, *Diversity and Motivation: Culturally Responsive Teaching in College*, 2nd ed. (San Francisco: Jossey-Bass, 2009).

20. Jack and Sathy, "It's Time to Cancel the Word 'Rigor.'"

21. Craig E. Nelson, "10 Dysfunctional Illusions of Rigor: Lessons from the Scholarship of Teaching and Learning," *To Improve the Academy* 28 (January 2010), https://doi.org/10.3998/tia.17063888.0028.014.

22. Andria F. Schwegler, "Academic Rigor: A Comprehensive Definition" (white paper, Quality Matters, 2019), https://www.qualitymatters.org/qa-resources/resource-center/articles-resources/academic-rigor-white-paper-part-one.

23. Derald Wing Sue et al., "Racial Microaggressions in Everyday Life," *American Psychologist* 62, no. 4 (May–June 2007): 276, https://doi.org/10.1037/0003-066X.62.4.271.

24. Sue et al., "Racial Microaggressions in Everyday Life," 273.

25. Emily Schnee, "'In the Real World No One Drops Their Standards for You': Academic Rigor in a College Worker Education Program," *Equity & Excellence in Education* 41, no. 1 (February 2008): 68, https://doi.org/10.1080/10665680701764502.

26. Zaretta Hammond, *Culturally Responsive Teaching and the Brain: Promoting Authentic Engagement and Rigor Among Culturally and Linguistically Diverse Students.* (Thousand Oaks, CA: Corwin Press, 2015).

27. Nicholas W. Papageorge, Seth Gershenson, and Kyung Min Kang, "Teacher Expectations Matter" (working paper 25255, National Bureau of Economic Research, Cambridge, MA, November 2018), http://www.nber.org/papers/w25255.

28. Daniel Solorzano, Miguel Ceja, and Tara Yosso, "Critical Race Theory, Racial Microaggressions, and Campus Racial Climate: The Experiences of African American College Students," *Journal of Negro Education* 69, no. 1/2 (2002): 60–73.

29. Givens, "Fugitive Pedagogy."

30. "Math Literacy as a 21st Century Civil Right // 2021 NCTM Annual Meeting Closing Plenary," video, 5:04, May 1, 2021, https://www.youtube.com/watch?v=HefIMcBz3wI&t=55s.

31. Hasan Kwame Jeffries, "Bob Moses Played Critical Role in Civil Rights Organizing and Math Literacy for Black Students," *The Conversation*, July 29, 2021, https://theconversation.com/bob-moses-played-critical-role-in-civil-rights-organizing-and-math-literacy-for-black-students-165149.

32. Courtland Milloy, "Bob Moses Saw Math as the Path to Equality," *Washington Post*, July 27, 2021, https://www.washingtonpost.com/local/bob-moses-algebra-math-black-students/2021/07/27/74e41f24-eef5-11eb-81d2-ffae0f931b8f_story.html.

33. The Algebra Project, "Overview of Research & Evaluation," April 10, 2007, http://www.algebra.org/articles/07AP_RESULTS.pdf.

34. Hammond, *Culturally Responsive Teaching and the Brain*, 15 (emphasis added).

35. Luke Wood, *Black Minds Matter* (San Diego: Montezuma Publishing, 2018), 101.

36. L. Dee Fink, *Creating Significant Learning Experiences: An Integrated Approach to Designing College Courses* (San Francisco: Jossey-Bass, 2003); CAST.org.

37. David E. Pritchard, Analia Barrantes, and Brian R. Belland, "What Else (besides the Syllabus) Should Students Learn in Introductory Physics?" (MIT Faculty Newsletter XXII, November/December 2009): 2.

38. Fink, *Creating Significant Learning Experiences*.

39. Isis Artze-Vega, Phillip M. Carter, and Heather Russell, "Attending to Local Context, Culture, and Language at Florida International University," in *Redesigning Liberal Education: Innovative Design for a Twenty-First-Century Undergraduate Education*, ed. William Moner, Phillip Motley, and Rebecca Pope-Ruark (Baltimore: Johns Hopkins University Press, 2020), https://doi.org/10.1353/book.76854.

40. Fink, *Creating Significant Learning Experiences*.

41. Fink, *Creating Significant Learning Experiences*, 31 (emphasis added).

42. Allison A. Parker, "The Myth of Diversity Training at the Community College," in *Beyond Equity at Community Colleges: Bringing Theory into Practice for Justice and Liberation*, ed. Sobia Azhar Khan and Kendra Unruh (New York: Routledge, 2022).

43. Steven A. Meyers, "Teaching Tips: Putting Social Justice into Practice in Psychology Courses," *Observer* 20, no. 9 (October 1, 2007), https://www.psychologicalscience.org/observer/putting-social-justice-into-practice-in-psychology-courses.

44. Beckie Supiano, "Teaching: Worried About Cutting Content? This Study Suggests It's OK," July 7, 2022, https://www.chronicle.com/newsletter/teaching/2022-07-07.

45. Joel Sipress and David Voelker, "The End of the History Survey Course: The Rise and Fall of the Coverage Model," *Journal of American History* 97, no. 4 (March 1, 2011): 1050–66.

46. Bryan M. Dewsbury et al., "Inclusive and Active Pedagogies Reduce Academic Outcome Gaps and Improve Long-Term Performance," *PLOS One* 17, no. 6 (June 15, 2022), https://doi.org/10.1371/journal.pone.0268620.

47. Meyers, "Teaching Tips."

Unit 2

1. Susan A. Ambrose et al., *How Learning Works*, The Jossey-Bass Higher and Adult Education Series (Chichester, England: Wiley, 2010).

2. Viji Sathy and Kelly A. Hogan, "How to Make Your Teaching More Inclusive: Advice Guide," *Chronicle of Higher Education*, https://www.chronicle.com/article/how-to-make-your-teaching-more-inclusive/.

3. Linda B. Nilson, *Specifications Grading: Restoring Rigor, Motivating Students, and Saving Faculty Time* (Sterling, VA: Stylus, 2015), 9.

4. Peter C. Brown, Henry L. Roediger, and Mark A. McDaniel, *Make It Stick: The Science of Successful Learning* (Cambridge, MA: Belknap Press, 2014).

5. Grant Wiggins, "Authenticity in Assessment, (Re-) Defined and Explained," *Granted, and . . . Thoughts on Education* (blog), January 26, 2014, https://grantwiggins.wordpress.com/2014/01/26/authenticity-in-assessment-re-defined-and-explained/.

6. Wiggins, "Authenticity in Assessment."

7. James M. Lang, *Cheating Lessons* (Cambridge, MA: Harvard University Press, 2013).

8. "Transparent Methods," Transparency in Learning and Teaching Project, accessed August 25, 2022, tilthighered.com/transparency.

9. Rebecca D. Cox, *The College Fear Factor: How Students and Professors Misunderstand One Another* (Cambridge, MA: Harvard University Press, 2009).

10. Jordynn Jack and Viji Sathy, "It's Time to Cancel the Word 'Rigor,'" *Chronicle of Higher Education*, September 24, 2021, https://www.chronicle.com/article/its-time-to-cancel-the-word-rigor.

11. Di Xu and Shanna S. Jaggars, "Performance Gaps between Online and Face-to-Face Courses: Differences across Types of Students and Academic Subject Areas," *The Journal of Higher Education* 85, no. 5 (2014): 633–59, https://doi.org/10.1080/00221546.2014.11777343.

12. Joe Feldman, *Grading for Equity: What It Is, Why It Matters, and How It Can Transform Schools and Classrooms* (Thousand Oaks, CA: Corwin, 2008), xxviii.

13. Asao B. Inoue, "Theorizing Failure in US Writing Assessments," *Research in the Teaching of English* 48, no. 3 (February 2014): 330–52.

14. Jeffrey K. Smith and Lisa F. Smith, "Grading in Higher Education," in *What We Know about Grading*, ed. Thomas R. Guskey and Susan M. Brookhart, Association for Supervision and Curriculum Development (Alexandria, VA: ASCD, 2019), 195–213; Daniel Starch and Edward C. Elliott, "Reliability of Grading Work in Mathematics," *The School Review* 21, no. 4 (April 1913): 254–59.

15. Robert Glaser, "Instructional Technology and the Measurement of Learning Outcomes: Some Questions," *American Psychologist* 18 (1963): 519–21.

16. Scott Jaschik, "Imagining College Without Grades," *Inside Higher Ed*, January 22, 2009, https://www.insidehighered.com/news/2009/01/22/imagining-college-without-grades.

17. Nilson, *Specifications Grading*.

18. Susan Blum, *Ungrading: Why Rating Students Undermines Learning (and What to Do Instead)* (Morgantown: West Virginia University Press, 2020).

19. Margery B. Ginsberg and Raymond J. Wlodkowski, *Diversity and Motivation: Culturally Responsive Teaching in College*, 2nd ed. (San Francisco: Jossey-Bass, 2009).

20. Jack and Sathy, "It's Time to Cancel the Word 'Rigor.'"

21. Adam Grant, "Why We Should Stop Grading Students on a Curve," *New York Times*, September 11, 2016, https://www.nytimes.com/2016/09/11/opinion/sunday/why-we-should-stop-grading-students-on-a-curve.html.

22. Joseph Feldman, "Grade Expectations: Why We Need to Rethink Grading in Our Schools," interview by Lory Hough, *Ed.* (*Harvard Ed. Magazine*), Summer 2019, https://www.gse.harvard.edu/news/ed/19/05/grade-expectations.

23. Michelle D. Miller, "Ungrading Light: 4 Simple Ways to Ease the Spotlight Off Points," *Chronicle of Higher Education*, April 2, 2022, https://www.chronicle.com/article/ungrading-light-4-simple-ways-to-ease-the-spotlight-off-points.

24. Jesse Stommel, "Ungrading: an FAQ," February 6, 2020, https://www.jessestommel.com/ungrading-an-faq/.

25. Chavella Pittman and Thomas J. Tobin, "Academe Has a Lot to Learn about How Inclusive Teaching Affects Instructors," *Chronicle of Higher Education*, February 7, 2022, https://www.chronicle.com/article/academe-has-a-lot-to-learn-about-how-inclusive-teaching-affects-instructors.

26. See https://onlinelearningconsortium.org/consult/oscqr-course-design-review/.

27. See https://www.qualitymatters.org/qa-resources/rubric-standards/higher-ed-rubric.

28. L. Dee Fink, *Creating Significant Learning Experiences: An Integrated Approach to Designing College Courses* (San Francisco: Jossey-Bass, 2003).

29. David E. Pritchard, Analia Barrantes, and Brian R. Belland, "What Else (Besides the Syllabus) Should Students Learn in Introductory Physics?" *MIT Faculty Newsletter* XXII, no. 2 (2009).

30. Brian Mooney, "Why I Dropped Everything and Started Teaching Kendrick Lamar's New Album," March 27, 2015, https://bemoons.wordpress.com/2015/03/27/why-i-dropped-everything-and-started-teaching-kendrick-lamars-new-album/.

31. Ginsberg and Wlodkowski, *Diversity and Motivation*.

32. Monica Anderson and Jingjing Jiang, "Teens, Social Media and Technology," Pew Research Center, May 31, 2018, https://www.pewresearch.org/internet/2018/05/31/teens-social-media-technology-2018/.

33. Andrew Perrin and Sara Atskep, "About Three in Ten U.S. Adults Say They Are 'Almost Constantly' Online," Pew Research Center, March 26, 2021, https://www.pewresearch.org/fact-tank/2021/03/26/about-three-in-ten-u-s-adults-say-they-are-almost-constantly-online/.

34. See https://tilthighered.com/tiltexamplesandresources.

35. Helenrose Fives and Nicole DiDonato-Barnes, "Classroom Test Construction: The Power of a Table of Specifications," *Practical Assessment, Research, and Evaluation* 18, no. 3 (2013),

https://doi.org/10.7275/cztt-7109; available at: https://scholarworks.umass.edu/pare/vol18/iss1/3.

36. See https://www.clemson.edu/otei/documents /Teaching%20Review%20Resources/Test _Blueprint_Guide_final.pdf.

37. See https://uwaterloo.ca/centre-for-teaching -excellence/teaching-resources/teaching-tips /developing-assignments/exams/exam-preparation.

38. Thomas Lancaster and Codrin Cotarlan, "Contract Cheating by STEM Students through a File Sharing Website: A COVID-19 Pandemic Perspective," *International Journal for Educational Integrity* 17, no. 3 (2021), https://doi.org/10.1007 /s40979-021-00070-0.

39. Anushka Patil and Jonah Engel Bromwich, "How It Feels When Software Watches You Take Tests," *New York Times*, September 29, 2020, https://www .nytimes.com/2020/09/29/style/testing-schools -proctorio.html.

40. Susan Blum, *My Word!: Plagiarism and College Culture* (Ithaca, NY: Cornell University Press, 2010). A good summary article is Blum's "Academic Integrity and Student Plagiarism: A Question of Education, Not Ethics," *Chronicle of Higher Education*, February 20, 2009, https://www.chronicle.com/article/academic -integrity-and-student-plagiarism-a-question-of -education-not-ethics.

41. Wendi Dew and Isis Artze-Vega, "Teaching for Equity: Introduction to Transparent Assessment," *The Grove*, October 29, 2020, http://thegrove.valenciacollege. edu/teaching-for-equity-introduction-to -transparent-assessment/.

42. Tiffany O. Howard, Mary-Ann Winkelmes, and Marya Shegog, "Transparency Teaching in the Virtual Classroom: Assessing the Opportunities and Challenges of Integrating Transparency Teaching Methods with Online Learning," *Journal of Political Science Education* 16, no. 2 (2020): 198–211, https://doi.org/10.1080/15512169.2018.1550420.

43. Feldman, "Grade Expectations."

44. Kimberly A. Fournier et al., "Using Collaborative Two-Stage Examinations to Address Test Anxiety in a Large Enrollment Gateway Course," *Anatomical Sciences Education* 10, no. 5 (2017): 409–22, https:// doi.org/10.1002/ase.1677.

45. Miller, "Ungrading Light."

46. Jack and Sathy, "It's Time to Cancel the Word 'Rigor.'"

47. Lisa M. Nunn, *College Belonging: How First-Year and First-Generation Students Navigate Campus Life* (New Brunswick, NJ: Rutgers University Press, 2021).

Unit 3

1. Terrence Collins, "For Openers . . . An Inclusive Syllabus," *in New Paradigms for College Teaching*, ed. William E. Campbell and Karl A. Smith (Edina, MN: Interaction Book, 1997).

2. James M. Dyer et al., "Laying Bare the Foundations: Examining and Confronting Language Expectations in a College Syllabus," *in Beyond Equity at Community Colleges*, ed. Sobia Azhar Khan and Kendra Unruh (New York: Routledge, 2022), 32.

3. William Germano and Kit Nicholls, *Syllabus: The Remarkable, Unremarkable Document That Changes Everything* (Princeton, NJ: Princeton University Press, 2020), 8.

4. Judith Grunert O'Brien, Barbara J. Mills, and Margaret W. Cohen, *The Course Syllabus: A Learning-Centered Approach*, 2nd ed. (San Francisco: Jossey-Bass, 2008).

5. Michael S. Palmer, Lindsay B. Wheeler, and Itiya Aneece, "Does the Document Matter? The Evolving Role of Syllabi in Higher Education," *Change: The Magazine of Higher Learning* 48, no. 4 (2016): 36–47.

6. Ken Bain, *What the Best College Teachers Do* (Cambridge, MA: Harvard University Press, 2004), 75.

7. Palmer, Wheeler, and Aneece, "Does the Document Matter?"

8. Robin Lightner and Ruth Benander, "First Impressions: Student and Faculty Feedback on Four Styles of Syllabi," *International Journal of Teaching and Learning in Higher Education* 30, no. 3 (2018): 443–53.

9. Richard J. Harnish and K. Robert Bridges, "Effect of Syllabus Tone: Students' Perceptions of Instructor and Course," *Social Psychology of Education* 14 (2011): 319–30.

10. Palmer, Wheeler, and Aneece, "Does the Document Matter?"

11. Rose M. Perrine, James Lisle, and Debbie Tucker, "Effects of a Syllabus Offer of Help, Student Age, and Class Size on College Students' Willingness to Seek Support from Faculty," *Journal of Experimental Education* 64, no. 1 (Fall 1995): 41–52, https://doi.org /10.1080/00220973.1995.9943794.

12. Rebecca A. Glazier and Heidi Skurat Harris, "How Teaching with Rapport Can Improve Online Student Success and Retention: Data from Two Empirical Studies," *Quarterly Review of Distance Education* 21, no. 4 (2020): 1–17.

13. Collins, "For Openers . . . An Inclusive Syllabus," 80.

14. Michelle Pacansky-Brock, "The Liquid Syllabus: An Anti-Racist Teaching Element," *C2C Digital Magazine* 1, no. 15 (Spring/Summer 2021), https://scalar.usc .edu/works/c2c-digital-magazine-spring-summer -2021/the-liquid-syllabus-anti-racist.

15. Sherria D. Taylor et al., "The Social Justice Syllabus Design Tool: A First Step in Doing Social Justice Pedagogy," *Journal Committed to Social Change on Race and Ethnicity* 5, no. 2 (Fall 2019): 133–66.

16. Milton A. Fuentes, David G. Zelaya, and Joshua W. Madsen, "Rethinking the Course Syllabus: Considerations for Promoting Equity, Diversity, and Inclusion," *Teaching of Psychology* 48, no. 1 (January 2021): 69–79.

17. Collins, "For Openers . . . An Inclusive Syllabus," 80.

18. L. Dee Fink, *Creating Significant Learning Experiences: An Integrated Approach to Designing College Course*s (San Francisco: Jossey-Bass, 2003).

19. Michelle Miller, *Minds Online: Teaching Effectively with Technology* (Cambridge, MA: Harvard University Press, 2014).

20. Fink, *Creating Significant Learning Experiences*.

21. Stephen J. Quaye and Shaun R. Harper, "Faculty Accountability for Culturally Inclusive Pedagogy and Curricula," *Liberal Education* (Summer 2007): 36, https://files.eric.ed.gov/fulltext/EJ775570.pdf.

22. Taylor et al., "The Social Justice Syllabus Design Tool."

23. Allison A. Parker, "The Myth of Diversity Training at the Community College," in *Beyond Equity at Community Colleges: Bringing Theory into Practice for Justice and Liberation*, ed. Sobia Azhar Khan and Kendra Unruh (New York: Routledge, 2022).

24. Michelle Pacansky-Brock, "Creating a Liquid Syllabus" (Canvas course, California Virtual Campus–Online Education Initiative), https://ccconlineed .instructure.com/courses/6771.

25. Pacansky-Brock, "The Liquid Syllabus."

26. Collins, "For Openers . . . An Inclusive Syllabus."

27. Chavella Pittman and Thomas J. Tobin, "Academe Has a Lot to Learn About How Inclusive Teaching Affects Instructors," *Chronicle of Higher Education*, February 7, 2022, https://www.chronicle.com /article/academe-has-a-lot-to-learn-about-how -inclusive-teaching-affects-instructors.

28. Brian Helmke, "BME 2240 Biotransport: Spring 2013 Learning Guide," Florida State University, https://fda. fsu.edu/sites/g/files/upcbnu636/files/Media /Files/Newsletter/Issue%205/Biotransport %20Syllabus.pdf.

29. Fuentes, Zelaya, and Madsen, "Rethinking the Course Syllabus."

30. Rebecca D. Cox, *The College Fear Factor: How Students and Professors Misunderstand One Another* (Cambridge, MA: Harvard University Press, 2009), 67.

31. Kim Case, "Syllabus Challenge: Infusing Inclusive Practices" (slideshow), accessed September 19, 2022, https://docs.google .com/presentation/d/1l6hihdEqbwN0_BkC _xhhtRLtBUV7YuPcymtoWn09uTE /edit#slide=id.p8.

32. Bridget Arend, "Transforming Your Syllabus with an Equity Mindset: The Role of Policy Statements," *Intentional College Teaching*, July 15, 2021, https://intentionalcollegeteaching.org/2021/07/15 /transforming-your-syllabus-with-an-equity -mindset/.

33. Matthew R. Johnson, "10 Course Policies to Rethink on Your Syllabus," *Chronicle of Higher Education*, August 11, 2021, https://www.chronicle.com /article/10-course-policies-to-rethink-on-your -fall-syllabus.

34. Pittman and Tobin, "Academe Has a Lot to Learn."

35. Arend, "Transforming Your Syllabus."

36. Dyer et al., "Laying Bare the Foundations," 36.

37. Isis Artze-Vega, Elizabeth I. Doud, and Belkys Torres, "*Más allá del inglés*: A Bilingual Approach to College Composition," in *Teaching Writing with Latino/a Students: Lessons Learned at Hispanic-Serving Institutions*, ed. Cristina Kirklighter, Diana Cárdenas, and Susan Wolff Murphy (Albany: State University of New York Press, 2007).

38. Monica Linden, in "Sample Syllabus Statements from Brown University," Diversity & Inclusion Syllabus Statements, Harriet W. Sheridan Center for Teaching

and Learning, accessed August 25, 2022, https://www.brown.edu/sheridan/teaching-learning-resources/inclusive-teaching/statements.

39. Collins, "For Openers . . . An Inclusive Syllabus."

40. Fuentes, Zelaya, and Madsen, "Rethinking the Course Syllabus."

41. Committee on CCCC Language Statement, "Students' Right to Their Own Language," *College Composition and Communication* 25, no. 3 (September 1974), updated August 2006, https://cdn.ncte.org/nctefiles/groups/cccc/newsrtol.pdf.

42. Diversity & Inclusion Syllabus Statements, Harriet W. Sheridan Center for Teaching and Learning, accessed August 25, 2022, https://www.brown.edu/sheridan/teaching-learning-resources/inclusive-teaching/statements.

43. Harnish and Bridges, "Effect of Syllabus Tone."

44. Maxine T. Roberts, "Appendix: The Syllabus: A Tool That Shapes Students' Academic Experiences," in Center for Urban Education, Rossier School of Education, *Syllabus Review Guide for Equity-Minded Practice* (Los Angeles: University of Southern California, 2017), 46.

45. Taylor et al., "The Social Justice Syllabus Design Tool."

46. Marcia D. Dixson et al., "Nonverbal Immediacy Behaviors and Online Student Engagement: Bringing Past Instructional Research into the Present Virtual Classroom," *Communication Education* 66, no. 1 (2017): 37–53, https://doi.org/10.1080/03634523.2016.1209222.

47. D. Randy Garrison, Terry Anderson, and Walter Archer, "Critical Inquiry in a Text-Based Environment: Computer Conferencing in Higher Education," *The Internet and Higher Education* 2, nos. 2–3 (Spring 1999) 87–105.

48. "CoI Framework," *Community of Inquiry*, accessed September 11, 2022, https://coi.athabascau.ca/coi-model/.

49. "Course Design Rubric Standards," *Quality Matters*, accessed September 19, 2022, https://www.qualitymatters.org/qa-resources/rubric-standards/higher-ed-rubric; "New OLC OSCQR Course Design Review," *Online Learning Consortium*, accessed September 19, 2022, https://onlinelearningconsortium.org/consult/oscqr-course-design-review/.

50. "Online Equity Rubric," Peralta Community College District, accessed September 19, 2022, https://www.peralta.edu/distance-education/online-equity-rubric. Version 3.0 was published in October 2020.

51. "Online Equity Training" (Canvas course, Peralta Community College District), Spring 2021, https://lor.instructure.com/resources/db1027485c2c45ec9cefd7c3443c8e25.

52. Glazier and Harris, "How Teaching with Rapport Can Improve Online Student Success and Retention."

53. Garrison, Anderson, and Archer, "Critical Inquiry in a Text-Based Environment"; Marti Cleveland-Innes and Prisca Campbell, "Emotional Presence, Learning, and the Online Learning Environment," *The International Review of Research in Open and Distance Learning* 13, no. 4 (October 2012): 269–92; Flower Darby and James M. Lang, *Small Teaching Online: Applying Learning Science in Online Classes* (San Francisco: Jossey-Bass, 2019).

54. Equity Unbound, "Community Building Activities," *OneHE*, accessed August 29, 2022, https://onehe.org/equity-unbound/.

55. Darby and Lang, *Small Teaching Online*.

56. Remi Kalir, "Annotate Your Syllabus 3.0," Kalir's blog, July 16, 2020, http://remikalir.com/blog/annotate-your-syllabus-3-0/.

57. Dyer et al., "Laying Bare the Foundations," 43.

Section Two Opener and Unit 4

1. Stephen D. Brookfield, *The Skillful Teacher: On Technique, Trust, and Responsiveness in the Classroom*, 3rd ed. (San Francisco: Jossey-Bass, 2015), 15.

2. Peter Felten and Leo M. Lambert, *Relationship-Rich Education: How Human Connections Drive Success in College* (Baltimore: Johns Hopkins University Press, 2020).

3. Laura I. Rendón, *Sentipensante (Sensing/Thinking) Pedagogy: Educating for Wholeness, Social Justice and Liberation* (Sterling, VA: Stylus), 15.

4. Zaretta Hammond, *Culturally Responsive Teaching and the Brain: Promoting Authentic Engagement and Rigor Among Culturally and Linguistically Diverse Students* (Thousand Oaks, CA: Corwin, 2015).

5. Stephen M. R. Covey, *The Speed of Trust: The One Thing That Changes Everything* (New York: Free Press, 2008), 29.

6. Zaretta Hammond, "The First Six Weeks: Building Trust," *Culturally Responsive Teaching and the Brain* (blog), September 3, 2014, https://crtandthebrain .com/the-first-six-weeks-building-trust/.

7. See Felten and Lambert, *Relationship-Rich Education*.

8. Peter Demerath et al., "A Grounded Model of How Educators Earn Students' Trust in a High Performing U.S. Urban High School," *Urban Review* 54, no. 5 (December 2022): 703–32, https://doi.org/10.1007 /s11256-022-00635-4.

9. Geneva Gay, *Culturally Responsive Teaching: Theory, Research, and Practice* (New York: Teachers College Press, 2010), 72.

10. Zaretta Hammond, "Culturally Responsive Teachers Create Counter Narratives for Students," *Valinda Kimmel* (blog), updated June 22, 2018, https://www.valindakimmel.com/thing-zaretta -hammond-culturally-responsive-teachers-create -counter-narratives-students/.

11. Hammond, *Culturally Responsive Teaching*, 72.

12. Hammond, *Culturally Responsive Teaching*, 17.

13. Bryan Dewsbury, "Deep Teaching in a College STEM Classroom," *Cultural Studies of Science Education* 15 (2020): 169–91.

14. bell hooks, *All About Love* (London: Womens, 2000), 3.

15. Mays Imad, "Reimagining STEM Education: Beauty, Wonder, and Connection," *Liberal Education* 105, no. 2 (Spring 2019): 30–37.

16. Stephen D. Brookfield, *The Skillful Teacher* (San Francisco: Jossey-Bass, 1990), 163.

17. Stephen L. Chew et al., "Trust in and Rapport with the Teacher as Separate Components of a Successful Student Mindset" (paper presentation, Annual Conference on Teaching, Phoenix, AZ, October 2018).

18. Roy F. Baumeister and Mark R. Leary, "The Need to Belong: Desire for Interpersonal Attachments as a Fundamental Human Motivation," *Psychological Bulletin* 117, no. 3 (1995): 497–529, https://doi .org/10.1037/0033-2909.117.3.497.

19. For example, Achim Peters, Bruce S. McEwan, and Karl Friston, "Uncertainty and Stress: Why It Causes Diseases and How It Is Mastered by the Brain," *Progress in Neurobiology* 156 (September 2017): 164– 88, https://doi.org/10.1016/j.pneurobio.2017.05.004.

20. Stephen L. Chew and William J. Cerbin, "The Cognitive Challenges of Effective Teaching," *The Journal of Economic Education* 52, no. 1 (2021): 17–40, https:// doi.org/10.1080/00220485.2020.1845266.

21. Estela Mara Bensimon and Lindsay Malcom, *Confronting Equity Issues on Campus: Implementing the Equity Scorecard in Theory and Practice* (Sterling, VA: Stylus, 2012).

22. Brookfield, *The Skillful Teacher* (2015), 49.

23. Stephen L. Chew, "Student Fear and Mistrust," *Taking Learning Seriously* (blog), accessed November 7, 2022, https://takinglearningseriously.com /barriers-to-learning/student-fear-and-mistrust/.

24. Stephen L. Chew, "The Importance of Building Student Trust" (paper presentation, Research on Teaching and Learning Summit, October 12, 2018). https://www.rotlsummit.com/sites/default/files /slides/2018-10-12-Chew-Summit-Keynote.pdf.

25. Hammond, "Culturally Responsive Teachers Create Counter Narratives."

26. Brookfield, *The Skillful Teacher* (2015), 162.

27. Rendón, *Sentipensante*, 33.

28. Kevin Fosnacht and Shannon Calderone, "Who Do Students Trust? An Exploratory Analysis of Undergraduates' Social Trust" (paper presentation, annual meeting of the Association for the Study of Higher Education, November 20, 2020).

29. Paulo Freire, *Pedagogy of the Oppressed* (1970), trans. Myra Bergman Ramos (New York: Continuum International Publishing Group, 2005).

30. Gloria Ladson-Billings, "Toward a Theory of Culturally Relevant Pedagogy," *American Educational Research Journal* 32, no. 3 (1995): 465–91.

31. Peter Miller, Tanya Brown, and Rodney Hopson, "Centering Love, Hope, and Trust in the Community: Transformative Urban Leadership Informed by Paulo Freire," *Urban Education* 26, no. 5 (January 2011): 1078–99, https://doi.org/10.1177/0042085910395951.

32. Fosnacht and Calderone, "Who Do Students Trust?"

33. Fosnacht and Calderone, "Who Do Students Trust?"

34. Fosnacht and Calderone, "Who Do Students Trust?"

35. David S. Yeager et al., "Loss of Institutional Trust Among Racial and Ethnic Minority Adolescents: A Consequence of Procedural Injustice and a Cause of Life-Span Outcomes," *Child Development* 88, no. 2 (March/April 2017): 658. It may surprise you that we're referencing a study conducted with middle

school students, yet, as Yeager and colleagues point out, mistrust accumulates during students' elementary and middle school education, and many students bring this mistrust to our colleges and universities.

36. National Center for Education Statistics, "Postbaccalaureate Enrollment," *Condition of Education*, July 8, 2022, https://nces.ed.gov /fastfacts/display.asp?id=98.

37. Yeager et al., "Loss of Institutional Trust," 659.

38. Margery B. Ginsberg and Raymond J. Wlodkowski, *Diversity and Motivation: Culturally Responsive Teaching in College* (San Francisco: Jossey-Bass, 2009), 1.

39. Yeager et al., "Loss of Institutional Trust," 658–76.

40. Hammond, *Culturally Responsive Teaching*, 73.

41. Brookfield, *The Skillful Teacher* (2015).

42. Demerath et al., "A Grounded Model of How Educators Earn Students' Trust."

43. Demerath et al., "A Grounded Model of How Educators Earn Students' Trust."

44. Demerath et al., "A Grounded Model of How Educators Earn Students' Trust"; Russell Bishop and Mere Berryman, *Culture Speaks: Cultural Relationships and Classroom Learning* (Wellington, New Zealand: Huia Publishers, 2006); and Andrew Brake, "Right from the Start: Critical Classroom Practices for Building Teacher-Student Trust in the First 10 Weeks of Ninth Grade," *The Urban Review* 52, no. 2 (June 2020): 277–98.

45. David Scott Yeager et al., "Breaking the Cycle of Mistrust: Wise Interventions to Provide Critical Feedback Across the Racial Divide," *Journal of Experimental Psychology: General* 143, no. 2 (April 2014): 804–24.

46. Jacqueline Jordan Irvine, *Educating Teachers for Diversity: Seeing with a Cultural Eye* (New York: Teachers College Press, 2003); James A. Vasquez, "Contexts of Learning for Minority Students," *The Educational Forum* 52, no. 3 (Spring 1988): 243–53, https://doi.org/10.1080/00131728809335490.

47. Synthesis of fixed and growth mindsets for faculty: https://tll.mit.edu/teaching-resources/inclusive -classroom/growth-mindset/; Mindset Toolkit for educators developed by Carol Dweck and colleagues: https://www.mindsetkit.org/about; Gregory M.

48. Susan Ambrose et al., *How Learning Works: Seven Research-Based Principles for Smart Teaching* (San Francisco: Jossey-Bass, 2010), 125.

49. Ambrose et al., *How Learning Works*.

50. Yeager et al., "Breaking the Cycle of Mistrust."

51. Geoffrey L. Cohen, Claude M. Steele, and Lee D. Ross, "The Mentor's Dilemma: Providing Critical Feedback across the Racial Divide," *Personality and Social Psychology Bulletin* 25, no. 10 (October 1999): 1302–18, doi:10.1177/ 0146167299258011.

52. Anne Gregory and Rhona S. Weinstein, "The Discipline Gap and African Americans: Defiance or Cooperation in the High School Classroom, Study 2," *Journal of School Psychology* 46, no. 4 (2008), 455–75.

53. Yeager et al., "Breaking the Cycle of Mistrust," 805.

54. Yeager et al., "Loss of Institutional Trust," 674.

55. Rosemary M. Lehman and Simone C. O. Conceição, *Creating a Sense of Presence in Online Teaching: How to Be "There" for Distance Learners* (San Francisco: Jossey-Bass, 2010).

56. Shanna Smith Jaggars and Di Xu, "How Do Online Course Design Features Influence Student Performance?," *Computers & Education* 95 (April 2016): 270–84, https://www.sciencedirect.com /science/article/abs/pii/S0360131516300203.

57. Harriet L. Schwartz, *Connected Teaching: Relationship, Power, and Mattering in Higher Education* (Sterling, VA: Stylus, 2019).

58. Harriet L. Schwartz, "Authentic Teaching and Connected Learning in the Age of COVID-19," *The Scholarly Teacher*, accessed October 6, 2022, https://www.scholarlyteacher.com/posts /Authentic-Teaching-and-Connected-Learning -in-the-Age-of-COVID-19.

59. Marcia D. Dixson et al., "Nonverbal Immediacy Behaviors and Online Student Engagement: Bringing Past Instructional Research into the Present Virtual Classroom," *Communication Education* 66, no. 1 (2016): 37–53, https://doi.org/10.1080/03634523 .2016.1209222.

60. Thomas Lancaster, "Contract Cheating by STEM Students Through a File Sharing Website: A Covid-19 Pandemic Perspective," *International Journal for*

Educational Integrity 17, no. 3 (2021), https://doi .org/10.1007/s40979-021-00070-0.

61. Flower Darby and James Lang, *Small Teaching Online: Applying Learning Science in Online Classes* (San Francisco: Jossey-Bass, 2019).

62. Susan Blum, *My Word!: Plagiarism and College Culture* (Ithaca, NY: Cornell University Press, 2010).

63. Mays Imad, "Leveraging the Neuroscience of Now," *Inside Higher Education*, June 3, 2020, https://www.insidehighered.com/advice /2020/06/03/seven-recommendations -helping-students-thrive-times-trauma.

64. Jane Tompkins, "Pedagogy of the Distressed," *College English* 52, no. 6 (October 1990): 653–60.

65. Michelle Pacansky-Brock, "How to Humanize Your Online Class, Version 2.0" (infographic), https:// brocansky.com/humanizing/infographic2.

66. Demerath et al., "A Grounded Model of How Educators Earn Students' Trust."

67. Tess L. Killpack and Laverne C. Melón, "First-Day Info Sheets: A Tool to Prompt Semester-Long Inclusive Teaching," *Journal of Microbiology & Biology Education* 21, no. 1 (2020), https://www.ncbi.nlm .nih.gov/pmc/articles/PMC7148150/.

68. Tracie Marcella Addy et al., *What Inclusive Instructors Do: Principles and Practices for Excellence in College Teaching* (Sterling, VA: Stylus, 2021). A copy of the form is available here: https://journals.asm.org /action/downloadSupplement?doi=10.1128%2Fjm be.00183-21&file=jmbe00183-21_supp_1_seq8.pdf.

69. See http://thisibelieve.org.

70. Sample lessons are available here: https://www .mindsetkit.org/topics/teaching-growth-mindset.

71. Anna M. Ortiz and Lori D. Patton, "Awareness of Self," in *Why Aren't We There Yet? Taking Personal Responsibility for Creating an Inclusive Campus*, ed. Jan Arminio, Vasti Torres, and Raechele L. Pope (Sterling, VA: Stylus, 2012), 26.

72. Patrick Turner and Efren Miranda Zepeda, "Welcoming Ain't Belonging: A Case Study That Explores How Two-Year Predominantly White Colleges Can Foster an Environment of Validation and Mattering for Men of Color," *Higher Education Studies* 11, no. 2 (2021): 127–38.

73. Hammond, *Culturally Responsive Teaching*.

74. Maha Bali, "Third Places for Ongoing Community Building," OneHE.org, accessed November 7, 2022, https://onehe.org/eu-activity/third-places-for -ongoing-community-building/.

75. Saundra McGuire and Stephanie McGuire, *Teach Students How to Learn* (Sterling, VA: Stylus, 2015).

76. Rudy Jean-Bart, "Reducing Bias by Getting to Know Your Students." Video. Association of College and University Educators, Microcredential in Inclusive and Effective Teaching, accessed October 3, 2022.

Unit 5

1. Linda Nilson, *Specifications Grading* (Sterling, VA: Stylus, 2015), 33.

2. Tracie Marcella Addy et al., *What Inclusive Instructors Do: Principles and Practices for Excellence in College Teaching* (Sterling, VA: Stylus, 2021).

3. Kelly-Ann Allen et al., "The Need to Belong: A Deep Dive into the Origins, Implications, and Future of a Foundational Construct," *Educational Psychology Review* 34, no. 2 (June 2022): 1133–56, https://doi .org/10.1007/s10648-021-09633-6.

4. Allen et al., "The Need to Belong," 1134.

5. Terrell Strayhorn, *College Students' Sense of Belonging: A Key to Educational Success*, 2nd ed. (New York: Routledge, 2019), 3.

6. Annemarie Vaccaro and Barbara M. Newman, "Development of a Sense of Belonging for Privileged and Minoritized Students: An Emergent Model," *Journal of College Student Development* 57, no. 8 (November 2016): 925–42, http://doi.org/10.1353 /csd.2016.0091.

7. Gregory M. Walton and Geoffrey L. Cohen, "A Question of Belonging: Race, Social Fit, and Achievement," *Journal of Personality and Social Psychology* 92, no. 1 (January 2007): 82–96.

8. Arthur Cohen, *The Shaping of American Higher Education: Emergence and Growth of the Contemporary System* (San Francisco: Jossey-Bass, 1998).

9. Jeffrey Jensen Arnett, "Emerging Adulthood: A Theory of Development from the Late Teens through the Twenties," *American Psychologist* 55, no. 5 (May 2000): 469–80, doi:10.1037/0003-066X.55.5.469. PMID 10842426.

10. U.S. Department of the Interior, "Minority Serving Institutions Program," accessed September 19, 2022, https://www.doi.gov/pmb/eeo /doi-minority-serving-institutions-program.

11. National Center for Education Statistics, "Characteristics of Postsecondary Faculty," *Condition of Education*, September 19, 2022, https://nces.ed.gov/fastfacts/display.asp?id=61.

12. Walton and Cohen, "A Question of Belonging," 82.

13. Walton and Cohen, "A Question of Belonging," 83.

14. For instance, in December of 2021 at a university in the western United States, individuals dressed in Ku Klux Klan outfits were seen in a residential hall, and human excrement was found smeared on the dormitory-room door of a Black student. In 2022, a noose was found hanging from a tree outside a dormitory at one of the nation's preeminent universities.

15. Andew Limbong, "Microaggressions Are a Big Deal: How to Talk Them Out and When to Walk Away," NPR, June 9, 2020, https://www.npr.org/2020/06/08/872371063/microaggressions-are-a-big-deal-how-to-talk-them-out-and-when-to-walk-away.

16. LaQuan Lunford, *What It's Like*, video, 5:38, August 29, 2019, Purdue University, https://mediaspace.itap.purdue.edu/media/What%27s+It+Like+-+LaQuan+Lunford/1_leh75pzu.

17. Claude M. Steele and Joshua Aronson, "Stereotype Threat and the Intellectual Test Performance of African Americans," *Journal of Personality and Social Psychology* 69, no. 5 (November 1995): 797–811, https://doi.org/10.1037/0022-3514.69.5.797.

18. Charlotte R. Pennington et al., "Twenty Years of Stereotype Threat Research: A Review of Psychological Mediators," *PLOS One* 11, no. 1 (2016), https://doi.org/10.1371/journal.pone.0146487.

19. Stanford Graduate School of Education, "Empirically Validated Strategies to Reduce Stereotype Threat," accessed September 19, 2022, https://ed.stanford.edu/sites/default/files/interventionshandout.pdf.

20. Sylvia Hurtado and Deborah Faye Carter, "Effects of College Transition and Perceptions of the Campus Racial Climate on Latino College Students' Sense of Belonging," *Sociology of Education* 70, no. 4 (October 1997): 324–45.

21. Anne-Marie Nuñez, "A Critical Paradox? Predictors of Latino Students' Sense of Belonging in College," *Journal of Diversity in Higher Education* 2, no. 1 (March 2009): 46–61, doi:10.1037/a0014099; Angela M. Locks et al., "Extending Notions of Campus Climate and Diversity to Students' Transition to College," *Review of Higher Education* 31, no. 3 (Spring 2008): 257–85; Dawn R. Johnson et al., "Examining Sense of Belonging among First-Year Undergraduates from Different Racial/Ethnic Groups," *Journal of College Student Development* 48, no. 5 (September/October 2007): 525–42; and Strayhorn, *College Students' Sense of Belonging*.

22. Lisa M. Nunn, *College Belonging: How First-Generation Students Navigate Campus Life* (New Brunswick, NJ: Rutgers University Press, 2021), 6.

23. Patrick Turner and Efren Miranda Zepeda, "Welcoming Ain't Belonging: A Case Study That Explores How Two-Year Predominantly White Colleges Can Foster an Environment of Validation and Mattering for Men of Color," *Higher Education Studies* 11, no. 2 (2021): 127–38.

24. Vaccaro and Newman, "Development of a Sense of Belonging," 932.

25. Turner and Miranda Zepeda, "Welcoming Ain't Belonging," 132.

26. Locks et al., "Extending Notions of Campus Climate"; Dina C. Maramba and Samuel D. Museus, "Examining the Effects of Campus Climate, Ethnic Group Cohesion, and Cross-Cultural Interaction on Filipino American Students' Sense of Belonging in College," *Journal of College Student Retention: Research, Theory & Practice* 14, no. 4 (February 2013): 495–522, https://doi.org/10.2190/CS.14.4.d; Anne-Marie Núñez, "Modeling the Effects of Diversity Experiences and Multiple Capitals on Latina/o College Students' Academic Self-Confidence," *Journal of Hispanic Higher Education* 8, no. 2 (April 2009): 179–96.

27. Leslie R. M. Hausmann, Janet Ward Schofield, and Rochelle L. Woods, "Sense of Belonging as a Predictor of Intentions to Persist among African American and White First-Year College Students," *Research in Higher Education* 48, no. 7 (November 2007): 803–39. "Intent to persist" is a characteristic commonly used to study retention.

28. Gloriana Trujillo and Kimberly Tanner, "Considering the Role of Affect in Learning: Monitoring Students' Self-Efficacy, Sense of Belonging, and Science Identity," *CBE—Life Sciences Education* 13, no. 1 (Spring 2014): 6–15.

29. Karen Gravett and Rola Ajjawi, "Belonging as Situated Practice," *Studies in Higher Education* 47, no. 2 (2022): 1.

30. Alison Cook-Sather, Peter Felten, Kayo Stewart, and Heidi Weston, "Reviving the Construct of 'Mattering'

in Pursuit of Equity and Justice in Higher Education: Illustrations from Mentoring and Partnership Programs," in *Creating Academic Belonging for Underrepresented Students: Models and Strategies for Faculty Success*, ed. Eréndira Rueda and Candice Lowe-Swift (Sterling, VA: Stylus, forthcoming).

31. Bettina Love, *We Want to Do More Than Survive: Abolitionist Teaching and the Pursuit of Educational Freedom* (Boston: Beacon, 2019), 2.

32. Susan A. Ambrose et al., *How Learning Works: Seven Research-Based Principles for Smart Teaching* (San Francisco: Jossey-Bass, 2010), 170.

33. Margery B. Ginsberg and Raymond J. Wlodkowski, *Diversity and Motivation: Culturally Responsive Teaching in College*, 2nd ed. (San Francisco: Jossey-Bass, 2009), 34.

34. John M. Braxton, Jeffrey F. Milem, and Anna Shaw Sullivan, "The Influence of Active Learning on the College Student Departure Process: Toward a Revision of Tinto's Theory," *The Journal of Higher Education* 71, no. 5 (September/October 2000): 569–90.

35. Braxton, Milem, and Sullivan, "The Influence of Active Learning."

36. Braxton, Milem, and Sullivan, "The Influence of Active Learning."

37. Walton and Cohen, "A Question of Belonging."

38. Nunn, *College Belonging*, 67.

39. Nunn, *College Belonging*, 95.

40. Ginsberg and Wlodkowski, *Diversity and Motivation*, 259.

41. Ginsberg and Wlodkowski, *Diversity and Motivation*, 263.

42. Laura I. Rendón, "Validating Culturally Diverse Students: Toward a New Model of Learning and Student Development," *Innovative Higher Education* 19, no. 1 (Fall 1994): 40.

43. Sylvia Hurtado, Adriana Ruiz Alvarado, and Chelsea Guillermo-Wann, "Creating Inclusive Environments: The Mediating Effect of Faculty and Staff Validation on the Relationship of Discrimination/Bias to Students' Sense of Belonging," *Journal Committed to Social Change on Race and Ethnicity* 1, no. 1 (Spring 2015): 65.

44. Krysti Ryan, Kathryn Boucher, Christine Logel, and Mary Murphy, "Creating a Belonging Story," *College Transition Collaborative*, accessed October 2, 2022, https://collegetransitioncollaborative.org/belonging-story/.

45. Ryan, Boucher, Logel, and Murphy, "Creating a Belonging Story."

46. Ryan, Boucher, Logel, and Murphy, "Creating a Belonging Story."

47. Saundra Yancy McGuire with Stephanie McGuire, *Teach Students How to Learn: Strategies You Can Incorporate Into Any Course to Improve Student Metacognition, Study Skills, and Motivation* (Sterling, VA: Stylus, 2015), 89.

48. Locks et al., "Extending Notions of Campus Climate"; Maramba and Museus, "Examining the Effects of Campus Climate"; and Núñez, "Modeling the Effects of Diversity Experiences and Multiple Capitals."

49. Ginsberg and Wlodkowski, *Diversity and Motivation*, 94. The authors refer to Elizabeth F. Barkley, K. Patricia Cross, and Claire Howell Major, *Collaborative Learning Techniques: A Handbook for College Faculty* (San Francisco: Jossey-Bass, 2005).

50. D. Randy Garrison, Terry Anderson, and Walter Archer, "Critical Inquiry in a Text-Based Environment: Computer Conferencing in Higher Education," *The Internet and Higher Education* 2, nos. 2–3 (Spring 1999): 87–105, https://doi.org/10.1016/S1096-7516(00)00016-6.

51. Ginsberg and Wlodkowski, *Diversity and Motivation*, 96.

52. Ambrose et al., *How Learning Works*.

53. Ginsberg and Wlodkowski, *Diversity and Motivation*, 271.

54. Hunter Gehlbach, *User Guide: Panorama Student Survey* (Boston: Panorama Education, 2015), https://www.panoramaed.com/panorama-student-survey. Although the questions in figure 5.1 were validated for students in sixth to twelfth grade, we find them equally useful for informally evaluating college students' sense of belonging. We replaced the word *teacher* with *professor* but otherwise left the questions unchanged.

55. Gregory M. Walton and Geoffrey L. Cohen, "A Brief Social-Belonging Intervention Improves Academic and Health Outcomes of Minority Students," *Science* 331, no. 6023 (March 2011): 1447–51.

56. Belonging for Educators, "Activity: Considering Belonging in Your Classroom," *The Mindset Kit*,

accessed September 19, 2022, https://www
.mindsetkit.org/belonging/about-belonging
/activity-considering-belonging-classroom.

57. Michelle Pacansky-Brock, "How and Why to Humanize
Your Online Class (Version 2.0—Condensed),"
accessed September 28, 2022, https://brocansky.
com/humanizing/infographic2-con.

Unit 6

1. Scott Freeman, David Haak, and Mary Pat Wenderoth,
"Increased Course Structure Improves Performance
in Introductory Biology," *CBE—Life Sciences
Education* 10, no. 2 (2011): 175–86,
https://doi.org/10.1187/cbe.10-08-0105.

2. Viji Sathy and Kelly A. Hogan, "Want to Reach All of Your
Students? Here's How to Make Your Teaching More
Inclusive: Advice Guide," *Chronicle of Higher Education*,
July 22, 2019, https://www.chronicle.com/article
/how-to-make-your-teaching-more-inclusive/.

3. Laura I. Rendón, *Sentipensante (Sensing/Thinking)
Pedagogy: Educating for Wholeness, Social Justice
and Liberation* (Sterling, VA: Stylus, 2009).

4. "Executive Functioning in Online Environments,"
CAST, accessed September 23, 2022, http://
udloncampus.cast.org/page/teach_executive.

5. Kimberly D. Tanner, "Structure Matters: Twenty-One
Teaching Strategies to Promote Student Engagement
and Cultivate Classroom Equity," *CBE–Life Sciences
Education* 12, no. 3 (Fall 2013): 322, https://doi
.org/10.1187%2Fcbe.13-06-0115.

6. Sathy and Hogan, "Want to Reach All of Your
Students?"

7. Sarah Eddy and Kelly Hogan, "Getting Under the
Hood: How and for Whom Does Increasing Course
Structure Work?," *CBE–Life Sciences Education* 13,
no. 3 (Fall 2014): 453–68, https://doi.org/10.1187
/cbe.14-03-0050.

8. Linda Nilson and Ludwika Goodson, *Online Teaching
at Its Best: Merging Instructional Design with
Teaching and Learning Research* (San Francisco:
Jossey-Bass, 2018), 38.

9. Nilson and Goodson, *Online Teaching at Its
Best*, 56.

10. Terry Doyle, *Learner-Centered Teaching: Putting the
Research on Learning into Practice* (Sterling, VA:
Stylus, 2011), 7.

11. Scott Freeman et al., "Active Learning Increases
Student Performance in Science, Engineering, and
Mathematics," *Proceedings of the National Academy
of Sciences* 111, no. 23 (2014): 8410–15, https://doi
.org/10.1073/pnas.1319030111.

12. Freeman, Haak, and Wenderoth, "Increased Course
Structure Improves Performance," 176.

13. Freeman, Haak, and Wenderoth, "Increased Course
Structure Improves Performance," 176.

14. L. Dee Fink, *Creating Significant Learning Experiences:
An Integrated Approach to Designing College Courses*
(San Francisco: Jossey-Bass, 2003).

15. Freeman, Haak, and Wenderoth, "Increased Course
Structure Improves Performance," 175.

16. Elli J. Theobald et al., "Active Learning Narrows
Achievement Gaps for Underrepresented Students
in Undergraduate Science, Technology, Engineering,
and Math," *Proceedings of the National Academy of
Sciences* 117, no. 12 (March 2020): 6476–83, https://
doi.org/10.1073/pnas.1916903117.

17. Theobald et al., "Active Learning," 6476.

18. Theobald et al., "Active Learning," 6479.

19. Bryan M. Dewsbury et al., "Inclusive and Active
Pedagogies Reduce Academic Outcome Gaps and
Improve Long-Term Performance," *PLOS One* 17,
no. 6 (June 2022), https://doi.org/10.1371/journal
.pone.0268620.

20. Andrew Estrada Phuong, Judy Nguyen, and Dena Marie,
"Evaluating an Adaptive Equity-Oriented Pedagogy: A
Study of Its Impacts in Higher Education," *Journal of
Effective Teaching* 17, no. 2 (2017): 5–44.

21. Flower Darby, "Planning a Great Online Class Through
Roundabout Design," *Faculty Focus*, January 11,
2021, https://www.facultyfocus.com/articles
/online-education/online-course-design-and
-preparation/planning-a-great-online-class
-through-roundabout-design/.

22. Darby, "Planning a Great Online Class."

23. Stephen M. Kosslyn, *Active Learning Online: Five
Principles That Make Online Courses Come Alive*
(Copenhagen: Alinea Learning, 2021).

24. Susan A. Ambrose et al., *How Learning Works: Seven
Research-Based Principles for Smart Teaching*, The
Jossey-Bass Higher and Adult Education Series
(Chichester, England: Wiley, 2010).

25. L. Dee Fink, "A Self-Directed Guide to Designing
Courses for Significant Learning," *Dee Fink &*

Associates, 27, https://www.bu.edu/sph/files
/2014/03/www.deefinkandassociates.com
_GuidetoCourseDesignAug05.pdf.

26. Barak Rosenshine and Carla Meister, "The Use of
Scaffolds for Teaching Higher-Level Cognitive
Strategies," *Educational Leadership* 49, no. 7
(April 1992): 26–33.

27. Eddy and Hogan, "Getting Under the Hood."

28. Nilson and Goodson, *Online Teaching at Its Best*, 40.

29. Betsy Barre, Allen Brown, and Justin Esarey,
"Workload Estimator 2.0," Wake Forest University,
accessed September 23, 2022, https://cat.wfu.edu
/resources/tools/estimator2/.

30. Jerod Quinn, Martha Burtiss, and Surita Jhangiani,
eds., *Toward a Critical Instructional Design* (Denver:
Hybrid Pedagogy, 2022); Jerod Quinn, Martha
Burtiss, and Surita Jhangiani, eds., *Designing for
Care* (Denver: Hybrid Pedagogy, 2022).

31. "OLC Quality Course Teaching and Instructional
Practice Scorecard," *Online Learning Consortium*,
accessed October 9, 2022, https://onlinelearning
consortium.org/consult/olc-quality-course-teaching
-instructional-practice/.

32. "5 Tips for Engaging Online Course Design," The K.
Patricia Cross Academy, accessed September 23,
2022, https://kpcrossacademy.org/engaging
-online-course-design/.

33. Stiliana Milkova, "Strategies for Effective Lesson
Planning," Center for Research on Learning and
Teaching, accessed September 23, 2022, https://crlt
.umich.edu/gsis/p2_5. The article includes a list of
great questions to ask yourself for each step.

34. Archy O. de Berker et al., "Computations of
Uncertainty Mediate Acute Stress Responses in
Humans," *Nature Communications* 7, no. 10996
(2016), https://doi.org/10.1038/ncomms10996;
J. Schomaker and M. Meeter, "Short- and Long-
Lasting Consequences of Novelty, Deviance and
Surprise on Brain and Cognition," *Neuroscience &
Biobehavioral Reviews*, 55 (August 2015): 268–79,
https://doi.org/10.1016/j.neubiorev.2015.05.002.

35. Sathy and Hogan, "Want to Reach All of Your
Students?"

36. Jan Meyer and Ray Land, "Threshold Concepts
and Troublesome Knowledge: Linkages to Ways
of Thinking and Practising within the Disciplines,"
*Occasional Report 4: Enhancing Teaching-Learning
Environments in Undergraduate Courses Project*,
Enhancing Teaching-Learning Environments
in Undergraduate Courses Project (Edinburgh:
University of Edinburgh, 2003), 1, http://www.etl.tla
.ed.ac.uk/docs/ETLreport4.pdf.

37. Flower Darby and James M. Lang, *Small Teaching
Online: Applying Learning Science in Online Classes*
(San Francisco: Jossey-Bass, 2019).

Unit 7

1. Michelle Pacansky-Brock, "How & Why to Humanize
Your Online Class, Version 2.0" (infographic),
brocansky.com, 2020, https://brocansky.com
/humanizing/infographic2; Michelle Pacansky
-Brock, "The Liquid Syllabus: An Anti-Racist Teaching
Element," *C2C Digital Magazine* 1, no. 15 (Spring/
Summer 2021), https://scalar.usc.edu/works/c2c
-digital-magazine-spring-summer-2021/the
-liquid-syllabus-anti-racist.

2. Michelle D. Miller, "Ungrading Light: 4 Simple Ways
to Ease the Spotlight off Points," *Chronicle of Higher
Education*, August 2, 2022, https://www.chronicle.
com/article/ungrading-light-4-simple-ways-to
-ease-the-spotlight-off-points.

3. Flower Darby and James M. Lang, *Small Teaching
Online: Applying Learning Science in Online Classes*
(San Francisco: Jossey-Bass, 2019).

4. Marcia D. Dixson et al., "Nonverbal Immediacy
Behaviors and Online Student Engagement: Bringing
Past Instructional Research into the Present Virtual
Classroom," *Communication Education* 66, no. 1
(2017): 37–53, https://doi.org/10.1080/03634523
.2016.1209222.

5. Flower Darby, "How to Be a Better Online Teacher,"
Chronicle of Higher Education, April 17, 2019, https://
www.chronicle.com/article/how-to-be-a-better
-online-teacher/.

6. Miller, "Ungrading Light."

7. Karen Costa, *99 Tips for Creating Simple and
Sustainable Educational Videos: A Guide for Online
Teachers and Flipped Classes* (Sterling, VA: Stylus,
2020).

8. Maha Bali, "Third Places for Ongoing Community
Building," OneHE.org, accessed September 26,
2022, https://onehe.org/eu-activity/third
-places-for-ongoing-community-building/.

9. Linda Nilson, *Specifications Grading: Restoring Rigor, Motivating Students, and Saving Faculty Time* (Sterling, VA: Stylus, 2014).

10. Since my institution at the time did not have an administratively run learning assistant program, students were chosen for this role based on a direct application to me at the end of each fall semester. To be selected as a learning assistant, students did not necessarily need to have gotten an A in the course. Instead, I am attentive to students who gravitate toward leadership roles, who show a certain comfort level in explaining course material to others, and most importantly, who show respect and humility in the ways in which they engage other students. To learn more about the learning assistant model, see the Learning Assistant Alliance website, https://www.learningassistantalliance.org.

11. See https://www.nsta.org/case-studies and https://serc.carleton.edu/index.html.

12. As described in Unit 1, cutting content can be an important part of equity-minded course design. See Bryan M. Dewsbury et al., "Inclusive and Active Pedagogies Reduce Academic Outcome Gaps and Improve Long-Term Performance," *PLOS One* 17, no. 6 (June 2022), https://doi.org/10.1371/journal.pone.0268620.

13. See https://elireview.com.

Section Three Opener and Unit 8

1. Parker J. Palmer, *The Courage to Teach: Exploring the Inner Landscape of a Teacher's Life* (San Francisco: Jossey-Bass, 1998), 2.

2. Maryellen Weimer, *Inspired College Teaching: A Career-Long Resource for Professional Growth* (San Francisco: Jossey-Bass, 2010), 23.

3. Lindsey Malcom-Piqueux and Estela Mara Bensimon, "Taking Equity-Minded Action to Close Equity Gaps," *Peer Review* 19, no. 2 (Spring 2017): 7.

4. Colleen Flaherty, "Zero Correlations Between Evaluations and Learning," *Inside Higher Education,* September 21, 2016, https://www.insidehighered.com/news/2016/09/21/new-study-could-be-another-nail-coffin-validity-student-evaluations-teaching; Kevin Gannon, "In Defense (Sort of) of Student Evaluations of Teaching," *Chronicle of Higher Education,* May 6, 2018, https://www.chronicle.com/article/in-defense-sort-of-of-student-evaluations-of-teaching/; and Anya

Kamenetz, "Student Course Evaluations Get an 'F,'" *NPR,* September 26, 2014, https://www.npr.org/sections/ed/2014/09/26/345515451/student-course-evaluations-get-an-f.

5. Colleen Flaherty, "Speaking Out Against Student Evals," *Inside Higher Education,* September 10, 2019, https://www.insidehighered.com/news/2019/09/10/sociologists-and-more-dozen-other-professional-groups-speak-out-against-student.

6. Nancy Bunge, "Students Evaluating Teachers Doesn't Just Hurt Teachers. It Hurts Students," *Chronicle of Higher Education,* November 27, 2018, https://www.chronicle.com/article/students-evaluating-teachers-doesnt-just-hurt-teachers-it-hurts-students/.

7. Stacey Patton, "Student Evaluations: Feared, Loathed, and Not Going Anywhere," *Chronicle of Higher Education,* May 19, 2015.

8. Tony Knight and Art Pearl, "Democratic Education and Critical Pedagogy," *The Urban Review* 32 (2000): 197–226, https://doi.org/10.1023/A:1005177227794.

9. Herbert W. Marsh, "Students' Evaluations of University Teaching: Research Findings, Methodological Issues and Directions for Future Research," *International Journal of Educational Research* 11, no. 3 (1987): 253–388, https://doi.org/10.1016/0883-0355(87)90001-2.

10. Fadia Nasser and Knut Hagtvet, "Multilevel Analysis of the Effects of Student and Instructor/Course Characteristics on Student Ratings," *Research in Higher Education* 47 (2006): 559–90, https://doi.org/10.1007/s11162-005-9007-y.

11. Jonathan Zimmerman, *The Amateur Hour: A History of College Teaching in America* (Baltimore: Johns Hopkins University Press, 2020).

12. Herbert W. Marsh, J. U. Overall, and Steven P. Kesler, "Validity of Student Evaluations of Instructional Effectiveness: A Comparison of Faculty Self-Evaluations and Evaluations by Their Students," *Journal of Educational Psychology* 71, no. 2 (April 1979): 149–60, https://doi.org/10.1037/0022-0663.71.2.149.

13. Justin Esarey and Natalie Valdes, "Unbiased, Reliable, and Valid Student Evaluations Can Still Be Unfair," *Assessment & Evaluation in Higher Education* 45, no. 8 (2020): 1106–20, https://doi.org/10.1080/02602938.2020.1724875.

14. For brevity's sake, we are not attempting a comprehensive review of the research related to gender, race/ethnicity, and other identities of

potential bias in SETs. Also, despite myriad studies, some potential areas for bias, such as ability/disability, gender conformity, sexuality, class, and nationality, need more exploration and study. A few of the more comprehensive surveys of research are Linse, "Interpreting and Using Student Ratings Data," Kreitzer and Sweet-Cushman, "Evaluating Student Evaluations" (both cited later in this unit), and Stephen L. Benton and William E. Cashin, "Student Ratings of Teaching: A Summary of Research and Literature," *IDEA Paper*, no. 50 (January 2, 2011).

15. Thomas A. Angelo and K. Patricia Cross, *Classroom Assessment Techniques: A Handbook for College Teachers* (San Francisco: Jossey-Bass, 1993), 317.

16. Michael Scriven, "Critical Issues in Faculty Evaluation: Valid Data and the Validity of Practice," in *Valid Faculty Evaluation Data: Are There Any?* (Montreal: 2005 AERA Symposium, April 14, 2005), 7, http://www.cedanet.com/metA.

17. Weimer, *Inspired College Teaching*, 51.

18. Karen A. Loveland and John P. Loveland, "Student Evaluations of Online Classes versus On-Campus Classes," *Journal of Business and Economics Research* 1, no. 4 (2003): 1–10.

19. Rebecca Kreitzer and Jennie Sweet-Cushman, "Evaluating Student Evaluations of Teaching: A Review of Measurement and Equity Bias in SETs and Recommendations for Ethical Reform," *Journal of Academic Ethics* 20 (2022): 73–84, https://doi.org/10.1007/s10805-021-09400-w.

20. Bob Uttl, Carmela White, and Daniela Wong Gonzalez, "Meta-Analysis of Faculty's Teaching Effectiveness: Student Evaluation of Teaching Ratings and Student Learning Are Not Related," *Studies in Educational Evaluation* 54 (September 2017): 22–42.

21. Kreitzer and Sweet-Cushman, "Evaluating Student Evaluations," 73.

22. Anne Boring, Kellie Ottoboni, and Philip Stark, "Student Evaluations of Teaching (Mostly) Do Not Measure Teaching Effectiveness," *ScienceOpen Research* (January 2016): 10.

23. Kreitzer and Sweet-Cushman, "Evaluating Student Evaluations," 76.

24. Sophie Adams et al., "Gender Bias in Student Evaluations of Teaching: 'Punish[ing] Those Who Fail to Do Their Gender Right,'" *Higher Education* 83 (2022): 787–807, https://doi.org/10.1007/s10734-021-00704-9.

25. Adams et al., "Gender Bias in Student Evaluations," 790.

26. Kreitzer and Sweet-Cushman, "Evaluating Student Evaluations," 76.

27. Langdon D. Reid, "The Role of Perceived Race and Gender in the Evaluation of College Teaching on RateMyProfessors.com," *Journal of Diversity in Higher Education* 3, no. 3 (September 2010): 137, https://doi.org/10.1037/a0019865.

28. Mara S. Aruguete, Joshua Slater, and Sekela R. Mwaikinda, "The Effects of Professors' Race and Clothing Style on Student Evaluations," *Journal of Negro Education* 86, no. 4 (Fall 2017): 499, https://doi.org/10.7709/jnegroeducation.86.4.0494.

29. Kreitzer and Sweet-Cushman, "Evaluating Student Evaluations," 80.

30. Susan A. Basow, Stephanie Codos, and Julie L. Martin, "The Effects of Professors' Race and Gender on Student Evaluations and Performance," *College Student Journal* 47 (2013): 352–63.

31. Kreitzer and Sweet-Cushman, "Evaluating Student Evaluations," 80.

32. Boring, Ottoboni, and Stark, "Student Evaluations of Teaching," 1.

33. Alfred P. Rovai et al., "Student Evaluation of Teaching in the Virtual and Traditional Classrooms: A Comparative Analysis," *The Internet and Higher Education* 9, no. 1 (2006): 23–35.

34. Henry F. Kelly, Michael K. Ponton, and Alfred P. Rovai, "A Comparison of Student Evaluations of Teaching between Online and Face-to-Face Courses," *The Internet and Higher Education* 10, no. 2 (2007): 89–101.

35. Loveland and Loveland, "Student Evaluations of Online Classes," 4.

36. Guy Boysen, "Student Evaluations of Teaching: Can Teaching Social Justice Negatively Affect One's Career?" in *Navigating Difficult Moments in Teaching Diversity and Social Justice*, ed. Mary E. Kite, Kim A. Case, and Wendy R. Williams (Washington, DC: American Psychological Association, 2021), 235–46, https://doi.org/10.1037/0000216-017.

37. Kimberly D. Tanner, "Promoting Student Metacognition," *CBE—Life Sciences Education* 11, no. 2 (June 2012): 113–99.

38. David D. Perlmutter, "How to Read a Student Evaluation of Your Teaching," *Chronicle of Higher*

Education, October 30, 2011, http://chronicle.com
/article/How-to-Read-a-Student/129553/.

39. Perlmutter, "How to Read a Student Evaluation," para.
4.

40. Charlie Blaich and Kathy Wise, email message to Mays
Imad, September 14, 2022.

41. Angela R. Linse, "Interpreting and Using Student
Ratings Data: Guidance for Faculty Serving as
Administrators and on Evaluation Committees,"
Studies in Educational Evaluation 54 (September
2017): 103.

42. David A. M. Peterson et al., "Mitigating Gender Bias
in Student Evaluations of Teaching," *PLOS One* 14,
no. 5 (2019), https://doi.org/10.1371/journal.pone
.0216241.

43. Peterson et al., "Mitigating Gender Bias," 3.

44. Malcom-Piqueux and Bensimon, "Taking Equity-
Minded Action," 7.

45. Linse, "Interpreting and Using Student Ratings Data,"
103.

46. Stephen Brookfield, *Becoming a Critically Reflective
Teacher* (San Francisco: Jossey-Bass, 1995).

47. Bettina L. Love, *We Want to Do More Than Survive:
Abolitionist Teaching and the Pursuit of Educational
Freedom* (Boston: Beacon, 2019).

Unit 9

1. Tia Brown McNair, Estela Mara Bensimon, and Lindsey
Malcolm-Piqueux, *From Equity Talk to Equity Walk:
Expanding Practitioner Knowledge for Racial Justice
in Higher Education* (Hoboken, NJ: Jossey-Bass,
2020).

2. Lindsey Malcolm-Piqueux and Estela Mara Bensimon,
"Taking Equity-Minded Action to Close Equity Gaps,"
Peer Review 19, no. 2 (Spring 2017): 5–8.

3. Iris Borch, Ragnhild Sandvoll, and Torsten Risør,
"Discrepancies in Purposes of Student Course
Evaluations: What Does It Mean to Be 'Satisfied'?,"
*Educational Assessment, Evaluation and
Accountability* 32 (2020): 83–102.

4. Bryan Dewsbury and Cynthia J. Brame, "Inclusive
Teaching," *CBE—Life Sciences Education* 18, no. 2
(2019), https://doi.org/10.1187/cbe.19-01-0021.

5. Peter Felten and Leo M. Lambert, *Relationship-Rich
Education: How Human Connections Drive Success in
College* (Baltimore: Johns Hopkins University Press,
2020).

6. Michele T. D. Tanaka, *Learning and Teaching Together:
Weaving Indigenous Ways of Knowing into Education*
(Vancouver, BC: UBC Press, 2016).

7. Bryan M. Dewsbury, "Deep Teaching in a College STEM
Classroom," *Cultural Studies of Science Education* 15
(March 2020): 179, https://doi.org/10.1007/s11422
-018-9891-z.

8. Maryellen Weimer, *Inspired College Teaching: A
Career-Long Resource for Professional Growth* (San
Francisco: Jossey-Bass, 2010), 76–77.

9. Center for Urban Education, *Data Tools,* Equity-Minded
Inquiry Series, Rossier School of Education,
University of Southern California, 2020, https://static1
.squarespace.com/static/5eb5c03682a92c5f96da4fc8
/t/5f3a1a566ced5e0ad47879fb/1597643354901
/Data+Tools_Summer2020.pdf.

10. "National Survey of Student Engagement," Center
for Postsecondary Research, Indiana University
Bloomington School of Education, accessed
September 23, 2022, https://nsse.indiana.edu
/nsse/.

11. "History: The Wabash National Study of Liberal Arts
Education," Center of Inquiry at Wabash College,
accessed September 23, 2022, https://
centerofinquiry.org/wabash-national-study-of
-liberal-arts-education/.

12. Ernest T. Pascarella and Charles Blaich, "Lessons
from the Wabash National Study of Liberal Arts
Education," *Change: The Magazine of Higher Learning*
45, no. 2 (March 2013): 6–15, https://doi.org/10.1080
/00091383.2013.764257.

13. "National Survey of Student Engagement
2008 [Sample]," Indiana University Center for
Postsecondary Research, accessed September 30,
2022, https://centerofinquiry.org/wp-content
/uploads/2017/04/NSSE2008_Sample.pdf.

14. Noelle Arnold, Keeley J. Pratt, and Carlotta Penn,
*Supplemental Evaluation of Inclusive Classroom
Instruction (Pilot 2020)* (Columbus: The Ohio State
University, College of Education and Human Ecology,
Office of Equity, Diversity and Global Engagement,
2020), https://edge.ehe.osu.edu/files/2021/03
/SEI_CI_AnnouncementWEB.pdf.

15. Tasha Souza, *Evaluation of Teaching Items in Course
Evaluations* (Boise: BUILD, Boise State University,

2022), https://www.boisestate.edu/build/inclusive
-excellence-resources/inclusive-resources
-evaluation-of-teaching-items-in-course
-evaluations/.

16. Max van Manen, *Researching Lived Experience:
Human Science for an Action Sensitive Pedagogy*
(Albany: State University of New York Press, 1990).

17. Amedeo Giorgi, ed., *Phenomenology and
Psychological Research* (Pittsburgh: Duquesne
University Press, 1991); Max van Manen,
"Phenomenology in Its Original Sense," *Qualitative
Health Research* 27, no. 6 (May 2017), https://doi
.org/10.1177/1049732317699381; Max van Manen,
*The Tact of Teaching: The Meaning of Pedagogical
Thoughtfulness* (Albany: State University of New
York Press, 1991); Max van Manen, *Researching
Lived Experience*; Max van Manen, *Phenomenology
of Practice: Meaning-Giving Methods in
Phenomenological Research and Writing* (New York:
Routledge, 2016); Kiymet Selvi, "Phenomenological
Approach in Education," in *Education in Human
Creative Existential Planning*, ed. Anna-Teresa
Tymieniecka and Analecta Husserliana (Heidelberg,
Netherlands: Springer, 2008): 95, https://doi
.org/10.1007/978-1-4020-6302-2_4; Allen
J. Heindel, "A Phenomenological Study of the
Experiences of Higher Education Students with
Disabilities" (PhD diss., University of South Florida,
May 2014), https://citeseerx.ist.psu.edu/viewdoc
/download?doi=10.1.1.679.4287&rep=rep1&type=pdf;
and Amy J. DeWitt, "Phenomenological Study
Examining the Challenges and Strategies of Students
Who Are Parents in the Higher Education Setting"
(PhD diss., Liberty University, 2021), https://
digitalcommons.liberty.edu/cgi/viewcontent
.cgi?article=3917&context=doctoral.

18. Andrea S. Webb and Ashley J. Welsh,
"Phenomenology as a Methodology for Scholarship
of Teaching and Learning Research," *Teaching &
Learning Inquiry* 7, no. 1 (2019): 170.

19. Mays Imad, "Reimagining STEM Education: Beauty,
Wonder, and Connection," *Liberal Education* 105, no. 2
(Spring 2019): 30–37.

20. Mays Imad, "In Their Own Voice: Reclaiming the Value
of Liberal Arts at Community Colleges," *Change: The
Magazine of Higher Learning* 51, no. 4 (July 2019):
55–58, https://doi.org/10.1080/00091383.2019
.1618146.

21. Imad, "In Their Own Voice."

22. For instance, Charles Blaich and Kathleen Wise, *From
Gathering to Using Assessment Results: Lessons
from the Wabash National Study*, National Institute
for Learning Outcomes Assessment Occasional Paper
No. 8 (Urbana, IL: University of Illinois at Urbana-
Champaign, January 2011), https://www
.bu.edu/provost/files/2015/09/From-Gathering
-to-Using-Assessment-Results_Lessons-from
-the-Wabash-Study-C.-Blaich-K.-Wise1.pdf.

23. Georgia L. Bauman, "Promoting Organizational
Learning in Higher Education to Achieve Equity in
Educational Outcomes," *New Directions for Higher
Education*, no. 131 (Fall 2005): 23–35, https://doi
.org/10.1002/he.184.

24. Center for Urban Education, *Data Tools* and Bauman,
"Promoting Organizational Learning."

25. Center for Urban Education, *Data Tools*.

26. McNair, Bensimon, and Malcolm-Piqueux, *From Equity
Talk to Equity Walk*, 54.

27. Bryan Dewsbury et al., "Inclusive and Active
Pedagogies Reduce Academic Outcome Gaps and
Improve Long-Term Performance," *PLOS One* 17, no. 6
(June 2022): 9.

Conclusion

1. Eboo Patel, "Teach Your Students to Be Builders, Not
Critics," *Inside Higher Ed*, September 6, 2022, https://
www.insidehighered.com/views/2022/09/06
/teach-students-be-builders-not-critics-opinion.

2. Sylvia Wynter, "The Pope Must Have Been Drunk,
the King of Castile a Madman: Culture as Actuality
and the Caribbean Rethinking of Modernity," in *The
Reordering of Culture: Latin America, the Caribbean
and Canada in the 'Hood* (Ottawa: Carleton University
Press, 1995), 17–42.

3. Mays Imad, "Leveraging the Neuroscience of Now,"
Inside Higher Education, June 3, 2020, https://
www.insidehighered.com/advice/2020/06/03
/seven-recommendations-helping-students-thrive
-times-trauma. The *learning sanctuary* is a concept
developed by coauthor Mays Imad and introduced in
this article.

4. Sandy Baum and Michael McPherson, *Can College
Level the Playing Field? Higher Education in an*

Unequal Society (Princeton, NJ: Princeton University Press, 2022), 1.

5. Baum and McPherson, *Can College Level the Playing Field?*, 28.

6. Lindsay Ahlman, "Casualties of College Debt: What Data Show and Experts Say about Who Defaults and Why," The Institute for College Access & Success, June 14, 2019, https://ticas.org/affordability-2/casualties-of-college-debt-what-data-show-and-experts-say-about-who-defaults-and-why/.

7. Ibram X. Kendi, *Stamped from the Beginning: The Definitive History of Racist Ideas in America* (London: Hachette, 2016); Khalil Gibran Muhammad, *The Condemnation of Blackness: Race, Crime, and the Making of Modern Urban America* (Cambridge, MA: Harvard University Press, 2019); Edward E. Baptist, *The Half Has Never Been Told: Slavery and the Making of American Capitalism* (New York: Basic Books, 2014).

8. Ruha Benjamin, *Race after Technology: Abolitionist Tools for the New Jim Code* (Cambridge, MA: Polity Press, 2019), 181–82.

9. Jarvis R. Givens, "Fugitive Pedagogy: The Longer Roots of Antiracist Teaching," *The Los Angeles Review of Books*, August 18, 2021, https://lareviewofbooks.org/article/fugitive-pedagogy-the-longer-roots-of-antiracist-teaching/.

10. bell hooks, *Teaching Community: A Pedagogy of Hope* (New York: Routledge, 2003), xv.

11. The Dalai Lama, Desmond Tutu, and Douglas Abrams, *The Book of Joy: Lasting Happiness in a Changing World* (New York: Random House, 2016), 60.

12. Sylvia Wynter, "'No Humans Involved': An Open Letter to My Colleagues," *Forum N.H.I.: Knowledge for the 21st Century* 1, no. 1 (Fall 1994), https://people.ucsc.edu/~nmitchel/sylvia.wynter_-_no.humans.allowed.pdf.

13. Baum and McPherson, *Can College Level the Playing Field?*.

14. Patel, "Teach Your Students to Be Builders, Not Critics."

15. Elan C. Hope and Margaret B. Spencer, "Civic Engagement as an Adaptive Coping Response to Conditions of Inequality: An Application of Phenomenological Variant of Ecological Systems Theory (PVEST)," in *Handbook on Positive Development of Minority Children and Youth*, ed. Natasha J. Cabrera and Birgit Leyendecker (New York: Springer, 2017), 421–35, http://doi.org/10.1007/978-3-319-43645-6_25.

16. J. Luke Wood, *Black Minds Matter: Realizing the Brilliance, Dignity, and Morality of Black Males in Education* (San Diego: Montezuma, 2018), 151.

17. Tracie M. Addy et al., "What Really Matters for Instructors Implementing Equitable and Inclusive Teaching Approaches," *To Improve the Academy: A Journal of Educational Development* 40, no. 1 (Fall 2021), https://doi.org/10.3998/tia.182.

18. Isabel Wilkerson, *Caste: The Origins of Our Discontents* (New York: Random House, 2020), 386.

19. Allison A. Parker, "The Myth of Diversity Training at the Community College," in *Beyond Equity at Community Colleges: Bringing Theory into Practice for Justice and Liberation*, ed. Sobia Azhar Khan and Kendra Unruh (New York: Routledge, 2022).

20. Peggy McIntosh, "White Privilege: Unpacking the Invisible Knapsack," *Peace and Freedom Magazine* (July/August 1989): 10–12.

21. Laura I. Rendón, *Sentipensante (Sensing/Thinking) Pedagogy: Educating for Wholeness, Social Justice, and Liberation* (Sterling, VA: Stylus, 2009), 48.

CREDITS

About the Authors

Artze-Vega photo: Valencia College; Darby photo: Cameron Clark; Dewsbury photo: Annette Grant Photography; Imad photo: MSSJF Photography.

Unit 3

Excerpts from the syllabus of Professor Heather Blatt: Reprinted by permission of Dr. Heather Blatt, PhD.

Excerpts from the syllabus of Professor Brian Helmke: Reprinted by permission of Dr. Brian Helmke, PhD.

Excerpts from the syllabus of Professor Monica Linden: Reprinted by permission of Dr. Monica Linden, PhD.

Excerpts from Professor Melonie Sexton's "About Your Instructor" page: Reprinted by permission of Dr. Melonie Sexton, PhD.

Unit 5

Table 5.1: Edited and reprinted by permission of The Eberly Center for Teaching Excellence and Educational Innovation at Carnegie Mellon University.

Unit 8

Excerpt from Kimberly D. Tanner: Used with permission of American Society for Cell Biology, from "Table 3: Sample Self-Questions to Promote Faculty Metacognition about Teaching" in "Feature: Approaches to Biology Teaching and Learning: 'Promoting Student Metacognition,'" *CBE–Life Sciences Education* vol. 11, no. 2 (June 2012): 113–20. © 2012; permission conveyed through Copyright Clearance Center, Inc.

Unit 9

Excerpts from Mays Imad, "Reimagining STEM Education: Beauty, Wonder, and Connection": Used with permission of the American Association of Colleges and Universities from *Liberal Education* vol. 105, no. 2 (Spring 2019): 30–36. © 2019 by the American Association of Colleges and Universities.

Appendix

The Grounded Model: Building Student-Teacher Trust in a "Beating the Odds" U.S. Urban High School: Adapted with permission from Springer Nature from Peter Demerath et al., "A Grounded Model of How Educators Earn Students' Trust in a High Performing U.S. Urban High School," *The Urban Review* 54, no. 5 (December 2022): 703–32. © 2022. https://www.springer.com/journal/11256.

The "Who's in Class?" Form: Adapted and reproduced by permission of the publisher Stylus Publishing, LLC (Sterling, VA) from *What Inclusive Instructors Do: Principles and Practices for Excellence in College Teaching* by Tracie Marcella Addy, Derek Dube, Khadijah A. Mitchell, and Mallory SoRelle. Copyright © 2021 Stylus Publishing, LLC.